Aviation and Airport Security

Terrorism and Safety Concerns

KATHLEEN M. SWEET, Esq.

Embry-Riddle Aeronautical University

PEARSON

Prentice
Hall

Upper Saddle River, New Jersey 07458

Cataloging-in-Publication Data is available at the Library of Congress.

Publisher: Stephen Helba
Executive Editor: Frank Mortimer, Jr.
Assistant Editor: Sarah Holle
Production Editor: Donna Lee Lurker, UG / GGS Information Services, Inc.
Production Liaison: Barbara Marttine Cappuccio
Director of Manufacturing and Production: Bruce Johnson
Managing Editor: Mary Carnis
Manufacturing Buyer: Cathleen Petersen
Creative Director: Cheryl Asherman
Cover Design Coordinator: Miguel Ortiz
Cover Designer: Carey Davies
Cover Image: David Lawrence/Corbis Stock Market
Editorial Assistant: Barbara Rosenberg
Marketing Manager: Tim Peyton
Formatting and Interior Design: UG / GGS Information Services, Inc.
Printing and Binding: R.R. Donnelley & Sons

Pearson Education LTD.
Pearson Education Singapore, Pte. Ltd
Pearson Education, Canada, Ltd
Pearson Education–Japan
Pearson Education Australia PTY, Limited
Pearson Education North Asia Ltd
Pearson Educaçion de Mexico, S.A. de C.V.
Pearson Education Malaysia, Pte. Ltd

10 9 8 7 6 5 4 3 2 1
ISBN 0-13-112289-4

This book is dedicated to Gretchen, Gus, Major, Angus and Barri, and especially to Myles and Tim.

Contents

chapter two
THE HISTORICAL HIJACKING THREAT AND GOVERNMENT RESPONSE: A PERSISTENT PROBLEM

18

chapter three
INTERNATIONAL SOLUTIONS AND REACTIONS: LOT OF TALK

45

chapter four
GROWTH AND CHANGE: AIRCRAFT AS MISSILES   **61**

chapter five
TERRORISM: THE ROOTS REMAIN   **81**

chapter six
INTERNATIONAL MAJOR COUNTERTERRORISM UNITS, LAW ENFORCEMENT, AND INTELLIGENCE AGENCIES: THE BEST DEFENSE   **110**

chapter seven
SCREENING: THE LAST LINE OF DEFENSE   142

chapter eight
PRIVATE SECURITY PERSONNEL VERSUS TRANSPORTATION ADMINISTRATION
SECURITY PERSONNEL: INCREASED SUPERVISION   176

chapter nine

chapter ten

chapter eleven
SECURITY AND THE RULES OF LAW: A SLIPPERY SLOPE   237

chapter twelve

FOREIGN AIRPORT SECURITY: US LAW AND FOREIGN DOMESTIC LAW COMPARISON: LESSONS LEARNED 275

chapter thirteen

TECHNOLOGICAL IMPROVEMENTS: SOME INTRUSIVE AND SOME NOT 296

chapter fourteen

AIRPORT OPERATOR CONCERNS AND OTHER SAFETY AND SECURITY ISSUES: THE FOUNDATIONS OF SECURITY 311

chapter fifteen

ACCESS CONTROL AND PERIMETER SECURITY: ANOTHER FOUNDATION   327

Preface

As I sit down to write these introductory words, in the peace of the English countryside in spring, the war against Saddam Hussein is probably hours away from its opening. Many of my friends and former colleagues in the British and American armed forces will be involved. I shall have to sit this one out and experience it only vicariously. The overall operational commander of the British forces is a former student of mine—the first one I ever launched on his first solo flight thirty-five years ago when I was an instructor pilot.

I have had this strange feeling of closeness, yet remoteness, during many previous conflicts: I was just completing training as a conscript back in 1956 when the Suez conflict ran its short course; I was on exchange duty at the USAF Air War College when my British colleagues fought to regain the Falkland Islands in 1982. But at least I knew what the airmen, sailors, and ground troops were engaged upon, and what their equipment could deliver. For the vast majority of the population of Britain and the United States, that kind of knowledge has for a long time been out of reach. The all-volunteer force, and reducing numbers of men and women in uniform, have combined to make the business of war a very specialist subject. Until 11 September 2001.

From that day on, when the terrorist threat brought bloodshed into the workplace, violence and death were transferred off the in-flight entertainment screen and right into your face—permanently and finally. We are all at risk. There is no sure hiding place.

Lt Col Sweet (Ret.) provides the templates for dealing with this acute challenge to our normal freedoms. She is ideally qualified to do so. She is certainly motivated to do so. I first met her when yet another conflict was claiming lives as I stood on the sidelines. We were both in Moscow in the mid-1990s, working as attachés in our respective embassies. Kathy was a ***mould***-breaker. The Russians were not entirely at ease with the idea of a female attaché, let alone one who seemed to know her way round aircraft. So they gave her more freedom than any of us poor mere men could ever hope for, and as a result she was let loose inside a Sukhoi fourth-generation jet fighter while the rest of us wondered if we could even get a photo of it! She demonstrated resilience and resourcefulness throughout a long tour of duty in Moscow, deploying all her manifold skills and talents: as intelligence gatherer and analyst, as linguist, as jurist, but above all as a woman of considerable energy and determination.

Thus, it comes as no surprise at all to me to be asked to write this Preface to her current examination of the terrorist threat to commercial airline and airport security. Her previously published review of the topic was thorough and—of its day—timely. But not even she is immune to fate. As the book went to print, the events of 11 September struck their grievous blows against the international community. The present volume takes the reader, amateur or concerned professional, through the history of air terrorism and the ways in which counter measures are developing. It reveals the dynamism with which international and national agencies are responding to the challenges of terrorism. It must surely be required reading for any air service operator, and will be invaluable to the traveling member of the public as well as the responsible legislator. In short, it is a key contribution to the current campaign against the terrorist.

Phil Wilkinson
Air Commodore, Royal Air Force (Ret.)
Hampshire, England

ABOUT THE AUTHOR

Kathleen M. Sweet, Lt. Col., Ret., USAF, JD, is currently on the faculty at Embry-Riddle Aeronautical University in Prescott, Arizona, in the Department of Global Intelligence and Security Studies, where she teaches courses in strategic intelligence, security, and terrorism. She was retired from the US Air Force in 1999. While in the military, she was an Instructor at the Air War College at Maxwell AFB, Alabama, and an Assistant Air Attache to the Russian Federation, an Intelligence Officer, and a Member of the Judge Advocate General's Department. Additionally, she was assigned as a Military/Political Affairs Officer to the 353rd Special Operations Wing located at Clark AFB, Republic of the Philippines. She is also presently a Consultant with International Risk Control Ltd, London, England. She is President and CEO of Risk Management Security Group, a transportation security consulting firm.

ACKNOWLEDGMENTS

I am especially grateful for the contributions of Air Commodore (Ret.) Phil Wilkinson, Hampshire, England, and Myles Patrick Doyle, Enniscorthy, Ireland, for their valuable contributions. I would like to thank Sarah Holle at Prentice Hall, as well as the following reviewers: Scott Watson, Liberty Regional Agency, Dover, NH; James Albrecht, Sam Houston University, Huntsville, TX; Robert Dolph, Security Sales & Integration Magazine, Maitland, FL; David Mullins, Security Analyst, Linden, NC; Dr. Tom Babcock, California State University—Fullerton, Fullerton, CA; and David McElreath, Washburn University, Topeka, KS. I also particularly would like to thank my husband, Timothy R. Sweet, for his dedication in proofreading this book.

Introduction

1. **19 April 1995:** Bomb rips through the Alfred P. Murrah Federal Building in Oklahoma City killing 168 and injuring over 500.
2. **25 June 1996:** Terrorists attack the US military complex at Khobar Towers in Saudi Arabia killing 19 and wounding another 100.
3. **7 August 1998:** Terrorists bomb US embassies in Kenya and Tanzania, killing 224 including 12 Americans.
4. **12 October 2000:** *USS Cole* was refueling in the Yemeni port of Aden when a small boat approaching the ship exploded killing 17 sailors and injuring 39 others.
5. **11 September 2001:** Four aircraft are hijacked in the United States. Two fly into and destroy the World Trade Center in New York City, one slams into the Pentagon, and a third crashes in Pennsylvania, apparently disrupting the terrorists hopes of also smashing into the White House.
6. **22 November 2001:** The US government allocates $13 billion in 2001 to prevent future terrorist attacks and to prepare adequately to respond to them.

Friedrich Nietzsche cautioned that, "Stare not into the Abyss, lest the Abyss stare back at you." The intelligence community must reorganize and refocus on the "war on terrorism." Problems that have plagued the intelligence community for decades still haunt the halls of the Central Intelligence Agency and other intelligence agencies. Basically, the increased importance of intelligence on terrorist networks has not been matched by increased understanding of what it is or how it can and should be used to improve policymaker's decisions and solutions. Efforts to enhance the assets in the intelligence-gathering toolbox have raised difficult questions about balancing the genuine needs of national security and the protection of individual liberties so rooted in democratic traditions.

Terrorism is ultimately any incident that involves the use of violence to achieve political ends. Nothing seems to strike fear into the hearts of people more than a term such as *terrorist attack*. Events, especially those in the United States and Israel during 2001/2002, have solidified the citizens of the world against those who would use terror to undermine a democratic way of life. In the "broken" new world, unthinkable thoughts and a kind of hierarchy of horribleness are emerging. Radiation, germs, and gas compete for the public's attention.

Using civilian airliners as guided missiles, terrorists slammed three aircraft filled with several hundred innocent civilians on board into the World Trade Center Towers in New York and the US military headquarters at the Pentagon in Washington, DC. Within a couple of hours, every US military base and installation around the world was at nearly the highest level of alert condition possible. Called DEFCON for Defense Condition in the military, the new threat condition known by civilians is now called Force Protection Condition (FPC). The FPC's range from the lowest, ALPHA, to the highest, DELTA. In a matter of less than an hour after the terrorist attack, military aircraft from the active force, the Guard, and the Reserves were airborne, flying combat air patrol (CAPS) missions over eight major US cities. Later primarily Army National Guard units were tasked to enhance security levels at US airports.

Contemplating the worst, US intelligence officials have confirmed the possibility that al-Q'aeda may well have acquired Soviet-era nuclear warheads or enough material for an atomic bomb. In response, sophisticated sensors have been deployed at US borders, overseas facilities, and points in and around the capital. Ordinary Geiger counters have been used for decades by the US Customs Service, but now newer radiation detectors, referred to as gamma ray and neutron flux detectors, are becoming familiar to the average citizen. With the aid of hindsight, it is patently clear that US intelligence agencies missed the transformation of al-Q'aeda from an obscure group of Islamic extremists to a sophisticated terrorist powerhouse. Additionally, the link between the 19 terrorists who participated in the attack, Mohammed Atta, has become a household name even though authorities previously overlooked his activities in the United States and Europe.

Regardless of advances in technology, the threat is real and the nation's transportation facilities, especially airports, remain at particular risk. This risk has been extended to include not only damage to airport facilities, aircraft both in flight and on the ground, but to the consequences of using the aircraft as missiles against other targets of opportunity. Additionally, air to ground missiles could destroy an aircraft from a ground position off the airport complex. Terrorists indeed tried to bring down an Israeli aircraft in Africa in 2002. Over the years, the threat to aviation security has changed dramatically. It has encompassed hijacking, on-board bombs, and even shifted to terminal assaults. The new tactic of actually commandeering and using aircraft as a lethal missile has only added to the mix of potentially dangerous scenarios. Even though the original concept of hijacking an aircraft has now witnessed several adaptations, the potential threat remains high for the industry. Cargo vulnerabilities are particularly acute. Terrorists have proved to be especially innovative in finding ways to publicize causes at the expense of the aviation community. They are wealthy, well organized, and capable. The future will likely encompass the use or threatened use of weapons of mass destruction to include chemical, biological, or nuclear weapons. Therefore, the procedures, equipment, and planning for adequate airport and aircraft security in the twenty-first century remain a priority for all air travelers and security practitioners alike. The nation failed in the past to acknowledge and adequately respond to terrorist intentions to attack democratic traditions by the use of aircraft. Unfortunately, history often repeats itself.

That failure to recognize and appropriately respond to Usama bin Ladin's public persistence to inflict pain on America has been all too graphically visible to the world since 9/11. Policymakers must think the unthinkable. For example, the sheer abundance of nuclear materials and expertise in the world makes a nuclear threat quite a viable one. Richard Garwin, who helped design the hydrogen bomb 50 years ago has said, "Instead of killing 5,000 people in New York, a bomb could kill 10,000 or 500,000 people in an instant." Bin Ladin, or terrorists like him, could steal a nuclear weapon, steal the materials to make one, spread radioactive material with a conventional bomb, or attempt to attack a nuclear power facility in order to cause massive release of radioactive material. Terrorists could even theoretically use a tactical nuclear or conventional weapon encased with radioactive material to destroy an aircraft in flight. Additionally, the use of biological and or chemical weapons is not outside the realm of possibility. To argue that there are better or easier targets out there forgets the concept that terrorists are not necessarily rational.

Some experts have believed for years that the government needs to be tasked with the job of screening passengers and bags, while continuing with the mandate of monitoring the work to test the system for violations. In fact, the system is already heading in that direction based on the November 2001 legislation. Steering in this direction does not mean that the legislation is a panacea for the industry's security challenges. The current legislation is likely not the long-term answer and needs to be evaluated more fully and periodically supplemented. However, some absolutely necessary precautions such as installing armor and locks on cockpit doors, changing aircraft electronics so that potential hijackers cannot shut off the transponder, and screening all airport employees for weapons when they report to work are currently being effectuated. Pressure to install explosive detection equipment at airports and consistent 100% screening of all passengers and cargo also needs to be fastidiously pursued. Even though the Transportation Security Administration has widely publicized the fact they are attempting to effectuate 100% screening, the means by which they are accomplishing this claim needs to be scrutinized.

This book seeks to present not just an historical analysis of the development of airport security but also to convince the reader of the importance of commercial aviation to the world economy. Efforts by the international community to attempt to resolve the complex issues related to airport security are also discussed; including specific references to domestic and international laws, treaties, and case law. The legal framework in which law enforcement personnel and the intelligence community are either constrained or set loose are detailed to provide the reader with the necessary parameters in which the entire security team must and will operate in the future. Legislation enacted since 9/11 is analyzed and the reader is provided with a critical review of the ongoing efforts of the Transportation Security Administration (TSA) and the Department of Homeland Security. Some of the procedures and policies are praised and others are criticized, leaving the reader the opportunity to make their own decisions as to what will improve security as it relates to their practitioner goals or student development. An attempt was also made to provide the reader with a comprehensive, but by no means exhaustive, review of terrorism, terrorist organizations, national and international law enforcement, counterterrorism, and intelligence units. The book additionally discusses changes in airport security from its beginnings to current trends, including TSA procedures as well as technology previously in use, still in use, and its potential use. A review of basic access control and perimeter security procedures and equipment provides the reader with a fundamental understanding of the minimum requirements for a security plan for individual airports not just covering physical requirements but also procedural and integrated enhancements.

Once again, the issue is not "if" but "when" the world witnesses another attack on the transportation industry. The challenge is whether security practitioners, academics, and policymakers will be prepared to meet it to the benefit of passengers and the economy alike.

chapter one

The Aviation Industry: A National Security Asset

NEWS

1. **April 1999**: Transportation Department tests conducted at airports revealed investigators successfully breached security 117 of 173 attempts, or 68% of the time.

2. **2000**: By the year 2010, aviation's impact on the world economy could exceed US $1800 billion with over 31 million jobs provided and passenger traffic topping 2.3 billion per year.

3. **March 2001**: The Federal Aviation Administration (FAA) released results of a safety audit, which gave some dreadful marks to the major airlines and was so problematic that the Department of Transportation has initiated its own investigation of the auditing process.

4. **April 2002:** Argenbright Security Inc. was fined $1 million for failing to meet security obligations and potentially putting the millions of people who fly on commercial aircraft every day at risk.

5. **2002**: Under a pending proposal, the US government wants to promote tips from citizens about suspicious conduct. The government denies the program called Terrorism Information and Prevention System would encourage people to spy on their neighbors.

■ IMPORTANCE OF AIR TRANSPORTATION

The entire age of air transportation is not yet older than the life span of an ordinary human being. On 17 December 1903, the Wright Brothers launched an airplane with controllable powered engines at Kitty Hawk, North Carolina, and changed the world forever. The historic flight covered only 120 feet, which is a shorter distance than an average flight attendant traverses in walking from the front end of a large commercial airliner to the other end. Several others, including Richard Pearse of New Zealand, flew first but failed to achieve powered sustainable controlled flight. The invention of the airplane enabled humans for the first time in history to travel rapidly and easily over land-dominated obstacles like mountains, deserts, and ice caps. It has since also provided speed not even imagined a generation ago. The greatest tribute to air transportation, however, may be the simple fact that it is taken so much for granted. Any passenger can walk into any scheduled airline service and purchase a ticket to virtually anywhere on the planet because of the airlines' intercarrier cooperative programs. The same service is available for freight shipments. The world depends on it. Unfortunately, there are signs that its infrastructure and security have been somewhat neglected and taken for granted.

Clearly, the hopes and dreams of future generations are dependent on air travel, and eventually the vastness and potential of space transportation. The air transport industry is one of the most vital and fastest paced economic forces in the global economy. In addition, commercial aviation will only increase in importance in the future and will continue to do so throughout the twenty-first century. As technology improves, so does air transportation and the ability to travel and move cargo over longer distances in shorter periods of time.

Air transportation is also a sterling example of applied technology. As technology improves, so must air transportation and the facilities that support it. The ability to provide safe air travel and freight carriage to the industry's patrons is a continuous challenge. These advances in technology must also enable authorities to secure the airport environment from those who would potentially disrupt it. At the same time, care needs to be taken that security measures do not delay air cargo to the point where it is noncompetitive with goods shipped by sea. The global economy depends on continued and uninterrupted service. Terrorists and other criminal activities threaten that safe environment.

■ AIRWAYS

Remarkably, air transport as a means of moving passengers and freight has gained an important place in the US civilian economy in only the past quarter century. Ferdinand Graf von Zeppelin created the world's first commercial airline in 1912 in Europe, using dirigibles to transport more than 34,000 passengers before the start of World War I. After the war, European governments heavily subsidized such now well-known airlines as British Airways, Air France, and the Royal Dutch Airline, KLM.

In the United States, the development of commercial airlines progressed more slowly. It was as recently as 1958 that US airlines finally carried more passengers, as measured by passenger miles, than the railroads. Admittedly, in comparison with rail and truck transport, the airlines still carry an insignificant proportion of the total volume of freight around the world. However, air cargo service is still vitally important because of its capabilities for rapid delivery over lengthy distances without the requirement of frequent transfer. The volume of air freight traffic has in fact been growing rapidly, particularly since the development of standardized containers, which greatly facilitate loading and unloading. As regards passenger carriage, no piece of equipment ever invented, other than the airplane, has impacted transportation on such a global scale so rapidly.

The interconnectivity of the airline industry has framed the perception that the planet seems smaller. It can be argued that the intermixture of cultures and peoples has changed the diversity of the world. Travelers can literally see the Pyramids at Giza, the Great Wall of China, the Golden Gate Bridge, and Westminster Abbey all within a few days if they are up to the trip. Air transportation, enhanced by advances in communications, has expanded the world's economy exponentially.

■ DEVELOPMENT OF THE AVIATION INDUSTRY

Flight as a practical means of transportation was highlighted with Charles A. Lindbergh's transatlantic flight in 1927. Improvements continued to be made in the design of commercial aircraft, but it was not until World War I that aviation came into its own as an industry. Out of necessity during the war, the United States had built almost 17,000 aircraft and over 10,000 people had learned to fly. After the war, surplus aircraft were converted to civilian commercial use. The idea of commercial flight started to catch on and regular mail service began in 1918 between Washington, DC, Philadelphia, and New York. The US Postal Service subsequently and greatly contributed to the creation of a nationwide system of airports, making transcontinental service soon available.

In 1925, the Air Mail Act authorized the US Postal Service to award airmail routes to private contractors. The practice continues today and raises unique problems pertaining to the needs of airport security personnel in inspecting sealed bags of mail. US Postal Service mail heavier than 16 ounces was banned on passenger airplanes after September 11, but such carriage has returned so long as the packages are screened by bomb sniffing dogs.

The US commercial air industry really began to grow when the US Army transferred some of the rail routes to commercial carriers. After that, the Air Commerce Act of 1926 gave further encouragement to the development of the airline industry. The law provided for the certification of aircraft and airmen, the drafting and implementation of air traffic rules, and the creation of civil airways. The government had stopped its own operation of airmail routes in 1927, transferring the business to the exploding aviation industry. Except for a short period in 1934, civilian air carriers have consistently been reimbursed for carriage of the mail, often making them quite a profit. Interestingly enough, in order to reduce the cost of this carriage, the government required the air carriers to provide space for passengers. Hence, significant development of the airline passenger industry was begun. The expansion of air travel on regularly scheduled airlines grew speedily, and has obviously resulted in tremendous convenience for the world traveler.

The Civil Aeronautics Act of 1938 further promoted the development of today's airline industry. The Act provided for the establishment of a Civilian Aeronautic Board (CAB) to set up routes, fares, and safety standards. Congress specifically intended to express a policy of encouraging the development of air transportation and to foster regulations to promote aviation. They sought to provide the public with air transportation at reasonable rates and as safely as possible. World War II also gave a tremendous boost to aviation as military improvements in aircraft eventually crossed over into commercial aviation. Some of these improvements and advancements had immediate civilian applications. Eventually, trunk lines were expanded, local lines multiplied, and scheduled air carriers instituted freight service. Soon thereafter, airlines carrying only cargo also made an appearance.

Aviation-related advancements are always in development. Increases in speed, range, capacities of aircraft, and navigation are constantly improving. Giant strides are additionally being made in the area of air traffic control. The control tower is one of the nerve centers of any airport. Air traffic controllers, who are constantly under pressure attempting to juggle aircraft traffic, can arguably be overtasked during peak hours. The controllers use radar, radio, signal lights, and innovations in communications and navigation to direct air traffic near the airport as well as on the ground. All of these systems are susceptible to interference, and the consequences of this would be potentially catastrophic. Enhancements were needed when the commercial jet era began in 1958 and had broadened to the evolution of the supersonic transport (SST), which reaches speeds of 1400 miles per hour. Even faster aircraft are currently under development by the National Aeronautic and Space Administration. Communication, navigation, and infrastructure capabilities must all match these advancements.

The industry got an additional boost during the late 1970s. The US government hoped further to enhance the rapid growth of aviation with the decision to deregulate the airlines in 1978. The Airline Deregulation Act of 1978 permitted air carriers to set their own routes. In 1982, they were allowed to set their own fares as well. The CAB was abolished and the Federal Aviation Administration (FAA) was tasked with regulating safety. Financial difficulties in the 1980s generated the consolidation of many of the larger air carriers, and smaller carriers subsequently created regional niche markets. "The industry continued to grow and in 1998, the 10 largest carriers transported 551 million passengers controlling 96% of the market" (Aviation Industry, *The Columbia Encyclopedia*, 6th ed., Columbia University Press, 2001, Pg. 2).

However, this deregulation also generated increased burdens on the FAA to provide safe, yet efficient, airports and aircraft standards without a corresponding increase in staff and budget. Two significant crashes, one over San Diego in 1978 and one at Chicago O'Hare in 1979, in conjunction with an increase in hijackings intensified public demand for more strict and expanded safety measures. At the same time, the FAA became embroiled in controversy over how to handle the multitask mandate of regulating a rapidly growing industry, facilitating that growth, and the briskly proliferating terrorist threat. They were tasked with handling all three.

Facilities

In the United States, cities, counties, states, or public corporations own most of the larger airports; however, many smaller airports are still privately owned. The FAA is the primary government agency, which regulates design and operations standards. They also regulate safety and security in conjunction with the Transportation Security Agency (TSA). Civilian airports are classified as either air carrier airports or general aviation airports. Military facilities fall into another category. Each has its own respective security requirements. Enhancements to improve security at general aviation airports is pending before the 108th US Congress.

Airway Routes

The routes of the airway system consist of designated air space through which the movement of aircraft is controlled. In the interest of safety, a highly technical system of navigation aids is used to guide aircraft and to control their movement.

Aircraft landing at Washington's Ronald Reagan Airport after restrictions were lifted post September 11, 2001. Many special security restrictions remain in force at the airport due to its proximity to Washington's government buildings and monuments. *Courtesy National Business Aviation Association.*

Adequate aircraft landing facilities, airports, and auxiliary services are critical. Two serious consequences of the rapid expansion of general aviation have been the heavy saturation of air space and the overloading of the capacity of many airports. According to some experts, this overcrowding has reached critical proportions. The situation has received much media attention, especially after tragic accidents and the release of government reports criticizing the FAA or the financial profit-making motives of the airline industry.

The airport facilities crisis has several facets. The increase in air traffic consisting of general aviation aircraft, large commercial airlines, commuter airlines, and freight traffic are progressively overburdening airports built decades ago. An air carrier airport may service commuter, regional, national, and freight only and international passenger and cargo airlines all at the same time. The 1978 deregulation had generated an increase in the number of commercial airlines using major airports as well as an increase in the flight schedules of all airlines using such airports without corresponding upgrades in facilities. The cycle of industry growth without infrastructure growth has been perpetuating itself for more than twenty years. On top of this, less crowded reliever airports have not adequately absorbed increases in general aviation traffic. Furthermore, the absence of adequate ground navigational facilities at these airports forces many light and medium-sized aircraft to use the larger airports, especially during bad weather, complicating the safe management of these airports.

Since air transport is one of the fastest growing sectors of the world economy, any blip in the carefully orchestrated daily movement of airborne aircraft has a ripple effect. When airports close or are restricted in any way, the entire worldwide system feels the effects in some manner. By the year 2010, aviation's impact could exceed US $1800 billion, with over 31 million jobs provided to the world's workforce. (Internet: http://www.atag.org/ECO, 4/22/01, Pg. 3.) Consequently, the financial effects can be significant when even a small disruption occurs. In addition, approximately one-third of the world's manufactured exports (by value) are now transported by air. The effects of the aviation industry on the global economy are significant. It is an indisputable fact that the shutdown of US aviation after 9/11 clearly negatively affected the global economy. Interruptions in service have major repercussions not only to the aviation industry but also to almost all facets of the world's economic productivity. So much so that governing political figures have frequently intervened in order to prevent strikes, bankruptcies, and mergers. Governments also interject demands on security requirements when the terrorist or criminal threat receives media attention and requires a public response.

The demand and the need for adequate and well-protected airports will only continue to increase. In the United States, a 1999 study indicated that strains on the airport infrastructure likely cost the airlines and the public more than US $4.5 billion that year (Air Transportation Association, 1999 Study). The Air Transportation Association of America has placed most of the blame on air traffic control delays, but such delays represent only part of the problem. Governments must soon recognize that future global economic growth is substantially threatened unless concrete investment in airport infrastructure comes about soon.

In 1998, the world's airlines carried more than 1600 million passengers and over 29 million tons of freight. The world's fleet of aircraft consists of about 18,000 aircraft operating over 15 million kilometers and serving nearly 10,000 airports. "Passenger and freight traffic are expected to increase an average annual rate of around 4-5% between 1998 and 2010, significantly greater than the growth of the global Gross Domestic Product" ("The Economic Benefits of Air Transport" Air Transportation Action Group, 2000 Edition, Pg. 4). These figures will only grow in the future and are indicative of the size and dimensions of the piece of the pie the air transportation industry encompasses. Such an important segment of the economy needs constant attention by the FAA, the TSA, the airlines, freight forwarders, and security professionals.

■ DEREGULATION

As discussed, few federal statutes for economic regulation of the air transportation industry existed between 1926 and 1938. The Air Mail Act of 1934 launched the appointment of a Federal Aviation Commission tasked with making recommendations to Congress on national aviation issues. The Civil Aeronautics Act of 1938 implemented many of the commission's recommendations and laid out the outline of economic regulation that existed until 1978, when Congress literally deregulated the entire industry.

The Civil Aeronautics Act of 1938 contained many controls that mirrored the economic regulations placed on the railroads and the trucking industries. Many experts have argued for the return of these kinds of regulation. First, air carriers were required to obtain certificates of public convenience and were required to provide necessary and adequate facilities on routes for which they had authorization. Routes could not be abandoned without the prior approval of the government. Second, carriers were obligated to charge just and reasonable rates and provide safe and adequate service and facilities. Rates and fares had to be published for public inspection and had to be filed with the appropriate government regulatory agency. The rates were published and changes required a 30-day notice period. In 1972, the CAB was even authorized to regulate rates to and from foreign countries. Today, a passenger can be sitting in a seat for which they paid $300; whereas the passenger seated directly next to them paid $800 or more. Another passenger may have purchased an Internet discount rate at $69 one way. The Civil Aeronautics Act also gave the corresponding regulatory agency the power to investigate alleged unfair and deceptive practices or unfair methods of competition and to issue "cease and desist" orders to air carriers (52 Statute. 973, Civil Aeronautics Act Annotated). The CAB also controlled consolidations and mergers of airline companies and acquisitions of control and leases of air carriers. Therefore, it previously played an important role in preventing monopolies.

Nonetheless, on 24 October 1978, the Airline Deregulation Act of 1978 was signed into law. The basic purpose of the airline deregulation legislation was to encourage an air transportation system that placed primary reliance upon competitive market forces as the basic determinant of commercial airline operations. The timetable called for a seven-year phase out. The Act allowed wide discretion in the setting of passenger fares. The confusing fares of today are a direct result of this decision and have created a situation many passengers resent. It also dismantled the governing board, CAB, and distributed its responsibilities between the Department of Transportation, the Department of Justice, and the US Postal Service (Mini-Brief, "Airline Deregulation: An Early Appraisal," Congressional Research Services, Library of Congress, 25 June 1980, No. MB 79247, Pg. 1). The *laissez faire* argument of competitive market prices benefiting the consumer has arguably not occurred in the minds of the traveling public. In fact, some passengers would claim the airlines actually engage in price-fixing and predatory pricing practices to drive competitors out of business. Both are detrimental to the consumer.

Many airline mergers have indeed reduced costs and expanded market shares. However, whether the savings are actually passed onto the consumer presents a different debate. Price fixing, forcing smaller airlines out of business and thereby reducing competition in a particular market, is not uncommon, as evidenced by the dismantlement of some regional airlines by larger ones. Furthermore, generally monopolistic acts and predatory pricing are also not unusual features of gigantic corporations, even the airlines.

CONSEQUENCES OF 9/11 TO THE INDUSTRY

After the tragedy of 9/11, the stock value of the major airlines provided a clear indication of the consequences of a single terrorist act that involved two major airlines and four aircraft. Two hijacked airliners destroyed the twin towers of New York's World Trade Center, another slammed into the Pentagon in Washington DC, and a fourth airliner, believed destined for the White House, crashed in Pennsylvania when several passengers overtook the hijackers in a last ditch and heroic effort to save American lives. All normal commercial and general aviation was suspended following the attacks.

Hence, the nation's commercial airlines and general aviation aircraft were grounded. For three full days, the skies above America were virtually silent except for military aircraft. Slowly, the airports were reopened and commercial flight was resumed.

Note: *The only permitted flights picked up and removed the relatives of Usama bin Ladin from the territory of the United States for their own safety at the request and funding of the Saudi Arabian government.*

On 20 December 2001, the Department of Transportation lifted flying restrictions on Class B airspace. This essentially restored Visual Flight Rules (VFR) to pre–September 11 conditions in major metropolitan areas. However, it was not until April 2002 that Ronald Reagan Washington Airport had the remaining restrictions on the operation of commercial aviation removed.

Between 31 December 2000 and 31 December 2001, the percentage negative change in the stock value of the two directly involved carriers was substantial. American Airlines stock was down 43.1% and United Airlines stock dropped 65.3%. The other airlines were significantly affected as well. Northwest stock plummeted 47.9%, Delta dropped 41.7%, and US Airways fell a whopping 84.4% (*Plane Business*, 2001 Stock Performance, Internet: http://www.planebusiness. com/stock performance/2001.html, 28 May 2002). The airline industry began to scream for assistance.

■ EMERGENCY FUNDING

In an effort to bail out the airlines, Congress passed the Air Transportation Safety and System Stabilization Act (ATSSA), which authorized $15 billion in expenditures. President George W. Bush, seeking to gain rapid approval of the Bill, announced that safe, viable, and effective commercial air traffic is important to the US way of life. In response, the House of Representatives quickly passed the Bill 356 to 54 votes and the Senate followed suit with a vote of 96 to 1 in probably the largest showing of bipartisanship since World War II. Specifically, the legislation gave the airlines $5 billion in immediate cash assistance and $10 billion in loan guarantees. Many Congressmen expressed concerns over bailing out an already

1-10	Baggage Belts	21	Lifts	32	The Kiosk Sweet Shop	43	Meeting Point
11	Aer Rianta Information	23	Airline Customer Service	33	Hughes & Hughes Bookshop	44	Chauffeur Meeting Point
12	Vodafone Store	24	Airline Customer Service	34	Disabled Toilets	46	Customs VAT Office
13	Hertz Car Rental	25	Airline Customer Service	35	Airline Baggage Enquiries	47	Vending Machines
14	Europcar Car Rental	26	Reed Aviation Cust Service	36	ICE Bureau de Change	48	Upper Crust Cafe
15	Budget Car Rental	27	Airline Customer Service	37	Car Park Ticket Station	49	Oversized Baggage
16	Avis Car Rental	28	Public Toilets	38	Cash Point	T	Public Telephones
17	National Car Rental	29	Nursery Toilets	39	CIE Bus & Rail Information		
18	Green Room Bar	30	Tax Refund Office	40	Tourist Information		
19	Cash Point	31	Arrival Gate	41	ICE Bureau de Change		
20	Pre-Booked Car Hire			42	Bar		

Layout of the arrivals level at Dublin International Airport, Dublin, Ireland. Proper airport design can be a crucial factor in thwarting terrorist activity especially in light of the historical terminal attacks on the Rome and Tel Aviv airports as well as the more recent attack at the El Al counter in Los Angeles. *Courtesy Aer Rianta.*

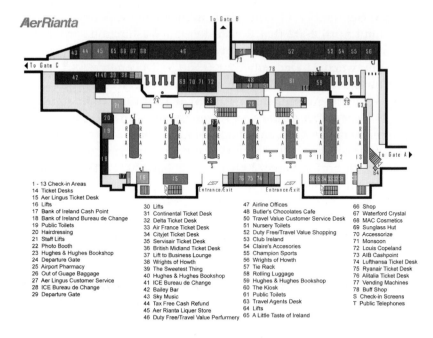

Layout of the departures level at Dublin Airport, Dublin, Ireland. Proper airport design and placement of security officers and screening equipment can be a crucial factor in defending both passengers and cargo from terrorist attack. *Courtesy Aer Rianta.*

financially insecure industry, but the pressure to do something quickly was too much for politically motivated leaders in Congress. At the time, it seemed unpatriotic to oppose the Bill; even though one lone Congressman did just that.

To address one apprehension, the bill contains a provision that limits the salaries of airline executives. Any airline that accepted the bailout money is prohibited from raising the salaries of its executives that make over $300,000 per year for a specific period of time. It was thought this provision would prevent the bailout money from ending up in the pockets of top executives instead of serving its intended purpose. Admittedly, the traveling public virtually stopped flying for a period of time immediately after the attack. It remains to be seen whether the significant losses the airlines allegedly incurred are an accounting fiction.

Airlines squealed that they were significantly struggling after the attack, complaining of empty planes and lost profits. They quickly laid off 80,000 workers and grounded 20% of their flights (Adams, Marilyn, *USA Today*, 26 December 2001). However, in December of 2001, approximately two months later, the financially desperate months seemed to be fading away. For example, American Airlines announced it intended to recall many reservations agents and decided to cancel the scheduled layoffs of numerous mechanics. The other airlines followed suit, and by mid-2002, it once again became difficult to find a seat on an aircraft. Once again, aircraft were full and the airlines began rescheduling previously canceled flights. The short-lived days of cheaper and more competitive airfares to regenerate passenger travel had already dissipated. For example, in the summer of 2002, it became almost impossible to find a really discounted fare to Europe, especially on short notice.

The airline industry is recovering from 9/11. However, statistics indicate that many passengers are flying at small regional airports rather than larger international ones. Some of the larger airports continue to have long security lines, especially during peak traveling times and dates. Northwest Airlines, the world's fourth largest airline, lost $264 million in the first half of 2002, which is actually less than most of the other major carriers. The year 2002 witnessed US Airways filing for bankruptcy, United Airlines lobbying for government support, and most airlines making major job cuts. According to the Air Transport Association, revenue declined for all major airlines during the first half of 2002. United Airlines dropped 22%, US Airways 24%, and American Airlines 16%. Holding on were Alaskan Airlines at 2.2%, Southwest at 8.5%, and Delta at 13.7% (Air Transport Association, "Percent Change in Operating Revenues First Six Months of 2002," *Star Tribune*, 8 September 2002, Pg. D8). On the other hand, the parent of American Airlines Stock gained a whopping 424% during the second quarter of 2003.

▓ PROTECTING PUBLIC AIR TRANSPORTATION

It is clear that airlines are a primary means of public transportation in large cities. Thousands of people may jam a terminal on any given day. Larger airports resemble small cities, and definitely present a particularly enticing target for terrorists for several logistical reasons. First of all, they typically are crowded with people every day. Second, airlines move on a scheduled basis in predictable geographic locations. Most importantly, they are public facilities providing a public service and are extremely difficult to harden as targets. Consequently, public transportation is an attractive target in terms of difficulty in providing adequate physical, personal, and operational security. The challenge is substantial and should not be neglected.

The threat can emanate from a terminal assault, a hijacking, the use of an aircraft as a weapon, and even the exposure of commercial aircraft to surface-to-air missiles. Congress seems to have reached the conclusion that lethal force must be met with lethal force. The Senate joined the House of Representatives in September 2002 in voting overwhelmingly to permit pilots to carry guns in the cockpit. The wisdom of this publicity-motivated vote remains fully to be evaluated. Training to arm pilots with .40 calibre semi-automatic handguns began on 13 April 2003. The government has engaged in many false starts over the years in protecting the public air transportation system. This is likely one of them.

In another rush to "defend the public," the government must not lower the standards for airport screeners in an attempt to meet Congressional mandated, but arbitrary, compliance dates for federal airport screening. The fact that 29 people were arrested in the fall of 2002 on federal charges of lying or offering false papers to get jobs at three Florida airports makes the point. The scenario of hiring screeners with criminal backgrounds has persisted up to the present. The following chapters will review the history behind the threats to airports, aircraft, and the airline industry in general. The book will also analyze local, national, and international efforts to protect the public and the air transportation industry.

▓ CONCLUSION

The horrific events of 9/11 have exemplified the potential results of terrorist attacks on not only the aviation industry but also the financial heartbeat of the nation and the global economy in general. The attack on the World Trade Center and the Pentagon will clearly be the most expensive aviation disaster in US history. The lingering costs, according to the airlines, came close to completely devastating the economic well-being of the industry, let alone the nation as a whole. From an equipment perspective alone, each of the four airplanes was insured for $2 billion; $50 million for the airframe and the remaining amount for damage and liability. These figures omit, of course, the incalculable loss of life. Regardless of any particular viewpoint on the exact extent of the damage, the concept of the airline industry as a strategic national asset was affirmed. Essentially the attacks threw an incredible wrench into the national and world economic machinery, reaching almost everyone in some manner, whether personal or economic.

The US Stock Exchange was closed for several days after the attack but eventually reopened on Monday, 18 September 2001. As perspective, it is significant to point out that the US stock markets had not been closed for three consecutive days since the Great Depression. When the markets reopened, the economic effects of the tragedy became self-evident. Airline stocks in particular plummeted. Other related industries were similarly affected. Warnings of additional threats continue to disrupt confidence in the markets, complementing previous unrelated economic woes. Consequently, investor faith in a quick economic recovery lingers behind previous expectations.

On 21 September 2001, the House and the Senate of the US Congress overwhelmingly approved a $15 billion bill aimed at rescuing the aviation industry from the immediate effects of the terrorist hijackings. The bill also contains a provision of an additional $3 billion in support of enhanced security upgrades. In May 2003, the TSA allocated 2.3 billion to US carriers to offset security costs. The continuing costs related to upgraded security will remain a hot topic of debate. Who should pay and exactly how much should be spent will affect both security and the gross national product for years to come in many ways.

Again, according to the airlines, the attacks allegedly have financially overwhelmed airlines worldwide. In response, in Minnesota, Northwest Airlines announced the company would lay off 10,000 employees. In Atlanta, Delta announced the furloughing of 13,000 employees. Industry executives invoked wartime powers to override no-layoff protections in employee contracts. The CEO of Northwest, Richard Anderson, summed the situation when he said, "The fact that our industry was essentially turned into a weapon of terrorism on September

11 causes us to take immediate action to be certain we preserve the long-time future of the airline" (Tom Kennedy and David Phelps, "NWA Will Lay Off 10,000; $15 Billion Airline Aid OK'd," *Star Tribune*, 22 September 2001, Pg. 1).

Whatever your perspective, it is no longer reasonable to argue that the airline industry is not a national and global asset. The aviation industry is clearly an asset that directly affects the employment of millions of aviation industry employees and indirectly affects many millions more. Security officials must also be cognizant of the threat to cargo and avoid focusing totally on screening passengers and luggage. The real question is how the world came to be in this predicament of terrorism and what can realistically be done about it on a global scale.

chapter two

The Historical Hijacking Threat and Government Response: A Persistent Problem

NEWS

1. **September 1970:** Palestinian terrorists hijacked several airliners forcing them to fly to the Jordanian desert. With the media present and cameras filming, the aircraft were destroyed in fiery explosions costing the airlines millions.

2. **1985:** During the height of the Christmas season, fanatical Japanese terrorists, in support of the Palestinian cause, open fire on helpless airline passengers at both the Vienna and Rome airports.

3. **1985:** Shi'ite gunmen hijack TWA flight 847 from Athens. The hijackers kill one of the passengers and disperse the rest of them throughout Beirut, making significant demands for their release.

4. **1988:** Libyan intelligence officers plant a bomb in the belly of Pan Am Flight 103, which explodes over Lockerbie, Scotland, killing hundreds.

5. **2001:** President Bush calls on US governors to mobilize the National Guard to help boost security at the nation's airports until tighter security can be put into place.

6. **4 July 2002:** A former Egyptian citizen living in California opens fire on passengers waiting in line at the El Al check-in counter. A security guard fatally shot the attacker.

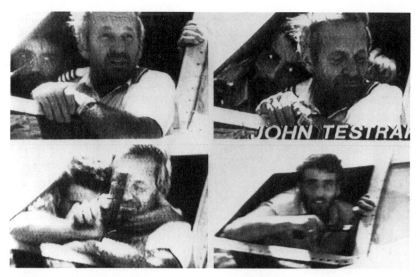

An armed terrorist holds a gun on Trans World Airline pilot John Testrake during an interview from the hijacked plane, TWA Flight 847, at the Beirut International Airport. Terrorists have become particularly adept at using the media to advertise their cause. *ABC NEWS/AP Laserphoto / CP Photo Assignment Services.*

▨ HIJACKING

Hijacking has been characterized as the forcible seizure of any vehicle in transit in order to commit robbery, extort money, kidnap passengers, or carry out other crimes. For many years, the term historically was used to indicate the illegal taking of property from someone traveling on a public road. In the United States, the term first came to mean the theft of goods in transit by truck. Eventually, the term *hijacking* grew to encompass the seizure of ships, usually for theft and extortion. The concept of "hijacking" was eventually extended to include the taking of airplanes.

More accurately, under the reign of Queen Elizabeth I of England, the Elizabethan Sea Dogs, privateer ships sailing under the protection of the English flag, committed repeated violent acts of piracy against the Spanish fleet. Under similar circumstances, American pirates significantly contributed to the American Revolution and the War of 1812. Both countries had strict laws against such conduct even though they unofficially resorted to analogous conduct themselves.

Sea piracy continues today, especially in the South China Sea where it has received international attention because of its frequency and operational proficiency. Westerners are, nonetheless, more familiar with the hijacking of the *Achille Lauro*, an Italian cruise ship hijacked off the Mediterranean coast of Egypt on 7 October 1985 by the Palestinian Liberation Organization. Egyptian President at the time, Hosni Mubarak, induced the hijackers to surrender after promising air passage to Tunisia. However, during the incident, the hijackers had shot to death a Jewish American passenger, 69-year-old Leon Klinghoffer. Consequently, President Ronald

Reagan sent US Navy jets to intercept the escaping hijacked aircraft and forced the plane to land at Naval Air Station Sigonella, Italy. Critics have alleged that US troops engaged in some piracy of their own. Modern terrorism continues to take the form of piracy, but it has expanded to include attacks in the air as well as on the sea.

Currently, hijacking, skyjacking, or air piracy is defined as the forcible commandeering of an aircraft while in flight. During the 1970s, the incidences of hijacking in the United States became intolerable. Cuban exiles, fleeing felons, and extortionists topped the list of hijackers. In 1973, the Federal Aviation Administration (FAA) consistently began searching all passengers and their carry-on luggage. Prior to such efforts, political terrorists had begun consistently to carry out hijackings either to gain publicity for their cause or to obtain the release of fellow terrorists from prison. US government figures for the past three decades show the highest number of hijackings took place in 1970 when the total reached 74 ("Jet Hijackings Decline but Still a Threat," *Associated Press*, 1 January 2000).

In the mid-1980s, the problem escalated further. In 1985, a Trans World Airlines flight departing from Athens was hijacked and diverted to Lebanon where the hostages were detained for 17 days. The TWA Boeing 727 had 153 people on board. Three Lebanese Shi'ite Muslims demanded the release of more than 750 Lebanese and Palestinians being held in Israel. In a cooperative effort, Israel released 31 prisoners, and the hostages were eventually released. Soon thereafter, the Italian ship the *Achille Lauro* was hijacked in the Mediterranean Sea, further highlighting the problem. In both instances, American citizens were killed. The situation demanded action and the FAA began to improve security measures while government leaders sought to improve international cooperation to combat the use of aircraft to further terrorism.

Regardless of massive security efforts on the part of authorities at the time, hijackings continued. In fact, twenty years later between the years of 1992 and 1996, although indicating a reduced number, 89 aircraft were still hijacked. According to FAA statistics, 40 planes were hijacked in 1990, 12 planes in 1992, 31 in 1993, 23 in 1994, 9 in 1995, and 14 more in 1996. (Federal Aviation Administration, "Criminal Acts Against Civil Aviation," Appendix F, 1996, Pg. 79). Increased security has indeed been productive and lifesaving, although it has not stopped, nor likely will ever stop the threat completely. Terrorists who will surely continue to exploit any lapses in security measures will always discover any reduction in such diligence. Furthermore, the public, especially since 9/11, has continued to demand even more innovative techniques to fight the continuing problem. Some of these innovations are arguably more intrusive than the now familiar metal detectors and x-ray machines. Therefore, much like in the past, and in spite of renewed demands by the public for safer airport security, some critics have pursued legal battles to stymie efforts to do so.

■ LEGAL RESPONSES TO EXPANDING SECURITY MEASURES

For example, Gregory T. Nojeim, legislative consultant to the American Civil Liberties Union (ACLU), presented a statement on the civil liberties implications of airport security measures before the White House Commission on Aviation and Security on 5 September 1996. Generally, the ACLU is devoted to protecting the principles of freedom, including the prohibition against unreasonable searches and seizures set forth in the Bill of Rights. The group has supported the need for appropriate measures to ensure that air travel is safe. On the other hand, the ACLU has publicly and persistently reminded the proponents of intrusive security procedures that civil liberties should not be sacrificed to make air travel safer. The statement made to the Commission outlines three basic premises and they remain pertinent today:

1. Passengers should not be detained, questioned, and searched as if they are potential criminals unless there are specific facts that indicate that they may commit a criminal act.

2. No passenger should be singled out on the basis of his or her perceived or actual race, religion, national origin, gender, sexual orientation, or political opinion.

3. Passengers not legitimately under suspicion should not have to fear that their private effects and private lives would be held up to public scrutiny or that personal data about them will be made accessible to others without their fully informed and genuinely noncoerced consent (Internet: http://www.aclu.org/congress/airtest.htm., 3/3/01, Pg. 2).

An example of a case, which exemplifies the concerns of civil libertarians, is highlighted in the case of *Brent vs. Ashley*, et al. 247 F.3d 1294, 2001. Rhonda Brent, the only black women arriving on a flight to the United States from Nigeria, alleged in a federal lawsuit a violation of her Fourth Amendment rights during a strip search and subsequent x-ray of her person. Two US Customs officers initially searched her baggage and found nothing. They decided to conduct a full-body pat down and strip search. The officers justified their search based on the nervousness of Brent and her arrival from a source country. The body pat down and strip search consisted of touching her crotch area, ordering her to pull down her clothes, removing and examining her sanitary napkin, squeezing her abdomen from the pubic to thorax, and monitoring her responsive actions. An electronic document search also revealed nothing. The Customs agents decided that an x-ray and pelvic examination at a hospital was appropriate. Brent was presented with a consent form and told that if she refused to sign it she could be held for 35 days or indefinitely until a judge ordered the x-ray. Brent requested to speak to an attorney and to call home. Both requests were denied. The pelvic exam and x-ray revealed the complete absence of drugs. After a ten-hour delay in her trip, she was returned to the airport. Brent filed suit against nine customs employees alleging the commission of common law torts and constitutional violations.

The court concluded that the decision to stop and search Brent was based upon the fact that she shook her head in disapproval upon seeing the way customs officials were treating a black male copassenger. Brent argues that a simple expression of disapproval does not provide reasonable suspicion to justify a search and the court agreed. However, the law is clear that "routine border searches of the persons and effects of entrants are not subject to any requirement of reasonable suspicion, probable cause or warrant." The court further reasoned that an invasive border search of someone's body requires a showing of reasonable suspicion. *US vs. Montoya de Hernandez*, 473 US 531, 538, 105 S Ct. 1300 (1985). The court ultimately held that because Brent had failed to demonstrate that the initial stop did not constitute more than a routine border search, the initial stop did not violate her Fourth Amendment rights. However, a nonintrusive search of Brent's person and her luggage revealed nothing; she presented verifiable residence and employment information and an electronic document search of her revealed nothing. The court, therefore, went on to find the strip search of Brent was unconstitutional. It is not likely many people would tolerate this kind of conduct and still want to spend money to fly. Although hopefully well intended, the conduct of these US Customs agents, with hindsight, appears to be out of proportion to the overall situation.

Other critics have focused on racial profiling, computerized passenger registries, and cameras that search through clothing. For example, the Centre for National Security Studies in Washington, DC believes that legislation signed into law by the Clinton Administration may pose serious threats to constitutional rights. This group had focused on the fact there had been only two international terrorist acts committed on US soil up to that time; namely, the notorious bombing of the World Trade Center in February 1993 and the occupation of the Iranian Mission in New York City in April of 1992. The massive attack of 9/11 changed the perceptions of many travelers, and reinforced the idea that the overwhelming number of American air travelers appear willing to submit to more technologically superior levels of security intrusion in order to keep the air travel environment safe from criminals and/or terrorists. This does not obviate the constitutional issues. Furthermore, since 9/11 Attorney General Donald Ashcroft has announced, in conjunction with Congressional approval, intentions to empower law enforcement with even broader powers.

Of note is that future threats may well emanate from within the United States. Post-September 11 dissemination of anthrax via the mail is a prime example of the possibility of such an internal threat. Domestic terrorist groups are proliferating, and international terrorists will still seek to carry their cause to the United States. It is a clear and present danger that sufficient threat still exists. Concurrently, travelers appear to support the continuation of appropriate security measures. That support, however, is dependent on the public's perception of the threat and the conduct of those administering them. Furthermore, the perceptions of the ACLU, the Centre for National Security studies, the Arab-American league, and others that constitutional guarantees are being put in danger will persist.

■ INTERNATIONAL PERSPECTIVES

International efforts to combat the problems related to air hijacking have been mixed. Some countries have matched or exceeded the efforts of the United States, mostly notable those in Europe and Israel. Other countries may recognize the threat but be totally unable to finance any improvement measures. Still others totally disregard the need for adequate security measures and tend to make air travel to and from those countries potentially dangerous. Admittedly, the temptations offered by a specific airport environment to terrorists will fluctuate and the approaches to counter the threat will vary as well.

Additionally, efforts to enforce and adequately make use of existing international treaties will also only progress when the international community is forced to recognize the need. Unfortunately, different commitment levels on the part of the signatories often limit the effectiveness of international treaties. Divergent interpretations of provisions, various attitudes toward the particular treaty, and the difficulty in appropriately enforcing them also affect the outcome of each effort to utilize the treaties. Overall, countries diverge in their perception of the threat. Their exposure to a particular threat also differs, and levels of international attention to fluctuating sets of circumstances often change. Consequently, although well intentioned, the treaties have been often proved to be ineffective.

■ THE TREND BEGINS

On November 24, the day before Thanksgiving 1971, a passenger calling himself Dan Cooper boarded Northwest Orient Flight 305 at Portland, Oregon. He looked like any other businessman. Only 36 other passengers were on board that day and the plane was, therefore, only partially filled. Just as the plane was taxiing for takeoff, Cooper handed a note to the flight attendant telling her to read it immediately. It concisely indicated, "I have a bomb in my briefcase." Cooper announced he would blow up the plane unless he was given $200,000 and four parachutes. In order to bolster his demand, he let two of the flight attendants see what he claimed was a bomb.

In Seattle, Washington, the authorities decided to comply. Cooper received the money and the parachutes, prepared at nearby McChord AFB. The hijacker permitted all the passengers and two of the flight attendants to deplane, but demanded the pilot fly on to Reno, Nevada, in spite of the fact he had earlier expressed a desire to proceed to Mexico. Surprising authorities, and as per Cooper's specific instructions, the plane headed for Reno at low altitude and minimum cruising speed with the flaps down and ventral stairs extended. When the crew landed at Reno he was not on board. Miraculously, he allegedly survived after parachuting out over rough terrain. He has never been officially found, although stories abound about both his success and alternatively about his possible death on impact.

With the ensuing publicity the incident received, Cooper became a bit of a folk hero, and his legend grows somewhat each time the tale is told. Nonetheless, airport authorities did sit up and take notice of his success and began to take measures to prevent the event from reccurring elsewhere. From a certain perspective, this was one of the first and only truly potentially successful hijackings. It was a simple criminal act. Even more deadly threats were soon to be improved upon and fine tuned by international terrorists. It was to take much more serious disasters to really get the attention of the public, the US government and the international community.

■ EARLY FEDERAL AVIATION REGULATIONS

It is generally understood that Federal Aviation Regulations (FARs) were designed to ensure the security of airports serving scheduled air carriers required to have screening programs. In other words, air carriers had the responsibility to prevent and deter carriage of weapons and explosives aboard their aircraft by potential hijackers. Where applicable, air carriers issued and carried out written security programs, which accomplished 100-percent screening of all passengers and searched all carry-on items (FAR Part 121.538 and Part 108.7. *Note: Current regulations are contained in 49 CFR Chapter XII, Parts 1540*). Post–9/11, this basic concept had been expanded to require all baggage be screened by explosive detection equipment before 31 December 2002, not by airlines but by the government.

Conversely, airports serving applicable air carriers were responsible for preventing and deterring unauthorized access to the air operations area, and for providing law enforcement support at passenger screening stations. Basically, FAR Parts 107 and 108 required airport operators and airlines to issue a security program incorporating the above procedures. Overall, the FARs set the general guidelines for all security assets and procedures at US airports and for US and foreign airlines servicing US airports.

Originally, the amount of security required effectively to deter hijacking was thought to be directly proportional to the size of the aircraft. This approach took into consideration the relationship between the amounts of publicity the hijacker could receive from the incident and the number of passengers on board; meaning the larger the aircraft, the more hostages and the bigger media event. Therefore, tighter security rules were originally developed for larger passenger aircraft.

To ensure consistent application of FAA's security rules and to achieve the necessary and appropriate level of security per aircraft, FAR Part 108 evolved. As stated, Part 108 based security requirements upon aircraft complexity instead of certification and categorized commercial airplanes into three groups according to configured seating capacities.

1. Over 60 seats
2. 31–60 seats
3. Less than 31 seats

Commercial aircraft with over 60 seats have the most stringent requirements. Concurrently, Part 108 required the adoption of a comprehensive security program for operations with 31 through 60 seats. The program was supposed to be comparable to that required for operations with airplanes having more than 60 seats, but normally the smaller operators were required only to have to implement those portions of the program that required the following:

1. Procedures for contacting a law enforcement agency and arranging for a response to an incident when needed.

2. Instruction for all crew members and internal employees in appropriate security procedures. Each operator was required to implement its full security program upon notification of specific threats by the FAA.

For operators of smaller aircraft, 1–30 seats, no security program was required unless passengers had uncontrolled access to a sterile area. The concept of sterile areas will be discussed in a later chapter. In all cases where passengers had uncontrolled access, or where passengers were discharged into a sterile area, provisions had to be made properly to screen the passengers. Carriers controlled access to the sterile area through surveillance and escort procedures or through the screening procedures of another carrier.

This has become a particularly sensitive issue, especially since 9/11. Experts agree that it is often fairly easy to circumvent security procedures at a small feeder airport and later gain access to the sterile concourse at a larger airport. Unfortunately, as recently as March 2002, one small airport in Minnesota had a brand new x-ray screening machine still visible in the terminal in its original box, but still not deployed for regular use.

■ AIRPORT SECURITY PROGRAMS

Where security programs were required by the FARs, both the airlines and the airport were required to have security programs in writing signed by the operators and approved by the FAA. Overall, the airport security program was at a minimum to include descriptions of the following:

1. The air operations area—that portion of the airport designed and used for landing, take-off, or surface maneuvering of aircraft

2. Areas on or adjacent to the airport, which affect security of the air operations area

3. Each exclusive area

4. The procedures, facilities, and equipment used to perform the control functions by the airport operator and by each air carrier

5. Notification procedures

6. Alternate security procedures for use in emergencies and other unusual conditions

7. The system for maintaining records of security related incidents

8. The law enforcement support system and the peace officer training program

> **Note:** *As opposed to the common notion of airport passenger security, the security provisions of FAR Part 139 are primarily concerned with public protection and appropriate safeguards against inadvertent entry of persons or large domestic animals into any air operations area. The provisions of FAR Part 107 Airport Security related to the control of access to air operations areas by unauthorized persons and ground vehicles. Like Part 107, Part 108 "Airplane and Airport Operator Security" was also concerned with the prevention of unauthorized persons and vehicles. In essence, FAR 107 and FAR 108 addressed issues of criminal violence and aircraft piracy, whereas Part 139 is concerned with the segregation of the public from air operations as a function of operational safety.*

Furthermore, as mentioned, Part 139 did not regulate security procedures at reliever or feeder airports, which flow into larger metropolitan airports. For example, like many small airports, Flying Cloud Airport in Eden Prairie, Minnesota, leaves the gates to the airport open at all times. Controversy has often developed between owners of aircraft that want aircraft secured and operators of a flight school that want easy access for students. On top of proprietary concerns, these smaller airports are far too accessible to the determined terrorist for a variety of reasons. Recent threats of potential biological attacks possibly by use of crop-dusting aircraft are a perfect example. The overall security situation at these facilities still poses a major loophole in a broader aviation security context. Additionally, the status of the student pilots has become an issue.

▩ NEW CARRIER RULES—1972

Part 121.538, the rule specifically pertaining to air carriers at the time, became effective on 31 January 1972 (*Federal Register* 37:2500, Docket 11432). It required each certificate holder to adopt and implement a screening system that would detect weapons and explosives in carry-on baggage or on the person of passengers. Because the public was screaming for action, the amendment to Part 121 was rapidly, some say hastily, put into effect with only three day's notice to the airlines. The Rules were also once again adjusted to require each carrier to submit its screening program to the FAA Administrator no later than 5 June 1972 (*Federal Register*, 37:4904, 7 March 1972). Procedures were inconsistent between airlines, and the rush was on to comply with the new rules.

Each carrier's program was to contain some minimum acceptable elements. They included:

1. The ability to prevent or deter unauthorized access to its aircraft
2. The means to ensure that baggage would be checked in by a responsible agent or representative of the certificate holder

3. The capability to prevent cargo and checked baggage from being loaded aboard its aircraft unless handled in accordance with the certificate holder's security procedures

How each of these requirements was implemented was varied depending on the airline. The airlines subsequently had many comments to submit, as was their right under the Administrative Procedures Act. Many useful suggestions were made based on airline experiences during this first trial and error period. Several other provisions were incorporated after receiving comments submitted as per the original notice of Proposed Rulemaking issued in September. The rules have been continually amended over the years, and are once again being closely reviewed and updated by the new Transportation Security Administration as part of 49 CFR Chapter XXII. The Rules had also undergone considerable review in the year 2000/2001.

Admittedly, in 1972, after President Richard M. Nixon issued a presidential decree declaring a renewed emphasis on air security, the rules were somewhat tumultuously put into place. Consequently, the rules were revamped again to reflect the perceived pressure to implement immediately the screening requirements. The new deadline for carrier screening programs was moved up to 8 May 1972. Further refinements took place in 1981 when Part 121.538 was rewritten as Part 108. Part 107 continued to pertain strictly to the airport operator. The Report of the President's Commission on Aviation Security and Terrorism, issued on 5 May 1990, became the catalyst for recommendations to again amend the rules in the 1990s.

Owing to pressure from the public and concerned government officials, the FAA originally had rushed to implement changes to the Federal Aviation Regulations. As stated, Part 121.538 was issued on 31 January 1972, and required each certificate holder to adopt and implement a screening system that would detect weapons and explosives in carry-on baggage or on the person of passengers, all with only three days notice. The rules, although not considered by the airlines and airport operators to be totally unnecessary, presented some huge obstacles. They were deeply concerned over their ability to achieve them within the required time frame. Equipment was scarce, the costs were likely to be high, and the airlines were concerned about passenger reactions to the delays. The same situation permeates the industry today in light of new rules mandating 100% screening by new explosive-detection equipment.

The development of airport and airline security regulations actually evolved over many years and months. Aviation bombings and hijackings are rare but represent a significant threat, especially if you are a passenger on board or involved on the ground. In an attempt to reduce the vulnerability of aircraft, implementation of the 1972 rules forced air carriers to bear the primary responsibility for applying security measures to passengers, flight and maintenance crews, carry-on baggage, and cargo. Furthermore, originally, Section 538 of the former Part 121 specifically required each scheduled carrier to develop and implement a security program designed to prevent or deter the carriage aboard aircraft of sabotage devices or weapons and to prevent or deter unauthorized access to aircraft. It also required passenger baggage to be checked and cleared in accordance with detailed security procedures, thereby resulting in the security checkpoints now so familiar at airports today.

Landmark revision of procedures and security measures after repeated hijacking incidents in the 1970s also gave rise to specifics of Part 107 and Part 108. Part 107 formally gave airport operators the responsibility for providing protection against unauthorized access to air operations areas. Furthermore, airports governed by state and local authorities were held responsible for assuming duties to maintain a secure ground environment and supported by official law enforcement personnel. Part 107 specifically applied to airport operators and Part 108 pertained to the airline carrier. Both parts have been amended from time to time and were first significantly amended as a result of the Report of the President's Commission on Aviation Security and Terrorism of 1972.

Part 108 rules have also gone through much iteration, but by the end of 1972, the increasing frequency of terrorist or criminal threat prompted the FAA to require at a minimum:

a. Screening of all persons and carry-on baggage before entering an airport's departure area (only authorized personnel should be able to enter restricted areas)

b. The availability of a sworn law enforcement officer at the screening point within a specific period of time

c. Development by both scheduled airline carriers and airport managers of security programs approved by the FAA

d. Development of an airport disaster plan

The use of the new procedures exposed some of the flaws. For example, an emergency order closed a glaring loophole in the law, which had originally excluded smaller aircraft from the screening procedures. After two hijackings of Pacific Southwest Airlines on 5 and 6 July 1972, respectively, the need to expand the screening requirements became self-evident. At the time, a California man received the unenviable distinction of being hijacked twice in a single trip. The emergency order was directed at high-density "shuttle flights" (*Aviation Daily*, 202:42, 11 July 1972, Washington, DC, Ziff-Davis Co.). This order was to become effective 30 days after issuance, and all carry-on baggage was to be screened for this level of travel as well. Passengers themselves were simply required to show two forms of identification, and those that could not were required to be screened. At the time, the smaller airlines claimed they were being discriminated against, because at the time larger airlines still had not been forced to conduct 100% screening of passengers and carry-on baggage. This set of circumstances, of course, would change in the very near future.

Additional revisions to FAR Parts 107, 108, and 139, effective in November 2001, filled in other loopholes in the initial rules. The rules increased the number of aircraft operators subject to the security program provisions. They now included all individuals who enplane or deplane into a sterile area and even pertained to certain helicopter operators. The rules also expanded the training requirements for these same aircraft operator security personnel and required them to participate in airport-sponsored contingency exercises. It should be pointed out that general aviation aircraft were not intended to be covered by Part 108, but these aircraft as well as Fixed Based Operators (FBOs) are covered as tenants under the rules contained in Part 107 and Part 139. The changes better defined the areas of an airport in which security interests are the most critical.

NEW AIRPORT OPERATOR RULES

The air carriers were not the only entities compelled quickly to provide a safe environment for aviation. The rewritten Part 107 required the airport operator to "immediately adopt and put into use facilities and procedures designed to prevent or deter persons and vehicles from unauthorized access to air operations" (*Federal Register*, 37:5689, 5691, 18 March 1972). In another hurried but necessary move, the FAA gave airport operators only 90 days in which to prepare and submit to the FAA Administrator an entire security plan for the airport facility. Airport operators all over the nation scrambled to comply. Again, the quality of the procedures varied from airport to airport. Some local authorities believed their airport was low risk and did not emphasize the need for real quality programs. Others immediately grasped the need and reacted appropriately.

Unfortunately, problems persisted. From the time period December 1998 through May 1999, the Inspector General of the FAA conducted approximately 173 tests at eight US airports. In a somewhat shocking discovery, the investigators gained unauthorized entry to restricted areas on 117 occasions. The Inspector General gained access by following authorized employees into restricted areas, riding unguarded elevators, going through unlocked gates and doors, and walking through cargo areas. Some of the problems that plagued airport operators in the past therefore endure today. The investigators concluded that airport operators and air carriers had not implemented effective access control procedures, engaged in improper training of employees, and the FAA did not coordinate appropriate oversight programs (Theresa Anderson, "Airport Security," *Security Management*, February 2000, Pgs. 73–74). History often repeats itself.

RESISTANCE FADES

The airlines abandoned their last bit of resistance to 100-percent mandatory screening ironically after two nonterrorist attempted hijackings in October 1972. In a twist of fate, the airlines were completely frustrated with the increasing numbers of fleeing felons seeking to escape by acquiring free airline transportation. In one particular case, an airline agent walked down a jetway to secure the aircraft door prior to taxiing and takeoff. Before the agent was finished securing the door, four late passengers followed him into the jetway and shot him. They also shot at a ramp serviceman, who was motioning to the flight crew and simply caught the attention of the escaping felons. He was trying to advise the flight crew that they had started the engines while the plane was still being refueled. The hijackers turned out to be a bank robber and three murder suspects. They professed no political cause; just a desire for a quick getaway, and the plane appeared to them to be a handy tool to do so.

Immediately on the heels of the first incident, three alleged rapists hijacked a Southern Airways DC-9 departing Birmingham, Alabama, in November 1973. They controlled the aircraft for almost thirty hours and eventually shot and wounded the copilot. A demand for $10 million was refused but authorities turned over $2 million to the hijackers, who subsequently diverted the plane to Havana, Cuba. Of particular note was that at one point the hijackers wanted the pilot to fly the aircraft into a nuclear facility. This comment alarmed a great many people, particularly the authorities at the Tennessee Valley Authority, who were alerted to the threat (Frank Brennan, "Anti-hijacking: Who Pays the Bill," *Chicago Daily News*, 23 February 1973). The instance did have a silver lining. Both federal authorities and airline security were unprepared for incidents of this type and the incidents provided a wake up call. At this point, the public, law enforcement, and airline/airport security officials were forced to collaborate on more effective ways to deal successfully with hijackers.

In another quickly implemented attempt to curb the tide of both terrorist and simply criminal attempts to commandeer aircraft, the FAA issued two emergency regulations on 5 December 1972. One gave carriers 30 days in which to institute a 100% search of all passengers and carry-on items and the other gave airport operators 60 days in which to station at least one law enforcement officer at each passenger checkpoint during boarding and preboarding. The airlines and airport operators again immediately scrambled to comply. The costs were considered to be prohibitive by the airlines and those entities operating the airports: private, local, and state alike. Local law enforcement often insisted that they had neither the resources nor the desire to accept such responsibility. Many believed hijacking was a federal issue. Consequently, airline and operator responses were instantaneous, vocal, and negative. This was in spite of the fact they knew that something had to be done. It was the burden of cost that was the critically disputed factor. What entities should actually bear these costs continues to be a controversial issue.

Regardless of all opposition, the airlines and airport operators attempted to implement the procedures on 5 January 1973. Passengers proved to be more resilient and infinitely more patient than the airlines had anticipated. The fear of terrorism had softened the public's attitude toward the benefits of improved and stringent security. Confusion, the absence of sufficient screening equipment, unfamiliarity with adequate security procedures, and the fear of legal repercussions from passengers all contributed to the general chaos regardless of everyone's good intentions. Somehow everyone survived and in time regular routines were established. The process became more orderly and the flow of passengers smoother.

■ HOW TO IMPLEMENT?

Regardless of general acceptance of the threat, not everyone agreed on how to meet the challenges the threat created. For example, the Airport Operators Council International (AOCI) initially sought a restraining order to stop the implementation of the new rules. They contended that hijacking was a chronic national problem and not an emergency. In response, they sought to overturn implementation of the new rules on an administrative technicality. They reasoned that the FAA, by not allowing time for comment before issuing the orders, was acting in violation of the Federal Administrative Procedures Act. A federal judge agreed based purely on the procedural error argument and issued a ten-day restraining order. Many people believe that the real issue was whether the required law enforcement was to be federal or local and who should pay for the increased security. At the time, the Department of Transportation (DOT) clearly advocated that the law enforcement responsibility remained with the local authorities. Undersecretary of the DOT, Egil Krogh, even testified before a congressional hearing that, "We see no rationale for distinguishing the airport from the bus depot or the train station in the provision of police protection" (*Aviation Daily*, 205:319, 28 February 1973). Although his comments sound like they hold a great deal of common sense, the comparison of a train station, bus depot, and airport is not quite valid considering the complexity of the airport environment. Airports differ significantly from other transportation hubs such as bus terminals or train depots. First, airports require considerably more land and they are generally located quite a distance from the cities they serve.

The controversy raged on, but on 12 February 1973, the judge vacated the restraining order that had earlier been issued purely on an administrative technicality. The court correctly decided that the safety of the traveling public was in jeopardy by failure to implement the regulations (*Aviation Daily*, 205:233, 13 February 1973). Regardless, the AOCI continued the fight in the US Court of Appeals. At that level, the court ruled that the FAA could continue to carry out the new rules but penalties were not to be imposed without a hearing if the airport operator cited was making a reasonable effort to comply with the requirement (*Aviation Daily*, 205–267, 10 February 1973). A good faith effort was required in light of the need and minor infractions could be overlooked for the time being. Basically, airport operators evidencing the proper efforts to comply were not to be fined.

At the time, airline carriers were not only confronted with the gigantic issues of who should pay and who exactly should be in charge of law enforcement but also with other procedural specifics as well. Topics relating to the legality of searches and seizures plagued the early compliance attempts. Some airlines had even forbidden their employees from performing personal searches of passengers, fearing lawsuits. Right from the beginning, the airlines perceived the dilemma of having to deny permission to board the aircraft to those passengers who could not be cleared by the available magnetometers; thereby returning their fares, losing their business, and reducing company profits. The airlines were also legitimately concerned over potential lawsuits from intrusive searches by passengers who were not just insulted by the searches but believed they invaded their personal privacy. They were right, and over the years untold numbers of lawsuits would be filed, settled, and litigated at great cost.

Jurisdictional issues also continue to arise. Who is really in charge is a familiar cliché. Back in 1973, the Civil Aeronautics Board Chairman, Secor Browne, had criticized the program arguing that airport security should be the purview of federal rather than local responsibility and that the federal government should allocate funds to cover the costs (*Aviation Daily*, 205:114, 14 January 1973). He did not have much support, however, and local law enforcement persevered while bearing the lion's share of the responsibility. In a cooperative effort, however, the FAA continued to station federal law enforcement agents at airports as part of a regulated FAA security program and the Federal Marshal Program.

As mentioned, consistency was another problem, and early in 1975, the Air Transportation Association sought to work out a single-standard security program. Their efforts produced the Air Carrier Standard Security Program (ACSSP), which attempted to bring some pattern to the diverse interpretations of the new rules. In 1976, all but a few of the carriers accepted the program and today it is mandatory.

■ PUBLIC LAW 93-366

By 1974, it became obvious that US law relating to hijacking needed strengthening. On 5 August 74, Public Law 93-366 was signed into law. Title I, better known as the Anti-Hijacking Act of 1974, and Title II, the Air Transportation Security Act of 1974, significantly changed the Federal Aviation Act of 1958. The law literally implemented the provisions of the Hague Convention for the Suppression of Unlawful Seizure of Aircraft agreed to by the international community.

To give some teeth to the new law, the international aspects of the legislation gave the President some broad statutory authority to regulate international air operations. For example, he could "without notice or hearing and for as long as he determines necessary" suspend the right of any carrier, either US or foreign, to engage in air transportation between the US and any nation permitting its territory to be used in furtherance of air piracy. In an additional broadening provision, the President also could suspend foreign air commerce between the US and any foreign carrier that continued air service between itself and a nation harboring terrorists. This broad regulatory power sounds good, but like many things is more complicated and difficult to enforce than it appears on the surface.

■ DISSEMINATION OF THREAT WARNINGS

After 30 years of implementation, some issues, such as the dissemination of threat warnings, have still completely to be resolved. The bomb that detonated in the belly of Pan Am Flight 103 over Lockerbie, Scotland, forced authorities to rethink the threat warning issue. On the other hand, the airlines do not want to alarm passengers unnecessarily. However, many passengers believe that they have the right to know. The Lockerbie bomb had been inserted into a Toshiba radio-cassette player and security officials had previously located two such bombs on other airlines.

It was later determined that some people within the system knew of the specific threat. Consequently, the real issue revolves around the idea of whether the right people get the right information when they need it to provide first-rate security. In October 1988, a similar Toshiba radio-cassette player was found in the possession of the Popular Front for the Liberation of Palestine. A second bomb was discovered inside a Toshiba Boom Box Model 453 in the automobile of a member of another terrorist group. It contained the same barometric triggering device used in the Pan Am bombing. The FAA did send out a warning on 18 November 1988; a month before Lockerbie. However, at least one airline official did not see the bulletin, because he had been on vacation. The warning had gone out to all US embassies and consulates, but the official who really needed the intelligence did not receive and therefore could not react in order to avoid the tragedy in Scotland. Procedures now require carriers to provide written confirmation of receipt of the threat information. How they are exactly required to handle the information is still under debate.

Police and investigators look at what remains of the flight deck of Pan Am 103 on a field in Lockerbie, Scotland, in this December 1988 photo. Two Libyan intelligence agents were eventually tried in a Scottish court in the Netherlands for this terrorist act. Only one was convicted and sentenced to 20 years imprisonment. *AP Photo / CP Photo Assignment Services.*

■ RECOMMENDATIONS OF THE PRESIDENT'S COMMISSION

The Report of the President's Commission on Aviation Security and Terrorism, dated 15 May 1990 and published by the Government Printing Office the same year, suggested more than 60 recommendations for improving airport and aircraft security procedures as part of the aftermath of the Lockerbie tragedy. The committee, of course, concluded that the United States should pursue a more vigorous counterterrorism policy, which was not a particularly controversial recommendation to make. The report did document some other suggested changes, including the following:

1. The federal government, not local government, should manage security at domestic airports through federal security managers, obviating any issues of jurisdiction between law enforcement agencies.
2. The State Department should pursue further negotiations with foreign governments to permit US carriers to comply with US law overseas requiring 100% screening and other security measures even when they conflict with local law.
3. The FAA should launch a priority research program to improve technological means to prevent terrorism, placing the costs of research and development on the federal government.
4. Public notification of threats to civil aviation should be made where appropriate.
5. Victims should qualify for special financial compensation.
6. The State Department must take major steps to ensure that the families of victims receive prompt, humane, and courteous treatment and service from airlines.

Some of these ideas sound good on paper but would not necessarily be easy to effectuate. For example, the United States cannot demand that overseas airports comply with US laws. The art of diplomacy is needed in persuading them of the needs involved. Some are more easily convinced than others. Additionally, public notification is riddled with problems. Who determines if the threat is real and who decides what action to take are really thorny issues which remain unresolved. The issue of jurisdiction between law enforcement agencies came back to haunt the nation in September 2001. Once again, the concept of federal managers was openly discussed and now has been implemented over a decade later.

■ AVIATION SECURITY IMPROVEMENT ACT OF 1990

Based on the above-mentioned recommendations, the US Congress moved swiftly. They enacted the Aviation Security Improvement Act of 1990, PL 101-604, dated 16 November 1990; a mere 6 months after the commission issued its report. The Act contributed to the successful implementation of many new and innovative security procedures. Title I of the law deals with general aviation security and Title II with appropriate US responses to terrorism affecting Americans abroad. In the aftermath of the Lockerbie disaster, the White House was eager to show the public that the government was responding to a perceived need. One of the findings contained in the new law was that, "the safety and security of passengers of United States air carriers against terrorists threats should be given the highest priority by the United States Government." Second, "the report of the President's Commission on Aviation Security and Terrorism, dated 15 May 1990, found that current aviation security systems are inadequate to provide such protection" (Internet: http://cas.faa.gov/reports/pl101604/pl101604.html.)

First, the legislation established a number of new offices and positions. Within the FAA and the Department of Transportation, it created a Director of Intelligence and Security as well as numerous federal security manager positions authorized to implement security programs throughout the United States. The Director of Intelligence and Security reported directly to the Secretary of Transportation. The director's duties included the following:

1. Receipt, assessment, and distribution of intelligence information relating to long-term transportation security
2. Development of policies, strategies, and plans for dealing with threats to transportation security
3. Other planning relating to transportation security, including coordination of countermeasures with appropriate federal agencies
4. Serving as the primary liaison of the Secretary with the intelligence and law enforcement communities
5. Such other duties as the Secretary may prescribe as necessary to ensure, to the extent possible, the security of the traveling public

The Act amended the Federal Aviation Act of 1958 (49 U.S.C. App 1341–1358). By doing so, it also created an Assistant Administrator of Civil Aviation Security. This individual became responsible for the day to day management of the FAA field security resources. The duties included, but were not limited to, the enforcement of security-related requirements, identification of research and development requirements of security-related activities, and assessment of threats to civil aviation, as well as the inspection of security systems. In essence, the position was designed to have one individual accountable for measures to strengthen air transportation security.

The legislation also sanctioned the positioning of Federal Security Managers at all Category X US airports and Liaison Officers at designated airports outside the United States. The general idea was to review and coordinate security on a global basis. The legislation also required an annual report to Congress, which solicits information on the successfulness of security at all levels of airport operations. Section 105 mandated background checks on airport and airline personnel. Additionally, Section 107 ordered a program to accelerate research and development and the rapid implementation of new technologies and procedures to counteract terrorist acts against civil aviation. In further response to the President's Commission, the law also required that US air carriers provide the Department of State the passenger manifest for any flight involved in an aviation disaster within one hour of notification; thereby hoping to accelerate timely notification of the next of kin.

■ THE FEDERAL AVIATION REAUTHORIZATION ACT OF 1996

More legislation followed with congressional passing of the Federal Aviation Reauthorization Act of 1996. President Bill Clinton approved Public Law 104-264 in October 1996. Title II contained Section 301 entitled Aviation Security, and included "Report on Proposed Legislation on Funding for Airport Security" which mandated that the FAA, in cooperation with other appropriate agencies, conduct a study and submit to Congress a report on, "whether and if so how to transfer certain responsibilities of air carriers under federal law for security activities conducted onsite at commercial service airports to airport operators or to the federal government or to provide for shared responsibilities between air carriers and airport operators or the federal government" (PL 104-264). The study examined the evolution of aviation security responsibilities. Overall, the study concluded that a system of shared responsibilities was the best model. It did not conclude, to the dismay of many local officials and airline corporate officers, that a transfer of air carrier responsibilities to another agency, entity, or the federal government was appropriate. This conclusion rankled those seeking to centralize security responsibilities with the federal government.

To soften the recommendations, the study details the incremental increases in federal government involvement in aircraft and airport security measures and predicts the proliferation of assistance would increase especially in the area of security training. The study also tackled the tough question of who pays for appropriate levels of security at American airports. In essence, they reasoned that any security measures taken or required in the future should be paid for by the users of the system; that is, the traveler. In reality, the traveler in the long run will determine just how much intrusion they will tolerate and just how much they are willing to pay for it via the legislative process. As a result of the compromise bill passed by Congress in November 2001, passengers can expect to pay the costs of the increased security. After January 2002, taxes and fees for passengers include a security fee of up to $10 per round trip ticket, a 7.5% domestic ticket tax, a $3.00 per person per flight segment fee, and a maximum of $18 in airport passenger facility charges. Taxes and fees can amount to 50% of the cost of the ticket. Additionally, airlines are required to pay about $4.00 per passenger to the government to cover security screening costs (*Air Transport News*, 16 November 2001). Passengers paid $977 million in the fiscal year ending September 2002: six times the amount the airline industry paid.

At the time of the study, annual US air carrier passenger traffic in the domestic system alone rose from 424 million to 523 million (Internet: http://cas.faa.gov/reports/98study/98study.html, Pg. 5). The commercial aircraft fleet had risen to 4,916 aircraft in 1996. The current aviation security regulations apply to 165 US air carriers, 164 foreign carriers, and numerous freight forwarders. For perspective, during the study (FY 1996), FAA aviation security special agents conducted 6317 US air carrier inspections and 643 foreign air carrier inspections at US airports. They also performed 870 US airport facility inspections, 267 facility security inspections, and 123 foreign airport assessments in addition to 223 random freight forwarder inspections. The TSA has already assumed this function.

It is indisputable that fairly stringent security measures had been in place for flights departing the US for many years. As the President directed in July 1996, air carriers are performing preflight security inspections on all international flights, "on every plane, every cabin, every cargo hold, and every time" (Internet: http://cas.faa.gov/reports/98study/98study.html, Pg. 6). During the mid-1990s, the FAA and the Office of the Secretary of Transportation worked closely with the National Security Council to refocus federal government attention on the needs to improve airport security. They were also successful in creating the Aviation Security Advisory Committee (ASAC) of the Baseline Working Group (BWG) on 17 July 1996, which has the unfortunate honor of sharing its inception date with the TWA Flight 800 disaster. Unfortunately, as is well documented, the security procedures in place proved to be insufficient either because the rules were deficient or the implementation left a great deal to be desired.

▪ CIVIL AVIATION SECURITY—TRANSPORTATION SECURITY ADMINISTRATION

The Federal Aviation Administration's Civil Aviation Security (CAS) Division was tasked with keeping civil aviation safe from terrorist attacks. Their mission was to "ensure and promote a secure and safe civil aviation system." Their goal was to be recognized as the world leader in civil aviation, identifying and countering aviation-related threats to US citizens worldwide. The Office of the FAA Associate Administrator for Civil Aviation Security developed and implemented regulatory policies, programs, and procedures to prevent criminal, terrorist, and other disruptive acts against civil aviation.

The organization was divided into two main sections, one handling internal issues and the other tasked to manage external security issues. The internal division had the responsibility for all security-related issues within the agency and included the following programs: internal investigations, drug investigation support, personnel security, industrial security, identification media, physical security, and communications information security. The internal division was responsible for establishing and enforcing regulations, policies, and procedures for all of these areas. They were also tasked to identify specific potential threats and establish appropriate countermeasures, deploy Federal Air Marshals (Civil Aviation Security Specialists) on selected US flights, and provide overall guidance to ensure security at airports. FAA personnel monitored and inspected air carrier and airport security and had the authority to assess civil penalties. The Civil Aviation Security Specialist program administered by the FAA was abolished 21 February 2003 and incorporated into the TSA.

The "investigations" program, now part of the Office of Security and Hazardous Materials, is considered to be an internal affairs division of the FAA and coordinates all matters that may involve the misconduct or malfeasance of an employee. Special Agents constitute an internal police force for the scrutiny of employee involvement in any criminal activity in order to supervise those who are supposed to be protecting the public. The potential for bribery, extortion, and intimidation of FAA employees by criminals is a constant threat. Organized crime will always pursue FAA employees who may be able to facilitate the introduction of contraband into civil aviation or other criminal activity. FAA employees are not immune from the financial pressures of the world or from the sophisticated and often brutal intimidation methods of drug cartels. Protecting its own assets and policing itself contributes to the maintenance and safety of the entire commercial aviation system. The job is huge and requires constant vigilance.

The drug investigations support program exists to assist and supplement law enforcement personnel in the ongoing efforts to control the gigantic flow of illegal drugs through many US airports. Agents seek to assist local, state, and federal law enforcement agents in all cases where civil aviation is involved. They are specially trained and provide law enforcement with additional expertise in aviation-related cases requiring a unique knowledge of carrier operations both on the ground and in the air. They work in very close cooperation with US Customs, the Drug Enforcement Agency, and the Federal Bureau of Investigation.

The personnel security program assesses the integrity of new employees. The program is responsible for "background checks" of prospective agency employees. The agency also ensures that designated personnel at air route control centers, terminal radar approach control facilities, and other staffed facilities are properly trained and equipped in security matters. Criminal and financial checks are routine and often military and medical records, when appropriate, are also reviewed. In conjunction, the industrial security program is tasked with providing security clearances for industry officials and companies that contract with US civil aviation. The program is supposed to ensure that contracting companies maintain the security of sensitive FAA information that the contractors generally have access. The potential for serious security violations is always present when civilian contractors are involved. This program attempts to keep civilian contractors aware of the need to maintain a constant state of security awareness and remain focused. Operational security requirements are often ignored for the sake of expediency and whenever the concept of profit versus expenses for security come into play. The old adage that "loose lips sink ships" can be easily forgotten in today's world of mass communications, cell phones, computers, and wireless communications.

The identification media program was assigned the task of developing and controlling all identification materials used by FAA employees. According to their Web site, there are currently no less than sixteen different types actively in use. The changes in technology in this field occur frequently, and the ability to counterfeit identification badges is a constant threat. The task of staying on top of changes and improvements is a daunting endeavor and presents some unique challenges. Access control is an essential part of any program, and just staying on top of the changing technology is a task unto itself.

The physical security program is in charge of keeping all FAA assets secure, including both tangible assets and personnel. The property and equipment in use by the FAA is of exceptional value and range from TACAN (Tactical Air Navigation) testing facilities to aircraft. The possibility of loss from theft and sabotage is an ever-present danger and constant vigilance is mandatory. In addition, the personnel in this program must be able to assess the threat both internally and externally.

The FAA is also a communications-intensive organization. The communications security program guarantees that the integrity of the FAA's telecommunications is maintained. This program is also involved in highly technical cryptographic operations in order to deny unauthorized users access to FAA communications. This particular function is absolutely critical to the safe operations of air traffic control operations and flight operations in general. The FAA also strives to provide effective air traffic control voice and data communications security as well as effective navigation system security, including Global Positioning Systems (GPS). Again, the rapid changes in technology make this task a daunting one. Sometimes the "bad guys" have more sophisticated equipment than the "good guys."

Arguably, one of the most important liaisons exists between the FAA and the Office of Intelligence and Security in the Office of the Secretary of Transportation. They coordinate security and intelligence between agencies. Continuing cooperation has been further encouraged by the formation of a Department of Transportation Security Working Group under the direction of the Director of the Office of Intelligence and Security. The FAA Office of Intelligence provided intelligence analysis of the threats to civil aviation as the basis for determining the application of aviation security measures. Similar to military intelligence units, the division routinely published synthesized intelligent and threat-assessment information. These products were used to evaluate security programs both domestically and internationally. Information was collected from open sources and from US government-classified sources.

Information of this type is disseminated to airport operators and airlines by means of documents called "information circulars" and "security directives" as provided for by FAR 108.18 or 14 CFR Sec 108.18. If a specific threat cannot be countered, either the specific flight will be canceled or public notification will be made. When this does occur, airlines are not pleased with the ensuing loss of passengers and profits.

Since 9/11 the FAA's Civil Aviation Security organization has been integrated into the newly founded Transportation Security Administration (TSA). President Bush signed the Aviation and Transportation Security Act (PL 107-71) on 19 November 2001. It, in part, created the TSA within the Department of Transportation. For the first time in history, even though considered as an option a decade earlier, transportation security will be performed and monitored by the federal government. As a direct federal responsibility, an Undersecretary of Transportation Security, who will formally report directly to the Secretary of Transportation, will manage the program.

Specifically, the TSA will operate the passenger-screening process but its overall mission is broader. It is tasked with analyzing threats that pertain to the entire transportation infrastructure—aviation related and otherwise. The agency's budget for FY 2003 will be $4.8 billion and will be funded through contributions and fees from the airline industry and passengers as authorized under the Act. As a result of 11 September 2001, as well as underscoring the importance of the aviation industry, the budget levels of this organization (CAS and now TSA) will jump from $1345 million in FY2002 to $4800 million in 2003 (Internet: http://www.dot.gov./bit/tsa.html, 6/6/02).

The TSA assumed all passenger/carry-on bag screening on 19 November 2002, replacing contract personnel with federal employees. Additionally, all major airports were operationally to use explosive detection equipment to accomplish 100% screening of all cargo by December 2002. However, airports and airlines repeatedly indicated that this is an unfeasible date to expect total compliance. Like the 1970s, airports scrambled to comply, but the equipment is very expensive and sufficient numbers of them still need to be manufactured. Compromising what was originally a great idea, the TSA softened the mandate and has temporarily agreed to permit airports to use explosive detection equipment, trace detection equipment, bomb-sniffing dogs, manual search or a combination of the above to meet the requirement. Consequently, they technically claimed compliance with the Congressional mandate.

The agency has also selected new security managers for the nation's major airports. Unfortunately, they seem to be hiring individuals with impressive law enforcement backgrounds but with little day-to-day security experience. How successful these people are will be critical to the security of the entire aviation transportation network.

■ AVIATION SECURITY RESEARCH AND DEVELOPMENT DIVISION

The Aviation Security Research and Development Division is the lead agency within the FAA for research and development programs related to civil aviation security. It was created as early as 1974 and has accomplished a great deal in the last several years. The goal is to develop and implement equipment designed to counteract criminal and terrorist attacks against civil aviation. The Division is technology oriented and is divided into four interrelated sections: Explosives and Weapons Detection, Aircraft Hardening, Human Factors, and Airport Security Technology Integration.

The Division continues to promote research and development, especially in the area of detection of explosives and weapons and their placement on board aircraft and inside airports. Other programs are focused on automated aviation security systems for the screening of both passengers and cargo that provide for the highest throughput in the least intrusive manner. Still other programs are directed at methods to harden aircraft in order to mitigate the damaging effects of bombs, weapons, missiles, and electromagnetic interference. Detection and deterrence are the ultimate goals, which are achieved by developing systems that address all potential vulnerabilities at the airport pertaining to passengers and cargo and at air traffic control facilities.

▦ COSTS

Since the 1970s, the federal government has proffered the argument that the costs related to aviation security are just another cost of doing business for the airlines. In the years when hijacking seemed to be a constant and everyday threat, the airlines were less reluctant to argue with the government over who should bear these expenses. However, for quite a long time, the airlines have engaged in an extensive lobbying campaign for an expansion of a federal security force to pick up the responsibilities legislated to the airlines. The government had repeatedly refused to accept accountability for this type of security in spite of making sweeping declarations regarding terrorism and the nation's airways as constituting a vital national interest. In a bold statement, Senator Frank Lautenberg, a member of the President's Commission on Aviation Security and Terrorism, stated in a speech on the Senate floor on 1 August 1996:

> Congress, our Nation's airlines, and our airports have been unwilling to make the investments necessary to protect the public. Terrorism is an act of war against an entire nation, with civilians on the tragic front lines, and we have got to confront it with the same commitment and fervor that we must reserve for other threats to our national security.

His words seem hauntingly prophetic.

The concept of the nation's airways as a national asset and consequently a national security issue has been made for quite some time. However, without the constant threat of imminent hijackings, the public has not been inclined to add the expense of adequate airport and airline security to federal budget requirements. This is particularly true in light of the level of the current federal debt. Since the threat of acts of domestic terrorism at US airports did not appear real to most Americans until 9/11, they were highly disinclined to pay for current needs, let alone future requirements. The White House Commission, as early as 1996 in its final report, went so far as to say,

> The federal government should consider aviation security as a national security issue, and provide substantial funding for capital improve-

ments. The Commission believes that terrorist attacks on civil aviation are directed at the United States, and that there should be an on-going federal commitment to reducing the threats they pose (Final Report to President Clinton, Internet: http://cas.faa.gov/reports/Whc97rpt.htm, Sec 3.1, Pg. 20).

In spite of all the rhetoric, not enough resources were committed in time to prevent the 9/11 tragedy. Renewed posturing has forced the US government to readdress the issue. Concerns over the proficiency of airport screeners and who should pay their salaries and their training have now been addressed in PL 107-71. Time will only tell how this plays out in the future, but the increasing costs will have to be shared by the aviation industry, the traveling public, and the federal government.

■ WHITE HOUSE COMMISSION ON AVIATION SAFETY AND SECURITY: THE DOT STATUS REPORT

During the 1990's the White House did take an active role in investigating ways to improve security for travelers at all transportation hubs. As mentioned, much debate was exchanged and bantered back and forth on the appropriate policy positions that the US government should take. For example, should the government consider aviation security as a national security issue? If the aviation industry is a strategic asset, then government should also correspondingly provide substantial funding for capital improvements to the aviation industry infrastructure.

It was also suggested that the FAA should establish federally mandated standards for security enhancements for such concepts as explosive detection. The Aviation Security Improvement Act of 1990 (PL 101-604), mentioned above, states that prior to a requirement for a deployment of explosives-detection systems (EDS), the FAA had to certify that EDS performance meets standards based upon the amount and types of explosives likely to be used to cause catastrophic damage to commercial aircraft. In 1992, the FAA issued the draft EDS standard and the National Academy of Sciences completed the final protocols a little less than a year later. In December 1994, the Invision CTX-5000 became certified as the first EDS approved by the FAA.

The Commission also reflected on the persistent problems pertaining to screening the US mail. Security experts had recommended that the US Postal Service (USPS) should advise customers that all packages weighing over 1 lb should be subject to examination for explosives if they are to be moved by air. The USPS initially responded negatively to the obligation and suggested that the procedure would impede the USPS's ability to provide timely, reliable low-cost mail service. As mentioned, this requirement was indeed implemented after 9/11. The USPS is also concerned whether or not the public would accept further intrusion on the privacy of mail, let alone routine intrusion. The USPS's Aviation Mail Security Committee continues to debate these issues.

In 1997, based on advice from the Aviation Security Advisory Committee Baseline Working Group, the White House report also reviewed the issue of needed improvements in the area of cargo security. Consequently, on 14 May 1997, the FAA proposed amendments to standard security programs for US carriers, couriers, freight forwarders, and cargo consolidators, as well as a model security program for foreign air carriers. The whole issue of cargo acceptance and handling procedures has been discussed on numerous occasions with much input from numerous sources being considered. Regardless, according to many experts, cargo continues to present a major vulnerability (White House Commission on Aviation Safety and Security the DOT Status Report, (Internet: http://cas.faa.gov/reports/Whc98s1.htm, 1 May 2001).

■ AIR TRANSPORTATION SECURITY ACT OF 2001: PL 107-71

As stated, the President signed into law the ATSA in an effort to improve the nation's transportation security system. The Act is intended fundamentally to change the way security is performed and overseen as regards the entire transportation industry. The Act contained some specific deadlines for its new administrators. One such deadline was to issue new qualification standards for airport screeners. On 31 December 2001, Secretary Norman Mineta, US Secretary for Transportation, announced the new but very similar to the already mandated requirements for federal airport screeners. They included the need for US citizenship, possession of a high school education or equivalent, the ability to pass a background and security investigation, including a criminal records check, and the necessity of passing a standardized examination. The standards have already been proven to be problematic.

Resorting back to the private sector for assistance, the TSA and FAA also published training plans for the new aviation security personnel, meeting the congressional mandate of doing so within 60 days of the Act. The TSA hoped also to meet the deadline of 19 November 2002 to deploy 30,000 trained screeners at over 400 airports, and has since claimed to do so. The challenge is a daunting one, and they are likely to run up against the same problems currently encountered by the private security firms presently doing the job. The TSA plans to:

- Screen all persons, baggage, and cargo
- Provide stress management conflict resolution programs
- Implement policies for professional interaction with passengers

The TSA had previously issued Requests for Proposals (RFPs) devoted to screener and law enforcement personnel qualification, recruitment, experience, and screener training. They sought to develop an appropriate training regimen including a minimum of 40 hours of instruction. As a first step, as of 30 April 2002, 200 federal employees had been deployed at the Baltimore-Washington Airport marking the initiation of the program. As of July 2002, the government was still struggling to locate enough people qualified to screen passengers at the nation's airports. The TSA had hired about 7,700 screeners and claimed it needed approximately 33,000 employees. By November, however, the TSA once again claimed success in meeting the Congressional mandate of a federal screener workforce. In a complete turnaround, Admiral James M. Loy, the chief TSA administrator, announced a program in April 2003 initiating a "rightsizing" program to reduce the number of screeners currently employed by 3,000.

The airlines were also required within 60 days to amend their training programs to incorporate the TSA standards. All airline personnel, particularly aircrews, were to receive the training within six months from enactment of the new legislation. The TSA also published the procedures for airports to seek portions of the $1.5 billion authorized by Congress to fund security improvements at airports.

■ CONCLUSION

The need to develop aircraft and airport security functions became readily apparent in the early 1970s. Various jurisdictions took various approaches to counter the threat. In the United States, the Federal Aviation Regulations Part 107 and Part 108 specifically addressed these issues. Those regulations were differentiated based on the size of the aircraft and the size of the airport. The public was somewhat slow to recognize the requirement to bypass their Fourth Amendment rights, and controversy still surrounds the procedures. Additionally, specific incidents of abuse catch the media's attention and bring the issues to the forefront.

The new TSA seeks to provide, in its own words, "excellence in public service." They hope to protect the nation's transportation infrastructure and to ensure freedom of movement of people and commerce. It took thirty years for the nation to recognize and to implement federal control of security at airports. It remains to be seen how effective administration of the system becomes under federal supervision. They face incredible challenges. The responsibility is almost too massive to imagine, and critics will be quick to jump on the slightest infraction or outright failure. Additionally, bureaucracies tend to perpetuate themselves, often to the detriment of the TSA's original mandate. The public's attention span is also quite short, especially if they perceive that the threat has dissipated. A return to apathy is a major problem. Just as important a problem is when a democracy goes too far in the name of security. Constant vigilance is needed to protect and preserve our fundamental constitutional freedoms. It is a very slippery slope to forget the democratic principles upon which this nation was founded—all in the name of perceived external or internal threats. The next chapter will cover international attempts to address these problems.

chapter three

International Solutions and Reactions: Lot of Talk

■ NEWS

1. **11 August 1982**: Mohammed Rashed planted a bomb on Pan Am Flight 830. It exploded just a few minutes before it landed in Honolulu. The bombing investigation linked the attack to Saddam Hussein. Rashid was charged under the Montreal Convention and stood trial in Athens, Greece.

2. **19 January 2001**: Abdel Basset Ali al-Megrahi and Lamen Khalifa Fhimah, brought to trial in the Netherlands, pled not guilty to prosecutor's claims that they planted a plastic explosive on board the airliner that blew up 1 December 1988 over Lockerbie, Scotland.

3. **1 March 2001**: A three-judge Scottish Court found Abdel Basset Ali al-Megrahi guilty of murder based on more than eight months of trial. The defendant received a mandatory sentence of life imprisonment. The court also concluded that prosecutors failed to present sufficient evidence to meet the burden of "proof beyond a reasonable doubt" in the case against Lamen Khalifa Fhimah.

4. **26 November 2002**: Richard Reid, the man accused of attempting to smuggle a bomb concealed in his shoe on board an American Airlines flight departing Paris, is a small-time British criminal who converted to Islam while incarcerated.

5. **8 January 2003**: A federal appeals court ruled President George W. Bush has the authority to designate US citizens as "enemy combatants" and detain them in military custody if they are deemed a threat to national security.

■ CRIMES AGAINST HUMANITY

Of course, terrorism and the aircraft hijacking problem is not limited to the United States. Recently, there have been two trends in international terrorism. The actual number of incidents has been decreasing, but the lethality of incidents has been increasing. After reaching a peak in 1987, international terrorist incidents overall have been declining according to statistics collected by the US State Department. For example, in 1992, the State Department recorded 364 terrorist incidents worldwide, which was down from 666 reported in 1987. A number of cooperative international efforts have been accomplished to assist in reducing the threat worldwide. However, as noted previously, the real level of effectiveness of some of these treaties is regrettably low, depending on the circumstances and in spite of the original good intentions of the drafters and signatories.

Clearly, the problem of hijacking and terrorist or criminal acts in general against aviation is not the enigma of a single nation. It pervades many peoples and many nations and cannot be effectively opposed by one nation alone. Consequently, multilateral action by the international community has resulted in the drafting and implementation of several treaties. Combined, these treaties have met with some success and at least forced the international community jointly to recognize a global problem.

The term *crimes against humanity*, popularized after World War II at the Nuremberg trials did not originate in the context of the laws of war but with laws used in peacetime. Centuries before, the term had been used to describe acts of piracy. Sir Edward Coke, an English jurist during the reign of James I, describes pirates as *hostis humanis generis*. The Latin term is generally translated as common enemies of mankind (Robert Friedlander, *Terrorism: Documents of International and Local Control*; Dobbs Ferry, NJ: Oceana, 1979, Pg. 18).

Early US case law substantiates the concept of piracy as an international crime. In 1820, the Supreme Court in *US* vs. *Smith* (18 US 5 Wheat. Pg. 71) determined that piracy was "an offense against the law of nations," and referred to pirates as enemies of the human race. The concept was affirmed in the World Court in the famous Lotus case (PCIJ Series A, No. 10 [1927], 2 Hudson World Court Rep 20). Piracy at sea and piracy in the air have historically been treated in a similar manner, although not exactly the same. It took centuries to codify the laws of the sea, and piracy at sea is clearly universally accepted as an international crime.

On the other hand, air piracy has received sporadic intensive attention, usually after some weighty tragedy. Three major and several minor agreements on aircraft hijacking have been signed and utilized to combat terrorism. They have met with varying degrees of success. Three main challenges to each convention revolve around determining exactly which nation has jurisdiction, defining the prosecutable offenses, and establishing effective procedures for extradition. A collateral, but important, goal is to somehow force or encourage nations actually to enforce the treaties they have committed to uphold.

The following section identifies the major terrorism conventions and protocols and provides a brief summary of each. In addition, other international agreements are relevant but are outside the scope of this text. They include bilateral extradition treaties, the 1961 Vienna Convention on Diplomatic Relations, the 1963 Vienna Convention on Consular Relations, and a number of related UN Security Council and General Assembly Resolutions.

■ THE TOKYO CONVENTION

One of the first international agreements was drafted and ratified as early as 14 September 1963 and applies to acts affecting in-flight safety. In essence, the Treaty authorizes the aircraft commander to impose reasonable measures, including restraint when necessary to protect the safety of the aircraft. This treaty recognizes the inviolability of a hijacked aircraft and passengers regardless of where the aircraft may be forced to land. The signatories to the Convention ultimately agreed that, in the event of a hijacking, the country where the aircraft lands must permit the aircraft, passengers, crew, and cargo to proceed to its destination as soon as practical. Precisely, the Convention on Offenses and Certain Other Acts Committed on Board Aircraft, or Tokyo Convention of September 1963, contained provisions detailing a commitment by the signatory nations to take custody of the alleged perpetrators of criminal acts aboard aircraft and expedite the continued journey of the aircraft, crew, and its passengers. PL 91-449 realized the law in the United States, but the treaty was also signed into law in 122 other countries.

The Treaty made an attempt to define some jurisdictional sore points between nations. Exactly who has legal authority to exercise control in any given situation is often disputed. Obviously, the hijacking of an aircraft is a criminal act that usually takes place en route between more than one country. On top of that, the aircraft may well be registered to a third country. Therefore, Article 3 of the Convention provides that the state of registration has primary jurisdiction. However, a significant loophole was inadvertently legislated. The Treaty failed to force that nation which had jurisdiction to actually prosecute the offenders. Therefore, a nation could accept jurisdiction and simply neglect to prosecute. Later conventions sought to remedy this situation, but nations that stubbornly intended not to prosecute continued to do so.

Another recognized shortcoming of the Convention revolves around another jurisdictional issue. In legalese, the fact that aircraft in flight are legally regarded as part of the territory of the State of registration of the aircraft, the State where the aircraft lands will treat offenses committed on board during the flight as committed on foreign territory unless it is the State of registration of the aircraft. In cases of piracy, this created heated jurisdictional disputes. For example, in cases of passenger misconduct not rising to the level of a hijacking, minor offenses will usually not be investigated or prosecuted at all. Basically, the Tokyo Convention obligates the contracting states to establish jurisdiction over offenses and crimes only when committed on board aircraft of its own nationality. In essence, a jurisdictional gap exists when it comes to less serious crimes and created at least concurrent jurisdiction in others.

■ HIJACKING CONVENTION

Owing to the increased incidents of seizure of aircraft in the late 1960s, many concerned nations met in 1970 at The Hague, Netherlands, for another discussion of the persistent problem. As a result, the Convention for the Suppression of Unlawful Seizure of Aircraft was completed on 16 December 1970. The terms of the Convention became effective thirty days after ratification by the tenth country. With the acceptance by the US Senate, ratification in the US was completed on 14 September 1971 and proclaimed by the President on 18 October 1971 (PL 93-366). The Convention entered into force on 14 October 1971.

Overall, this agreement sought to tackle the difficult issues of extradition and prosecution of offenders neglected in the earlier Tokyo Convention. The main provision requires that every Signatory State in which a hijacker is discovered must either extradite the offender to the State whose aircraft is hijacked or prosecute the hijacker; potentially subjecting them to severe penalties. Problems have been encountered even among nations willing to take a strong stand against terrorism. For example, some nations vehemently opposed to the death penalty will not extradite terrorists to the United States on moral grounds. The conviction and sentence of the one convicted perpetrator of the Lockerbie disaster are a perfect example.

Theoretically, the signatory states must also provide "severe penalties" for the criminal offense of hijacking. As is common regarding international treaties, the exact interpretations of certain specific clauses in this Treaty are also controversial. What the term *severe penalties* precisely means to one nation might not seem so to another. Other interpretations are also open to dispute. For example, the trial of two suspected Libyan terrorists, both former intelligence officers who were accused of bombing Pan Am Flight 103 over Scotland, has created much debate over the sufficiency of the findings of the court. Both individuals were eventually tried in the Netherlands where the death penalty is illegal. One individual was acquitted and the other received a life sentence—much to the disappointment of many of the surviving relatives and legal observers in the United States. However, the ability of one country to get another country to do what it wants has been a thorny diplomatic issue for centuries.

The Treaty definitively requires that each nation make the offense of unlawful seizure of an aircraft a crime. Article 1 offers a definition of the actions that may constitute the offense of hijacking. Specifically, Article 1 states that any person commits an offense, who on board an aircraft in flight:

1. Unlawfully, by force or threat thereof, or by any other means of intimidation, seizes, or exercises control of that aircraft, or attempts to perform any such act
2. Is an accomplice of a person who performs or attempts to perform any such acts

The Convention also revisited the issue of jurisdiction. Simply providing that the state of registration had primary jurisdiction was not working. Delegates decided a system of concurrent jurisdiction might be more effective and just such a system was formalized. Three states were legally given the responsibility for jurisdiction in a specific order of precedence:

1. The State of registration
2. The State of first landing
3. The State in which the lessee has its principal place of business or permanent residence (Convention for the Suppression of Unlawful Seizure of Aircraft, Article 1).

In more legalese, the Convention mandated that each contracting state take steps to actually establish jurisdiction if the offender is within its territory and will not be extradited. The intention of the change was to force the signatories to accept jurisdiction and actually take action once a crime has been committed.

The Convention also sought to toughen up language requiring states to consistently prosecute. The language obligates each state either to extradite or to submit the case, "without exception whatsoever to its competent authorities for the purpose of prosecution." Many countries were uncomfortable with the language; viewing it as an infringement on sovereignty. Therefore, the Convention did not go so far as to create an absolute obligation to extradite, but it came as close as possible without several countries refusing to sign. It also requires parties to assist each other in connection with criminal proceedings brought under the Convention.

■ MONTREAL CONVENTION

The Convention for the Suppression of Unlawful Acts against the Safety of Civil Aviation, the third major treaty, entered into force on 26 January 1973. It is also known as the Montreal Convention of September 1971, or the "Sabotage Convention," and applies to acts of aviation sabotage such as bombings aboard aircraft in flight. The specific legislation in the United States gives effect to the earlier Hijacking Convention by providing the President with authority to suspend air service to any country which he determines is encouraging hijacking in opposition to the Hijacking Convention. The law orders the government to provide regulations requiring that detection devices must screen all air carrier passengers and their carry-on baggage. Also, it requires a federal air transportation security force to be stationed at major airports under the auspices of the Federal Aviation Administration (FAA). Basically, the convention provides for the precise applications of the overall principles of The Hague Convention to all crimes committed on board commercial aircraft. For example, the Treaty defines acts which are criminally punishable as:

1. Acts of violence against a person on board an aircraft in flight if that act is likely to endanger the safety of that aircraft
2. Destruction of an aircraft in service or damage to such an aircraft which renders it incapable of flight or which is likely to endanger its safety in flight
3. Placing or causing to be placed on an aircraft in service, by any means whatsoever, a device or substance which is likely to destroy that aircraft, or to cause damage to it which is likely to endanger its safety in flight
4. Destruction or damage of air navigation facilities or interference with their operation, if any such act is likely to endanger the safety of the aircraft in flight
5. Communication of information which is known to be false, thereby endangering the safety of the aircraft in flight (Convention for the Suppression of Unlawful Acts against the Safety of Civil Aviation, signed in Montreal on September 23, 1971).

This particular Treaty also mandated that all signatory parties agree to take all practicable measures to prevent the commission of these offenses. This concept has been unevenly implemented depending on the interpretation of the language in the Treaty and the financial resources of the host country. It unequivocally mandates the apprehension and prosecution or extradition of aircraft saboteurs, and provides for severe penalties for the perpetrators of these crimes. It also dictated that the 128 party signatory nations engage in all practical efforts to prevent hijacking and to forewarn other nations when it had reason to believe a crime might take place within their jurisdiction. Such cooperative efforts are well intentioned but often difficult to effectuate.

On 14 December 1973, the United Nations supplemented the Tokyo Convention upon recommendation of the 24th Session of the International Law Commission. The Convention on the Prevention and Punishment of Crimes Against Internationally Protected Persons, including diplomatic agents, requires each signatory to criminalize the intentional murder, kidnapping, or other attack upon the person or property of an internationally protected person. It specifically outlawed attacks on senior government officials and diplomats, and also made it a crime to engage in violent attacks on official premises, private accommodations, or the means of transport of such person. Generally, the Treaty was offered and supported in response to the activities of the Irish Republican Army in the United Kingdom. The commission had been actively studying the question of the protection and inviolability of diplomatic agents and other persons entitled to special protection under international law. The British wanted to have international approval of legal measures taken against suspected IRA members, and this Treaty was clearly supportive (UN Resolution 3166).

TOKYO SUMMIT

Later in May 1986, seven major democracies completed the Tokyo Summit on International Terrorism. In part, they were responding to the misuse of diplomatic privileges by some "rogue nations." The Tokyo Summit attempted to close another loophole in the international maze of international law.

Signatories each committed to "make maximum efforts to fight against the scourge." The conference developed the following guidelines jointly, believing that the commission of such crimes is a matter of grave concern to the international community:

1. Mutual refusal to export arms to rogue states which sponsor or support terrorism.
2. Strictly limit the size of diplomatic missions and other official bodies abroad of rogue states, which engage in terrorist activities and to control the travel of members of such, missions, and bodies. Close, where appropriate, or make radical reductions in, such missions and bodies.
3. Deny entry to all persons, including diplomatic personnel, who are suspected of terrorist activities or who have been convicted of a terrorist offense.
4. Improve extradition procedures using domestic laws to expeditiously bring to trial those individuals who have perpetrated acts of terrorism.
5. Employ stricter immigration and visa requirements with respect to nationals of rogue States, which support or sponsor terrorism.
6. Improve bilateral and multilateral law enforcement efforts.

Unfortunately, these recommendations were not immediately acted upon. It would take more tragic incidents to get the United States and other nations to cooperate more fully with each other and to improve their collective response plans to such incidents.

FURTHER EFFORTS

By 1973, it was clear that the combined treaties had still not stopped the steady stream of hijackings. Taken collectively, the three major treaties should have ensured the safety of internationally registered aircraft, but unfortunately did not.

In reality, some countries still simply refused to extradite. Others only imposed slight penalties for crimes "generally considered" to be serious offenses by a host of other nations. Still others, like Libya, actually offered a safe haven to terrorists perceived to share a commonly held political persuasion. Some critics also recognized that some signatories had signed the treaties for only political reasons and never had any intention of respecting the spirit of the international law developed. In reality, there are no sanctions or enforcement procedures in any of the three Treaties. Actual enforcement of any particular Treaty has been a problem and will remain so. In essence, they are "gentlemen's agreements" dependent on enforcement solely on the integrity of each signatory nation. Efforts were made during the International Civil Aviation Organization (ICAO) Extraordinary Assembly in September 1973 to achieve some enforcement consensus, but it ended in failure. Furthermore, a proposal to convene another multinational convention creating an international commission with the authority to investigate alleged violations of the three major treaties and to enforce sanctions never came about.

In addition, although well intentioned, the Treaties current at the time still contained some loopholes. For example, they failed to cover procedures relating to airports and ticket offices. Terrorists who choose simply to assault and murder people in the airport terminal did not fall under the Treaties, but instead local law. Consequently, after terrorist attacks at the Rome and Vienna airports in 1987, the Montreal Protocol of 1988 was signed. This additional and additive document provided the means for procedures for handling acts of violence of all civil aviation facilities to include airports and ticket offices. Additional changes were still needed.

The Blue and White flag of the United Nations—symbol of the union of all peoples in search of a permanent, durable peace. The UN has passed several anti-terrorist measures but lacks enforcement capability. The UN recognized the Palestinian Liberation Organization with observer status in order to facilitate discussion with the Israeli government and to take note of the Palestinian refugee issue. *UN / DPI.*

■ BONN AGREEMENT

Soon thereafter, Prime Minister Pierre Trudeau of Canada pressed for even more sanctions in the form of a joint declaration against rogue nations. Another effort, the Bonn Agreement of 1978, was thereupon signed by the heads of State of Britain, Canada, France, West Germany, Italy, Japan, and the United States. This agreement was never ratified by corresponding legislatures but exhibited an attempt by the leading democratic nations jointly to tighten efforts to combat aviation-related terrorism. Analysts described the effort as a formal attempt on the part of major Heads of State to publically denounce terrorism and hijacking in particular. This effort was the first where several nations banded together to arrange mutually to agree that in cases where a rogue country refused to extradite or legally prosecute hijackers and/or give back aircraft, the respective governments unanimously agreed to take immediate action to cease all flights to that country. Alternatively, incoming flights from the offending country were also to be banned. In a collateral move, the United States urged that the Bonn Declaration adopt an annex declaring that all signatories halt air carrier service to nations where attacks on airports and airline offices went unpunished.

Deplorably, except for some saber rattling toward South Africa for offering refuge to the mercenaries who attempted to overthrow the government of the Seychelles and a collective suspension of service to Afghanistan for its failure to prosecute suspected hijackers, the Bonn Agreement has never been collectively used. This is unfortunate in that the concept provided a significant economic tool to combat air piracy.

Note: *In 1973, after numerous attempts to hijack US carrier aircraft to Cuba, US and Cuban authorities correspondingly and respectively agreed that hijackers were to be "returned to the party of registry of the aircraft or vessel or be brought before the courts of the party whose territory he reached for trial." The Agreement had also stated that Cuba was to facilitate "without delay the continuation of the journey of the passengers and crew innocent of the hijacking." The Cuban government retracted the agreement a mere four years later. In spite of the denunciation of the agreement by Cuba in 1976, there had been a rather substantial record of cooperation between the two countries.*

Senior Vice-President and General Counsel of the Air Transport Association, James E. Landry, suggested the following measures in the United States during a speech to the National Forum Foundation's Conference on Terrorism and Transportation on 12 May 1986. Although his comments fell on deaf ears, he reasoned that additional measures were necessary and recommended the following:

1. Expand the scope of the Bonn Declaration to encompass acts other than hijackings.
2. Establish the means to monitor incidents to assure proper and timely actions are pursued in other countries.
3. Refine and expand appropriate sanctions.
4. Collaborate with such organizations as ICAO for promulgating international security standards, drawing upon their expertise to improve countermeasures.
5. Authorize and provide resources for ICAO to evaluate the extent and methods of states in applying the Security Standards and Recommended Practices.
6. Convene a subsequent sanctions conference.

The Bonn Conference, which was part of a G-7 Summit in July 1978, attempted to get the major powers to halt bilateral air traffic with countries which refused to extradite and prosecute hijackers. Essentially they failed. As stated, the agreement was effectively invoked only once in 1982 when Britain, West Germany, and France terminated all air traffic with Afghanistan (Caleb M. Pilgram, "Terrorism in National and International Law," 8 *Dickinson Journal of International Law 147*, 198, 1990). The issue of terrorism is discussed routinely at these conferences. In a collateral Treaty during the same time frame, the International Convention Against the Taking of Hostages, signed in New York on 18 December 1979, provided that any person who seizes and detains and threatens to kill, to injure, or to continue to detain another person is subject to the law. Therefore, any person committing an act of hostage taking was supposed to be either prosecuted or extradited under international law. However, these documents in reality generally achieve little more than the usual condemnation of terrorism and pledge to cooperate.

▧ DIPLOMATIC CONFERENCE ON AIR LAW

One effort to more easily identify explosives utilizes the concept of taggants. It has been proven to be highly effective while showing how the efforts of the International Civil Aviation Organization (ICAO) can be an effective means of initiating international aviation cooperation. On 12 January 1990, a subcommittee of the ICAO drafted a treaty to require the addition of taggants to explosives manufactured by contracting states. Taggants are additives to explosives that make them easily visible to various scanners. Essentially, the taggants make explosives detectable by use of gas analysis procedures, which are readily available on the market. Taggants can be either chemical or physical compounds. They individually identify explosive devices by manufacturer, lot number, and type. Physical taggants are either plastic, metal, or ceramic tags directly attached to the device. On 2 April 1990, the United States actively participated in a meeting of the full legal committee of ICAO dealing with this issue. The committee presented the proposed treaty at the full convention in early 1991. The Convention accepted the new international treaty on the Marking of Plastic Explosives for the Purpose of Detection in March of the same year.

The Treaty was designed to control and limit the use of unmarked and undetectable plastic explosives. Generally speaking, it requires each party to take necessary and effective measures to prohibit and prevent the manufacture of unmarked plastic explosives. They are also expected to prevent the movement of unmarked plastic explosives into or out of its territory and to exercise strict and effective control over possession and transfer of unmarked explosives. The Treaty also mandated that all stocks of unmarked explosives not in the possession of the police or the military be destroyed or marked within three years.

Ten years earlier, the Convention on the Physical Protection of Nuclear Material was signed on 3 March 1980. It required each party to take appropriate steps within the framework of its national law to ensure as far as practicable that during international transportation nuclear material within its territory is protected to certain minimal levels defined in the Act. Unfortunately, every nation with nuclear material has some unaccounted for material, including the United States.

▓ G-7 SUMMIT 1995

This conference, held in June 1995, followed on the heels of the bombing at Oklahoma City and the subway gas attack in Tokyo. They pledged to instruct a task force of terrorism experts to report on the best methods of combating terrorism in an offensive mode as opposed to defensive (G-7 Summit Chechnya War: *Dow Jones International News Service*, 17 June 1995). One year later in Lyon, France, they again addressed the issue of terrorism. This time the conference took place in the wake of the bombing on the US military installation in Saudi Arabia and an IRA bombing in Manchester, England.

▓ LYON SUMMIT 1996

At a conference held in Lyon, France, in 1996, the world's security ministers once again met to discuss international cooperation in fighting terrorism. They were quick to acknowledge the effectiveness of military and spy satellites in tracking down terrorists, but recognized the need for even more cooperation between nations and their law enforcement and security agencies. The ministers ultimately agreed on approximately 25 measures further to enhance efforts to track down and bring to justice known terrorists.

The group agreed that each nation could improve its counterterrorism cooperation and capabilities. They concluded that nations will have to accelerate the research and development of methods adequately to detect explosives and other harmful substances. In keeping with new laws in the United States, other nations need to investigate organizations and groups that purport to be charitable organizations but in reality serve as cover for terrorist organizations collecting money for their causes. These groups must be targeted and outlawed, thereby shutting down a source of legal revenue for terrorist endeavors. The conference noted that many nations still have laws that make it legal to export weapons and explosives without any controls. Export control laws need to be reformed as well as antiterror legislation to give them more teeth.

An important issue discussed was that of political asylum. The conference encouraged countries to ensure that the rights and freedoms of their nations are not taken advantage of by terrorists who seek to plan and finance terrorist activities within their borders. As always, the exchange of information was also considered to be crucial to the success of antiterrorist cooperative efforts. Direct exchange of information was encouraged with the realization that most intelligence agencies and national law enforcement agencies are hesitant to release such information. The conference identified the information that explicitly needs to be shared. They included:

1. The actions and movements of known terrorists
2. The discovery of forged travel documents
3. Information relating to explosives and arms trafficking
4. Detection of the use of state of the art communications technologies by terrorists
5. Any information relating to the possible use of weapons of mass destruction including nuclear, chemical, and biological weapons

It is clear that it has been known for decades what needs to be done to prevent the proliferation of terrorism; it is just extremely difficult and challenging actually to have the reforms come about on an international scale.

■ MINISTERIAL CONFERENCE ON TERRORISM

On 30 July 1996, the leaders of the major world powers announced cooperative action against terrorism. They hoped to tighten security to prevent terrorist activity before it happened. They wanted to make it easier to identify terrorist suspects. The conference adopted a 25-point antiterrorism plan. The plan included coordinated airline security measures, curbs on terrorist fund raising, better exchange of intelligence, policing the Internet, setting global standards for detecting bombs, improving extradition arrangements, outlawing possession of biological weapons, drafting a treaty requiring countries to try suspected bombers or extradite them, and tightening border checks (Bill Nichols, and Jay McCormick, "Anti-Terror Action Slows; Plan Outlined in Paris," *USA Today*, 31 July 1996, 1A). The conference, overall, was a bit of a defeat for US leadership in policymaking. The European and Japanese representatives strongly criticized US support of economic sanctions against countries such as Iran and Libya. US opponents were responding to US action penalizing countries that have traded with Cuba, and because they believe that it is better to target the terrorist group rather than alienating the host country. The European Union has repeatedly objected to the United States penalizing non-US companies in pursuit of US foreign policy goals.

INTERNATIONAL CONVENTION FOR THE SUPPRESSION OF THE FINANCING OF TERRORISM

In 1999, in a further effort to combat terrorism, the International Convention for the Suppression of the Financing of Terrorism was drafted. It requires the parties to take all necessary steps to prevent and counteract the financing of terrorists. These preventive efforts are meant to encompass not just those groups that are openly terrorist in nature but also other more innocuous groups as well. The Treaty covers all groups supporting terrorist efforts, whether directly or indirectly, even groups claiming to have just charitable or cultural goals. The Treaty also covers groups that also engage in such illicit activities as drug trafficking or arms dealing in order to finance their terrorist pursuits. In addition to holding those who finance terrorism accountable, the Treaty provides for the identification, freezing, and seizure of funds allocated for terrorist activities. Bank secrecy is no longer an acceptable excuse for refusing to cooperate even though it has been tolerated for years.

UNITED NATIONS

Of course, the United Nations has repeatedly condemned terrorist activities. For example, after a series of terrorist acts worldwide, the General Assembly unanimously passed a resolution that:

1. Unequivocally condemns, as criminals, all acts, methods and practices of terrorism wherever and by whoever committed, including those which jeopardize friendly relations among States and their security

2. Appeals to all States that have not yet done so to consider becoming party to the existing international conventions relating to various aspects of international terrorism

3. Calls upon all States to fulfill their obligations under international law to refrain from organizing, instigating, assisting, or participating in terrorist acts in other States or acquiescing in activities within their territories directed toward the commission of such acts (Louis Henkin, et al, *International Law: Cases and Materials*, 3d Edition, 1993 Pg. 392).

The UN Security Council votes in this photo on a six month extension of the UN humanitarian program in Iraq in 1999 in UN Headquarters. The UN has repeatedly intervened in countries that act as sources of terrorism in efforts to combat the roots of terrorism, both in the Middle East and around the world. *U.N., Evab Schneider / AP/Wide World Photos.*

Additionally, the Security Council adopted a resolution in December 1985 condemning all acts of hostage taking and abduction. They also agreed that all States are obligated to prevent such acts. In 1996, the General Assembly readdressed the issue of terrorism. In the Declaration on Measures to Eliminate International Terrorism, they resolved:

States must fulfill their obligations under the Charter of the United Nations and other provisions of international law with respect to combating terrorism and are urged to take effective and resolute measures, in particular

a. To refrain from organizing, facilitating, financing, or tolerating terrorist activities
b. To ensure the apprehension and prosecution or extradition of perpetrators of terrorist acts
c. To cooperate with one another in exchanging relevant information
d. To take appropriate measures, before granting asylum, for the purpose of ensuring that the asylum seeker has not engaged in terrorist activities (General Assembly Resolution 49/60, UNGAOR 6th Comm. 84th meeting, UN Document A/49/743, 1994).

Basically, all the resolutions and declarations made by the UN are focused on nation states implementing the provisions of treaties already in existence. The UN is attempting to get those countries actually to enforce them or to sign them in the first place. The UN has no real enforcement powers of its own; however, they can be a powerful force in the area of delicate international maneuvering.

Most recently, on 26 October 2001, the UN published the requirements that all of its 189 members must now follow when combating terrorism on their own soil. Member states that fail to follow the guidelines will be subject to sanctions under Resolution 1373, which was passed by the Security Council on 28 September 2001. Under the guidelines, all states must demonstrate the legislative and executive measures they have taken to combat terrorism. Specifically, each state must show their law enforcement agencies are making efforts to freeze the assets of terrorists and take appropriate action to punish the supporters or terrorists. Furthermore, the UN is asking that countries document their procedures to ensure that terrorists do not seek refuge on their soil and how they intend to prevent future terrorist attacks. One UN diplomat has been quoted as saying, "It's a steady raising of the bar" (Carola Hoyos, "UN Sets Out Rules for States Battling Terrorism," *Financial Times*, 28 October 2001, Pg. 3).

ICAO/ECAC

All countries are individually responsible for implementing effective aviation security systems. Since terrorism is an international issue and can affect several nations within the time span of a few hours, nations have banned together to establish standard procedures. The first efforts to work out international civil aviation agreements were first made in Europe at about the same time the Wright Brothers made their historic flight at Kitty Hawk, North Carolina. However, it was not until 1944 that any significant progress was made. In November 1944, over fifty nations met in Chicago to examine the problems of international civil aviation. The result was the Convention on International Civil Aviation. The preamble of the Convention stipulates that the ratifying governments have, ". . . agreed on certain principles and arrangements in order that international civil aviation may be developed in a safe and orderly manner and that international air transportation services may be established on the basis of equality of opportunity and operated soundly and economically" (International Civil Aviation Organization, ICAO, Pgs. 13–17).

In less than 24 months, the required numbers of nations signed the convention on 4 April 1947, and the ICAO was created. It replaced the temporary organization set up in 1944. The ICAO has two main elements, the Assembly, which is the policymaking body, and the Council, a governing body, which is responsible to the Assembly. A 27-member council provides overall direction to the organization. The Air Navigation Commission, the Air Transport Committee, and the Committee on Joint Support of Air Navigation Services, and a Finance Committee supplement their efforts.

One of the ICAO's main duties is to adopt international standards and recommendations and to incorporate them into the convention as annexes. Annex 17 deals directly with airport security standards. No legal action can realistically be brought against violators of the association rules, but if a country does not obey the rules, airliners from that state may be denied landing and other services. Regardless of the success of ICAO and Annex 17 precautions, soon after the Annex was adopted by a majority of nations, there were 31 hijackings in 1978, 27 in 1979, and 40 hijackings in 1980.

The European Civil Aviation Conference (ECAC) is an international organization that works with various governments to develop measures, standards, and recommended practices solely within Europe. It operates with the active support of the ICAO. It has been in operation for many years, and it has three basic principles which sum up the current status of the mutual agreements:

1. That the threat of unlawful interference with civil aviation in its many forms of violence is likely to persist.
2. That ICAO Standards and Recommended Practices in aviation security have to take into account the widely varying provisions available for their implementation in more than 180 participating countries.
3. Mutual understanding and close and constant cooperation between all state authorities concerned are necessary to achieve and maintain a high standard of aviation security (Alan Panghorn, "How Far Has Europe Come Since Pan Am 103." *Intersec*, *Intersec* Publishing Ltd, Three Bridges Publishing, 5 May 1996, Vol. 6, Pg. 195).

■ CONCLUSION

International treaties including the Tokyo, Hague, and Montreal Conventions all remain hallmarks of international efforts to combat terrorism. Unfortunately, years of cooperation have proved that once the Treaties are in effect they often fail to be effective. Nations react depending on the attitude of each nation, all of whom can still exercise their own sovereignty over suspected terrorists regardless of the language in the existing treaties. One of the newest undertakings involves the attempt to track terrorists by following the money trail. After 9/11, cooperative efforts in the financial realm are critical to the success of the ongoing "War on Terrorism." Terrorist operations are expensive and the money has to come from somewhere and it moves along with the terrorist operators. The trail the money leaves is the best way to document who the actual perpetrators were and how they organized the attack. Similar patterns of financing can be monitored hopefully to prevent future attacks.

Efforts will likely continue to fine tune the Treaties as the need arises. However, enforcement, as always, will remain a problem. Even recent efforts by the UN to "raise the bar" for its member states recognizes that efforts to combat terrorism will suffer from an inability to enforce any sanctions levied against violators of the guidelines. A silver lining to the tragic events of 9/11, however, is the renewed attention of the global community for the need actively to pursue the perpetrators of terrorism jointly. Hopefully, the enthusiasm to stop terrorism at an international level will not turn to apathy again and remain active.

chapter four

Growth and Change: Aircraft as Missiles

1. **30 May 2001**: CNN announced that an Algerian terrorist, arrested after he attempted to smuggle explosives into the United States in December 1999, admitted he intended to blow up the Los Angeles International Airport.

2. **6 August 2001**: The CIA briefs President Bush that al-Q'aeda operatives might try to hijack US aircraft.

3. **10 August 2001**: Phoenix FBI agent writes letter noting that Middle Eastern men were attending flight schools in the United States and that bin Laden may have sent them. The memo proposed a nationwide canvass of flight schools.

4. **11 September 2001**: American Airlines Flight 11 crashes into the North Tower of the World Trade Center, United Airlines Flight 175 crashes into the South Tower, and American Airlines Flight 77 crashes into the Pentagon.

5. **April 2002**: About 130,000 former law enforcement officers, federal agents, and general citizens have applied to become federal Air Marshals since the government began advertising the jobs after 9/11.

■ EARLY HIJACKINGS

One of the earliest known acts of air piracy, or skyjacking, occurred in 1930 when hijackers took over a Peruvian aircraft. The incident received little attention and never resulted in any international efforts to combat a potential threat to international aviation. In fact, some authorities, depending on their own political viewpoints, actually praised some hijackers based on purely political sympathies even in the West. To illustrate, numerous individuals attempted to escape across the Iron Curtain were welcomed with open arms by Western European governments. Any attempt to flee Soviet-perceived oppression was accepted as being legal and praiseworthy conduct. Of course, the attempts were not viewed from the Eastern Bloc countries from the same perspective. Similarly, support for air piracy continues from rogue countries supportive of terrorism in the Middle East and elsewhere. The terrorists are received as heroes in the fight against perceived Western tyranny and past repressive colonialism.

From 1930 to 1967, only 12 US commercial aircraft hijackings were attempted and only seven were semisuccessful. However, in 1968, a deluge of hijackings began to plague the nation. Many Americans traveling the Caribbean were repeatedly detoured to Havana, Cuba. Of the 22 hijackings in 1968, 19 were directed to fly to Cuba. By 1969, the number of US passengers and crewmembers who made the Cuban detour totaled 1359. Americans, and the airlines that often suffered the financial loss of the aircraft, were increasingly agitated. Something clearly had to be done. It was merely too easy to board an aircraft and commandeer it. As is often the case, there are two sides to every story. Many nations and specific groups perceived hijackings as permissible expressions of political viewpoints warranting their support. Some of these nations continue to attempt to ignore the criminality of such conduct.

There have been hijackings of general aviation aircraft as well. In 1962, two individuals kidnapped at gunpoint the pilot of a private Cessna 172 and compelled him to transport them from Florida to Cuba. The perpetrators were charged with commission of "aircraft piracy" in violation of a 1961 Amendment to Section 902 of the Federal Aviation Act of 1958 (49 USC Supp. IV Section 1472 I). As used in this subsection, the term *aircraft piracy* was defined as "any seizure or exercise of control, by force or violence or threat of force or violence and with wrongful intent, of an aircraft in flight in air commerce." The defense argued that a private plane was not an aircraft in flight in air commerce. The lower court initially held for the defendants and dismissed the indictments; however, the Supreme Court disagreed (*US vs. Healy*, 376 U.S. 75, 1964). They reasoned that the phrase "an aircraft" is on its face an all-inclusive term. They went on to express the opinion that Section 902 (1) of the amended act (49 USC Supp. IV Sec 1472 [l] made it a crime to carry a concealed weapon "while on board an aircraft being operated by an air carrier in air transportation." By that language the court concluded that Congress knew how to choose words solely to refer to commercial airlines when it wanted to do so.

At the other end of the Cuba hijackings, although not really sympathetic to the plight of the passengers, crew, or airline (usually Eastern Airlines), the Cuban authorities were not really hospitable to the hijackers either. They made no distinction between large aircraft and small aircraft hijackings. Considering the political realities between the governments of Cuba and the United States, little cooperation between the two initially took place. However, the hijackers were not welcomed with victory parades. An armed reception committee generally greeted the hijackers, and they could expect months of interrogation and harsh imprisonment. Furthermore, the interrogation and imprisonment were often under severely brutal conditions. Almost all of the hijackers were kept under close arrest in spite of their professed Cuban sympathies and later often expressed extreme disillusionment with their chosen refuge.

Worsening the problem for the United States, Fidel Castro initiated the Mariel Boatlift in April 1980. Castro had decided to empty his prisons and mental hospitals and literally export them to the United States. He hoped to relieve his own government of the obligation to support them. Approximately 125,000 refugees, mostly those convicted of crimes or who were mentally unstable, eventually made it to US territory, often under extreme hardship. Many individuals, however, were not pleased with their forced change in homelands and sought to return to Cuba by any means possible. This consequently prompted a series of "homesick hijackings," especially at Christmas time. The emotional drive to return to family and friends was unexpectedly great. The problem was so distinct and created such a nuisance that the situation reached a point where the Federal Aviation Administration even put commercials on TV in Florida warning would be hijackers that Castro's response to hijacking was jail and not *Felize Navidade*. These initial "emotional" hijackings were the prelude to more severe terrorist activities to come.

▨ TERRORIST HIJACKINGS SPREAD

The early 1970s saw a continuing series of aircraft hijackings. In a coordinated effort, on 6 September 1970, a terrorist group hijacked TWA flight 707 on a scheduled flight from Frankfurt to New York. The flight was full, carrying 145 passengers plus the crew. They seized the plane over Belgium and ordered the pilot to fly to Jordan. On the same day, Palestinian guerillas also hijacked a Swissair DC-8 flight outbound from Zurich and a Pan Am 747 aircraft out of Amsterdam. A Swiss Air DC-8 aircraft was commandeered over France and also ordered to fly to Dawson Field in Jordan. The Pan Am flight turned out to be an afterthought. Earlier, the terrorists made an attempt to hijack an El Al flight en route from Tel Aviv to Amsterdam. The original hijack team, including Leila Khaled, Patrick Arguello, and a third Arab initiated a violent conflict when the pilot refused their demands. One flight attendant was shot and an Israeli Sky Marshal managed to kill one of the hijackers. The other two hijackers were subdued and eventually flown to London. Left off of the original plane, the remaining members of the team hijacked the Pan Am flight.

Three days later, a BOAC VC-10 was hijacked; completing the series. The Pan Am flight was directed to Beirut and Cairo where the plane was eventually destroyed. The other aircraft were forced to fly to Zarca in the Jordanian desert by members of the Popular Front for the Liberation of Palestine (PFLP). The nearly 500 passengers and crew suffered six days of terrible confinement inside the plane. The remaining three planes were blown up in full view of media cameras. This was the first extensively televised terrorist hijacking. Terrorists had discovered the media. Some reports of the incident even claim the terrorists prepositioned the cameras. After more than 20 days of negotiations, the Jordanian army freed the last of the hostages, and the seven political prisoners the hijackers demanded to be released were in fact released. They had also demanded the release of three members of the PFLP in a Swiss jail, other terrorists being held in West Germany, and the release of Leila Khaled in London. The British, with Prime Minister Edward Health at the helm, were in turmoil over the events. The hijacked BOAC V-10 aircraft had 110 British citizens on board. The British capitulated and released Khaled, but vowed never to submit to terrorism again.

Hijacking an aircraft greatly appealed to extortionists and terrorists with a cause that they sought to publicize. The incidents were accomplished to achieve both political and personal gains, and were successfully used as a dramatic method of attempting to enforce their demands. The sensationalism of an aircraft being blown up or captive hostages huddled in an aircraft cabin was an assured draw for the cameras. In addition, the Palestinians wanted to send a statement to the Egyptian government. They wished to express their displeasure with Egypt's participation in a Middle Eastern peace plan.

US government response to the threat was swift but not totally effective. Initially, the government response, publicly announced by President Richard Nixon, proposed the placement of "specially trained, armed US government personnel on flights of US commercial airliners." In reality, the placement on all "threatened" aircraft was unattainable. It simply was not possible to put an agent on every flight. On top of that, the costs were prohibitive and the airlines balked at the "freeloaders" on board. The Nixon administration's plan also called for the use of electronic screening equipment at airports and urged the Department of Transportation (DOT), Department of Defense, (DOD), Department of Treasury, CIA, and FBI to accelerate their present efforts to develop security measures. Research and development in the field of access control, explosive detection, and screening equipment began to proliferate.

▪ INITIAL PUBLIC RESPONSES

Initially, much was written and debated as how to best deal with the growing problem. Suggestions ranged from the reasonable to the bizarre. The public was even asked to forward suggestions to authorities in the hopes of canvassing methods, which would have broad-based public appeal. One unique proposal opined that the planes should be equipped with a sleeping gas that would be pumped into the cabin in the event of an attempted hijack. Thankfully, cooler heads prevailed, and the Joint Airline/Government Task Force, commissioned at the time to analyze possible solutions, warned that a gas strong enough to disable hijackers could cause the death of passengers with certain chronic diseases. Such a method was not feasible, or even reliable, and was quickly discarded.

Any and all ideas were considered. Some of the more unusual examples now appear humorous. For instance, one suggestion involved the use of a hypodermic needle filled with a poison or drug that would be installed in each airline seat. Should a hijacker or hijackers seek to take over an airborne aircraft, the pilot could activate the mechanism and disable the perpetrators. How this was to work if the terrorists were standing up when they seized the aircraft was unclear. Regardless, the idea appealed to some, but the potential liability associated with misuse or accidental use soon caused the rejection of such an idea. The potential for inadvertent use on regular passengers, of course, also doomed this idea from the beginning.

Another humorous, although impractical, proposition suggested that all passengers strip down naked prior to flight. Each passenger would then be required to wear an issued flight suit, thereby supposedly eliminating the ability of a passenger to smuggle a weapon or explosive device onto the aircraft on their person. The issue of discovering dangerous weapons potentially hidden in body orifices was never addressed. Again, the concept of changing clothes fell in disfavor.

By far the author's favorite and most hilarious idea was proffered on the former sitcom *All in the Family*. The family patriarch, Archie, believed that each passenger should be issued a gun enabling the entire plane of passengers to deal with the bad guys. As much as this sounds pretty far-fetched, the concept of passengers becoming involved in subduing terrorists or simply unruly passengers is an issue worthy of discussion. The idea of life imitating art has unfortunately occurred. The concept of passenger involvement in the subduing of unruly passengers was later to have some significant negative repercussions when fellow passengers inadvertently killed a passenger in an attempt to control him. The overtaking of the hijackers of United Airlines Flight 93, which crashed into the Pennsylvania countryside on 9/11, reflects a positive example of passenger involvement. But such "cooperation" by passengers is not really to be encouraged except under extreme circumstances.

■ COCKPIT DOORS

Another more serious proposal argued for the development of an inaccessible bulletproof pilot's compartment. Initially, the Airline Pilot's Association came out in favor of the inaccessible cockpit, but the FAA came to concur with the reasoning that a bulletproof cockpit would be vulnerable to hostage threats. No pilot would realistically let a passenger be sacrificed by refusing to open the cockpit door. Even though today access to the cockpit is supposed to be accessible only to the crew, terrorists and unruly passengers have not found it particularly difficult to overcome this obstacle. There remain neither really good answers nor appropriate alternatives in a hostage scenario for the pilot. Denying terrorist's access to the cockpit in order to fly the plane themselves and use it as a weapon is a completely different matter. The Israeli airlines have had secure cockpits for years, and the requirement for denied access will likely become standard law in the United States in response to this new twist.

Since 9/11 the government, has decided to force all aircraft flying through its airspace to make their flight deck doors virtually impenetrable. On 15 January 2002, the FAA published new standards for flight deck doors to protect airline and cargo crews from intrusion and small arms fire or fragmentation devices. The regulations require the doors to be resistant to force, small arms fire, and hand grenades. The FAA gave US airlines only 45 days to strengthen the locking devices on current doors. A deadline of April 2003 was set to make all cockpit doors bulletproof and resistant to explosives on aircraft with 20 or more seats. The rules also apply to the more than 500 international carriers that provide service in and out of the United States. Beginning on 9 October 2001, the FAA also issued a series of regulations that allowed near-term door reinforcement as a stop gap measure until the new rules were fully implemented (Internet: http://www.faa.gov/avr/arm/nprm.cfm). The ICAO has stated that its members would install doors that meet security standards similar to those adopted in the United States but not until 1 November 2003. The ICAO is also not requiring any temporary fixes until that date. As in the 1970s when rules were also hastily implemented, the airline industry has bulked regarding the costs. Cargo carriers, such as the United Parcel Service, have been particularly vocal, commenting that they are at little risk of hijacking. Some airlines have estimated the cost per aircraft will be $50,000 or £35,000. The US Transport Association hopes to lobby the US Congress to foot the bill, which they estimate to be about $250 million. So far, the US government has provided $100 million to compensate airlines for costs associated with cockpit doors or about $13,000 per aircraft.

Aviation industry suppliers, including Alcoa Aerospace, Boeing, and AAR competed for the business. AAR claimed to have produced the cheapest, ThreatDefense, at approximately $18,000. In Britain, British Airways has used reinforced metal to strengthen doors. Additionally, Virgin Air installed Permaglass armor plating on its 25 aircraft. It is still important to consider the dilemma to pilots when a hijacker screams, "Open the door or I'll kill ten of the passengers every ten minutes until you do." By April 2003, Boeing had won the initial contract and supplied 4,300 kits to the airlines. Airbus Industries has also delivered 557 kits to US operators and about 1,800 worldwide.

Other suggestions included the initiation of photo ID cards. After careful consideration, however, the issuance of photo ID cards to passengers was determined to be a potential administrative nightmare. Essentially, who should get one and who should not opens the door for not just harmless administrative errors but also screaming passengers with complaints of discrimination. Decisions regarding who should get "a pass" and how the determination was to be made would likely have been totally mired in a swamp of legal pitfalls. Setting aside the problems of the size of sheer administration of such a program, the likely plethora of accusations of discrimination, which would surely arise, made any attempts to implement such a program impractical. Nonetheless, the current Director of Homeland Security has publicly advocated a "trusted traveler" program. Passengers would agree in advance to submit personal information in exchange for an alleged counterfeit-resistant ID card that would permit them to be exempt from some portion of security. The details remain unclear and conflicting. Efforts also to use biometric means of identification in order to provide frequent travelers quick access is undergoing testing and will present a new set of challenges.

The determination of just exactly what a "hijacker" looks like or acts like constantly lends itself to questions of prejudice based on race, national origin, and religious preference. US law strictly prohibits any such discrimination. Law enforcement, however, continues to argue that some citizens can be identified as potential hijackers, thereby segregating them from the general population. Such a concept is known as profiling.

■ PROFILE OF A HIJACKER

In the 1970s an FAA Task Force study encompassed motivational and behavioral characteristics of hijackers, identification of the weapons used, and an analysis of the origin and intended destination of hijacked flights. Later, the FAA adopted a profile-screening program tested by Eastern Airlines owing to its apparent consistent vulnerability. The results of the test indicated that between 80 and 90% of hijackers appeared to fit the profile established by the commission. Unfortunately, so did a lot of innocent passengers.

Government authorities are relooking at the issue of profiling. *Racial profiling* is certainly a term that is frowned upon by civil libertarians. Realistically, however, security experts argue that profiling should simply be a process in which information in some sort of a database can be used to separate passengers into two groups. The two groups would include those who present little or no risk and those who merit additional attention from the appropriate security personnel. Profiling has been used successfully by other government agencies, including the FBI and the Customs Service, although not without generating some heated controversy. Currently, in spite of recommendations by security professionals that automated passenger profiling be used at airports as complementary to other security procedures, the idea is still extremely controversial and has not been universally implemented. Many groups, including the American Civil Liberties Union, have argued that such a set of records violates citizens' civil liberties.

Regardless of the controversy, the FAA originally assisted three major airlines in implementing just such a system. The FAA had, through a grant to Northwest Airlines, developed a prototype system known as Computer Assisted Passenger Screening (CAPS). The automated system uses information from the reservation system to screen out passengers for whom additional security procedures are unnecessary. On the other hand, if the system determines that a certain passenger is high risk, that person is subject to additional security procedures when they arrive at the airport and present a ticket. The system also randomly selects passengers for additional screening. Even though the criteria for selection are secret, sometimes the criteria can select a person clearly not a threat. Assuming some of the criteria include one-way traveler's, travelers who pay with someone else's credit card, unemployed travelers, last-minute travelers, or simply someone who is not a frequent traveler "mistakes" seem evident. For example, a seven-year-old boy selected by CAPS was forced to drink pond water he collected for a science project, which ultimately made him sick.

The legality of the system has yet to be challenged in the courts but surely will be in the future. Civil rights groups as well as Arab-American groups have specifically raised questions regarding the singling out of minorities and specifically Arab-American passengers. All of these groups raise issues of discrimination and invasion of a passenger's privacy. To address these concerns, the Department of Transportation did submit the entire profiling system parameters to the Department of Justice (DOJ) Civil Rights Division for critical review. In October 1997, the DOJ issued a report. The document concluded that CAPS did not violate the Fourth Amendment prohibition against unreasonable searches and seizures nor an individual's right to personal privacy. The report also concluded that there was no evidence that the system recorded an individual's race, color, national or ethnic origin, religion, or even gender when conducting a profile. It should be noted that these conclusions are contained in a DOJ report and do not necessarily mean they would survive judicial scrutiny. The Supreme Court of the United States will likely get to have the last word on the issue.

Most recently, airlines have acutely become aware of the fact that passengers are frustrated with the cumbersome and often seemingly irritating security systems at airports. To date, airport security officers have treated every single passenger as a suspected terrorist until proven otherwise. The alternatives suggested include renewed emphasis on profiling, trusted-traveler programs, and last, but not least, the simple use of common sense.

■ SKY MARSHAL PROGRAM/FEDERAL AIR MARSHAL PROGRAM

FAA Order 1650.6 formerly governed the program, which had been authorized in the Federal Aviation Act of 1958, the Anti-Hijacking Act of 1974, and the International Security and Development Cooperation Act of 1985 (Public Law 99-83). The program established a covert, armed security force capable of rapid deployment. The precursor of the Federal Air Marshal Program (FAM), formerly known as the Sky Marshal Program, was announced in a Department of Treasury news release dated October 1970. When the perceived need for armed agents first arose, Secretary of the Treasury David M. Kennedy and Secretary of Transportation John A. Vople were responding to President Nixon's call in

September 1970 for armed personnel on US commercial flights. John Cashman, in an article entitled, "Sky Marshals—How They Train and What They Do" (*Parade*, 19 November 1970, Pg. 7), wrote that the original members were a temporary force recruited from the Bureau of Customs, the FAA, FBI, CIA, and military. Eventually a permanent force of 1500 civilians was established. The team became known as Customs Security Officers (CSOs), who were trained by the former Bureau of Customs and attached to the FAA.

Unfortunately, it did not work. The program clearly enjoyed some success but proved to be incapable of stopping the continuing attempts to hijack aircraft. Early on, the Director of Civil Aviation Security for the Department of Transportation, Lt. Gen. Benjamin O. Davis (USAF Ret.), recognized the need to switch primary security efforts from the aircraft to the ground. Time would prove that even aircraft with both an FBI agent and a Sky Marshal on board were not immune from incident. Once the aircraft is in flight, the hijackers are already on board and the presence of agents did little to deter the attempts. It was therefore determined fairly early that the better security solution was preventive in nature and better pursued on the ground. Prevention of access to the airport or aircraft was and remains a crucial key to safety. Apparently, that lesson will have to be relearned.

Furthermore, the airlines considered the coverage too sparse and feared a midair shoot out. The debate over the Sky Marshall program in the 1970s raged for many years (Albert R. Karr, "Policing the Skies," *The Wall Street Journal*, Vol. II, No. 238, 21 Sept 1971). The FAA responded to complaints from the air carriers by charging the airlines with being solely preoccupied with efforts not to inconvenience the passengers instead of focusing on safety. When mandatory 100 percent passenger screening became effective in deterring hijacking, the need for these airborne law enforcement agents seemed to lose support. Eventually, the program fell into disrepair. The number of agents was reduced to as little as three dozen active agents prior to September 2001. The government now considers a revitalized training program as key to the success of an upgraded Federal Air Marshal Program.

Currently, the FAMs aboard aircraft are some of the best marksman in the world. They are highly trained, and their firearms training currency requirements are some of the most stringent in law enforcement. The Certified Protection Professional Certification Program (American Society for Industrial Security) has been acknowledged by the TSA as the only "security management designation" which will be recognized on the application form. Other certifications include sworn civilian law enforcement, emergency medical technician, private pilot, and licensed attorney. As mentioned, it was still considered prudent in March of 1976 to formalize the FAM Program, and it continues to provide extra security aboard high-risk routes with renewed vigor since 9/11 with less than enthusiastic support from the airlines. The agents themselves are deputized as Special Deputy US Marshals.

The FAM Program also received a great deal of attention after the hijacking of TWA Flight 847 on 14 June 1985. Captain Jake Testrake and his crew were hijacked,

A pistol wielding Federal Air Marshal runs between seats during a simulated hijacking aboard a retired L-1011 aircraft at the training facility in Pomona, New Jersey. The program has received extensive funding since the 9/11 tragedy but has also received considerable criticism regarding its training and scheduling practices. ©*Tim Shaffer/Reuters/NewMedia Inc. / CORBIS BETTMANN.*

and the media plastered the real-time photographs of the event all over the world, indicating to the terrorists that the media and the public could not get enough of it. In response to the dramatic events relating to Flight 847, the FAA drafted and implemented FAR 108.14, which required scheduled carriers and public charter operators to carry federal marshals on a priority basis, without charge, even if it required bumping a paying customer. The new regulation also corrected a gap in the regulations, which had not provided for the deadheading of agents; that is, how did they get back home after completing a working flight in one direction only.

The FAM Program currently has its training facility and airline security research facility located at the William J. Hughes Technical Center, Atlantic City International Airport and falls under the purview of the new Transportation Security Administration (TSA: 49 CFR Chapter XII Part 1544.223). Using a wall full of computer-generated maps, the TSA tracks the flight path of each flight with an air marshal on board, and supporting documents indicate the travel schedule of each marshal. They currently employ 45,000 people and are financed with a $4 billion supplemental spending bill from Congress. The agents receive special training and regularly travel on US air carriers on high-risk routes. They represent some of the very few people who are authorized to carry firearms on board aircraft and use them if necessary. Additionally, as federal agents, they are permitted to make arrests without a warrant when certain felony offenses against the United States can be reasonably shown to have been or are being committed.

Today, the FAM Program is just one of the tools used by air carriers, airport security officials, and law enforcement agents in combating the threats to civil aviation. The FAM agents continue to fly millions of miles a year, blending into the crowd of other passengers unbeknownst to a vast majority of them. However, the debate is back. Representative John Sweeney (R, NY), a member of the House Appropriations Subcommittee, has been quoted as saying, "We need to start seeing some results that are equal to the huge investment that we're making" (CNN, 8 May 2002). The FAM Program always seems to gain attention and support after a significant event. Administrations use the public's fear to support the need for the air marshals, but after the hullabaloo dies down, the practical usefulness, aside from a perception of safety on the part of the traveling public, dims considerably.

■ HISTORY OF SIGNIFICANT AIR HIJACKINGS SINCE 1972

Both the public and airline officials were eventually forced to recognize the need for balanced, yet more stringent, airport and airline security measures as early as the 1970s. However, the battle to control the commercial airways witnessed much tragedy before they jointly reached this conclusion. As is often the case, it takes a tragedy to get the legislative processes moving to implement the necessary security measures and plans to provide an adequate defense against those who would use innocent airline passengers and crews to serve the needs of their political causes. The task of ensuring the safety of US international and domestic air travel is clearly a monumental task. Typically, in one day, security professionals are required to screen more than 1.5 million passengers and their carry-on baggage. Both passengers and baggage are now routinely screened for metallic weapons and other dangerous materials. This was unfortunately not always the case. Consequently, the window of opportunity was open to terrorists. They recognized the window and boldly stepped through it on repeated occasions.

In order better to understand why the current procedures are in effect and tolerated, a general review of the hijacking problem is useful. Its evolution and destructiveness has been momentous, and has grabbed the attention of the media owing to the sensational nature of the incidents. There have been numerous events that have mesmerized the public; however, some stand out in importance. News reports reveal that terrorism continues to take different twists and turns. Some security efforts have succeeded, but nonetheless terrorism has not been stopped. Security was in many ways totally reactive and continues to be so. Authorities were reacting to the horrific hijackings at the end of the 1960s and early 1970s and now the monumental event of 9/11. It is safe to say the aftermath of the hijackings has changed the face of aviation for years to come. Airports are by their very function open and public places, and therefore all that more difficult to protect. Today, the threat extends from the airport facilities, the aircraft, and use of the aircraft as a weapon to even more horrific possibilities.

31 May 1972—Lod Airport

Israel has always been a significant target and will likely remain so. On 31 May 1972, at Lod Airport in Tel Aviv, three seemingly regular Japanese passengers, but who were terrorists, disembarked from an Air France flight arriving in Israel from Paris and Rome. After proceeding to the baggage pick-up area, the terrorists retrieved their bags. Inside their luggage were grenades and machine guns. They began firing the guns and throwing the grenades randomly throughout the waiting area. The terminal area, however, was crowded with travelers on a Christian pilgrimage vacation and not the intended target of Israelis. The rampage resulted in the deaths of 26 people and the wounding of another 78. Later, the three terrorists announced they were members of the Army of the Red Star and claimed the attack was an act of reprisal. The group was pledged to a Marxist revolution and was heavily involved in the Palestinian struggle in the Middle East (Grant Wardlaw, "Political Terrorism, Theory, Tactics and Counter Terrorism," Cambridge University Press, London, 1982, Pg. 38). Earlier that month an Israeli security team killed two Arab terrorists who had failed to hijack a Belgian plane at the same airport. The violence was to contribute to a cycle of attack and reprisal that survives today. Seven hardcore JRA (Japanese Red Army) members remained at large as recently as 2001 (Clifford E. Simonsen and Jeremy R. Spendlove, *Terrorism Today, The Past, The Players The Future*, Prentice Hall, Upper Saddle River, NJ, 2000, Pg. 240).

27 June 1976—Entebbe

In 1976, Israeli commandos executed a raid at Entebbe's airport, Uganda, where they freed 103 Israeli hostages from a plane hijacked by Palestinian and German terrorists. The Air France Airbus was originally enroute from Tel Aviv to Paris but had made a stop in Athens. It was forced to fly to Benghazi, Libya, where it refueled and proceeded on to Uganda's Entebbe International Airport. In conjunction with the rescue effort, eleven Ugandan Soviet-made MIG fighter aircraft were destroyed as well as most of the airport. Previously, on 27 June 1976, Palestinian terrorists working with the Baader-Meinhof Gang hijacked an Air France plane enroute from Israel to France. The terrorists had also demanded the release of about 53 of their comrades from prisons in West Germany, France, Switzerland, Israel and Kenya. The Palestinians freed many of the 258 original passengers who did not appear to be Israeli. Debriefing of these released hostages provided the authorities with vital information on the hijacker's numbers and organization. The remaining 106 hostages, merely suspected of being Jewish, were retained. Since the hijackers had separated those of the Jewish faith from other passengers, it indicated their intent to intimidate Israel.

In a bold move, the Israeli's decided not to succumb to the terrorist's demands. They decided on a course of action that turned out to be a spectacular rescue operation. On 3 July 1976, they dispatched four Hercules C-130 H cargo planes from Ophira Air Force Base loaded with almost 200 soldiers escorted by several F-4 phantom jets. Major General Dan Shomron, the Israeli Director of Infantry and Paratroopers, designed the plan, originally named Operation Thunderball. After successfully flying the 2500 miles to Uganda from Israel, commandos swiftly took back the hostages during a ninety-minute raid. The Israeli Defense Forces, in a brilliant tactical deception move, approached the aircraft in a convoy headed by a black Mercedes limousine. They hoped to fool the Ugandan soldiers surrounding the plane into believing that Idi Amin, the Ugandan president, was making a surprise visit. One soldier and three hostages were killed during the operation. The killed hostages apparently did not hear or understand the commando's command to lie down. The only Israeli military casualty was the team's leader, Colonel Jonathan Netanyahu. A Ugandan soldier tragically shot him in the back. The seven terrorists killed included two Germans, Wilford Bose and Gabriele Krocher-Tiedemann, and five Palestinian members of the PFLP. During the entire incident, thirty people were killed and 42 were injured, because the Ugandans sought to prevent the Israelis from leaving with the hostages. The entire operation lasted only three minutes (Major Louis Williams, "Thunderball at Entebbe," *Israeli Defense Force Journal*, May 1985) However, the Israelis set the tone for any future attempts on their citizens or aircraft. They now have the most stringent aircraft/airport security in the world.

14 June 1985—TWA Flight 847

In one of the most infamous hijacking scenarios, two Lebanese Shi'ite Muslim terrorists boarded Trans World Airlines Flight 847 departing Athens, Greece, on 14 June 1985. The Boeing 727 was scheduled to fly to Rome when in midair two hijackers seized the aircraft. In a quirk of fate, a third terrorist was unable to get a seat and, therefore, was not boarded onto the aircraft. President Ronald Reagan had taken a hard line against terrorism, and this incidence evidenced a renewed assault against US commercial carriers not seen since the 1970s. Nabih Berri, the spokesman for the Amal Militia, also jumped into the fray and sought expertly to choreograph the entire incident for the best media effect possible.

After being diverted, the plane was permitted to land in Beirut, Lebanon, with 145 passengers and 8 crewmembers aboard. The terrorists demanded that over 700 Shi'ite persons in Israeli jails be released. The hijackers subsequently released 17 American women and 2 children, but additional gunman came aboard. The pilot, John Testrake, was forced to fly the aircraft to Algeria where 19 more American women, 1 child, and 3 people of non-Israeli nationality were permitted to disembark. On 15 June, the plane returned to Beirut where yet another 10 Americans were released. However, tragically, after reviewing travel documents and discovering a US military member, the hijackers beat unconscious a US Navy diver, Robert Dean Stethem, executed him, and threw his body out the door of the plane. On the move once again, the plane returned to Algiers, and in return for the release of a comrade arrested at the Athens airport, an additional 53 passengers and 5 flight attendants were freed.

On 16 June, after flying back to Beirut again, the hijackers now threatened to blow up the plane if 50 Lebanese held in Israeli jails were not released. Simultaneously, the US Navy's Sixth Fleet was ordered into the Mediterranean Sea and the elite US Army Delta Force was deployed to the area. The Amal Militia now demanded the release of 800 other Lebanese prisoners while the hijackers reiterated their earlier demand for the release of 50 Lebanese prisoners, as well as 2 Shi'ites held in Madrid for attempted murder. At this point, the demands were not met, and the remaining passengers are removed from the plane as hostages, leaving a crew of three on board. Nabih Berri announced that the hostages were to be split up to thwart a suspected rescue mission. To meet the suspected threat, the Amal Militia allegedly put 6000 men on alert. Furthermore, the hostages with Jewish-"sounding" names were retained by a radical Iranian terrorist group, Hezbollah. One ailing American, Robert Peel, was released.

The details of the situation were broadcast around the world in real time. Nabih Berri, on 18 June, continued to very publicly pressure Israel into releasing hundreds of Lebanese, most of them Shi'ites. At a news conference, President Reagan announced that any retaliation would be risky, and also chastised the Greek government for lax security procedures. Meanwhile, the British and Italian Ambassadors to Lebanon, as well as the Syrians, declared they were involved in negotiations, whereas Reagan considered forcing the Lebanese to close the Beirut airport if diplomatic moves failed. The incident received global attention. Even the Russians jumped into the act. Soviet spokesman Vladimir Lomeiko condemned the hijacking, but suggested that the United States created the conditions that foster terrorism.

Eventually, on 29 June, the Syrians announced they had negotiated a settlement to the crisis. That same evening, the hostages were taken to a hotel for dinner, and are seen leaving with roses from their captors. The next day, seventeen days after the hijacking began, the hostages are handed over to the International Red Cross and driven to Damascus, Syria, where they board a US military aircraft bound for Rhein-Main Air Base in Frankfurt, Germany. Two of the hijackers were never caught, although all three, Mohammed Hamadei, Ali Atwa, and Hasan Izz Din, had prior outstanding arrest warrants issued in 1985. Mohammed Ali Hamadi, age 22, was arrested trying to enter West Germany with liquid explosives on 15 January 1987. Approximately two years after that, the German Hesse State Supreme Court convicted him of hijacking, the murder of Robert Stethem, and the possession of explosives. He received a sentence of life imprisonment. Eventually efforts to use international law, namely, The Hague and Montreal Conventions, all failed, and two of the three hijackers have never been brought to justice.

21 December 1988—Pan American Flight 103

The actual aircraft for Pan American Flight 103, a Boeing 747, N739PA, had originated in San Francisco. Many of the passengers arrived in London from Frankfurt, West Germany, on a Boeing 727, which had been positioned on stand Kilo 16 next to the Boeing 747. The passengers were transferred with their baggage to N739PA,

The Pan Am flight 103 airliner with its destroyed shell in Scotland. A worker looks out of the doorway at the wreckage. The photo is a pictorial reminder of the need to focus attention on cargo security and the consequences of neglecting to do so. *CORBIS BETTMANN.*

which was to fly to New York. After a six-hour turnaround, the aircraft left Heathrow airport at 6:04 PM with 243 passengers and a crew of 16 on board. The aircraft also carried 20 tons of cargo and 43 bags of military mail. As it was approaching the Burnham VOR, it took up a radar heading of 350 degrees and flew below the Bovingdon holding point at 600 feet. At 31,000 feet, slightly northwest of Pole Hill VOR and approximately seven minutes later, Shanwick Oceanic Control transmitted the aircraft's clearance. This transmission was not acknowledged. Subsequently, radar showed multiple primary returns fanning out downward.

The aircraft literally exploded over Lockerbie, Scotland (55 degrees 07 minutes N, 003 degrees 21 minutes W) and fell to the ground in pieces, killing 11 more innocent people on the ground. Major portions of the wreckage fell over the town of Lockerbie and to the east. Smaller debris was strewn along two trails; the longest extended approximately 130 kilometers to the coast of England. A complete primary wing structure, incorporating the center section of Pan Am 103 impacted on the southern edge of Lockerbie. The weight of the material displaced by the wing structure was estimated to be well in excess of 1500 tons. The impact of the crashing plane was so strong that the British Geological Survey recorded a seismic event measuring 1.6 on the Richter scale. The crash received international attention. The families of the victims banded together, and have pursued the facts and issues surrounding the crash with extreme tenacity. This aspect alone makes this particular crash especially unique.

Responsibility was originally thought to fall on the PFLP because of radio cassette bombs discovered in the hands of the PFLP-GC (General Command) prior to the bombing. Many intelligence analysts were convinced that the

Iranians were retaliating for the accidental shoot down of one of their commercial carriers. The latest evidence, however, indicates Muammar Khadaffi, the notorious dictator of Libya, was really responsible. Law enforcement later discovered a significant clue. A link was established between an obscure case involving the arrest of Mohammed Marzouk and Mansour Omran Saber, both Libyan intelligence agents, at Dakar, Senegal, airport in 1988 and the Lockerbie explosive device. It turns out they had in their possession 20 pounds of Semtex plastic, TNT explosives, weapons, and some triggering devices. One of the triggering devices matched a microchip fragment from the Pan Am bomb. The circuit board fragment recovered from the crash was actually part of a sophisticated electronic timer. Senegalese authorities discovered the same type of electronic timer in the possession of the two Libyan terrorists who had been arrested in February 1988. Meister et Bollier, a Swiss electronics firm, specially manufactured the timers, designated as MST-13, and all 13 timers had been delivered to the Libyans.

Further investigation revealed that Abd al-Basit Al-Megrahi, a senior Libyan intelligence official, and Lamen Fhimah, the former manager of the Libyan Arab Airlines office of Malta, conspired to bomb Pan Am Flight 103. The perpetrators made use of the Czech-made explosive and very powerful Semtex. A double-detonator device was used. The first trigger was activated by barometric pressure, which in turn activated a timing device. The actual bomb was encased in a Toshiba radio cassette player. The terrorists were able to obtain and attach an appropriately marked Air Malta tag that enabled the luggage to circumvent baggage security measures and to be directly routed to the Pan Am feeder flight.

Forensic experts identified the bag that contained the bomb as a brown, hard-sided Samsonite suitcase. One of the defendants, Al-Megrahi, arrived in Valletta's Luqa Airport with the other defendant, Fhimah from Libya, on the evening of 20 December 1988. Because Fhimah had been the former manager of the Maltese airport, he had somehow retained full access to the airport. Scottish investigators traced the clothing that had been packed in the bag to a shop in Malta. Frankfurt airport records show that an unaccompanied bag was routed from the Air Malta Flight 180 to Frankfurt where it was eventually loaded onto the Pan Am Flight 103 feeder flight, as per perfectly legal procedures in effect at the time.

A warning bulletin describing the device was sent by the FAA on 18 November 1988. The bulletin was delivered at US Embassies and Consulates around the world. However, the one airline official designated to read such material at Pan Am first saw the bulletin after a three-week vacation and after the crash. The issue of who should be advised of these warnings is controversial. For example, many telephone threats are fraudulent, and it is often difficult to separate the real threats from the false ones. As a result of that, such procedures have been changed so that carriers now provide written acknowledgement to the FAA of the receipt of such bulletins and the action they are taking. Procedures have not significantly changed regarding whom actually has access to the information.

Other safety and security issues were also involved. Apparently a telephone threat received from an anonymous caller on 5 December 1988 at the American

Embassy in Helsinki, Finland, warned of the impending disaster. The caller claimed a Finnish woman would carry a bomb aboard a Pan Am flight from Frankfurt to the US sometime during the next two weeks. The US State Department sent out diplomatic traffic notifying its own personnel. Even though notice again was disseminated to all US consulates and embassies, since Finnish police determined it was a hoax, the information was not passed on to the FAA. The procedure of nondisclosure, which emerged from this incident and was persistently raised by the families of the victims, posed the question of exactly who should be advised in the event of threat information. The recommendation of the President's Commission on Aviation Security and Terrorism in May 1990 was in favor of public notification of threats to civil aviation. However, security officials and the air carriers had reaffirmed an overall policy of nondisclosure. Nonetheless, Section 109 of the Aviation Security Act of 1990 now directs that Title II of the Federal Aviation Act of 1958 be amended to provide that the President shall develop guidelines for ensuring notification to the public of threats to civil aviation in appropriate cases. What the term *appropriate cases* means is not quite clear.

The Lockerbie incident also raised the issue of passenger/baggage reconciliation. The President's Commission reported and concluded that passenger/baggage reconciliation is a bedrock component of any heightened security program. In 1988, Pan Am was x-raying all interline bags rather than identifying and physically searching unaccompanied interline bags. Pan Am additionally claimed it had FAA approval to do this even though the FAA insisted it did not. Investigation disclosed the presence of an extra bag when the flight left Frankfurt, which had not been physically searched. Also as a direct consequence of the Lockerbie tragedy, the Air Carrier Standard Security Program (ACSSP) now requires both a positive match and an x-ray or a hand search of all checked baggage in specific designated countries.

11 September 2001

In an unprecedented act of massive terrorism, a hijacked commercial airliner, American Airlines Flight 11, was purposively diverted to impact the north tower of the World Trade Center in New York City. A second hijacked aircraft, United Airlines Flight 175 from Boston, crashed into the south tower and exploded upon impact. At approximately 9:17 AM, the FAA shut down all New York City airports and the Port Authority of New York and New Jersey ordered all bridges and tunnels in the New York area closed. A few minutes later, the FAA halted all flight operations at all US airports nationwide. For the first time in US history, commercial flight operations in the United States came to a screeching halt. On top of the devastation in New York, at 9:43 AM, American Airlines Flight 77 hurtled into the Pentagon in Washington, DC. At 10:05 AM, the south tower of the World Trade Center collapsed, and five minutes later, United Flight 93 was hijacked and crashed in Somerset County, Pennsylvania, after several passengers forcibly sought to reclaim the jet from the hijackers. In another unprecedented move, the

FAA diverted all trans-Atlantic flights inbound from overseas to the United States to Canada. Suddenly, the 50 remaining aircraft still aloft in US airspace was of concern.

Soon thereafter, in a massive release of debris and smoke, the north tower of the World Trade Center collapsed. Americans and members of 62 other nations lost friends and family in the ensuing devastation. Whatever the exact total loss of life amounts to it is unbearable. That evening Americans and the rest of the world learn that the well-coordinated, well-financed, and unfortunately well-executed attacks are likely the work of Usama bin Ladin's al-Q'aeda terrorist network. Apparently, three to five hijackers commandeered each aircraft armed simply with knives and box cutters.

Prior to the tragic events, there were clues about impending terrorist attacks; however, they were not sufficiently connected in order to prevent the attacks. In the April/May time frame, the government learned that Usama bin Ladin's network was targeting the US. In July 2001, the FBI advised law enforcement agencies of threats to US interests overseas and domestic. Additionally, the Phoenix FBI office notified Washington that men of Middle Eastern heritage were attending flight schools in Arizona, and that it was likely bin Ladin was involved. About a month later, the CIA formally told the President that al-Q'aeda operatives could be targeting the US aviation industry. Soon thereafter, Zacarias Moussaoui was arrested in Minnesota on a visa violation. He had raised suspicions at an Eagen, Minnesota, flight school after he was seeking training on a 747 jet but did not even have a pilot's license. Minnesota's FBI office was denied permission to search his computer. It was later found to contain references to al-Q'aeda operatives in Malaysia and Germany, the 9/11 hijackers, and crop dusting aircraft. On August 17, a Minneapolis FBI agent even surmised in a prophetic letter to headquarters that Moussaoui might be the type of person who would fly an aircraft into the World Trade Center. The National Security Agency had also intercepted messages the day before the attack referencing some big event.

After the attacks, the President of the United States announced that the US government will make no distinction between the terrorists who committed the acts and those who harbor them. Considering the horrific events, which are labeled "acts of war," a new war on terrorism has begun. The public has also been made aware of the fact that the effort to combat all forms of terrorism will not be a short one.

■ CONCLUSION

As hijackings continued to increase, authorities explored the options available to them to combat it. The Federal Aviation Security Regulations were eventually proposed and implemented. The Federal Aviation Act of 1958 had to be amended accordingly. The regulations have repeatedly been amended to accommodate innovations in technology and to close previously missed loopholes. All sorts of alternatives to improve the program were openly discussed over the years—

some adopted and some quickly and thankfully discarded. Eventually the public came to recognize that some drastic measures were required. Security programs, the Federal Air Marshall Program, and passenger screening were all initial attempts to control the threat at both domestic and international airports. It is still unsettled just how far the public and the courts will permit security officials to go to protect the air transportation industry—both cargo and passengers. Profiling being one of those methods continually being reviewed.

The US government has repeatedly sought to maintain and upgrade security standards at airports. The early rules may have been implemented in haste, but they have subsequently been revised and amended in order to fill loopholes and improve security at the nation's airports. Initially, the rules met with significant resistance from the airlines and even from some consumer groups. However, the US government has continuously sought to improve the safety and security of US airports. Both the Aviation Security and Improvement Act and the Federal Aviation Reauthorization Act of 1996 have appropriated money to be used in implementing the latest technology available in the field of airport security. Exactly who or what agency is responsible to foot the bill for the nation's airport security will remain under debate. The newest legislation addresses some of those questions but not all. The airlines have repeatedly argued that terrorism is a threat to national security and should be addressed and financed by the government. The government on the other hand had insisted prior to 9/11 that the cost of security is another cost of doing business in America and should be absorbed by the airlines, and hence the traveling public. Of note is the fact that the newest technology is also the most expensive technology.

The TSA is now challenged with overseeing the programs that assess whether airlines and airport operators provide adequate security measures at all airports. They assess both US and overseas facilities. They also continue to propose changes to the federal regulations as they deem appropriate. The most recent issues involve cargo, airmail, background checks on screeners, and explosive general aviation airport detection equipment. The government will also continue to assess the level of threat and to disseminate that information to the airlines.

In spite of the hijackings of 9/11 and interim efforts to place National Guardsmen at the nation's airports, significant long-term changes have yet fully to be implemented. Additional resources will have to be committed, and additionally more analysis as to what will be successful in the future will need to be researched. The ASTA of 2001 represents another knee-jerk reaction to air piracy. It was hastily enacted post-9/11 and will likely undergo needed changes as certain realities set in. General aviation airport and cargo issues also need to be immediately addressed by the 108th Congress.

Air piracy remains a security threat to international air travel. A constant trail of incidents evidences the point right up to the present. Repeated instances of hijacking over the years have proven time and time again that aircraft and airports are public, accessible, and somewhat easy targets for terrorists. They seek to publicize their cause and are guaranteed instant media coverage for their efforts. Politically volatile regions continue to produce emotionally driven terrorists who feel their actions are justified. Some very tragic results have been viewed by millions of people exposed to the media frenzies that follow major incidents. No geographical region has escaped the problem. However, responses from governments have varied from jurisdiction to jurisdiction. There is no question that additional hijackings and or other forms of attacks will plague the aviation industry. As mentioned, new forms of using the transportation industry to disrupt the US economy are likely. The use of aircraft to torpedo symbols of American democracy and strength was expanded to include not only hijacking and attacking airport terminals but also to include commandeering aircraft to destroy major targets. The governments of the world are therefore challenged not only to provide adequate security at all airports for both commercial and general aviation but also to address the underlying causes of the terrorism in the first place. The next chapter will explain the historical bases of these problem regions that generate terrorist conduct.

chapter five

Terrorism: The Roots Remain

■ NEWS

1. **January 2001**: A trial began in the Southern District of New York of four suspects in connection with the bombings at US Embassies in Kenya and Tanzania. Three of the four were extradited to the United States in 1999 to stand trial.

2. **10 October 2001**: Three small bombs exploded in Zamboanga City in the Philippines on 8 October, allegedly detonated by Aby Sayyaf, a group of Islamic militants with ties to Usama bin Ladin.

3. **May 2002**: Spurred by concerns about terrorism, federal authorities are investigating whether private guards hired by major airlines in Los Angeles have smuggled passengers from the Middle East into the United States. The State Department also branded seven countries as promoters of terrorism: Iran, Sudan, Libya, Cuba, Iraq, North Korea, and Syria.

4. **28 November 2002**: A suicide bombing at the Israeli-owned Paradise Hotel near Mombasa, Kenya, killed 16 people, including the three attackers. On the same morning, a failed missile attack on an Israeli airliner taking off from Mombasa airport was carried out.

5. **9 January 2003**: Islamic Jihad claimed responsibility for a suicide bombing that killed 17 Israelis, including 13 soldiers, at Megiddo Junction in northern Israel. The attack prompted former Palestinian Authority President Yasser Arafat to order the arrest of leaders of the militant group.

■ INTRODUCTION

Throughout the world, terrorist organizations often threaten any possibility of peace among and within nations. Terrorism itself has a deep history and, when analyzed, each terrorist group has a unique historical view of its own. Whether groups hold emotional left-wing, right-wing, or single-issue perspectives, the problems for reconciliation are often slim. Each is similar in that they will fight mercilessly for their own causes. This fight has historically included many instances of hijacking, airport raids, and now commandeering aircraft for use as passenger-filled missiles.

The *sine qua non* of terrorism is the media. The airplane provides a capsule container of ready-made hostages, all organized, sitting in rows, strapped into their seats, and basically defenseless. Terrorists have sought frequently to exploit this made-to-order situation in order to publicize their causes. From a terrorist's viewpoint, aircraft are a preferable target because of their international flavor and the likelihood the press will focus on the incident. Overall, most terrorist incidents in the United States have been bombing attacks involving detonated and undetonated explosive devices, tear gas, and pipe and fire bombs. The targets are not limited to aircraft and airports, and the effects can vary significantly from loss of life and injuries to property damage and disruptions in services such as electricity, water supply, public transportation, and communications. The primary way to reduce vulnerability to terrorist attacks is by increasing security at airports and other public domains. The aviation industry, however, is at particular risk.

Generally, the concept of terrorism has been defined as the use of force or violence against persons or property in violation of the criminal laws for purposes of intimidation, coercion, or ransom. No one definition has been universally accepted and the diversity of the term defies one simple definition. The Federal Bureau of Investigation categorizes terrorist activity as either domestic or international. Domestic terrorism involves groups or individuals whose terrorist activities are directed at elements of the government or population without foreign direction. International terrorism involves groups or individuals whose terrorist activities are foreign based and directed by countries or groups outside the United States or whose activities transcend national boundaries. The State Department defines terrorism as, "premeditated, politically motivated violence against noncombatant targets by sub-national groups or clandestine agents, usually intended to influence an audience" (Title 22 USC Section 2656f[d]). Clearly, it is a difficult concept to express in one definition.

Ironically, the term *terrorism* first appeared during the years of the French Revolution (1789–1795). Edmund Burke, a British philosopher in the 1700s, used the word to describe the political scene in revolutionary Paris. The violence became known as the "Reign of Terror" and applied to the conduct of the legal government at the time. The concept of terrorism has been around since the discovery that people can be influenced by intimidation. The earliest documented terrorist group was arguably the Sicarii, a Jewish group that used savage methods against the occupation force of the Roman Empire around 70 CE. The Ismaili, or Assassins, lashed out against perceived religious oppression from the eleventh to the thirteenth century throughout the Islamic world.

Today, the US Congress requires the Department of State to provide Congress a full and complete annual report on terrorism regarding those countries and groups deemed involved in such activities. The law requiring the report was amended in 1996 to also require information on the extent to which other countries cooperate with the United States in apprehending, convicting, and punishing terrorists responsible for attacking US citizens or interests. The report also contains information describing the extent to which foreign governments are cooperating or have cooperated during the previous five years in preventing future acts of terrorism.

Experts have attempted to differentiate between historical terrorism and modern terrorism. According to many scholars, modern terrorists strike at governments by killing their citizens not just at government or military targets. For example, they strike at aircraft containing innocent noncombatants with no vested interest in the outcome of whatever political goal the terrorists are seeking. Simply put, modern terrorists sensationalize the murder of innocents, and capturing an aircraft is a dramatic way of doing it. The causes behind the terrorism vary from region to region and country to country. In order to combat the problems, a basic knowledge of the issues, policies, and causes are important. The following sections summarize the historical reasons why many of the world's most notorious terrorist groups arose and eventually felt it necessary to jump from verbal rhetoric to violence.

■ CAUSES OF TERRORISM

Acts of terrorism directed at aircraft and airports was once again placed on page one of US news reports in May 2001. An Algerian terrorist admitted he was smuggling explosives across the US/Canadian border back in December 1999 in order to attempt to blow up the Los Angeles International Airport. His conduct reinforced the concept that the threat was still significant and authorities could not afford to relax security procedures already in place and enter into a state of apathy. Terrorism was and is alive and well. There were also major clues that went unnoticed prior to 9/11 that unfortunately were missed. Before discussing many of the groups actively engaged in terrorism it is relevant to point out US policy in negotiating with terrorists. The stated policy is as follows:

- **First**, make no concession to terrorists and strike no deals.
- **Second**, bring terrorists to justice for their crimes.
- **Third**, isolate and apply pressure on states that sponsor terrorism to force them to change their behavior.
- **Fourth**, bolster the counterterrorist capabilities of those countries that work with the US and require assistance (Patterns of Global Terrorism, 2000 US Department of State, Office of the Coordinator for Counterterrorism, April 2001, Pg. 1).

A thorough understanding of the background of some of the most treacherous groups will assist students and practitioners in this field in their efforts to remedy potentially dangerous and lethal situations. As mentioned, experts in the field have pondered the best definition of the term *terrorism*. Many agencies and scholars have sought a workable definition for their respective investigative purposes, and all agree it is an illusive term to pin down. The Omnibus Diplomatic Security and Anti-Terrorism Act of 1986 defines terrorism as the unlawful use of force or violence designed to intimidate or coerce a government or a civilian population in the furtherance of political or social objectives. Later legislation further defined a terrorist group as any organization that engages in, or has engaged in, terrorist activity as defined by the Secretary of State after consultation with the Secretary of the Treasury. Law enforcement agencies including the Federal Bureau of Investigation and the Central Intelligence Agency as well as the United Nations all have distinctive definitions which relate to their particular missions.

■ MIDDLE EAST

The current crisis in the Middle East is a direct result of political maneuvering by the West immediately preceding and during World War I. The Europeans sought to defeat Turkish influence in the area and to establish their own. In order to do so, they were willing to make promises they could not keep. At the turn of the century, the American naval strategist Alfred Mahan first coined the term *Middle East*. Since that time the violence in the region has been extraordinary in the sense that it has had repercussions around the world and continues to do so. Many Westerners have failed to understand the basic historical, social, religious, and economic factors that are the cause of such violence. First of all, the region is the focal point of the world's three major religions. That fact alone provides the local populations, and the faithful living elsewhere, with the fuel rapidly to incite emotionally charged responses to all sorts of political and economic issues.

To better understand terrorism in the Middle East and the subsequent requirements to promote security at worldwide airports, one must first appreciate some highly pertinent historical turning points. For 30 years prior to the establishment of the State of Israel, the Middle East conflict was a constant drain on Great Britain's ability to protect its national interests. The results of European imperialism and

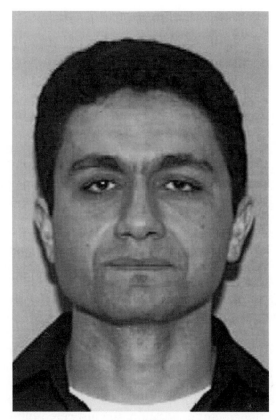

Mohammed Atta photo released 11/12/01 in a State of Florida, Division of Motor Vehicles photo. Atta is one of two men who received flight training in Florida and was one of the masterminds behind the 9/11 attack. *AP/Wide World Photos.*

intervention are one of the primary causes of the continuation of an almost universal hatred of Israel in the region. Efforts to resolve the issues have always failed, because the grounds for compromise acceptable to the parties involved have not been reached and the superpowers have been either unwilling or unable to impose solutions from the outside. Both sides blame the other, and pinpointing the real causes of the terror is like deciding what came first, the chicken or the egg.

During World War I, the Turks were allied with the Germans. Consequently, the British encouraged the Arabs to revolt against the Turks. In return for this revolt, the Arabs were promised their freedom. In reality, the British never really had any intention of ever granting full autonomy to the Arabs. In point of fact, the Europeans sought to carve up the riches of the region, especially oil reserves, and create new imperial colonies. As history has shown, the British not only deceived the Arabs, they also misled the Jews. Partially in response to the Zionist movement, the British also promised the Zionists a Jewish homeland in Palestine. Meanwhile, at the other end of the geographical region, the British approached the Russians with a deal to divide modern Iran into three parts. The Russians were to control the northern part and the British the south, leaving only the center to the Iranians. When World War I ended, the Middle East had become a powder keg of competing interests. It remains so today.

■ RIVAL CLAIMS

For more than 50 years, the critical issue has been, and continues to be, who is entitled to live in the land historically called Palestine. Even though the British had verbally made a promise to the Arabs to support an independent Arab state, they did so without the consent of the French. The French had their own set of goals and eventually signed the Sykes-Picot Agreement with the British that divided the Middle East into spheres of interest. In the alternative, the British also publicly issued the Balfour Declaration, promising Palestine as the future Jewish homeland.

At the end of the war, several traditional Arab families sought to unite Islam under their own banner. The result was the establishment of Syria, Iraq, Saudi Arabia, Jordan, Egypt, and Libya as the most powerful emerging Arab states. All considered the creation of a Pan Islamic state as a goal, but none of them was willing to concede their own chances to be the leading voice of this concept in the region. On top of traditional Arab families rivaling each other for control, Great Britain also acquired permission from the League of Nations to create the Protectorate of Transjordan. The British received their wish to be an influence in the Middle East, but it came at a price. Neither the Arabs nor Jews were satisfied with the arrangement. In addition, the insecure political atmosphere in the Arab states, born of many years of weakness, frustration, and mutual suspicion, precluded the emergence of even a moderate consensus between the Arabs.

It was tragic that the Arabs could not reach agreement among themselves even though it was clearly within their best interests. The tragedy was further compounded by the failure of the great powers at the time to help. The moral and diplomatic support given by President Harry S Truman to Israel has proven to be shortsighted. It has had the effect of making a permanent moral commitment from the United States to the eventual State of Israel. Throughout the next several decades, although American president's have sometimes opposed Israeli actions, when it comes to the fundamental question affecting the existence of the Israeli state, no American president has been in a strong enough position to call Israel's basic politics into question. The United States is still dealing with the repercussions of this initial commitment.

Both Jews and Arabs fought the British, but each envisioned a Palestine without the other. In 1936, the Arabs openly revolted. It was outwardly toward the British, but hatred of the Jews was festering and growing. At the time of the Balfour Declaration, the actual population of Palestine was about 600,000 Palestinians and approximately 70,000 Jews. However, in late 1945, thousands of Jews sought a place to settle after the Nazi Holocaust. The British had officially banned Jewish immigration, but pressure was building to open the Jewish settlement of Palestine. The United Nations eventually partitioned the area in 1947, because the situation was, in reality, out of British control. Today, the Middle East is witnessing a reverse Zionism on behalf of the Palestinians, who are insisting on the right to return to their homeland.

Prior to 1947, the Jews were also in open revolt against the British. The Irgun Zvai Leumi, a Jewish terrorist organization attacked both British soldiers and Arab Palestinians alike. Founding member of the Irgun, Menachim Begin, masterminded an attack on the King David Hotel in Jerusalem in 1946. The explosion left 91 people dead. He went on to become a member of the Knesset from 1949 to 1984 and later served as Prime Minister of Israel (George Rosie, *The Directory of International Terrorism, Paragon House*, New York, 1987, Pg. 39). The Arabs formed their own terrorist groups. By May 15, 1948, the United Nations recognized the modern state of Israel. The Palestinians, now displaced themselves, sought to get the land back by whatever means it took, including hijacking aircraft.

■ PALESTINIAN LIBERATION ORGANIZATION

As discussed, much of the conflict in the Middle East started during the 1800s when revolts by nationalists, Turks, and Arab familial groups inflamed the region while they pursued their own interests. The conflict ultimately was a battle over who would control Palestine and who would be the voice of the Palestinians. The situation was further complicated by the thousands of Jews seeking a homeland after the Nazi Holocaust. When Zionists occupied Israel, the Palestinians fled their traditional lands. Al-Fatah, later the Palestinian Liberation Organization (PLO), was born. After the Six-Day War in 1967, the Arab cause was in disarray. No one except the PLO was inclined to fight the Israelis. The PLO was prepared to fight back regardless of being underequipped and essentially no match for the Israeli army. They attacked the Israelis in unconventional ways including "terrorist acts" against schoolchildren, farms, and whatever they could reach.

Initially, the PLO had organized and matured while hiding out in Jordan and infiltrating Israel to raid settlements in the Gaza Strip and West Bank. However, in a bold gesture, the Israelis struck back and attacked a small village known as Karamah. The Israelis were repelled with the help of the Jordanian army. King Hussein of Jordan was not necessarily interested in protecting the PLO, but he was interested in protecting his own sovereign territory from invasion. Afterwards and in spite of the fact that he may not even have been present and his forces were really not victorious on their own, Yasser Arafat becomes a hero. He was born Abdel-Rahman Abdel-Raouf Arafat at-Qudwa al-Hussein. In time he would be viewed both as a revolutionary hero and as a bloodthirsty terrorist depending on your perspective. Whatever your viewpoint, the PLO would bring violence and terror to the region.

Al-Fatah was made up of holy warriors, or fedayeen. The founders included Yassar Arafat, Salah Khala, and Khalil Wazir. They were young, active, and humiliated after the 1967 Six-Day War. Its members did not often agree on how to respond to the perceived threat from Israel. Meanwhile, King Hussein was becoming more and more apprehensive about the PLO's continued presence in his country, and Arafat ignored the King's warnings to stop infiltrating Israel. In reality, Arafat increased his operations. In September 1970, after the PLO had successfully attacked civilians, hijacked aircraft, and assassinated many people, King Hussein had had enough. Much to Arafat's surprise, King Hussein attacked the PLO and forced the organization to flee to Lebanon. The event became known as Black September.

Soon thereafter, a militant faction of the PLO assumed the name Black September commemorating the eviction of the organization from Jordan. They eventually attacked the Israeli athletes at the Munich Olympics in 1972, and as a result were hunted down by the Israeli Mossad and assassinated. The conflict raged on for years with splinter groups seeking the assistance and support of rival Arab nations, all hoping to be the true voice of the Arab world. Many individuals within the PLO began to regard Yassar Arafat as a liability, considering him soft on Israel. About this time, Iraq recruited Sabri al-Banna, who later became known as Abu Nidal. Abu Nidal was to later lose his strictly Palestinian political motivations and turn mercenary. He even made several attempts on Arafat's life.

The overall situation defied compromise. The Israelis decided forcibly to remove the PLO from southern Lebanon and invaded. Thousands were massacred at Sabra and Shatila. Arafat once again was forced to flee. This time he went to Tunisia. Many experts at the time thought him finished; however, he was repeatedly to surprise everyone.

In 1987, the Intifada, or Arab uprising, took place. The uprising represented a spontaneous revolt by young Palestinians frustrated with life in refugee camps. The US media, in reporting on the Palestinians, pictured them as stone-throwing youths fighting heavily armed Israeli military forces. The West suddenly viewed the Palestinian revolt in a more sympathetic light. The United Nations even recognized the PLO as the official representatives of the Palestinian people. The fast-paced changes were too much for Arafat. In fact, in 1988, he recognized Israel and denounced terrorism. On 13 September 1993, a Declaration of Principles between the Israelis and the Palestinians was signed establishing a tentative peace at best.

Others were not to follow his leadership. The tangled web of Middle Eastern terrorism involves many more players than the members of the PLO. Terrorism was to continue and repeatedly to interfere with the peace process. Groups like Abu Nidal, Hamas, Hezbollah, and Islamic Jihad were to flourish. Any future negotiated peace settlement will depend on the control or placation of still extremely militant factions active in the region.

■ ABU NIDAL

Names like Al-Iqab (the punishment), Al-Asifa (the storm), and many others represent one group named for a single leader, Abu Nidal. This group, known especially for its brutal acts of terrorism, has managed to survive nearly three decades. The group's history, ideology, and structure revolve around a Palestinian formerly known as Sabri al-Banna. Al-Banna, known today as Abu Nidal, was the sole leader and proprietor of a highly volatile terrorist organization.

Soon after Sabri al-Banna entered the fourth grade, his family was forced from Jaffa as a result of the 1947 partition of Palestine and the fighting that followed. The family was eventually forced into a refugee camp after their homes and holdings were confiscated by the Zionist government. This experience was likely the driving force behind al-Banna's violent and angry future. Later he joined the Ba'ath Party of Jordan and the Fatah, both illegal in Saudi Arabia. He was eventually arrested, imprisoned, tortured, and expelled. After the 1967 Six-Day War, a formerly passive member of the Fatah became Abu Nidal, a master terrorist.

Within months of his arrival, Abu Nidal began to ignore directives from Fatah leaders. With the help of the Iraqis, by 1973, he had established his own terrorist organization. In 1974, he was expelled from the Fatah and sentenced to death for ordering an assassination attempt on Yasser Arafat. Nidal's defiance of the PLO was the result of Nidal's perceived laxness of PLO policies toward Israel. He was drawn to Bagdad because of its rejectionist approach to Israel. Using the resources provided by the Iraqi government, Nidal began his own terrorist campaign. Together Nidal and the Iraqis rejected all peaceful attempts to resolve the Palestinian problem. In his first major campaign, he hijacked a British airliner en route from Dubai to Tunis.

With the structure of his group in place, Nidal began to focus on his two main objectives. First he wanted Israel destroyed and second the punishment of all those who disagreed with him. No one was safe. From his base in Iraq, Nidal's organization focused on the moderate Arab states of Syria and Jordan, destroying embassies and assassinating Arab leaders. In the late 1970s, he moved his operation to Syria after being ejected from Iraq. He executed hundreds of terrorist acts both in Israel and Western Europe; targeting Israeli and Jewish sites. It is alleged that Abu Nidal has carried out operations in over 20 countries and caused the death of over 900 people. As part of this effort, the group coordinated an attack at two major international airports, Rome and Vienna, in December 1985. They intended to discredit Arafat and the PLO. Later, after also alienating himself from the Syrians, he moved the entire operation again to Libya, seeking financial support from Moammar Khaddaffi.

As stated, Abu Nidal is considered by many as being nothing more than a mercenary group. During the 1990s, Abu Nidal was reported to be dead or dying. It was also reported he had been captured by the Egyptians in 1998. The rumors were premature, and the group continued to terrorize the Middle East, although he had been behind the scenes for many years. However, in August 2002, he apparently died in Damascus. It was reported he had committed suicide, but it was unclear why the body had four bullet wounds.

■ HAMAS

One of more militant groups still active is the Islamic Resistance Movement, or Harakat-Al-Muqawama Al-Islamiyyah, also known as Hamas. To its members, the destruction of Israel is the only answer to the tenuous situation in the Middle

East. They see Israel, and anyone who recognizes Israel, as the enemy, and they will never recognize any claims the Israelis have also to have a right to a homeland in Palestine. They represent a continuing struggle, and are headquartered in the Gaza Strip. The Israelis incarcerated the founder of Hamas, Aheikh Ahmed Yassin, in 1989 for killing Palestinians who collaborated with the Israeli army. He was later released in a trade for two Israeli agents held in Jordan. It is composed of charitable, political (Al-Majd), and military (Izz Al-Din Al Qassam) elements. Hamas originated in the 1980s as part of the Palestinian Muslim Brotherhood, another rejectionist organization; one that is not likely to relinquish its desire to be the voice not only of Palestine but also of all the Arab peoples.

The Hamas movement considers Arafat to be a traitor. It supports complete Israeli withdrawal from the occupied territories. Hamas has dispatched most of the more than 92 suicide bombers who have killed hundreds of Israelis. They have the ability perpetually to disrupt any efforts for a peaceful compromise in the Middle East. They are well financed and extremely well organized. In 2002, Hamas published the following statement on its Web site, "We call on the Arabs and Muslims to burn the land under the feet of the American invaders, especially our brothers in Saudi Arabia because this war is not against Iraq, its against the Islamic nation" (Internet: http://www.hamas.org.uk/). So long as there is dissatisfaction with the Palestinian government, groups as radical as Hamas will flourish.

■ IRANIAN SUPPORT OF TERRORISM

The US government maintains a list of seven foreign governments that they accuse of sponsoring international terrorism. Of those seven nations, Iran, remains one of the most active sponsors of international terrorism. The sponsoring of international terror is the main reason that Iran is still isolated from the mainstream international community to the degree that it is.

The roots of Iranian terror can be traced back to the Iranian revolution and the rise to power of the late Ayatollah Khomeini. Starting in the early twentieth century, Iran began to want to be free of imperialistic rule. Fearing that if Iran went about eliminating imperialism incorrectly, they would become a communist state, the CIA and the US government decided to help the Shah. Whereas Americans felt that they were helping Iran, the Iranian population "viewed America's actions as part of the long history of imperialism" (Jonathan White, *Terrorism: An Introduction*, Wadsworth Publishers, Belmont, CA, 1998, Pg. 116). Because of how discontent his followers were becoming with the Shah's actions, he created a secret police to destroy his enemies, the SAVAK. The SAVAK was one of the first Iranian-sponsored terrorist organizations. They would often kidnap the Shah's political enemies and either torture or murder them. The SAVAK was also famous for arresting and beating demonstrators. Often those demonstrators would be imprisoned for long periods of time. In what proved later to be a fatal mistake, one of those prisoners, Hojatalislam Khomeini, would come back to haunt the Shah. Instead of executing Khomeini, the Shah had him deported to Iraq.

From Iraq, Khomeini's influence over Iran began to grow. While in Iraq, he ran a campaign to rid Iran of the Shah, and he was promoted to the rank of Ayatollah. After the election of President Jimmy Carter, Khomeini increased his anti-Shah campaign because he felt the West held excessive sway over the Shah. At about this time, Khomeini was forced to leave Iraq and moved his base of operations to Paris. While in Paris, ironically he grew even stronger, because he now had a direct telephone connection to Teheran. Khomeini eventually returned to Iran in 1978, and by February 1979, he was in power. Once in power, he initiated a "holy war against the West and the traitors to Islam" (White, 1998: Pg. 117).

An understanding of Islamic fundamentalism is critical to an understanding of Iranian sponsorship of terrorism in the Middle East. Some basic precepts include:

1. Islam is the answer to all the problems of their society, country, and region. Relative weakness compared to the West, slow or stagnant economic development, the failure to destroy Israel, domestic and inter-Arab disunity, inequality and injustice, and anything else are all due to the failure to implement Islam.

2. Implementing Islam and resolving the huge problems of the people and states requires the seizure and holding of power by radical Islamic groups and not by any other type of government or political group.

3. The only proper interpretation of Islam is the one offered by a specific political group and its leaders (Rubin Rubin, "Islamic Radicalism in the Middle East: A Survey and Balance Sheet," *Middle East Review of International Affairs*, May 1998). (Internet: http://www.biu.ac.il/besa/meria/journal/1998/issue2/jv2n2a3.html.)

The religious views of Iran are only one of the reasons that they are a sponsor of terrorism. By supporting terrorism through the 1980s, Iran gained important strategic, political, and economic assets. One of the main benefits resulted in the removal of American and French troops from Lebanon; enhancing their standing in the Middle East and all over the Muslim community, at least from their perspective. Officials also wished to export many fanatical revolutionary guards to the Bekoa Valley keeping them out of mainstream politics in Iran.

In 1996, while addressing officers of the Iranian Air Force, President Ali Kameini was quoted as saying, "The government and people of Iran are of the opinion that the Israeli entity is false and artificial. In fact, there is no nation named Israel. The Zionists scraped together some people from all over the world, and based on racism, brought about the Zionist regime by virtue of the conquest of Palestine" (Israeli Foreign Ministry, "Iran and Hezbollah," 3 March 2000, Internet: http://www.israel-mfa.gov.ilgopher://israel-info.gov.il). The Iranians will continue to export terrorism as long as they believe it serves their national interests.

▓ HEZBOLLAH

No terrorist organization in the world has received more assistance from Iran than Hezbollah. The International Policy Institute for Counter-Terrorism describes the group as the "spearhead for Iran in its use of terrorism in general, and its fight against Israel in particular" (Magnus Ranstorp, "Hezbollah's Command Leadership," *Terrorism and Political Violence*, Frank Cass, London, 1994, Vol. 6, No. 3, Pg. 304). Each year Hezbollah receives millions of dollars from the Iranian government to help what they believe is the legitimate struggle against Israel. Some have estimated the support to reach levels of $80 to $100 million dollars every year.

Hezbollah is also active in the United States. FBI agents arrested 18 Hezbollah supporters in North Carolina in July 2000. An FBI affidavit said investigators were searching for evidence that the defendants were providing resources to the terrorist group. The resources included night vision goggles, global positioning systems, and digital photograph equipment and computers. The goal of Hezbollah is to establish an Islamic state in Lebanon (Alexander Yonah, "Hezbollah: The Most Dangerous Terrorist Movement," *Intersec*, Intersec Publishing Ltd., Three Bridges Publishing Ltd., Vol. 4, Issue 10, Oct 1994, Pg. 393). As stated, their efforts were completely supported by the government of Iran and controlled by radical Shi'ite clerics. Hezbollah mainly targets Israel but considers the US and Western assets as legitimate targets. They represent an additional wild card in the region capable of disrupting any efforts toward peace. Additionally, they have recently been tied to the al-Q'aeda organization.

▓ AFGHANISTAN: USAMA BIN LADIN

Usama bin Ladin is discussed separately from the other Middle Eastern terrorists because of his uniqueness. He is an Arab, and he was headquartered in Afghanistan, but his cause is purely anti-Western. He was born into a wealthy Saudi family and is the seventeenth son of 52 children. He attended Abdul Aziz University. While at the University Usama bin Ladin was influenced by one of his instructors, Sheikh Abdallah Azzam, who was extremely disenchanted with the alleged corruption of the PLO. Usama bin Ladin and Azzam were both interested in the intertwined worlds of Arab politics and religion. The Soviet Union's invasion of Afghanistan embroiled Usama bin Ladin in a guerilla conflict backed by Saudi money and US weapons. He became an ardent anti-Western advocate and a combat veteran.

Bin Ladin's father, Mohammed bin Ladin, moved his family from Yemen to Saudi Arabia and gradually built the largest construction company in the country. In turn, the Saudi royal family gave the Usama bin Ladin family exclusive rights to all construction of a religious nature, whether in Mecca, Medina, or elsewhere. From this background, he somehow became obsessed with the US presence on the Arabian Peninsula. Usama bin Ladin believes that the United States has been occupying the lands of Islam in the holiest of places, including Jerusalem, Mecca, and Medina. The goal for Usama bin Ladin is to unite all Muslims and to establish an Islamic government in the entire Middle East. When the war against the

Soviets in Afghanistan ended, Usama bin Ladin was seen as a leader of religious fundamentalists who oppose non-Islamic governments.

In the mid-1990s, Usama bin Ladin cofounded an organization with Azzam named the Maktab-al Khidamat (MAK). Allegedly, the MAK acted as a recruiting center and clearinghouse for Islamic charities worldwide, but it has a more sinister, quieter goal directly related to terrorism. Unbelievably, the MAK had offices in Detroit and Brooklyn. Usama bin Ladin has since issued a Fatwa, or religious decree, against the United States (Hans H Chen and David Eberhardt, "Web of Terror," bin Ladin's International Terror Network, Internet: http://www.apbonlin.com/newscenter/majorcases/binladen/index.html) The Fatwa makes it the duty of every Muslim to kill Americans and their allies. The group is also active in espousing the need to liberate Moslem holy sites from the grips of the West.

In 1989, a car bomb killed Azzam. The extremist faction of MAK directly allied with bin Ladin's efforts, and they relocated to the Sudan. After being asso-

Saudi dissident Usama bin Ladin in an undisclosed location inside Afghanistan before the fall of the Taliban regime. He remains illusive and on the top of the world's most wanted list for his part in the September 2001 attacks in New York and Washington as well as elsewhere. *AFP Photo / CORBIS BETTMANN.*

ciated with several terrorist events, Usama bin Ladin was stripped of this Saudi citizenship. The Sudan eventually expelled him under pressure from the West, after which he relocated his entire organization (al-Q'aeda) back to Afghanistan. The Taliban regime protected him. In spite of efforts by the United Nations to force the Taliban government to assist in his apprehension, they have failed to do so. Pressure was increased after the bombing of two US embassies in Africa. Some intelligence officers would also argue that he was behind the World Trade Center bombing in 1993 and the attack on the *USS Cole* in Yemen. The conviction in May 2001 of four members of the group responsible for the US African Embassy bombings bolstered US government's legal battle to bring down bin Ladin. Barry Mawn, the assistant FBI director in charge of the New York office, said after the trial, " the verdict puts on notice any individual or group of individuals who seek to attack US persons or interests abroad, that the rule of law is more powerful than any terrorist bomb" (Charisse Jones and Martha T. Moorem, "US vs. bin Ladin Just Beginning," *USA Today*, 30 May 2001, Pgs. 1A, 3A). The 1998 bombings of the US Embassies in East Africa marked the declaration of jihad which sparked a relentless campaign aimed at the indiscriminate killing of Americans.

The World Trade Center bombing in 1993 and the convictions of others charged with plotting to plant bombs around New York City revealed that the international terrorist threat within the United States is more serious and more extensive than before. The events of 11 September 2001 made this a certainty. Usama bin Ladin has a well-organized and extremely well-financed organization with an infrastructure capable of attacking targets inside the United States. Those infrastructures still include airports (GAO/RCED-94–38, 27 March 1994). The group likely acquired its real operational sophistication around 1998 when it merged with other radical groups. For example, it significantly strengthened its ties with the Armed Vanguards of Conquest, an Egyptian cell of extremists whose leader, Ayman al-Zawahri, was involved in the assassination of former Egyptian President Anwar Sadat in 1981. Perhaps the most lethal turn in bin Ladin's conduct was his decision to financially and logistically to support the efforts of these other groups. US intelligence now speculates that Mohammed Atta was likely the prime coordinator and initiator of the 9/11 attack. He took his plan to al- Q'aeda and Usama bin Ladin approved and supported it. Such associations are likely to proliferate in the future.

■ EUROPE

Germany

The threat of terrorism unfortunately spread beyond the Middle East in the 1960s. Some of the most dramatic events took place in Europe, where transition from authoritarian rule to democracy after World War II had been traumatic to say the least. The terrorists sought to bring about the collapse of European governments and hoped to establish a new order based on the teachings of Karl Marx and Mao Tse Tung.

During the 1970s, terrorism in Europe was one of the greatest scourges facing both the United States and its NATO allies. Marxist groups, anxious to spread their message, engaged in a campaign of killings and terror attacks against civilian and military targets. One of these groups in Europe, the West German Red Army Faction (RAF), or the Baader-Meinhof Gang, originated among a group of militant extremists at the Free University of Berlin. Students Andreas Baader, Gudrun Ensslin, and Ulricke Meinhof joined together and agreed upon a campaign of direct action. They repeatedly robbed banks and kidnapped and assassinated political leaders and wealthy business leaders. Most notably, they cooperated with Palestinian terrorists in the murder of Israeli athletes at the Munich Olympic Games and the hijacking of an Air France plane to Entebbe, Uganda. The German police slowly began to close in on the gang, and the Baader-Meinhof Gang would begin a cycle of collapse and rebirth extending until the present.

Born out of the student protest movements of the 1960s, the RAF was a contradiction unto itself. Although the creators of the RAF espoused the downfall of capitalism, they were generally the children of successful and wealthy people. The RAF eventually became a model upon which new generations of terrorist groups would base their organization.

The RAF began in the summer of 1967 when Andreas Baader and Gudrun Ensslin, a leader of the student protest movements, met on 2 April 1968, the two young revolutionaries had begun their reign of terror by bombing upscale department stores in Frankfurt. Instead of staying in Germany, however, the group eventually traveled to Jordan, where they received a variety of training. Upon their return to Germany, the Baader-Meinhof Gang again began robbing banks, causing both fear and panic in Germany, especially among the banking industry.

Although Baader and Ensslin were the masterminds behind the criminal operations, Meinhof was nonetheless able to spur the cause through her literary talent. In 1971, Meinhof wrote *The Concept of the Urban Guerilla*, a mixture of strategic and tactical doctrine for terrorist activities in cities. Although the ideas may not have been entirely original, formulating them in one comprehensive manual was. The doctrine for asymmetrical warfare discussed in the manual is still used today, providing would be terrorists with a concise manual designed for achieving devastating results on a budget with limited resources.

At the same time as Meinhof began writing the manual, the Baader-Meinhof Gang officially became the Red Army Faction. Although the name change may seem purely aesthetic, it actually meant a broader change for its members. For the first time, the RAF could now publicly support its cause of Marxist revolution rather than portraying itself as a group of small-time criminals.

Although as quickly as the RAF adopted its new name, the German police, frustrated with their uncoordinated and unsuccessful efforts to catch the group, formed the Bundeskriminalamt (BKA), or Federal Criminal Investigation Office. For the German people and its government, the creation of the BKA was a dynamic shift in domestic policy. For the first time since World War II, Germany now had a unified federal police agency, with more power and discretion than local departments. This was the first time the allies permitted the Germans to have a unified national police force since the downfall of the Nazi regime.

In some ways, the creation of the BKA is exactly what the RAF wanted. Part of the manual stipulated that the short-term goal of terrorist activities was to force the government to take repressive measures. To the people of Germany, terrified of their own historical examples of a strong, unified police force, the creation of the BKA should have evoked feelings of resentment and fostered a sense of rebellion toward the government. However, just the opposite happened. Instead of the public despising the government, it fully supported efforts to stop to the activities of the RAF. The RAF had overstayed its welcome and the novelty of its cause had worn off.

As the BKA began to close in on the RAF, an all-out war ensued in 1971 and 1972. Over the course of 1971, shootouts between the police and members of the RAF were a monthly occurrence, with both sides taking casualties. In the month of May, five separate bombing incidents shocked the citizens of Germany and the American servicemen stationed there. Of the five incidents, two were directed at American installations. The speed and stealth with which the bombings were carried out demonstrated the resolve of the RAF and the effectiveness of its tactics.

Devastated by the ferocity of the RAF attacks, the BKA began to use radical tactics to close in on the leaders. The public, scared and tired of the RAF, supported the actions of the police. Finally, in June, after months of searching for the leaders, the police managed to catch Baader, Meinhof, and Ensslin. In 1975, following the imprisonment of the leaders of the RAF, the Baader-Meinhof laws were passed, repressing the rights of prisoners and defendants in Germany. Although the laws represent the type of repressive measures the RAF wanted, the people of Germany again supported the government's tactics.

Desperate to free their leaders, in September 1977, the remaining members of the RAF kidnapped Hans-Martin Schleyer, a wealthy businessman and president of the Employers Association. In an attempt to amplify their earlier kidnapping successes, the RAF conducted a joint operation with Palestinian terrorists. Meinhof eventually committed suicide, and Baader and other leaders shot themselves after a rescue attempt by their compatriots failed. Following the death of their leaders, the remaining members of the RAF executed Schleyer. Regardless, the group continued to exist, and in the 1980s, it focused on an anti-NATO campaign with a new generation of terrorists. Trying to regain their previous status, they attempted several terrorist acts with Action Direct (a French terrorist group), bombing three NATO buildings in the 1980s. After the fall of the Berlin Wall and the reunification of Germany, the public largely ignored and disapproved of the methods behind the RAF's messages.

The group again gained momentum in the 1990s after a member of the Grenzschutzgruppe-9 (GSG-9), an elite counterterrorist unit, allegedly executed a captured RAF member after he had been arrested. In 1993, further to demonstrate that it was still capable of attacks and was still alive, the RAF destroyed a brand new women's prison. Although the attack was a success, the perpetrators behind it were captured soon after the attack. It appeared that the RAF was breathing its last breath. Even though renewed anti-American and anti-NATO attitudes remain strong in Europe the group no longer wields the power it once did. On the other hand, the negativity generated by the recent G-7 Economic Conference in Genoa, July 2001, once again reinforced the possibility that the group, or one similar to it, could rise again.

Efforts to round up left-wing terrorists in Europe were enhanced by the uncovered files of the East German police, the Stasi, after the fall of communism in Eastern Europe. The Baader-Meinhof Gang, or Red Army Faction, no longer presents a viable threat, however; its terrorist activities greatly contributed to public support for various governments around the world to enhance their airport security. For many years, pictures of the members of the group were posted in public places throughout Germany and the world. Their legacy includes implementation of stringent airport security measures and a national police force for Germany.

Italy

Italy has experienced a decline of terrorism; at least from radical left terrorists as opposed to Mafia-type acts of terror. In Italy, the Red Brigade launched brutal attacks on politicians, police, and journalists. The most widely publicized attacks resulted in the kidnapping and murder of former Italian Prime Minister Aldo Moro and the kidnapping of Brigidier General James Dozier. The founders of the group, Renato Curcio and Margherita Cagol, students in the sociology department at Trent University in Milan, sought to make the cities of Italy unsafe. Originally, the group was mostly centered in Milan. Later, the group was thought to have approximately 500 members and another 1000 supporters. The Red Brigade eventually disintegrated as police arrested most members of the group. However, like the Baader-Meinhof Gang, the Italian Red Brigade seemed repeatedly to rise from the ashes. The group continued its left-wing objectives even after the demise of its original leaders. They even conducted a series of terrorist attacks in reaction to efforts by Italian law enforcement to arrest leading Mafia figures.

Italian terrorist groups had literally perfected the art of kidnapping, somewhat with the inadvertent help of Italian insurance companies, who were willing to issue insurance against such events. The kidnapping of leader of the Christian Democratic Party, Aldo Moro, turned the nation against the group. Moro was a creature of habit and followed the exact same route to work every day. He was easily ambushed on 16 March 1978. The well-organized attackers shot his five bodyguards. Italy's firm policy of "no deals" with terrorists, which ironically had been introduced by Moro himself, forbad the Italian government from negotiating for his release. Moro was found dead in the trunk of a car in Rome 54 days later. The Red Brigade also kidnapped Brigadier General James Dozier, then Deputy Chief of Staff of NATO. He had admitted some professed "plumbers" to his apartment when they captured him. He was held in Padua above a grocery store. In an extremely well-executed rescue attempt, he was freed. It was the beginning of the end for the Red Brigade (William Gutteridge, *Contemporary Terrorism*, 1986, Pg. 127).

Spain

The struggle for independence and autonomy is something that the Basque people have been fighting for since the sixth century. At that time, the Visigoths drove the Basque tribe into the mountainous regions of north-central Spain. The Basque were a very unique and individualistic people, and are said to be the oldest surviving ethnic group in all of Europe.

The Basque country (Euzkadi) is located in the northern region of Spain and southwestern France. There are seven different provinces, four of which are in Spain. Whereas the Basque of France are struggling for survival, the Basque of Spain are flourishing in a wealthy and expanding industrial economy. The Basque people make up about 5 percent of the population, but produce about 10 percent of the country's exports.

Student activists established the Euskadi Ta Askatasuna (ETA), the Basque Fatherland and Liberty, in 1959. With loose ties to Marxism, the group wished to create an independent homeland in Spain's Basque region. Prior to this, Generalissimo Francisco Franco closed all Basque schools and newspapers, and even outlawed the Basque language. In 1937, he enlisted the help of Hitler's Luftwaffe and demolished the Basque historic city of Gernika. The Spanish Civil War took the lives of 50,000 Basque and sent another 300,000 more to prison and exile.

General Franco died in 1976 and a new democratic government came to power. The Basque regained some of their lost autonomy. However, the ETA sought complete independence. They turned violent in 1968 and separated into political and military branches. Members have ordinary jobs during the week as lawyers, academics, and journalists. Unique among most terrorist organizations, they engage in terrorist activity usually only on weekends. One author has stated, "Most members only engage in terrorism for three years . . . before returning to their full-time occupation" (White, 1998, Pg. 195).

Clearly, the ETA is a highly structured and organized unit. In 1997, the ETA was listed by the US State Department as one of the best-organized terrorist groups in the world (Internet: http://www.ict.org.il/, 1999: Pg. 1). The ETA has about 20 hard-core members and hundreds of supporters. According to their own publications, the ETA targets, "the oppressive symbols of the Spanish State." Additionally, the ETA was armed, trained, and supported by the Russian's during the Spanish Civil War. After Soviet aid stopped, it was rumored that Muommar Khaddaffi has been supplying the ETA with assistance.

Allegedly, the Grupos Anti-terroristas de Liberacion (GAL) existed for many years as a covert police operation set up to kill members of the ETA. From December 1983 to February 1986, a series of assassinations and kidnappings were undertaken in which 27 people were killed and another 30 injured by activities of the GAL.

Today, the Basque people may use their own language, maintain aspects of their culture, and even have representation and participation in the Spanish Parliament. Such accommodations have greatly reduced tension in the area but they are still relatively high. Anxiety is still prevalent, and the ETA has become quite proficient at attacking airports. Their intent is to disrupt tourist flights along the coast during the summer season, scaring thousands of vacationing Spanish tourists. After sending warnings to the local papers, the ETA put an explosive device in a paper bag inside a woman's bathroom. All together 24 people were injured.

Northern Ireland

Even though the Irish Republican Army (IRA) has not been known routinely to hijack aircraft, they constitute a major terrorist organization and deserve some attention in the study of airport security. Additionally, although Ireland is one large landmass, it is split into two sections, north and south, both by the diversity of its people and by British mandate. The Irish Republicans, primarily Catholics, occupy the south and the Unionists, primarily Protestants, reside in the north. The split has existed since the Reformation and continues today.

Ireland was strongly influenced and may have originated from the Celts. The Irish formed strongly bonded tribal groups and there was no central governing body. Later, Christianity was introduced and accepted in 500 AD. This unified the Irish under one religion but did not really unify them under one central government. Ireland has not really been ruled by the Irish since a series of Viking incursions in 800 AD. When the Vikings invaded, the Irish were unable to defend their island in a collective manner and eventually fell.

Additionally, Ireland's history was filled with turmoil for hundreds of years after the Normans conquered Ireland, subjugating the Irish to British rule. The Protestant Reformation in the 1500s had long lasting consequences that are still felt in Ireland today. The Reformation was brought about by Henry VIII to allow himself to divorce his wife and remarry, after which he hoped to secure the thrown with a male heir. He established the Church of England, which was pretty much rejected by the Irish but was embraced by his daughter, who eventually became Queen Elizabeth I. She started an English colony known as the Plantation of Ulster in Northern Ireland and granted titled lands to wealthy British and Scottish subjects, thereby displacing native born Irish from the region.

In the years of 1845–1848, Ireland, experienced what became known as the Potato Famine. Shortly after the Famine, the British proposed a series of home rule plans. The Unionists who lived in Northern Ireland were opposed to home rule, because Northern Ireland was the center of power and felt that Ireland would be destabilized. The Republicans, mainly Irish Catholics in southern Ireland, were in favor of home rule but, their wishes were never realized.

In 1916, the British again proffered a plan to grant Ireland home rule. The Unionists and Republicans each feared the opposing side would gain the upper hand. Admittedly, by 1916, Britain had its attention focused on Germany. During

Easter 1916, Padraic Pearse and James Connolly led a revolt against the Unionists and British. The Easter rebellion was a huge surprise to the British, who were heavily engaged in World War I. Even though the rebellion had successfully taken over some federal buildings in Dublin, the revolt was doomed to failure. The Irish wanted home rule, but the British brutally put down the revolt, which they considered treasonous considering the timing. The Irish Republican Brotherhood (IRB) surrendered and became known as the IRA from that day forward.

The people of Ireland held Pearse and Connolly responsible for the destruction of Dublin. After defeating the Irish, the British military executed the Republican leaders they had captured, creating martyrs for the Republican cause. This proved to be a gigantic mistake. Owing to the harshness of the British response, the IRA enjoyed a renewed popularity.

Later, the Provisional IRA developed into an organized, sophisticated and effective terrorist group. By October 1972, they had allegedly killed 132 British soldiers, and by May of the same year the number had risen to 214. In response, on Bloody Sunday, 30 January 1972, British soldiers killed 13 protesters who were marching in a civil rights parade. The IRA continued the violence by responding in kind. On 21 July 1972, 22 bombs were planted in Belfast, killing nine civilians. With both sides exhausted with the violence, in 1981, Gerry Adams attempts to get the IRA to engage in less violence and more political discussion. The first cease-fire began in August 1994. The British insisted the IRA disarm. Since they refused, the attempted cease-fire lasted only until February

A masked Irish Republican Army gunman stands holding a machine gun next to a barbed wire roadblock with a sign reading Provisional IRA in Londonderry, Northern Ireland. Ireland remains divided and the seeds of continuing violence persist in spite of diplomatic efforts to conclude this chapter in Ireland's history. *Michael McQueen / Getty Images Inc.—Hulton Archive Photos.*

1996. In December 1997, the Irish Republican leader finally met with the British Prime Minister in still another attempt to stop the violence. The IRA is still well armed and financed. Most of the IRA's money comes from illegal activities including racketeering, extortion, and blackmail.

Throughout Irish history, the people have been invaded, subjected to foreign rule, and have had little to say about how they have been governed. The IRA, since its inception has taken hundreds of lives to obtain its goal, and now that they have an opportunity to attain it, they refuse to surrender their weapons out of mistrust. This may stem from the way violence has become a way of life for the Irish people. Violence is glorified in murals, song and poetry and martyrs of the IRA's cause are seen as heroes. In spite of the repeated instances of terrible tragedy on both sides, the violence continues, somewhat unabated. It will likely continue until Ireland is free and united.

■ JAPAN

Red Army Faction

The Japanese Red Army is a terrorist group, which sought the fastest, most simple means to achieve its goals. The JRA had a ruthless and somewhat successful history. Formed out of the 1960s' anti-Vietnam War movement, the JRA promoted the end of capitalism influenced by the United States. The group based its philosophy on a mix of feudal Japanese samurai warrior customs and Marxism. In 1971, a young former member of the Japanese Red Army Faction (JRAF), Fusako Shigenobu, broke from the group along with fellow radical Tsuneo Mori. Parting because the JRAF focused more on a national revolution, Shigenobu aimed for a more global transformation in forming the Japanese Red Army.

As she established her separate goals, Shigenobu decided to locate in Lebanon's Bekaa Valley in order to have closer contacts with the Popular Front for the Liberation of Palestine (PFLP). In doing so, the JRA now relies almost entirely on the PFLP for funds, arms, and training. However, Shigenobu had a central plan to promote the JRA's self-sufficiency by implementing the groups' capabilities as terrorist guns-for-hire.

In 1972, the JRA performed their first and perhaps most notorious venture at the Lod Airport in Tel Aviv. Three members armed with hand grenades and machine guns attacked the airport on a suicide mission, killing 26 and wounding 78 people in the joint JRA/PFLP mission. Establishing a ruthless reputation, the JRA proved itself in battle and continued its notorious rampage to achieve more funding through several hijackings. The JRA moved on to extort millions from the French and Japanese governments through such hijackings between 1973 and 1977.

Later in 1988, the JRA attempted an ambitious plan to initiate simultaneous attacks on US military targets both in Europe and the United States to mark the second anniversary of a US air strike against Libya in 1986. This previous US air strike had targeted Tripoli and Benghazi as a result of Libya's purported involvement in terrorist attacks on a West Berlin club popular with US soldiers. Libyan leader Colonel Muommar Khaddaffi had turned to the JRA for help, desperate for revenge. However, the plan simultaneously to bomb US military targets failed when a New Jersey police officer arrested JRA veteran Yu Kikumura while en route to bomb a US target.

The last major JRA incident occurred in Naples in 1988. Shigenobu herself was captured on 8 November 2000 in Osaka, Japan, after she had been on the run for over 30 years. She was charged with suspicion of conspiracy related to her participation in the seizure of the French Embassy in The Hague in 1974. She was also charged with attempted murder and passport fraud.

Four other members were returned to Japan in March 2000 after being deported from Lebanon. The Japanese charged them with attempted murder and forgery of official documents. A fifth member of the group, Kozo Okamoto, was not extradited, since he received political asylum from Lebanon for his participation in terrorist acts against Israel. However, Yoshimi Tanaka was successfully extradited from Thailand and charged with hijacking a Japanese Airlines plane to North Korea in 1970. As the JRA seems currently to be an inactive terrorist group, their strong beliefs persist among dwindling JRA members.

Aum Shinrikyo

Aum Shinrikyo most notably conducted the sarin nerve agent attack in the Tokyo subway on 20 March 1995, becoming one of the first groups to use a chemical agent in a terrorist attack. Members carried sarin, a deadly nerve gas originally produced by the Nazis, in two or three small plastic bags each and released them into five different subway cars. The plastic bags were covered with newspaper and later punctured by umbrellas to release the agent. In 1999 and 2000, a Tokyo court sentenced four of the five members of the group to death. A fifth participant received a reduced sentence. The professed religious cult leader Shoko Asahara is in police custody. The group has apologized and agreed to pay $40 million in damages to the victims of the attack.

Aum Shinrikyo members were not individuals seeking social release or some nebulous political revenge; they were an organized religious cult trying actively to destroy the Japanese government. They included a middle-aged surgeon, three physicists, and an electrical engineer—some very bright and educated minds (White 1998, Pg. 233). Their compound, located near Mt. Fuji, included a building known as Satyam 7, which was a large three-story prefabricated structure for the "secret work" of the science unit. The building contained millions of dollars of highly advanced equipment, most of which was purchased in the United States.

Cult members received extensive military training. They were also extensively brainwashed. Within the group there existed a strict spiritual hierarchy. Simply joining made the initiate a Zaike, or member, and then the pressure was applied to become a Shukke, who theoretically could use supernatural power. Shoko Asahara, the self-professed leader, was supposedly the most enlightened of the group and also head of the vast corporate empire behind the business of religion, including a chain of computer stores (Internet: http://www.pals.msus.edu/cgi-bin/ pals-cgi...142/te%20%shinrikyo/di%200001/txt).

Ashara was arrested in 1995 at the headquarters of the group near Mt. Fuji. He was hiding alone in a dark space about the size of a coffin. Police searched for hours before locating a hollow wall containing a hidden compartment about 10 by 3 feet. He had a cassette player, some medicine, and $106,000 in cash. His arrest does not stop the threat from the technological terrorist. Even though technological terrorism is not the course of action of a rational attacker, lack of rationality is no barrier to successful terrorist attacks. This was a group that had combined religious eschatology with violence supported by high tech weapons; a seriously dangerous hybrid. The conduct of this group represents a window on what is to come. It is a loud and clear warning for airports and airport security to be better equipped to handle potential biological, chemical, and maybe even nuclear attacks.

■ PERU

Tupac Amaru Revolutionary Movement/Movimiento Revolucionario Tupac Amaru (MRTA)

Terrorist activity has continued in Peru but declined sharply despite the fragile state of the current government after the precipitate resignation of President Fujimori. The Tupac Amaru Revolutionary Movement is a Peruvian Marxist-Leninist revolutionary movement started in 1984 by organizations from the radical left. Its stated objective is to rid Peru of imperialism and establish a Marxist regime. The group, which is estimated to have between 300 and 600 members, operates mainly in the Upper Haulage Valley, a vast jungle area in eastern Peru controlled mostly by guerillas and drug traffickers. Its activities include bombings, kidnappings, and assassinations. They have been known for their anti-American sentiments.

MRTA was named for the eighteenth century rebel leader who fought the Spanish in attempting to acquire freedom from oppression and colonialism. The goal of the current organization is to replace the representative democracy with the power of the people; a leftist concept. They launched their armed struggle in San Martin province, where conditions were in their estimation most favorable. In 1987, they were even able, for the first time, to take over a provisional capital, Juan, a city of approximately 25,000 inhabitants.

In addition, Peruvian forces captured their leader, Victor Play, in 1992. In a rather defiant event, his supporters attacked the Japanese Ambassador's residence in Lima in 1996. Four hundred guests had just sat down for a meal when over a dozen men stormed the compound. The situation was delicate, to say the least, considering all the foreign diplomats involved. Nonetheless, President Fujimori steadfastly refused the terrorists demands to release Play. After a four-month crisis, Peruvian special security forces tunneled into the compound.

Within less than an hour, the terrorists were dead and the hostages were freed. The incident reminds security forces everywhere that diplomats are high-risk targets for those seeking immediate media attention.

Shining Path/Sendero Luminoso

Peruvian authorities captured one of the remaining commanders of the Shining Path in April 2000. Jose Arcola Chiloquin or Romano led some significant terrorist acts mostly in the Upper Haulage Valley where they continue their efforts despite the loss of their leaders. Their founder, Abimael Guzman, received his indoctrination and training in China at the start of the Chinese Cultural Revolution. After returning to Peru, and as a university professor, he was working on research regarding the exploitation of the Peruvian Indians when he recruited his students into the Maoist Party and sent them out to "agitate" (Sam Dillon, "As Peru Votes, Insurgent's Mystique Casts Shadows," *Miami Herald*, 10 June 1998, Pgs. 1A, 26H). Since that time, he has led a highly successful insurgent group bent on creating a classless society in Peru.

The group was particularly vicious in its tactics. Members were known to use children to deliver bombs to public buildings and police stations, who were of course killed in the following explosions. Guzman had created a cultlike atmosphere, and he became known locally as the Fourth Sword of Marxism ("The Shining Path Comes Back," *The Economist*, 17 August 1996, Pg. 35). His dream fell apart when he was captured in 1992.

Terrorism in Latin America persists because of poverty, unequal land distribution among segments of the population, and of course repressive regimes. The danger remains that they will bring their causes to the United States.

■ RUSSIA

Although terrorism is looked upon by many as "senseless acts of violence carried out by madmen," there are many instances in which it is brought about by great injustice. According to one author, "a core element in any account of terrorism is that it involves the use of violence to achieve political ends" (Maxwell Taylor and Ethel Quay, *Terrorist Lives*, Bracey's UK Ltd., 1994, Pg. 9). It is not simply a tool used by a single individual to retaliate or eliminate on a personal level. Most terrorist acts have deep-rooted histories that are so sensitive that no one outside the group can really relate to the feelings that cause people to commit these acts. Like the old saying goes, one person's terrorist is another person's freedom fighter.

To understand fully what is really happening in the Russian-Chechen conflict, one must recognize the history of the region. Chechnya is located in the Caucasus Mountains along its northern slopes. Before the 1994 to 1996 war, Chechnya had a population of about 1.2 million, including 400,000 ethnic Russians. Although this area represents only a sliver of Russian territory, it is strategically located on the route of oil from the Caspian Sea to Europe.

The root of the problems between the Russians and the Chechens goes back as far as three centuries. By 1585, the region had been incorporated into the Ottoman Empire and had adopted Islam. In the early 1700s, Tsar Peter the Great invaded the area and claimed it as part of all the Russias. Between 1785 and 1792, the Moslem Chechens began to rise up against the Eastern Orthodox Russians when the Cossack settlers moved into the region in large numbers. During the first half of the 1800s, Chechnya was one of many groups of Islamic rebels trying to win independence. The Chechens, in fact, led a holy war against Russia as early as 1834 to 1859. They again rebelled during the Russian civil war after 1917. In 1934, the Chechens joined with neighboring Ingusheita to form an autonomous republic. However, Stalin deported 600,000 of them to Siberia and the Far East before World War II. It is documented that nearly 200,000 of these people perished on the way. Stalin feared the Chechens would welcome the Germans and hinder the Russian war effort. The survivors of the exodus were not allowed to return home until 1957 when Nikita Khrushchev finally permitted it. When they did return, they quickly discovered the ethnic Russians had taken over much of their valuable land.

On 2 November 1991, newly elected President Dzhokar Dudayev, a former Russian Air Force General, proclaimed Chechen independence. In response, Russian President Boris Yeltsin announced a state of emergency and sent troops. The Chechens mobilized 60,000 volunteers to retaliate, and the war dragged on through 1996. The Russians have temporarily withdrawn but have not politically given into any Chechen demands. In frustration, the Chechens have turned to terrorism. The hostility of the Chechen people toward Russia is deeply rooted. The viciousness of the war only intensified the problem and will not be easily ameliorated.

Acts of terrorism continue today, including several hijacking efforts. In December 2002, Chechen rebels took 700 people hostage in a daring terror attack on a Moscow theater that would end with 128 hostages dead, many as a result of the Russian rescue effort. This is significant, because the Chechen people believe the world has forgotten them. CIA director George Tenet has speculated that Chechnya is breeding a new generation of terrorists who threaten the West, just as many Afghanistan-bred fighters in the 1970s and 1980s went on to become foot soldiers for al-Q'aeda. Consequently, air piracy appears to them to be a reasonable means by which to return to the headlines. Another perplexing problem pertains to the former Soviet Union's nuclear stockpile. Clearly, they have been unable to account for all of it. In the hands of terrorists, this provides a powerful tool whether they actually have the weapons or not. The threat is enough.

■ US DOMESTIC TERRORISM

The concept of domestic terrorism in the United States changed dramatically after the bombing of the Murrah building in Oklahoma City. The incident proved that it does not take a significantly large number of people to affect history. The

US has seen its own proliferation of prolife terrorists, militias, white supremacist organizations, and environmental terrorists just to name a few. However, since 9/11, hate groups and other antigovernment groups have used the horrific events to recruit new members. Additionally, foreign terrorists seek to bring their causes to US soil. Either way, security personnel need to study the threat and be prepared.

The Order

The Silent Brotherhood, or the Order, was formed in September 1983 and was officially known as the Order Bruder Schweigen. Robert Jay Matthews formed the group in upstate Washington. Matthews, whose drive was to "quit talking and start acting" for total Aryan victory, led the group into becoming the most dangerous underground group since the Ku Klux Klan in a little under a fifteen-month timeframe. (Internet: http://www.front14.org/rac/theorder2.htm). The Order is one of the most well-known right-wing extremist groups in America and is best characterized as being neo-Nazi and racist. They consider themselves very patriotic and have self-labeled themselves as red neck, white skin, and blue collar.

Members of this group believe that God chose white Europeans to be leaders of the Aryan nation. The claim to follow the "14 words" (We must secure the existence of our people and a future for White children). With Matthews as their leader, the Order set out on a grand plan. They would exterminate the blacks, kill all the Jews, and drive the enemy into the sea. They are bound to follow the "88 precepts" as written by David Lane, a follower. Some of the teachings include the following:

1. Any religion or teaching which denies the Natural Laws of the Universe is false.
2. In accord with Nature's Laws, nothing is more right than the preservation of one's own race.
3. The White race has suffered invasions and brutality from Africa and Asia for thousands of years. . . . So the attempted guilt trip placed on the White race by civilization's executioners is invalid under both historical circumstances and the Natural Law which denies interspecies compassion.
4. The concept of a multiracial society violates every Natural Law for species preservation.

The group was not opposed to violence. They recorded the largest armored car robbery in history, with the hold up of a Brink's car and the acquisition of $3.8 million. During the Brink's hold-up, leader David Matthews dropped a pistol that was traced to another Order member's house. Additionally, one of the members turned FBI informant. Matthew's was tracked down, and in a firebombing incident, he was burned alive. After his death, many of his followers were arrested. The continued existence of this particular group is in dispute. The pro-liferation of white supremist groups around the globe is not. In a 1999 shooting at a California Jewish community center, the gunman claimed to be a member. Regardless, it is well accepted that much of the $3.8 million continues to fund the activities of white supremacist groups. The Aryan Nation, Militia of Montana, and many other extremists associated with right-wing groups and special interest groups will persist in challenging security officials.

■ NUCLEAR TERRORISM

Most Americans are well aware of the fact that terrorists are capable of executing a nuclear, biological, or chemical attack against the United States. However, most of them are also very apathetic about the possibility. In 1996, a nationwide survey found 72% believe there is a chance that terrorists could use a weapon of mass destruction to attack a US city, but only 13% worry a great deal about this, and 27% are somewhat worried. A full 59% profess not to be worried at all ("Terrorism Threat Assessments," Internet: http://www.fas.org/irp/threat/terror.htm). Times have changed considerably.

The issue of mass-destructive terrorism has caused concern to an unprecedented degree in the post–Cold War era. It is the argument of such scholars as Gavin Cameron that the real driving force behind the heightened danger of nuclear terrorism lies not with the increased opportunities for prolif-eration, but rather with the changing nature of political violence and the psy-chological and organizational characteristics of terrorism itself. To date, there have been few incidents of mass destruction and no major nuclear terrorism. The question for analysis is, given the conservatism of most terrorist groups, will they make the leap to nuclear, chemical, or biological weapons. Setting the theoretical debate aside: After 9/11, the US Coast Guard set up security zones around at least two nuclear power plants to prohibit ships from approaching the plants. Critics persist, however, in warning that many nuclear-powered plants remain vulnerable.

Modern technology has opened the doors to a new wave of terrorism. Most primitive weapons have been replaced with sophisticated silent and deadlier ones. The emergence of the computer as a technological device associated with terrorism is a rather new phenomenon, whereas the use of chemical and biologi-cal weapons have been around a lot longer, although they have been significantly enhanced. It is recent technological innovations that have made them more viable weapons. The sheer volume of such activities and their destructive poten-tial makes these kinds of terrorism more problematic. One of the most important points about any analysis of terrorism is why the numbers of incidents are down, yet the lethality has reached frightening degrees (Hoffman, Bruce, "Responding to Terrorism across the Technological Spectrum," *Terrorism and Political Violence,* Vol. 6, No. 3, Autumn 1994, Pg. 385). Those responsible for airport security must recognize the threat and prepare accordingly.

Biological and Chemical Warfare

Building or stealing a weapon of mass destruction is a difficult, complex, and risky task, but the basic technical requirements for building biological and chemical weapons are well established and not difficult to acquire. Biological and chemical weapons are actually becoming easier commodities to access. The materials, equipment, and expertise necessary to use them are no longer significant challenges for many terrorists. The latent ability of terrorists to build or use weapons of this type is increasing (Gordon M. Burck and Charles C. Flowerree, *International Handbook on Chemical Weapons Proliferation*, New York: Greenwood Press, 1991). In the aftermath of 9/11, Secretary of Defense Donald Rumsfeld publicly announced that the United States was taking seriously the possibility that terrorists might launch an attack of this sort.

Specifically, the FBI ordered crop-dusting planes to be grounded for 24 hours on 23 September 2001, and urged agricultural pilots to be vigilant of any suspicious activity they observed. Secretary Rumsfeld also reiterated that state sponsors of terrorism have very active chemical and biological warfare programs. Biological agents are much deadlier than their chemical counterparts and their effects are longer lasting. The lethality of biological weapons is such that 10 grams of anthrax could produce over one million deaths. Biological weapons challenge the conventional modes of thinking about the contemporary terrorist threat and indicate another degree to which technology has transformed terrorism.

The assumption of traditional terrorism was that a small number of casualties would have a dramatic impact on the much larger general audience. Modern terrorists now seek to kill large numbers of innocent victims in a single blow. Among the most readily available biological agents is anthrax. It is extremely lethal and contact causes an 80% mortality rate. Documented cases of criminals attempting to sell the agent have been repeatedly documented (C. L. Staten, "Two Men Arrested in Las Vegas in WMD Plot," *Emergency New Net*, 19 February 1998; Internet: www.emergency.com/lv-anthrax.htm). Fatalities at an airport would be momentous ranging from thousands to tens of thousands, assuming an effective dissemination of the agent and the absence of timely, effective medical care.

Although the production process for chemical weapons is longer than that of biological weapons, they can be designed to kill much faster. Binary weapons are one of the most significant developments in the evolution of chemical weapons terrorism. These devices consist of a chemical for which individual components may be stored separately. When the components are assembled, the elements are combined for an agent of great lethality. These binary weapons ease the storage risks for the terrorists, and with proper engineering enable the terrorist to remove themselves from the threat area. Technology has put at the terrorist's disposal a varied array of very lethal and definitely indiscriminate weapons. The sarin toxic nerve gas released in the Tokyo subway was only a sample of what is likely to come.

■ CONCLUSION

To succeed, terrorist operations require detailed information for planning and executing an attack. If an airport asset is the target, they can often acquire sufficient information to plan the attack by simply visiting the airport and testing its security procedures. Access is generally considered not to be difficult to achieve.

One private pilot, expressing his views on the Internet, claimed, "I have yet to encounter an airfield I could not enter" (Ian Blair Fries, Internet: http://www.flyer-online.com/Articles/flyer, Pg. 1). He believes that fences pose no obstacles to would be intruders and airport operators have little interest in constructing good ones. He reasons that a fence provides nothing in financial return to the airport tenant. He repeated the story,"

> The closest I came to having a fence stop me was at Duluth International Airport late one winter night. No one was home when I landed. Even the tower had closed. The gates were all locked and welded shut by the ice. However, airport plows had conveniently piled snow mountains on both sides of the fence. I simply climbed up on the snow, stepped across the fence and descended the packed snow on the other side" (Pg. 2).

Additionally, the events of 9/11 seemed to represent the ultimate attack. However, continuing attacks are not a question of if but when. The lesson for Americans is undeniable. Usama bin Ladin and his organization intend to continue to engage in terrorist acts against Americans in America. For example, not long after 9/11, Richard Reid, a British citizen, attempted to blow up American Airlines Flight 63 from Paris to Miami with a bomb in his shoe. In all likelihood he was not acting alone, and some of the detainees in Quantanamo Bay, Cuba, claim to recognize him from al-Q'aeda training camps in Afghanistan. On 22 December, only three months after the tragic events in New York, Washington DC, and Pennsylvania, he tried to board the aircraft with 10 ounces of PETN-based material (pentaerythritol tetranitrate), which is similar to Semtex.

This chapter has really provided only a cursory review of some of the more famous terrorist organizations at play both in the past and at present. There are numerous others. There are even terrorists who consist of either a party of one or a very small cellular group. Timothy McVeigh, who bombed the federal building in Oklahoma City and was executed in 2001, was just such an individual. He could have easily chosen an airport as his primary target, even though he had mistakenly chosen the Murrah Building as the source of decision making regarding the Branch Davidian incident at Waco, Texas.

chapter six

International Major Counterterrorism Units, Law Enforcement, and Intelligence Agencies: The Best Defense

▇ NEWS

1. **September 1985**: An Egypt Air flight was hijacked to Malta. The Egyptian government dispatched Force 777 to assist with hostage rescue operations. During the operation, snipers outside the aircraft mistook some escaping passengers for terrorists and gunned them down.

2. **11 June 1985**: Fawaz Yunis and four others boarded Royal Jordanian Airlines Flight 402 armed with grenades and automatic weapons. Eventually, the terrorists blew up the aircraft. "Operation Goldenrod" lured Yunis to a yacht in the Mediterranean under the pretense of a drug deal, and he was arrested and transferred to a US Navy ship.

3. **June 1994**: A member of the GSG-9 German counterterrorism unit sought to apprehend one of the leaders of the Red Army Faction, Wolfgang Grams. Police reports indicated that he had been killed in a shootout with the unit. However, there is speculation that he may have been summarily executed after he had been subdued.

4. **May 2002:** The FBI is actively engaging in recruiting agents with the critical skills of computer science, engineering, counterintelligence, and foreign language ability; especially Arabic, Farsi, Urdu, and Pashtu.

5. **19 June 2002**: The National Security Agency had intercepted two messages in Arabic on 10 September 2002, which referred to the next day as "zero hour." The messages were not translated until 12 September.

▓ INTRODUCTION

In light of the fact that modern terrorism has proliferated exponentially during the last half of the twentieth century, counterterrorist and counterinsurgency units have been established around the globe. It is fascinating to investigate the means by which governments have sought to fight the battle against internal terrorism in addition to terror inflicted on citizenry abroad. The efforts by some authorities have become quite controversial, especially in Israel and Northern Ireland. This is in part due to the fact that the civilian population seems to have accepted the loss of certain civil liberties in order to attempt to win the "war on terrorism." The loss of democratic safeguards, on the other hand, has disturbed some civil libertarians. They see governments becoming more terroristic in their methodology, with normal democratic procedural safeguards being pushed aside.

However, conventional police forces deployed in large and sometimes cumbersome formations are not capable of combating small, clandestine, mobile, and speedy terrorist units. Furthermore, using massive force in hostage situations proved to be unrealistic. New tactics were needed. The need was amplified after the terrorist attack on the 1972 Olympic Games in Munich, where it became woefully apparent that the police forces of Europe were not properly trained or equipped to deal with terrorists.

By legal tradition, this is a slippery slope for democracies. It is deplorable when the terrorist fighters become the terrorists. It is, therefore, mandatory that nations create counterterrorist forces that are highly trained in responding to terrorism, but also does so on a scale acceptable to the public and compatible with democratic traditions. This chapter will review the development of some of the most well-known units as well as some of their successes and failures. Some governments have incorporated their units into national police forces and others into the military. Generally, they all have a flexible command structure, special tactical training, the right people for the job with appropriate personal characteristics, and specific equipment. Most units are designated as either counterterrorist units (CTUs) or hostage rescue units (HRUs). They usually consist of a headquarters unit, several combat units, a training unit, a support unit, and a logistics operation.

Cooperation among various law enforcement agencies is crucial to the successful protection of any transportation facility. The protection of airports, because of the unique environment, presents its own specific challenges. Airports and the facilities and equipment that support such a facility are complex to say the least. They also present a packaged scenario for terrorists to acquire quite a lot of attention with one huge attention-getting gesture. Owing to the open and public nature of the airport surroundings, access to an airport is easy. However, once people are participants in the busy day-to-day operations of an airport, police and private security are tasked with protecting large numbers of people in an almost unprotectable situation. This exclusive and demanding situation has required the imposition of special rules and training on policing units.

The Federal Aviation Administration (FAA) recognized early that an airport with constantly moving people, aircraft, and ground vehicles would mandate some special controls. Initially, during the period that terrorist hijackings and assaults seemed all too commonplace, it was thought large numbers of police stationed at the airport would solve the problems. It did not. Other alternatives had to be conceptualized and put into use. The FAA has detailed who is a qualified airport law enforcement officer, what their training should entail, and when an airport operator can ask and receive federal agent assistance.

The daily, behind the scenes operations of many other local, state, federal, and international agencies enhances ongoing security at an airport. All must work in tandem to combat the continuing terrorist threat and to address issues of various criminal operations, including organized crime, drug trafficking, and most recently the trafficking in human cargo. Jurisdictions overlap and coordination of the big picture is a difficult job. The success of that job depends on the active intervention and support of the federal government. On top of all this, thousands of positions in law enforcement remain unfulfilled, and agencies nationwide are seeking to answer the question of where to acquire qualified law enforcement personnel to meet the growing need.

■ COUNTERTERRORIST UNITS

Austrian Special Counterterrorist Intervention Unit

The Cobra unit, or Gendarmerieeinsatzkommando (GEK), was developed in Austria over twenty years ago to combat terrorism and serious crime. The specialized tactical intervention unit was created within the Austrian Federal Gendarmerie. As many other European police forces discovered, they were not equipped to protect their citizens in the 1970s from terrorist assaults. Although not as well known as the British SAS or the German GSG-9, the unit is one of the best-trained and best-equipped units in Europe.

Two incidents reinforced and highlighted the need for this type of unit in Austria: a terrorist attack on Jewish immigrants traveling from Russia to Israel via Vienna, and the assault on OPEC headquarters in 1975. The terrorist's expertise at urban warfare also surprised the Austrians. New strategies were needed to combat the tactical realities of the new threat. Brigadier Johannes Pechter, a member of the Austrian Gendarmerie, was instrumental in developing apropos special operations, and his new unit was authorized to have national jurisdiction. Its highest priority is fighting terrorism.

The GEK, however, is specifically tasked with the following:

1. Intervention in extreme terrorist attacks involving hijackings and hostage taking
2. Assisting other security agencies in dealing with violent criminal organizations
3. Protection of the president and the prime minister as well as foreign presidents and heads of state visiting Austria
4. Protection of Austrian diplomatic missions abroad during periods of crisis or extreme violence (Eitan Meyr, "Elite Gendarmes," *S.W.A.T.*, May 2000).

The unit consists of approximately 170 members. Its facilities are located at Weiner Neustadt near the Austrian capital. The command structure runs directly to the Minister of Interior through the General Secretary of Security. Approximately 10 senior officers are part of the command staff. The main body of the unit consists of four operational platoons and one training platoon. They train in various mixtures of two-, three- and five-man tactical units. Training is heavily emphasized, and each member's marksmanship and physical capabilities are tested monthly. Competition remains tough, and members who become "unfit" are returned to their former regular police units, although they are permitted to recompete for a place on the team.

Note: *In 2000, unfortunately, France declined a request from the Austrian government to extradite Illich Ramieriz Sanchez, also known as Carlos the Jackal, to Austria to face charges based on the attack on OPEC (Patterns of Global Terrorism: 30 April 2001, European Overview, Pg. 2). United States Department of State, Department of State Publication.*

Canadian Armed Forces Joint Task Force 2

News reports have described the Canadian counterterrorism unit as a ". . . highly skilled counter-terrorist force of undetermined size, based somewhere near Ottawa with an anonymous commanding officer." (Paul Mooney, "Anti-Terrorism Unit Efficient, But Low Profile," *The Chronicle-Herald/the Mail Star*, 4 May 1995, Pg. A10). The task force was created in April 1993 when it became a unit separate and distinct from the Canadian Royal Mounted Police. The unit has a mandate ". . . to be ready to respond as a force of last resort to terrorist events or major disturbances of the peace affecting national security" (Mooney: 1995, Pg. A10). The unit is made up of strictly volunteers drawn from all the branches of the armed services and is commanded by a lieutenant colonel. Its size is estimated to be between 200 and 250 strong with part of the force on alert at all times. The government of Canada officially provided approximately $20 million to start and equip the unit.

The unit received national attention when it allegedly was sent to Bosnia to free some Canadian hostages from their Serb captors in 1995. Other events at least monitored by the unit were the Commonwealth Games and the G-7 conference during the same year. More, but probably unwanted, media attention was received after an exercise was supposedly conducted in the suburbs of Montreal much to the surprise of residents. Otherwise, the unit has remained discreet and out of the public eye.

Great Britain: Special Air Service (SAS)

Great Britain formed and trained one of the best-known antiterrorist special force units in the world. It is quietly headquartered at a Royal Air Force base at Creedenhill. It was formed over forty years ago and has survived and seen significant success by relying on the basics of secrecy and surprise. Their founding father, Lieutenant David Stirling of the Scots Guard, originated the concept of the standard "stick," a small unit of highly trained men to be utilized in volatile terrorist situations. Conventional army theoreticians attacked his theories during World War II, but he was adamant that specially trained units could be especially effective behind enemy lines. An army commando officer, Captain Robert Laycock, and a Welsh Guardsman, Jock Lewis, also envisioned the concept. Most of the original members were of Scottish Roman Catholic descent, whose heritage for generations has been to cultivate warriors who were specialists in guerilla warfare wrapped in the traditions of secrecy. The very first unit saw action in North Africa and became known as L Detachment, Special Air Service Brigade. All SAS members are volunteers, and they are all seasoned dedicated soldiers.

Proof of their dedication to the unit is evidenced by the fact that when they are accepted into the group, they give up whatever rank they have received and return to the basic rank of trooper. At the average age of 27, they choose to join the elite unit in spite of reduction in rank and reduction in pay. The competition and training to remain an SAS member is brutal. Several people have died during training. Members become proficient in explosives, battlefield medicine, use of state of the art communication equipment, and special weapons. They are trained to operate in every sort of environment including the jungle, the desert, mountains, and underwater. Training for members is constant. One squadron is always on alert to deploy at a moment's notice. A special Operations Research Unit supports all SAS deployments and is particularly accomplished in developing weapons specific to the needs of the unit.

For example, the elite force began testing the Canadian C-7 gun in 1999. In comparison to the US manufactured M-16, it is a rather expensive weapon. It is a complete weapons system that includes sights, laser targeting, grenade launcher, and maintenance, all for the price of about 5500 British pounds each; twice the cost of the M-16. The gun can be adapted to be used as a machine gun or sniper weapon, and according to one member of the SAS, "This weapon is worth its weight in gold" (John Harding, "SAS Carries 'Ultimate' Weapon," *The Daily Telegraph*, 27 October 2001, Pg. 4).

Operation Nimrod was conducted on 5 May 1980. The Special Air Service Regiment, or SAS, in conjunction with some additional special police units, carried out an assault against the Iranian Embassy in London. With the public watching, the team entered the building and methodically moved through it freeing hostages and throwing stun grenades mixed with gas. This stun grenade is now widely used by similar units around the world.

The SAS has sometimes come under a great deal of criticism. Like the Israeli team, Sarayat Mat'kal, the SAS has been called into service more frequently than most. SAS has regularly served as a back-up force for the Royal Ulster Constabulary in Northern Ireland, who are considered to be quite unpopular themselves in some Irish circles. On occasion, public indignation has been rapid and vocal. In fact, the efficiency and brutality of the SAS when they became involved in the urban warfare of Northern Ireland stunned the Irish terrorists.

Of particular note was an operation conducted in Gibraltar in 1988. The SAS had followed an IRA squad to the island. Intelligence information seemed to indicate that they intended to detonate a bomb during a military parade. The SAS launched a preemptive attack on the unit. Military experts would call it a precision maneuver, but civilians labeled it cold-blooded murder. Even though Britons overwhelming support counterterrorist efforts, the outcry against a government authorizing a "shoot first and ask questions later" was too much for such a democratic society. The European Court of Justice condemned the incident and provided the IRA with three more martyrs.

The British authorities have taken a strong stand against any actions by the SAS that have been considered to be excessive or have resulted in the needless loss of life. Members of the SAS, locally referred to as Sassmen, have even been prosecuted in local criminal court. Two members were actually tried criminally for the death of a civilian. Because of the length and breath of experience of the team, it is one of the most respected in Europe. It is rumored that the SAS has been present at every terrorist incident in Europe to determine what went well and what did not. In fact, the team has frequently trained with the equivalent group in Germany, GSG-9, and provided consulting to hostage situations around the world.

Germany: Grenzschutzgruppe 9 (GSG-9)

Grenzschutzgruppe 9 (GSG-9) was a direct outgrowth of the failure of the regular German police to deal with the Munich Olympic attack on Israeli athletes. The German police were woefully unprepared to handle the incident. Consequently, GSG-9 became operational on 17 April 1973, six months after the massacre in Munich. The Federal Border Guard was the parent unit of the team; in part because it reported directly to the central government. As mentioned, the Allies in Europe at the time tolerated the formation of a German national police force for the first time since the end of World War II. The group is headquartered in

St. Augustine near Bonn, and it was the brainchild of Colonel Ulrich Wegener, who envisioned the small and highly flexible antiterrorist unit.

GSG-9 is organized into three separate groups: GSG-9/1, GSG-9/2, and GSG-9/3. The group consists of a headquarters unit, a communications unit, and a documentation unit. GSG-9/1 is the traditional counterterrorist's assault group. GSG-9/2 consists of experts in maritime terrorism; GSG-9/3 is made up of aviation experts. The first two groups have approximately 100 members, and the aviation unit has about 50. Further broken down, each of the three strike forces has a command section and five Special Tactical Sections composed of four men and an officer, known as the five-man stick. (Christopher Dobson, and Ronald Payne, *Counterattack: The West's Battle Against Terrorists,* New York: Facts on File, 1982, Pg. 96).

GSG-9 is not a military organization; it is a civilian police force. Members of the German Armed Forces who wish to join the team must resign from the military first and join the Border Police. It is unique, especially in its training in the knowledge of the law as it relates to counterterrorism. The team constantly studies all active terrorist groups. It is also trained in the usual counterterrorism techniques, and it possesses one of the most complete arsenals in the world. Each member is an expert marksman.

GSG-9 is particularly well trained in the rescue assault of aircraft. The training served them well in their most famous rescue effort in Mogadishu, Somalia, in 1977. The team successfully raided a terrorist-held Lufthansa 707 after two men and two women hijacked the plane demanding the release of Baader-Meinhof prisoners in German jails. Zohair Akache's terrorist team hijacked the aircraft with 82 passengers on board and roamed the Middle East for a place to land, ending up in Mogadishu. The Somalis were more than willing to let the Germans take the lead, especially after the terrorists killed the German pilot. Twenty-eight team members stormed the aircraft and killed the terrorists with no loss of life to the hostages.

The team has been highly successful regardless of the fact that its reputation was slightly soiled in 1993 when an operation directed at the Red Army Faction went bad. The team captured Wolfgang Grams, and after he was in custody, one of the team members fatally shot him. An investigation concluded that Grams had shot himself, but the rumor of abusive conduct almost ended in the disbanding of the team. The operation involved an attempt to arrest both Wolfgang Grams and his girlfriend, Birgit Hogefeld, at a train station in Bad Kleinen. The original police report indicated that as police had closed in on the terrorists, Grams had pulled a gun and killed an officer. According to the report, the police took down Grams. Eyewitnesses, however, did not support that version of events. In fact, they claimed that Grams was shot while he lay helpless on the train tracks at the station.

One witness claimed, " Two policemen walked up to Grams, who was lying motionless. One bent over and shot him several times from closeup. Then the second officer shot at Grams, but more at his stomach and legs. He was shot several times" (James O. Jackson, "Death on Track 4," *Time,* 23 August 1993). The coroner's report authenticated the eyewitness accounts, and concluded that Grams had been shot at close range. In addition, the incident had disrupted efforts to negotiate a peace settlement with the Red Army Faction. As a result of the alleged murder and cover up, Interior Minister Rudolph Seiters resigned followed soon after by a chief federal prosecutor.

Later, exhibiting incredible restraint, the team captured a hijacker who had commandeered a KLM flight from Tunis to Amsterdam. The hijacker demanded that Skeikh Omar Abdel Rahman, on trial for the World Trade Center bombing in New York in 1993, be immediately released. GSG-9 was able to capture the hijacker without firing a single shot. GSG-9, in part because of its success, may not survive for very much longer. With the decrease in terrorist incidents in Germany and costs constraints coming into play, the team may be replaced with new SWAT-type units. Hopefully, its expertise and legacy will remain within the German antiterrorism effort.

Israel: Sayeret Mat'Kal

The Israelis have been combating terrorism for longer than almost any other country. Because of the abundance of terrorist attacks, the State of Israel swiftly developed the technological means, military doctrines, and general policy for counterterrorism efforts. Golda Meir, Prime Minister for many years, wholeheartedly supported the concept of secret strike teams after the attack on the Israeli team at the Munich Olympics. The whole country was seeking revenge, and the leadership of the country settled on a policy of "seek out and destroy" terrorists. They have perfected the concept of strike teams and have been actively involved in activities labeled both excessive and possibly illegal. The team's purpose was redefined in 1989 when Itzhak Rabin, then Minister of Defense, stated that, "The goal we set ourselves in the campaign against terror is not one of elimination, but to minimize our vulnerability and delivery of the strongest possible blows against terrorists" ("Israeli Counter-Terrorists Activity," Internet: http://www.ict.org.il/counter_ter/is_ct.htm, Pg. 1).

The team, officially known as the Sayeret Mat'kal, but also known as the General Staff Reconnaissance Unit 269, has embraced the Talmudic concept that if someone arrives to kill you, you should rise up and kill them first. Officially, the team was established in 1957 and was given both a peacetime mission relating to counterterrorism and a wartime mission dealing with intelligence gathering. Their overall approach is three pronged. It involves operative measures designed to combat terrorist targets in the area directly and defensive measures meant to foil any attempts. Finally, the strategy of punitive measures involves the legal, and some would say not so legal, concepts to punish the members and supporters of terrorist organizations. The three approaches are similar, but can be distinguished. The offensive activities seek to prevent the implementation of any terrorist attack by intervening during the planning and organizational stages of the attack. The defensive activities aim to disrupt an attack immediately after it is initiated. The punitive measures apply at all stages of the attack.

The strike team has been particularly successful, and it was especially effective during the raid into Entebbe, Uganda, in 1972 and in executing raids against Palestinian terrorists in neighboring Arab countries. Initially, forerunners of today's team embraced the rage sweeping Israel after the Olympic Games attack and sought to kill those responsible at all costs. Unfortunately, in their zeal, one of the hit teams, which had been unleashed, assassinated an innocent waiter in front of his pregnant wife. The Israelis were hunting for Ali Hassan Salameh, the architect of the Munich massacre. However, one of the intelligence team members mistakenly identified a Moroccan man married to a Norwegian woman as Salameh. The Israelis were embarrassed after the man was gunned down, and international pressure forced Israel to use restraint in killing alleged Palestinian terrorists.

Regardless of the international indignation, the team eventually found Salameh and killed him with a radio-controlled car bomb in Beirut. The incident precipitated another outcry from the international community, because the bomb killed four bodyguards and five innocent bystanders. The team also claimed to have been responsible for the assassination of Khalil al-Wazir, one of the leading Palestinian Liberation Organization strategists, in Tunis in September 1985.

In spite of some initial "media" setbacks, the Sayeret Mat'kal is one of the best-trained and best-equipped special forces units in the world. As previously discussed, the Irgun, a terrorist organization in its own right in the Israeli dispute with the British, was the successor of the team. The Irgun is best known for the bombing of the King David Hotel on 22 July 1946. The bomb killed 91 people: Arab, British, and Jewish alike. Some of the initial efforts of the team focused on efforts to prevent Palestinian terrorists from mounting attacks from Lebanon into Israel. The Israelis were retaliating for a Palestinian hijacking of an El Al airliner en route from Rome to Tel Aviv and a second incident at the Athens airport.

In retaliation, the Sayeret Mat'kal launched a commando raid directly against the Beirut International Airport in hopes of stopping intrusive Palestinian raids. The team completely destroyed thirteen empty aircraft. No one was injured. However, international reaction was still negative. Specifically, the French condemned the attack and used the raid as a reason for suspending arms shipments to Israel. The United States expressed its displeasure over the raid into another nation's sovereign territory, but did not cut off arms sales. In another unwanted twist of events, the Palestinians seemed to gain a bit of global sympathy, and the aircraft were replaced and upgraded as a result of claimed insurance money.

Regardless, strikes into Entebbe and elsewhere have made the team famous. In 1972, they successfully ended the hijacking of a Sabena Boeing 707 on a flight from Brussels to Tel Aviv. The hijackers, members of the Black September group, forced the plane to land in Tel Aviv and threatened to blow it up with everyone on board. The team stormed the aircraft with minimal loss of life. Many other counterterrorist squads quickly adopted their procedures in the years to come as the textbook way to conduct an aircraft rescue operation. Overall, the team has been very effective, and generally their efforts have been applauded, especially when viewed in humanitarian terms.

Civil Guard Less known and not as flamboyant as the Sayeret Mat'kal is Israel's Civil Guard (INP). With increasing criminal and terrorist activity, the Guard has become very important in the fight against terrorism. It was founded on 9 June 1974 and has grown into a significant force. The 50,000 strong force consists totally of volunteers. They participate in maintaining roadblocks, conducting security searches of public transportation, and operating emergency teams on a 24-hour basis. After terrorists murdered 22 school children at a school in Ma'alot in 1974, the response from the public to assist the police in internal security matters was immediate and has remained constant. The volunteer units have become fully incorporated into the national police force at all levels. They are activated in two main operational forms. First by means of local units deployed from neighborhood operational bases, and second by special units assisting the police in specific law enforcement and security operations.

The second operational form includes specially trained sharpshooter units and bomb-disposal support units. The national police confirm that, "Sharpshooters are primarily deployed in the assistance to INP units engaged in counter terrorist activities, ambushes and preventive operations" (Eitan Meyr, "The Israeli Civil Guard", *S.W.A.T.*, January 2001, Pg. 27). The bomb-disposal unit also assists the INP in surveillance of likely terrorist targets, evacuation of bomb victims, and driving bomb-disposal vehicles, as well as providing aid in the disposal of bombs. The integration of the Civil Guard into the INP has greatly facilitated their efforts in controlling the aftermath of terrorist attacks as well as aiding the prevention of them. The volunteer human resources potential is immense, and other governments could benefit from such a program in the counterterrorist arena.

Border Guard Force The Israeli Border Guard Force is a semimilitary force that possesses police powers and is worthy of mention in this context. The members of this force are referred to as the Green Police because of their easily recognizable green uniforms. It is a part of the national police and is answerable to the Israeli Police Commissioner. Its primary mission, since its inception in 1953, is to protect the borders of Israel. However, since terrorists have repeatedly attempted to infiltrate the border, the Border Guard Force's importance and amount of responsibility have increased.

Immediately after the Six-Day War, units of the organization were sent into the newly occupied territories. The Guard is now formally tasked with guarding airports and seaports in addition to other vital installations. It is approximately 8000 members strong, and uniquely 12% come from minorities such as Bedouin, Circasians, Christians, Druze, and Moslems (Eitan Meyr, "Protector if Internal Security," *S.W.A.T.*, May 2000). The Guard is also tasked with protecting the green line between Israel and the West Bank, a highly volatile area. In addition, the Border Guard Force also operates a number of special units like the Counterterrorism Hostage Rescue Unit, or YAMAM, which was set up in 1974. In conjunction, the YAMAS, or Mista'arvim Unit, conducts special undercover operations against terrorists in Judea and Sumaria.

Ireland: Army Ranger Wing (ARW)

The Army Ranger Wing (ARW) has the principal task of leading the tactical fight against terrorism in Ireland. Its headquarters is located at Camp Curraugh in County Kildare. The organization is directly subordinate to the army's Chief of Staff. The organization includes a command group, two assault platoons, and a support platoon composed of explosive experts, medical officers, and other specialists. As the primary counterterrorist force in Ireland, it is tasked with intervening in any extreme terrorist attack to include hijackings. For intervention purposes, each of the assault platoons can be subdivided into smaller tactical teams depending on the operational need.

France: Groupment d'intervention de la Gendarmerie Nationale (GIGN)

The GIGN has become one of the world's busiest counterterrorism units. The organization was founded as early as 1974 and consisted of a relatively small number of members. It was created following the attack at the Munich Olympic Games and the takeover of the Saudi Embassy in Paris. After so much experience, they have significantly honed their skills in combating the activities of terrorists. Between the years 1974 and 1985, ". . . they have participated in over 650 operations that freed over 500 hostages and eliminated dozens of terrorists" ("France's GIGN"; Internet: http://www.specwarnet.com/europe/gign.htm, Pg. 2). Different from the British SAS, the unit is a police unit, not a military one. Consequently, they are called upon to handle not only terrorist incidents but also nonpolitical criminal circumstances as well.

 The original organizers realized that the small number of officers assigned to the group was one of its advantages. Since its creation, therefore, it generally has had about 90 to 100 members. Additionally, the team has been noted for its creativity. Like American police departments that have sent lottery award notifications to individuals with outstanding warrants against them in order to have them claim the prize in person only to be arrested, the French have also pulled off some exceptional ruses of their own. In 1976, for example, in a hostage situation involving children, the GIGN sent drugged sandwiches to the terrorists. They fed the sandwiches to the hostages, having them immediately fall asleep. After the hostages lay down, the police had an open field of view for the GIGN snipers.

 Because the French have former colonies all over the world, the GIGN has been known effectively to operate everywhere from Djibouti to the Sudan. However, one of their most famous deployments involved the storming of an Air France Airbus in Marseilles, wherein all 13 hijackers were fatally shot. They are a particularly heavily armed unit, preferring as many other counterterrorism units, the Heckler and Koch MP5 submachine gun plus an assortment of handguns.

The members of GIGN are correspondingly well trained in all sorts of environments from alpine to ocean diving. They are recruited from the national police, the Gendarmerie. All officers have had at least five years of regular police experience. Once accepted, they receive an additional ten months of training in order to master the weapons of their adversaries. They also become experts in evasive driving, parachuting, mountain operations, marksmanship, and marine operations. The organization is broken down into four 15-man units and is supplemented by a command and support unit, including specialists in hostage negotiation. The commanding officer is a major and the command staff consists of a total of five officers. The staff consists of a deputy commander, three captains, and three lieutenants. Their headquarters is located at Maison Airport outside Paris.

Overall, the French have continued to conduct an all-out effort against terrorists. They have a nationwide "Vigi-Pirate" plan that combines military forces and the police as reinforcements for each other in part specifically to counterattacks by Algerian terrorists in the Paris metro and other major cities. The combined teams are highly successfully in increasing security at metro and train stations, bolstering security at borders, and expanding identity checks throughout the country. Additionally, in a cooperative effort with the Spanish, they launched an aggressive cross-border operation to shut down operations and supply lines of the ETA.

Spain: Grupo Especial de Operaciones (GEO)

In light of the fact that Spain has recently been inundated by significant acts of domestic terrorism, the government has not regretted its decision to establish a counterterrorism unit. The unit, assembled in 1978, initially suffered from a lack of political support and minimal fiscal resources.

Spain has suffered from attacks from both left-wing and right-wing terrorist groups, but most notably the Basque Fatherland and Liberty, Euskadi Ta Askatasuna (ETA). The ETA has historically targeted police, military personnel, and politicians. Initially, the GEO unit received some meaningful advice and assistance from German's GSG-9 unit after their repeated successes, and it has since become an elite unit that has been proven to be effective. One incident involved a terrorist takeover of the Central Bank of Barcelona, which involved over 200 innocent hostages. The 24-member terrorist team had occupied the bank and threatened to kill the hostages. The GEO stormed the bank. One hostage was injured, 10 terrorists were captured, and 1 killed. The remaining terrorists blended into the hostages fleeing the building and escaped.

The unit has been repeatedly called upon on numerous occasions, as Spain was wrenched by terrorism in the years 2000 to 2001 after a cease fire with the ETA fell apart. Additionally, a group that had been quiet for many years reappeared. The First of October Anti-Fascist Resistance Group (GRAPO) murdered a Spanish policeman following the arrest of seven of their members in Paris. The group also killed two security guards during an armed robbery and detonated seven bombs. The GEO was consequently busy during the year 2000 to 2001 assisting in quite a few antiterrorist deployments, justifying their continued existence.

United States: Armed Forces Teams

The home bases of American military counterterrorist forces are located in the United States, away from most previous international terrorist attacks. The Joint Operations Command, located at Fort Bragg, North Carolina, is generally believed to be tasked with the mission of repelling terrorist attacks or launching rescue operations of American citizens held as hostages. The Command brings together units from all of the branches of the Armed Forces, with the most publicly well known being Delta Force and Task Force 100. The Navy and Air Force have their own respective teams; namely, Seal Team Six (now the Naval Special Warfare Development Group, NSWDG) and AF Special Operations Command. They all have some unique expertise to bring to the mix such as the MC-130's at Hurlbert Air Force Base. The Navy's team is specifically tasked to deal with any terrorist activity in a maritime environment. Many critics of the teams, as well as many military officers, recognize the lack of cohesion of any effort that is "joint." On top of that, the founding father of Seal Team Six, Commander Richard Marcinko, was criminally tried for fraud and bribery; hence, the name change of the unit.

Unseemingly, the teams are best known for the failed attempt to rescue the US hostages being held in Teheran, Iran, also known as Operation Eagle's Claw. It failed miserably. Shrouded in so much "classified material," some of the military officers involved did not know what the mission they were preparing for was to accomplish. The effort proved the point that what can go wrong will go wrong. First, too many people held command authority, and their lack of ability to work together effectively contributed to the failed effort. The supposed overall commander, Army Major General James Vaught, was theoretically in command of Air Force Colonel James Kyle, Marine Colonel Charles Pitman, and Delta Force Commander Colonel Charles Beckwith. Personalities coupled with interservice rivalry contributed to mixed signals and ultimate disaster. A huge dust storm and the fact that one of the helicopters on the mission crashed into a C-130 loaded with munitions resulted in the death of eight marines, which has been touted as the tangible reason for the mission being aborted mid-effort.

Partly as a result of the "debacle in desert," the United States still lacks the political will and senior military support to create a truly single unit to combat terrorism. The US experience reinforces the point that it is not sufficient just to possess a force. There must also be a commitment to train, equip, and, most importantly, command them properly. They need to be equipped with high-tech, real-time information and refined weaponry to meet the ever-increasing sophistication of the terrorists.

Local, state, and national law enforcement officers generally handle incidents of domestic terrorism. At least, they are frequently, if not always, the first to be called to the scene of an incident. The FBI is also the lead agency tasked to collect intelligence on domestic terrorists, not the Central Intelligence Agency, which has an overseas mandate.

Operation Ice Eagle   In the aftermath of 9/11, airline travel in the United States and abroad dropped dramatically. While long-term plans to heighten airport security were underway, an interim solution was needed to restore public confidence in air travel. A visible increase in security was recommended. As a result, President George W. Bush offered federal funds to state governors if they would use those funds to place National Guard troops at security checkpoints.

Although public reaction was mixed, National Guard troops in Minnesota and many other states were activated and ready for duty by 6 October 2001. The mission was the subset of Operation Noble Eagle with a Minnesota twist, Operation Ice Eagle. Operational orders were cut and the state Adjutant General, 1st Brigade of the 34th ID (MECH), was assigned the task of placing troops at the Duluth, Minneapolis/St. Paul, and Rochester airports. Normally, the 34th Military Police Company would cover civilian law enforcement–related missions, but there were insufficient personnel. Consequently, combat arms units were used to fill the gap. On 30 September 2001, the 2nd Battalion 135th Infantry Air Assault and the 1st Battalion 194th Armor Regiment were given the duties of securing the airports in Minnesota.

Because the Posse Comitatus Act forbids the use of the US military from engaging in law enforcement duties against US citizens, the activation of the troops remained at the state level. Authorization came from 32 US Code Section 502, which authorizes the use of National Guard troops by the governor of a state for whatever purposes he or she deems fit. The authorization was not based on Title 10 of the US Code which would have given the troops federal jurisdiction, placing them in federal service. Guard units remained at US airports, with little training, under very unusual conditions, sometimes without normal federal benefits but serving with distinction until 17 May 2002.

■ ENFORCEMENT

Exactly who is a law enforcement officer, as it relates to aviation, was expressly defined in FAR 107. Section 107.15: Law Enforcement Support states,

> (a) Each airport operator shall provide law enforcement officers in the number and in a manner adequate to support
> (1) Its security program; and
> (2) Each passenger screening system required by Part 108 (Internet: http://www.faa.gov/avr/AFS/FARS/far-107.txt, April 2001, Pgs. 9, 22.

What this means is often debated. How many officers are needed and their precise function will vary from airport to airport. First, of course, law enforcement officers are appointed by a government entity and have statutory authority to engage in certain conduct. As already discussed, they possess the authority to arrest and detain under circumstances completely different than a private security guard or a private citizen. For example, a police officer has the authority to arrest an individual without a warrant for a crime committed in his or her presence or for a felony for which there is probable cause to arrest. That standard duty is applicable on and off an airport complex. Airport police are also tasked with assisting security personnel in the prevention and investigation of any terrorist threat. This special duty requires them to meet special criteria and to have special training. Private security and law enforcement must have a seamless working relationship. In fulfilling both their duties, there are, of course, many differences and some similarities between airport security personnel and a governmental police force.

Private and public police officers may both wear uniforms and badges and carry weapons. Both seek to compel obedience, prevent crime, and apprehend criminals. They are both apt to be sued as well. Therefore, it is absolutely mandatory that both groups understand what acceptable behavior is under the law and what is not. Because public officers and airport security guards should receive respect and cooperation does not make it so. In reality, they may face hostility and aggression that they need to be trained to handle.

Under the Federal Aviation Act of 1958, it is illegal to attempt to board an aircraft while having concealed on or about one's person a deadly or dangerous weapon. Private security officers routinely conduct the required regulatory searches. More and more federal employees will be assuming these duties. Furthermore, the regulations require that passengers or visitors discovered to be carrying an undeclared weapon, whether on their person or inside carry-on baggage, must be referred to a duly appointed law enforcement officer. Hence, the combined efforts of security and law enforcement are essential to the overall endeavor.

TSA 49 CFR Chapter XII, Part 1542.217 (a) Law Enforcement Personnel, formerly, Section 107.17 of the FARs, defines an airport-qualified law enforcement officer as follows:

1. Has the authority to arrest;
2. Is readily identifiable by uniform and displays or carries a badge or other indicia of authority;
3. Is armed with a firearm and authorized to use it; and
4. Has completed a training program that meets the requirements.
5. The law enforcement officer must, while on duty on the airport, have the authority to arrest, with or without a warrant, for the following violations of the criminal laws of the State and local jurisdictions in which the airport is located:
   (a) A crime committed in the officer's presence;
   (b) A felony, when the officer has reason to believe that the suspect has committed it (Internet: http://www.faa.gov/avr/AFS/FARS/far-107.txt, 22 August 2001).

Under the Federal Aviation Act of 1958, the law enforcement officer was originally supposed to be immediately available at the screening point. This concept was eventually discarded. The Flexible Response concept permitted the law enforcement officer to be available but not necessarily present. Historically and depending on the size of the airport, the response time varied considerably. Previously,

> At Category I airports the response time may not exceed five minutes, and at selected Category IA airports may not exceed one minute. At Category II airports the response time was 10 minutes; at Category II the response time was 15 minutes. At Category III airports the response time could have been as much as 20 minutes. (Laurence E. Gesell, *The Administration of Public Airports*, Coast Aire Publications, 1981 Pg. IX-15).

For security reasons, response times are no longer so readily available, although a common-sense approach recognizes that a qualified law enforcement officer is probably only a few minutes away if needed. Not all airports are large enough to justify an entire "airport police" contingent directly at the airport. Other small airports, when necessary, have to call local police to the scene.

Training

When the airport and airline security rules were implemented in the early 1970s, the FAA also established a special training program for local law enforcement officers. FAR 107.17 specifically required and TSA 49 CFR Chapter XII, Part 1542.217 (c) requires that each officer complete an appropriate training program. The training program must include training in:

1. The use of firearms;
2. The courteous and efficient treatment of persons subject to inspection, detention, search, arrest, and other aviation security activities;
3. The responsibilities of a law enforcement officer under the airport operator's approved security program; and
4. Any other subject the Administrator determines is necessary (Internet: http://www.faa.gov/avr/AFS/FARS/far-107.txt, 22 August 2001, Pg. 11)

Airport police officer training is conducted at the FAA facilities in Oklahoma City. The first class of officers was graduated as early as 26 Jan 1973, but since that time, thousands of law enforcement officers, private security professions, FAA employees, and international students have been graduated. The school, known as the Transportation Safety Institute, is still in existence and continuously provides officers with classes directly related to airport security techniques. Funded by the FAA to meet the expanded need to provide highly trained people at airports, the school's availability was extended to include FAA inspectors and special agents and not just local law enforcement. The school is internationally recognized, and also provides training to aviation and security professionals from around the world.

Over the years, the curriculum offered by the school has also been greatly expanded. They now conduct courses not only in basic civil aviation security but also more explicit and detailed seminars. Training now also includes courses in hijacking, terrorism, explosive detection, K-9 units, investigations, rule compliance, and inspections.

Training is also available at the FBI Academy in Quantico, Virginia. It is one of the world's most respected law enforcement training centers. Police training programs include the FBI National Academy, an eleven-week multidisciplinary program for seasoned law enforcement managers; the Executive Training Program; and the Operational Assistance Program, which specifically trains law enforcement personnel how to respond in certain emergency situations, including terrorist acts. Many agencies engage in cooperative efforts to maintain security at airports. They incorporate but are not limited to the US Customs Service, the Drug Enforcement Agency (DEA), the FBI, the US Marshals, the Immigration and Naturalization Service (INS), Interpol, and the US Postal Inspection Service (USPIS). All make distinct and unique contributions to the fight against terrorism.

One of the greatest detriments to the ongoing battle against the scourge of hijacking and airport assaults is when these organizations become proprietary and do not cooperate. Secrecy between agencies only assists the terrorist. If one agency does not wish to share its knowledge with another, critical information often fails to reach the person or officers who may need it most. In the future, the government has to ensure better interagency communication at all levels of government. All data accumulated must be shared so that they can be correlated and used as sources of predictive information.

The FAA also maintains their own staff of exceptionally trained security officers to supplement the policing of airports. FAR Section 107.19: Use of Federal Law Enforcement Officers (TSA 49 CFR 1542.219: Supplementing Law Enforcement Personnel) states:

> (a) Whenever TSA decides, after being notified by an airport operator prescribed in this section, that not enough qualified State, local and private law enforcement personnel are available to carry out the requirements of Sec. 1542.215 the TSA may authorize the airport operator to use, on a reimbursable basis, personnel employed by the TSA. . . .

Consequently, the FAA, the TSA, and many other agencies are considered to be necessary to provide overall security for airports in what is hopefully a cooperative team effort. Jurisdictional disputes and personalities must not interfere with the protection of the public. Providing a safe working environment for airport employees and the traveling public is a very high priority and requires constant vigilance. A short description of some of these agencies follows.

Customs officer checks declaration and packages for a passenger arriving at Los Angeles International Airport. US Customs continues to play a critical role in the overall environment and quality of airport security.
Phil McCarten / PhotoEdit.

US Customs Service

The US Customs Service is one of the oldest agencies of the US government. It was established in 1789 and is an integral part of the Department of the Treasury. It is the primary enforcement agency charged with the protection of US borders at 300 ports of entry. Specifically, the US Customs Service has a mission to assess and collect customs duties on imported merchandise, prevent fraud and smuggling, and control carriers, people, and articles entering and departing the United States. The Service is broken down into the offices of Assistant Commissioner for Enforcement, Inspection and Control, Commercial Operations, International Affairs, and Internal Affairs.

The current commissioner is in charge of over 19,000 employees and is responsible for protecting US citizens from everything from mad cow disease to explosives. Customs boosts a gigantic source of revenue for the government. In 2000, Customs returned $22.1 billion to the US Treasury in confiscated goods and currency and $23.8 in 2001. In a typical day, officers examine approximately 1.3 million passengers, 2661 aircraft, 60,196 trucks, 348,205 vehicles, and 522 vessels. Approximately 472 million pedestrians and passengers were examined in 2001 alone. The number of individual transactions increased from 23.5 billion in FY 2000 to 23.7 billion in FY 2001 (US Customs Annual Report 2001, Internet: http://www.customs.ustreasury.gov/reports 2001). In fiscal year 2002, U.S. Custom's staff arrested 12,570 people and seized 6.4 million rounds of ammunition and 39,643 firearms. (CBP Statistics and Accomplishments, Internet: http://www. customs.ustreas.gov/xp/cgov/toolbox/about/accomplish/accomplishments.xml)

The US Customs Service is the federal agency responsible for preventing the smuggling of contraband across US borders. It is well known as the primary enforcement agency protecting US borders from the particular threat of drugs, illegal immigration, and more recently of bondaged humans. The agency is equipped with extensive air, land, and marine interdiction forces. The assets conduct continual surveillance over water and all types of terrain. Customs agents have widespread authority to investigate and search all international passengers, including those arriving at airports. In a cooperative effort to stop, or at least minimize, the international flow of illegal drugs through the nation's borders, customs agents often work in tandem with the DEA.

The challenges facing the US Customs Service continue to evolve with the times. Currently, they are also deeply involved in targeting the illegal export of weapons and weapons technology to countries that support terrorism. They are also focusing on the transfer of money used in drug trafficking to offshore banks. Such scrutiny, however, requires time, and most passengers are focused on arriving at their aircraft before it takes off, continuing with their trip, or simply getting home. In recognition of the desires of most of the law-abiding traveling public, the agency has publicly announced they hope to process most international air passengers through inspection in 30 minutes or less while improving enforcement and regulatory processes. In addition, they have pledged, in partnership with the airlines, to obtain advance biographical information on 80% of all international air travelers through the use of the Advance Passenger Information System (APIS), expediting the processing of passengers.

Customs officials have also developed the Target Flight Connector System (TFCS), which provides analysis of data elements relating to flights, which have the most potential for an enforcement threat. They also use the Interagency Border Inspection System (IBIS), which encompasses more than 24,000 computer terminals located at air, land, and sea ports of entry. The service also uses a sophisticated air surveillance system developed by Decision Science Applications. It is designed quickly to identify legal fliers versus smugglers. The system is operated by radar controllers and is supposed to detect any suspicious flight. Controllers can immediately acquire the plane's identification number, altitude, direction of flight, and air speed. Appropriate law enforcement officers can then be contacted and their pursuit efforts coordinated.

Drug Enforcement Agency

Owing to a continuing concern about the growing problem of illegal drug infiltration into the United States, the Drug Enforcement Administration (DEA) is one of the fastest growing law enforcement agencies in the United States. DEA agents are an ever-present force at both domestic and international airports. Its mission is to enforce domestic drug laws and regulations and to assist other federal and foreign agencies in combating illegal drug production, sale, and transfer. The DEA is also assigned the explicit task of enforcing the provisions of the

Controlled Substance Act, which monitors the manufacture, distribution, and dispensing of prescription drugs. The agency was preceded by the Federal Bureau of Narcotics, which had been established by President Herbert Hoover in 1930 to supervise the proliferation of cocaine and heroin. The level of illegal drug usage has expanded exponentially since that era. Therefore, President Richard M. Nixon formed the DEA in 1973 as a "superagency" to combat the rapidly proliferating problem. Overall, it is the primary agency for domestic enforcement of federal drug laws and also coordinates and participates in drug investigations overseas.

In one particular aviation-related case, creatively called "Operation Green Air," the DEA completed an important marijuana trafficking investigation in April 2000. This case was especially unique, because it successfully terminated the illegal drug transportation of an organization that used FedEx, a commercial air shipment company, as its exclusive transportation source. The DEA reported that it is, of course, common for drug traffickers to use air transport in their logistics schemes to move quantities of drugs; however, solely to use one company had not been detected prior to this particular operation. The DEA uncovered evidence that a Los Angeles–based criminal group had bribed a number of FedEx employees, mostly drivers but some customer service representatives as well, to facilitate in the delivery of marijuana. The employees were paid to make sure that marijuana shipments were appropriately loaded on aircraft traveling between several major distribution areas. The bribed employees also provided security for the shipments while they were under FedEx control. Other employees manipulated corporate billing and accounting to provide for free shipping services. The DEA estimates that over 4000 packages were successfully airlifted in this manner, with the FedEx guarantee of pick up by 4 PM and next day delivery by 10 AM.

The DEA conducted an extensive 18-month investigation to unravel the scheme. According to DEA officials, ". . . over 100 individuals, including 25 FedEx employees, and the seizure of 34,000 pounds of marijuana and $4.2 million in currency and assets" were involved. In addition, it effectively dismantled the target organizations, which had shipped at least 121 tons of marijuana valued at $145 million over the past two years" (Internet: http://www.usdoj.gov/dea/major/greenair.htm, 4 July 2001).

The Director of the DEA since 8 August 2001, Asa Hutchinson has recently publicly accepted the challenge regarding the reorganization of the FBI and the establishment of a cabinet position for Homeland Security, which will directly affect the agency. Currently, the DEA has 4763 support employees and 4625 special agents. The government plans to divert more than 400 agents currently assigned to narcotics investigations to counterterrorism activities.

Federal Bureau of Investigation

The Federal Bureau of Investigation (FBI) was originally known as the Bureau of Investigation (BOI). Attorney General Charles J. Bonaparte, at the request of President Theodore Roosevelt, ordered the creation of an investigative arm of the

Department of Justice in 1908. The BOI began operations with nine special agents. By 1924, at the time J. Edgar Hoover was named Director, the BOI had approximately 650 employees, including 441 special agents. Shortly thereafter, Director Hoover fired special agents he considered to be unqualified and began to professionalize the organization. He abolished the seniority rule of promotion and introduced uniform performance appraisals. The BOI doubled in size in the 1930s.

The BOI became the FBI in 1935, and it has become one of the primary investigative agencies in the US government. It too plays an important role in airport security. The FBI in recent times has jurisdiction over nearly 200 federal crimes. The agency is especially well known for its professionalism, which is perpetuated by the extensive training of its agents and thousands of local law enforcement officers who receive supplemental training at the FBI National Academy. As of the year 2000, the agency had over 11,000 active agents and a budget of over $3 billion. The agency has five priorities including terrorism, organized crime, foreign intelligence operations in the US, federal drug offenses, and white-collar crime.

International terrorism came directly to the shores of the United States in the 1990s, and the Anti-Terrorism and Effective Death Penalty Act of 1996 gave the FBI additional resources to meet the increased demands. Several Presidential Decision Directives issued during the later part of the decade delineated the FBI's leadership role in countering terrorism. The federal structure had come under considerable criticism for failing to coordinate antiterrorism activity, assess and analyze accurate intelligence, and act quickly to prevent incidents. Acts of international terrorism at the World Trade Center in 1993 and the Atlanta Olympics as well as several poorly handled hostage situations had forced the FBI to bolster its mission in this area. At the time, the FBI had assigned approximately 500 agents to contend with the heightened domestic threat (Internet: http://www.fbi.gov). The predictive deficiencies of the program at the FBI were once again self-evident on 9/11, and may have contributed to the tragedy.

As a result, Director Robert S. Mueller has announced plans further to reorganize the FBI. Its new strategic focus will be to protect the United States from terrorist attacks. He plans to restructure the Counterterrorism Division to "redefine the relationship between Headquarters and the field" and to "shift from reactive to preventive orientation." The proposed shift in manning will move 400 agents from narcotics, 59 agents from white-collar crime, and 59 agents from violent crime units to 480 counterterrorism field agents and another 38 agents to security and training divisions (Internet: http://www.fbi.gov/terrorinfo/terrorism.htm, 11 June 2002, Pg. 1).

In the past 10 years, the FBI has already had its budget relating to terrorism tripled. The number of agents has also significantly increased as well as efforts to improve cross communication between agencies in order exchange information on terrorists. The CIA passed the names of over 100 suspected associates of Usama bin Ladin just in the last several years. Two of them, Khalid Al-Midhar and

Nawaq Alhazmi, later crashed an airplane into the Pentagon on 9/11. As has long been the case at the FBI, the agency is at its best in collecting evidence against known criminals. They have not been as successful in gathering intelligence and anticipating criminal activity before it happens. As discussed in a previous chapter, there is no universally accepted single definition of terrorism. The FBI defines terrorism as "the unlawful use of force or violence against persons or property to intimidate or coerce a government, the civilian population, or any segment thereof, in furtherance of political or social objectives." The FBI further describes terrorism as either domestic or international, depending on the origin, base, and objectives of the terrorist organization.

> Domestic terrorism involves groups or individuals who are based and operate entirely within the United States and Puerto Rico without foreign direction and whose acts are directed at elements of the US Government or population.
>
> International terrorism is the unlawful use of force or violence committed by a group or individual, who has some connection to a foreign power or whose activities transcend national boundaries, against persons or property to intimidate or coerce a government, the civilian population, or any segment thereof, in furtherance of political or social objectives (Internet: http://www.fbi.gov).

The FBI assists airport operations in several other unique ways. For example, the FBI's identification division is often called in to identify victims of major airline crashes. The FBI laboratory is one of the largest crime laboratories in the world. These services are provided free of charge to all law enforcement agencies in the United States. The ability quickly to identify passengers who are victims of a terrorist attack is particularly useful to aviation security personnel. The Automated Fingerprint Identification System (AFIS) converts fingerprints into algorithms. That is, it uses the converted algorithms, or sets of mathematical equations, and compares them to fingerprints of individuals who need to be identified. Using the automated program, law enforcement agencies can search and compare millions of samples in minutes. When combined with another new tool, Live Scan, which electronically scans fingerprints instead of using printer's ink, combinations can be made quickly and easily. Of course, the system is of no assistance in identifying victims unless they have a fingerprint on file. Millions of Americans do, however, as a result of job applications, military service, and the like.

The FBI is also an integral part of the National Domestic Preparedness Office, which is the clearinghouse for state, local, and federal weapons of mass destruction information and assistance. Other members include the Federal Emergency Management Agency (FEMA), the Environmental Protection Agency (EPA), the Department of Energy, the Department of Defense, and Health and Human Resources. Contact can be made with this organization at FBI, National Domestic Preparedness Office, RM 5214, 935 Pennsylvania Avenue, Washington, DC, 202-324-9026 (Internet: http://www.ndpo@leo.gov).

US Marshals

The US Marshal Service is the oldest federal law enforcement agency in existence. Congress created the Service over 200 years ago by means of the Judiciary Act of 1789. As the part of the federal judicial system, the agency is charged with carrying out all lawful orders issued by federal judges, the Congress, or the President. Their primary mission is to protect the Federal Courts and ensure effective operation of the judicial system. As an interesting footnote, during the Cold War, they were also responsible for swapping spies with the former Soviet Union. Today the service supports the needs of 94 districts spanning the continent and Guam, the Northern Mariana Islands, Puerto Rico, and the Virgin Islands. Headquartered in Arlington, Virginia, the agency employs more than 4000 deputy marshals.

They also provide a particularly unique service as regards aviation and the transportation of prisoners. "The U.S. Marshals Service assumes custody of individuals arrested by all federal agencies and is responsible for the housing and transportation of prisoners from the time they are brought into federal custody until they are either acquitted or incarcerated" (Internet: http://www.usdoj.gov/marshals/prisoner.html). Once a prisoner is convicted, the US Marshals retain the responsibility of delivering the prisoner to a specific institution for service of sentence. Carriage of passengers under the control of armed law enforcement escorts was provided for in FAR Section 108.21 and now TSA 49 CFR Chapter XII, Part 1544.221.

In 1995, the Immigration and Naturalization Service and the US Marshals combined their air fleet assets to create the Justice Prisoner and Alien Transportation System (JPATS). Costs and the consolidation of federal resources necessitated the move and have established a very effective and coordinated system for transporting both prisoners and criminal aliens. Most of the prisoners are transported aboard Service-owned aircraft, but not all. Some are still transported by commercial aircraft even though JPATS provides the more economical and secure means for transportation. When JPATS is not utilized, the TSA regulations apply to the transportation of prisoners aboard commercial aircraft.

JPATS acquired many of their airplanes at no cost from the Government Surplus Property Program and the Asset Seizure and Forfeiture Program. It is, aside from the military, the only government-owned scheduled prisoner transport system in the world. The system serves over 40 cities and has some unique aspects. Deputy Marshals, Aviation Enforcement Officers, and Aviation Safety Officers are all involved. They are strategically positioned throughout the aircraft during flight. In addition, the prisoners all wear handcuffs and leg irons. Local law enforcement assists in ground security and is stationed at each airport transfer point (Internet: http://www.usdoj.gov/marshals/usmshist.html).

As stated, the airlines, however, are often tasked with transporting alleged nonviolent prisoners and illegal aliens. Problems arise if the individual being transferred does not turn out to be nonviolent after all. The airlines and supporting ground security and law enforcement officers simply are not equipped to handle an unruly prisoner or illegal alien if they really want to escape. Additionally, once the aircraft becomes airborne, the problems are even more acute. Other passengers and aircrew are readily available hostages. Plus firing a weapon inside a pressurized aircraft is an extremely dangerous maneuver that limits the options available to the escort officer.

Recently, on 24 January 2002, John Walker Lindh, the alleged American Taliban, appeared in US Magistrates Court in Alexandria, Virginia. US Marshals accompanied him. Currently, the Marshals are responsible for the detention and transportation of both John Walker Lindh and Zackarius Moussaoui, the first defendant charged in the 9/11 attack (Internet: http://www.usdoj.gov/marshals, 11 June 2002, Pg. 1).

US Immigration and Naturalization Service

The Immigration and Naturalization Service (INS) is charged with the task of monitoring and policing the flow of immigrants into the United States. They have the almost Herculean task of patrolling the borders of the continental United States and American territories to ensure that illegal immigrants do not enter the country. Their jurisdiction encompasses in the vicinity of 8000 miles of border. Consecutively, they apprehend and deport illegal aliens who have not complied with US naturalization laws. Border management units consist of Border Patrol and Inspections as well as Interior Enforcement units.

The Inspections unit is the uniformed branch assigned the task of enforcing and administering US immigration laws by inspecting all persons seeking admission to or transiting the US at air, land, and seaport facilities. Inspectors make determinations regarding the eligibility of applicants seeking admission to the United States on a daily basis. Each inspector is charged with intercepting terrorists, smugglers, criminals, and undocumented aliens. As mentioned earlier in the text, inspectors are authorized to search the applicant and their possessions without a warrant. The program also provides for the preinspection of passengers overseas prior to flights destined for the United States. In detail, INS personnel work directly with foreign governments and air carriers to assist them in identifying passengers without the proper paperwork from boarding aircraft destined for the US. The inspectors are involved in the training of domestic and international air carrier personnel.

The INS, as does other law enforcement agencies, possesses the tool of prosecutorial discretion. This discretion authorizes the agency to decide when to exercise its enforcement authority. They exercise this discretion every day in one form or another. However, attention was focused on the INS after passage of the Illegal Immigration Reformation Immigrant Responsibility Act in 1996 due to allegations of discriminatory abuse (Internet: http://www.ins.usdoj.gov/graphics/lawenfor/index.htm). It was alleged INS personnel were using their discretion arbitrarily, singling out minorities for detention and intrusive searches. The INS has since gone to great lengths to train their personnel to restrict their activities to be in conformance with all applicable laws.

It has been reported that the INS deports more than 23,000 illegal immigrants a year on commercial air carriers. The Detention and Deportation branch is responsible for safely and humanely detaining and deporting illegal aliens or aliens who have violated US laws and are being deported. Most of the individuals deported have been indicted for criminal misconduct. Some high-risk deportees are considered such a risk that armed INS agents escort them. All other deportees travel on board the aircraft unescorted to the dismay of the airlines. INS policy is to escort deportees when they consist of a group larger than 12 people; groups of 11 or fewer travel unescorted, again placing a burden on the airlines.

It is not surprising that the transport of these people often presents security problems. Even if the deportees are not violent offenders, they are being sent somewhere against their will, automatically placing them in the category of a potential escape risk. It is not entirely unimaginable that a group or an individual could take over an aircraft or attempt to do so. The Airline Pilots Association (ALPA) has in the past expressed profound concerns over the INS practice of deporting individuals on commercial flights without an escort. In testimony before Congress, an ALPA representative made the following statement, which glowingly describes the irony of current policy.

> Ironically, the INS's own deportee escorts refuse to operate their deportee transport vehicles unless there are at least two of them in each vehicle, even though the deportees are handcuffed and often in leg irons. There is an obvious problem when these vehicles are allowed to pull up alongside of our aircraft and unload deportees, who moments before were in handcuffs, to ride unescorted in the seat next to Grandma (Internet: http://www.alpa.org/internet/tm/tm061198.htm, 14 July 2001, Pg. 5).

Prior to 9/11, the system was completely geared toward easing the way for commerce either in the form of tourism, business, or education. The INS manual still requires customs to exclude immigrants who incite or direct terrorist activity. Statements by immigrants of a general nature that do not directly advance specific acts of terrorism are not automatically a basis for exclusion however offensive the statements might be. Therefore, Hani Hanjour, identified as the pilot who flew the jet that slammed into the Pentagon, began blending in the American landscape started with a $110 application for a four-week English course. He only had to prove that he had paid for the lessons. He never turned up for class. Two other hijackers who crashed planes into the World Trade Center, Mohammed Atta and Marwan al-Shehhi, entered the United States on tourist visas. While their application for student visas were pending, they had already completed flight training at a school in Florida. Much to the embarrassment of INS, those visas were in fact granted six months after the 9/11 tragedy. Clearly change is required.

Unfortunately, there is currently, an exceptionally high employee turnover rate at the INS. The agency has about 15,000 officers; about 1500 fewer than authorized. Admittedly, it hired 1499 agents during this fiscal year but also lost 1459 veterans to the TSA. Employees' moral is not at an all-time high, and care needs to be taken to maintain the proficiency of the INS.

Department of Homeland Security

The Bush Administration announced on 6 June 2002 an attempt to revolutionize the method by which the government seeks to protect the United States from internal and external forces. The agency consolidated many existing agencies, including the entire INS, into one department. The new department will be divided into five divisions to include Border Transportation, and Security, Emergency Preparedness, Information Analysis and Infrastructure Protection, and Chemical, Biological, and Nuclear Countermeasures.

> *Border Transportation and Security* will likely envelop the entire Immigration and Naturalization Service from within the Department of Justice; the Customs Services from the Department of the Treasury; the Coast Guard from the Department of Transportation; Animal and Plant Health Inspection Service for the Department of Agriculture; and the Federal Protective Service from the General Services Administration and the new Transportation Security Administration.

> *Emergency Preparedness* will consolidate the Federal Emergency Management Agency; Chemical, Biological, Nuclear Response Services from Health and Human Services; the Emergency Support Team from the Department of Justice; the Office of Domestic Preparedness from the Department of Justice; the Nuclear Incident Response Section from the Department of Energy; and the National Domestic Preparedness Office from the FBI.

> *Information Analysis and Infrastructure Protection* will analyze intelligence from both the FBI and CIA, and will combine the Critical Infrastructure Assurance Office from the Department of Commerce; the Federal Computer Incident Response Center from the General Services Administration; the National Communications Systems division from the Department of Defense; and the National Infrastructure Protection Center from the FBI.

> *Chemical, Biological, and Nuclear Countermeasures* will include the Lawrence Livermore National Laboratory, Civilian bio-defense research programs from Health and Human Services, and the Plum Island Animal Disease Center from the Department of Agriculture.

Interpol

International police cooperation has been in use since the creation of the International Criminal Police Organization (Interpol). Interpol exists to facilitate the maintenance of a safer world community, especially within the 178 member countries. The organization plays a critical role in tracking terrorists and relating the information to the appropriate law enforcement agency. Interpol has a fundamental objective of overcoming national boundaries to coordinate international efforts to combat crime in whatever form. The development of rapid travel has made it far easier for criminals to move around the world. Additionally, the complex structures of modern societies and the constant growth of international exchanges provide more and more opportunities for international criminal activity. Interpol's mission specifically challenges the organization to be the world's preeminent organization dedicated to preventing and detecting international crime, including terrorism. It aims to "ensure and promote the widest mutual assistance between all criminal police authorities, within the limits of the laws existing in the different countries and in the spirit of the Universal Declaration of Human Rights and to establish and develop all institutions likely to contribute effectively to the prevention and suppression of ordinary law crimes" (Michael Fooner, *Interpol Issues in World Crime and International Criminal Justice*, New York: Plenum Press, 1989).

As early as April 1914, during the First International Criminal Police Congress held in Monaco, legal experts and police officers from 14 different countries and territories studied the possibility of establishing an international criminal records office and harmonizing extradition procedures. The outbreak of World War I prevented any further progress until 1923. The second International Criminal Police Congress met in Vienna, Austria, and was established as the International Criminal Police Commission. The organization, still essentially a European organization, was created after World War I, at which time counterfeit money was posing a big threat to the economic welfare of European countries. US participation began when J. Edgar Hoover was appointed Director of the FBI. He began receiving reports from Interpol in 1925 and increased the FBI's involvement by the late 1930s.

After World War II, another conference, held in Brussels, Belgium, revived the International Criminal Police Commission and the name *Interpol* was officially recognized. However, during the first 15 years, it was mainly a central European organization. The agency consists of a General Assembly, an Executive Committee, and the Secretary General, who is elected by the General Assembly. The current Secretary General, Ronald K. Noble began a five-year term in the year 2000.

Interpol investigates crimes including trafficking in human beings, crimes against minors, theft of art work, organized crime, counterfeiting, illicit drug trafficking, technology-related crime, environmental crime, and of course terrorism. They define terrorism as "a crime, characterized by violence or intimidation, usually against innocent victims in order to obtain a political or social objective." Interpol became extensively involved in the fight against terrorism as a result of a resolution passed at the 54th General Assembly in Washington DC in 1985. The resolution, AGN/54/RES/1, created a specialized group within the then Police Division to ". . . coordinate and enhance cooperation in combating international terrorism" (Internet: http://interpol.int/Public/Terrorism/default.asp).

The Anti-Terrorism Branch began operations in 1987 and is tasked with matters related to terrorism, firearms and explosives, attacks and threats against civil aviation, maritime piracy, and weapons of mass destruction. The unit seeks to disseminate information on terrorists and terrorists groups by responding to inquiries from member countries and coordinates sophisticated analysis. They attempt to keep the lines of communication between national police forces, military units involved in battling terrorism, and governments open. Interpol possesses a database called Interpol Weapons and Explosives Tracking System (IWETS) that maintains information on firearms and explosives. It provides current data on firearms manufacturers, identification of firearms, and information on stolen and recovered weapons. It must be remembered that Interpol has no arrest power or the authority to search and seize. It is purely an organization that facilitates cooperation between other police organizations. Interpol has recognized that the effort to combat terrorism must include coordinated efforts to disrupt funding to the terrorists. They have supported the concept that the frequency and seriousness of international terrorist acts are often, ". . . proportionate to the funding the terrorists might get" (Internet: http://www.interpol.com/public/Terror/finance.asp, 11 June 2002, Pgs. 1, 2).

The US National Central Bureau (USNCB) was established in order to promote a seamless working relationship between the United States and Interpol. The USNCB is the point of contact for international law enforcement within the United States and acts as the US representative to Interpol on behalf of the US Attorney General. It was authorized by 22 U.S.C. 263a and is officially part of the Department of Justice as well as being closely affiliated with the Department of Treasury. The published functions of the USNCB are to transmit information of a criminal justice, humanitarian, or other law enforcement–related nature between the National Central Bureaus of Interpol member countries and law enforcement agencies of the United States and to respond to requests by law enforcement agencies and other legitimate requests by appropriate organizations, institutions, and individuals.

It should be pointed out that for more than a decade, the National Institute for Standards and Technology (NIST) has advocated the development of data exchange within the law enforcement community. In the year 2000, the Institute adopted ANSI/NIST-ITL 1–2000, which uses a database format for the interchange of fingerprint, facial, and scar/tattoo information. The standard defines a structured framework for representing and exchanging rap sheets, photos, and arrest records into virtually all commercial fingerprint identification systems. Its impact, in conjunction with agencies such as Interpol, and the accessibility, connectivity, and mobility afforded by the Worldwide Web will prove to be dynamic.

United States Postal Inspection Service

The mission of the US Postal Inspection Service (USPIS) is to "protect the US Postal Service, its employees and its customers from criminal attack, and protect the nation's mail system from criminal misuse" (Internet: http://www.usps.gov/websites/depart/inspect). The USPIS inspection service is particularly interested in mail bombs. Even though the Postal Service processes over 170 billion pieces of mail annually, less than one in a billion will contain a bomb. In light of the fact that the mail is frequently carried on commercial aircraft, even one piece of mail is significant. The USPIS has disseminated a list of characteristics of mail bombs, which have repeatedly been observed. They include the following:

1. May have excessive postage. Normally, a bomber does not want to mail a parcel over-the-counter and have to deal face-to-face with a postal clerk.
2. Return address may be fictitious or nonexistent.
3. Postmark may show a different location than the return address.
4. May bear restricted endorsements, such as "Personal" or "Private." This is particularly important when the addressee does not usually receive personal mail at the office.
5. May display distorted handwriting, or the name and address may be prepared with homemade labels or cut-and-paste lettering.
6. May be professionally wrapped with several combinations of tape used to secure the package, and may be endorsed "Fragile-Handle with Care" or "Rush—Do Not Delay."
7. May feel rigid or appear uneven or lopsided.
8. May have an irregular shape, soft spots, or bulges.
9. May have protruding wires, aluminum foil, or oil stains, and may emit a peculiar odor (Internet: http://www.usps.gov/websites/depart/inspect/bombs.htm).

The advice that the postal inspectors give to their employees applies just as well to security officers who may encounter a suspicious package. First, do not open the package. Second, isolate the suspect package and evacuate the immediate area. Employees are further instructed not to put the package in water or a confined space. If possible, all windows in the immediate area should be opened to assist in venting the potential explosion. Finally, do not hesitate to check any suspicious package further, and never be embarrassed about a false alarm. It is always better to inspect harmless packages instead of ignoring a dangerous one.

Congress empowered postal inspectors to ". . . investigate postal offenses and civil matters relating to the Postal Service." Approximately 2000 postal inspectors work closely with other law enforcement agencies and local prosecutors to investigate cases. They are federal officers who carry firearms, make arrests, and serve warrants. They operate five forensic crime laboratories, which have been put to significant use during the last few years. A coordinated and intensive criminal investigation continues to focus on the anthrax-tainted letters processed through the postal service in late 2001, which resulted in the death of five people. By the end of June 2002, the FBI and the US Postal Service were offering a $2.5 million dollar reward for information leading to the arrest and conviction of the perpetrator. The investigation combines a criminal investigation with public health concerns. Additionally, pipe bombs discovered in Iowa and Illinois in rural mailboxes and injured five people occupied many agents during April 2002 until the bomber was apprehended on 7 May of that year.

CENTRAL INTELLIGENCE AGENCY/DEFENSE INTELLIGENCE AGENCY/NATIONAL SECURITY AGENCY

The Director of the Central Intelligence Agency (CIA) is the manager of the CIA, the Defense Intelligence Agency (DIA), and the National Security Agency (NSA). The CIA was established in 1947 when President Truman signed into law the National Security Act. The Act tasked the Director of the Central Intelligence Agency (DCI) with coordinating the nation's intelligence activities and evaluating and disseminating intelligence that affects the security of the United States. The CIA is an independent agency. It is responsible to the President and accountable to all Americans, generally through the intelligence oversight committees of the US Congress. Specifically, the CIA's mission is to ". . . provide accurate, comprehensive and timely intelligence on national security topics and to conduct counterintelligence activities, special activities and other functions related to intelligence and national security, as directed by the President (Internet: http://www.cia.gov/cia/information/info.html).

NSA, known as the eavesdropping and code-breaking agency, collects an incredible amount of traffic everyday. Unfortunately, on 10 September 2001, it intercepted some messages from Afghanistan in Arabic referring to 11 September as "the big match" and "zero hour." They were not translated until 12 September 2001. The NSA is equipped with an amazing amount of computer power. It intercepts millions of conversations and transmissions every single day. It coordinates traffic from everything from satellites to simple listening devices. The challenge is to identify which intercepted message is of value and which can be ignored. Translation is a huge problem. Nuances, dialects, and simple familiarity among the terrorists/criminals make it difficult to correctly and appropriately understand the exact meaning of a particular conversation. It takes years of training and specialization to accomplish this and a massive artificial intelligence network in addition.

The Defense Intelligence Agency is a Department of Defense combat support agency. With over 7000 military and civilian employees worldwide, DIA is a major producer and manager of foreign military intelligence. The agency is tasked to provide military intelligence to warfighters, defense policymakers and force planners, in the Department of Defense and the Intelligence Community, in support of US military planning and operations and weapon systems acquisition.

DIA became operational on October 1, 1961 as the nation's primary producer of foreign military intelligence. The agency relies heavily on the collection of intelligence by overt means and maintains an extensive program of military attaches.

All three agencies are facing intense public scrutiny for apparently missing potential signals of a gigantic attack on American soil. The debate has sparked a discussion about revamping the intelligence community and improving coordination and information sharing inside the government. This would constitute a herculean task, especially in light of the classified nature of the information. The critical problem facing all of these agencies is the sheer volume of information that they collect. It is virtually impossible to analyze it all in a timely manner, let alone effectuate policy based on it.

▨ CONCLUSION

The coordination of all law enforcement efforts at an airport is something like choreographing an intricate dance. The same can be said of law enforcement agencies nationwide. All the players need to be working in tandem, but they might not know who the other players are or even if they are present in the airport at any particular time. On top of that, they might not know exactly what kind of case each agency is currently working on at any particular time. Airport security officers must be worked into the mix. For example, if a DEA agent is following drug trafficker and the officer is carrying a weapon, it is highly detrimental to the operation for airport security to discover the weapon, thereby exposing the agent as being law enforcement. Precise synchronization is essential regardless of the territorial proclivities of some law enforcement officials.

A significant second problem relates to the lack of communication between agencies. There is a serious laxity in disseminating information that may not relate to an immediate threat. When the agencies fail to share information, the big picture is eluded. Worse yet, when they have the information, they often do not know what to make of it. The series of events and information acquired prior to 9/11 is an unfortunate example. The FBI had been collecting information on international terrorists who were attending US flight schools to learn to fly large aircraft. However, when a Minnesota flight school alerted the FBI of a suspicious student, no bells went off. Based on the events of 9/11, it is safe to surmise that the biggest problem the United States faces is not the simple number of law enforcement personnel on the job, but rather to which organization they belong and where they are deployed. The greatest difficulty is communication. They must learn to overcome the bureaucratic tendency to protect territory and not share databases; in short, multiple agencies that really are not working together.

Additionally, this chapter does not begin to detail all of the counterterrorist units deployed around the world. However, it is meant at least to recognize the most famous ones and to reemphasize some of their successes. Some have been exceptionally productive. Budget restraints have the power to erode the overall effectiveness of these units. Airport security and local airport police cannot really begin to match the expertise of types of units discussed. Efforts to make sure they remain an instrument in the antiterrorism toolbox will be essential in the future. Complacency is the terrorist's friend.

Not enough commitment to the concept can result in flawed missions, and too much zeal can result in the loss of innocent lives. Too little training and inappropriate equipment for the task are also recipes for disaster. Last but not least, the philosophy of the use of force in retaliation is a slippery slope. The protection of the average citizen's civil liberties must be preserved. Whenever the police or the military become judge and jury, the foundations of a democratic state could be in jeopardy. Much care should be given to make sure that the terrorist hunters not become the terrorists.

chapter seven

Screening: The Last Line of Defense

■ NEWS

1. **02 November 2001**: In Miami, a federal investigator sneaked three knives past airport screeners; in Fort Lauderdale, undercover sheriff's deputies took a pocketknife and a box cutter through the airport metal detectors and x-ray machines.

2. **22 November 2001**: The baggage screening firm at Boston's Logan Airport was reinstated after being fired for hiring criminals and allowing security breaches. Argenbright argued it did not get a hearing before losing its license.

3. **26 April 2002**: The US Transportation Security Administration announced the selection of three companies to develop plans for the federal takeover of airline passenger screening.

4. **7 June 2002**: Bomb-sniffing dogs were called into JFK airport in New York after a suspicious package was found in a men's bathroom. Passengers were permitted to return to the terminal in about 20 minutes after it was discovered the package contained only electrical circuit breakers.

5. **14 June 2002**: Government officials insist they can meet congressional deadlines to put security screeners into all airports by 19 November 2002 and to subject all baggage to the security of bomb-detention devices by 31 December 2002. They declare success in November.

■ INTRODUCTION

An airport is a unique transportation center used for the landing and takeoff of aircraft. Their primary purpose is to provide transportation for passengers and also freight and US mail. Generally, an airport consists of numerous structures designed to facilitate the needs of both aircraft and passengers. Runways provide the means for aircraft to takeoff and land. Taxiways are paths the aircraft use to reach the terminal building where passengers are boarded and off-loaded. The aircraft parking area at the gates of the terminal is known as the loading apron. The terminal also contains ticket and baggage counters, vendor operations, and security operations. A control tower is usually located near the terminal where air traffic controllers coordinate the movement of aircraft and maintenance and refueling personnel. Hangers, maintenance facilities, refueling facilities, and navigational equipment complete the basic layout of an airport. Of course, airports also need to offer passenger parking. All of these areas and people must be patrolled and protected by adequate security forces.

Because airports are among the busiest transportation centers in the world, the unhindered continuation of operations is vital to the world economy. In the United States alone, over 500 airports provide services to over 500 million passengers every year. These airports also move over 9 million metric tons of air cargo. Some economists estimate the total annual economic impact on the nation to be approximately $600 billion dollars annually. Ensuring the safety of all these passengers, freight, and personnel is a crucial part of airport operations. The Transportation Security Administration (TSA) requires that airports provide security measures to ensure the safety of everyone and everything involved. Most passengers are generally aware that security personnel operate metal detectors and x-ray machines that screen baggage for possible weapons or, serendipitously, illegal substances. Air carriers now also require that each passenger show photo identification before entering an aircraft. However, the job of providing overall security to an airport entails a great deal more.

As stated previously, air carriers, in conjunction with the TSA, routinely exercise 100-percent screening of all passengers and carry-on baggage, and were supposed to be able to screen all cargo by December 2002. The main terminal is one of the primary security challenges of security officials. Initially, there were three general security concepts for the physical arrangements of the main terminal facility: (1) the sterile concourse, (2) the sterile boarding area, and (3) departure gate screening.

As discussed, the courts have consistently upheld the reasonableness of subjecting anyone who travels on an airplane to a search by a metal detector and

A female screener checks a male traveler with a handheld metal detector at a security checkpoint. The quality and capabilities of all metal detectors have continued to improve since their standard incorporation into airport security practice. *Jack Hollingsworth / Getty Images, Inc.—Photodisc.*

their baggage by x-rays before the person is allowed to board the airplane. The rationale is simply explained in one case and provides that:

1. It is necessary to prevent hijackings and bombings.
2. The passenger "consents" to the search.
3. The intrusion is administratively limited only to a search for weapons and explosives. *US* vs. *Biswell*, 406 US 311 (1972). The questions related to the best way to conduct the searches, by what method, where, and for how long were to be determined by trial and error by airlines and airport operators alike. Recently, even the luggage manufacturers have gotten into the mix. Samsonite's engineers, immediately after 9/11, were working on a bag that doubles as a seat for those caught in airport security lines. After being notified that passengers would only be allowed one carry-on item and a

personal item, the company came up with an overnight bag with a sturdy pouch that can carry a laptop.

TSA 49 CFR Chapter XII, Part 1540.107, formerly, Section 107.20, relates to submission by travelers to the screening process. It specifically states, "No person may enter a sterile area without submitting to the screening and inspection of his or her person and property in accordance with the procedures being applied to control access to that area" (Internet: http://ccfr.access.gpo.gov/otcgi/cgr, 19 June 2002, Pg. 1). The process of screening is subject to many restrictions, and security personnel have perfected the most expeditious method of processing passengers, accompanying friends, family, vendors, and airline employees through the procedures. The TSA monitors the screening on a regular basis. Even though it has been criticized heavily, the process is currently serving a basic public need. Any process can always be improved, and the TSA will continue to make adjustments to policies and procedures as needed.

As a result of 9/11, a 19 November 2002 deadline was established for the federal government to assume the responsibilities for screening at airports. In April 2002, the TSA announced that three companies were selected to develop plans for the takeover. Fluor Enterprises, Inc., Hensel Phelps Construction Co., and Lockheed Martin Corporation were to receive $8.9 million for the plans. Each company was tasked to design plans for replacing the private screener at checkpoints with an all-federal work force. The TSA reviewed the plans and selected one of the companies, Lockheed Martin Systems, to implement it. The company and the TSA were all working under a congressionally mandated 19 November 2002 deadline for the complete replacement of employees. Unfortunately, in haste, the security of airports may still be at risk for many reasons.

■ THE FACILITIES

Sterile Concourse

The sterile concourse establishes an area to which access is controlled by the inspection of persons and property in accordance with an approved security program. Passengers have come to accept this as the normal course of business in an airport. At most US airports, security operations are located at a central screening point at the central access point to a concourse that serves several gates. This negates the need for airport authorities to bear the costs of maintaining security personnel at each gate or to station a law enforcement officer at each gate. This simple change of location from the gate to the choke point before the concourse entrance eventually made the practicality of x-ray machines to search baggage practical. Previously, the cost of an x-ray machine at each gate was a severely costly proposition. X-ray screening only became practical with the improvement of technology and the increase in number of businesses manufacturing them.

Now all sorts of x-ray machines and walk-through or hand-held metal detectors have resulted in a tremendous economy of equipment and personnel. Fewer

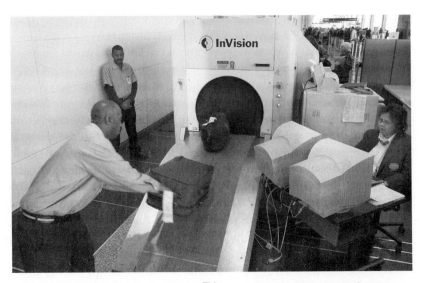

Baggage is sent through an InVision™ scanner at Washington's Ronald Reagan National Airport in 2002. A law went into effect in December 2003 requiring that all cargo, both domestic and international, be checked for explosives by use of a myriad number of detection devices and techniques. *AP/Wide World Photos.*

pieces of equipment and, more importantly, the need to employ fewer people to operate them, has arguably furnished the greatest savings. Cost-related problems have, however, resurfaced with the high cost of explosive detection systems and the requirement to screen all checked baggage by the end of 2002. The future process will likely be based on a combination of processes to include the use of trace detection equipment and manual searches. It has become clear that airport baggage areas, not the ticket counters, provide a better venue for the location of the newly mandated explosive-detection equipment. This will require extensive renovations to some airports. However, placing the explosive-detection equipment in the baggage area makes the screening invisible to the passenger and eliminates unnecessary congestion at the check-in and passenger screening points. This sequence has become part of the normal process of transferring the baggage from the ticket counter to the airplane.

Improvements made during the initial years of implementation of the rules also greatly increased the distance between the screening checkpoint and the boarding gate. Should an individual attempt to smuggle weapons or explosives, their physical presence is a good distance from the gate. This clearly provides a benefit to security personnel and law enforcement agents, who are afforded the advantage of time and distance. The potential hijacker is deterred from attempting to storm the aircraft directly and gives authorities some precious time and geography to prevent it.

Sometimes the checkpoint screening procedures fail to work. In spite of years of perfecting the screening of all passengers, people who are in possession of dangerous contraband are able to slip by undetected. Some of those people who side step security are in a hurry, some are evading the security, and some are inspectors testing the procedures. For example, outgoing flights at the Minneapolis/St. Paul Airport in July 2001 were grounded for about an hour. The airport police conducted a search for a man who bypassed a checkpoint after ticketing and before reaching the sterile concourse and gates. The police failed to locate the man, and a regular flight schedule was resumed after airlines were pressured for the continuation of operations. Had he been a terrorist, a catastrophe could have occurred.

A number of breakdowns to the system contributed to the incident. It was reported that a security officer failed to follow the man who walked pass the metal detectors and also failed to report it to the airport police to seek assistance for a full 20 minutes. Additionally, the surveillance camera installed at this particular checkpoint, which could have given an image of the man, did not have any film in it. Even though nothing seems to have come of the incident as stated, the threat could have been consequential ("Security Breach at Airport," Internet: http://www.kstp.com/index.cfm?viewer, 3 July 2001).

The simple movement of passenger and baggage screening to a central point has contributed other advantages, some directly to the airlines. Predeparture screening is accomplished gradually as passengers arrive at the terminal rather than being delayed until the aircraft is prepared to depart. This hugely cuts back on the annoyance factor to passengers. The quantities of passengers and visitors who must be processed each day are spread out. They are permitted to arrive at the airport gauging in advance the time they will need to process security and arrive at the gate. The flow of passengers and accompanying public is markedly quicker, avoiding long lines just at boarding time. Once at the gate, passengers will be permitted to board the aircraft directly, giving them a sense of rapidity to the process, whether it is a true perception or not. Processing at the main terminal entrance to the concourse also prevents crowding in the concourses and around gate areas, denying a terrorist or gunman the ability to mingle with and hide in a crowd. This concept is even truer today, because only ticketed passengers may enter the sterile concourse.

When first initiated, airport managers considered the main disadvantage to this arrangement as being the floor space needed to accommodate the equipment and personnel. However, the other advantages mentioned above soon became self-evident. Thereafter, make-shift screening facilities were turned into permanent better-arranged security operations. The only unhappy people at the time were vendors and concessionaires, who thought that the choke-point screening would somehow adversely affect sales. Their worries proved to be unfounded, and screening at the entrance to the concourse has become a bedrock element of airport planners. In addition, vendors have flourished on both sides of the screening checkpoints. Airport terminals on both sides of the security checkpoint now have everything from restaurants to retail outlets to spas. All of them need to be staffed, and all of them require the delivery of merchandise and supplies, providing an opportunity to smuggle dangerous instrumentalities into the sterile area.

Of continuing concern is the need to keep the concourse sterile. If the airport is not large enough to maintain a twenty-four–hour operation, a thorough search must be made for any weapons or dangerous objects that may have been secretly deposited during closed periods. Security personnel must conduct a very thorough search of the entire sterile area for any objects that should not be present. A cursory search is unacceptable. All restroom facilities, airport lounges, gate areas, and concessionaire operations need to be checked. This can be tedious work, but is an absolute necessity. Vast amounts of money invested in sophisticated screening equipment is useless if a weapon or dangerous device is already in the concourse readily accessible to potential terrorists who have cleared security. Bomb-sniffing dogs are an increasingly useful tool in this capacity. All airport employees should receive some minimal security training no matter how unrelated their job function within the airport complex may appear.

In order to assist in securing the sterile concourse, consideration must be given to the adequacy of physical barriers at the perimeters. Nonscreened individuals must not have easy access to the concourse. Nor should it be easy to pass

Massachusetts State Police trooper Daniel Griffin watches as his bomb-detecting dog sniffs baggage at Boston's Logan International Airport. Dogs are a critical component of any airport security management plan and offer a mobile and reliable means of explosive detection. *Susan Walsh / AP / Wide World Photos.*

dangerous items from someone outside the area to someone inside the area. Except for authorized personnel, access to the concourse must be restricted to passage through the security checkpoint. Additionally, passengers must not be permitted to have access to baggage or anything else that has not been screened. Even if someone clears security but seeks to return to the sterile concourse, they must be screened again regardless of any protestations from the passenger, vendor, or airline employee.

Also of concern is the sometimes flagrant abuse by airline employees of the door from the field to the jetway. Airline employees believe it is a major imposition to use security procedures at these entry points and other access points to the concourse. Any efforts by security personnel to protect the aircraft and aircrew from inadvertent incursion by potential hijackers or terrorists are nullified if the attackers can bypass all the screening requirements. If they can gain access at a weak airfield perimeter point and walk into the jetway or other access door with hostile intentions, security has failed. Airline personnel are also notoriously guilty of opening a door to a restricted area and permitting someone else to piggyback, so to speak, onto their entrance credentials.

Sterile Boarding Areas

A second option available to airport planners and security was the sterile boarding area or sterile holding area at the gate. Once passengers completed flight check and were screened, they would be isolated from physical contact with persons outside the area. Constructing these isolated sanctuaries presented challenges. Often the areas were relatively small and, if the waiting period was extended, they became confining and were difficult to make attractive and keep well ventilated. Passengers were not pleased with the arrangements, and the costs could be prohibitive. Admittedly, timing was critical for the advantage of screening passengers arriving at the boarding gate rather than after an aircraft was available for loading. Regardless, many European and non-Western airports have determined this method of screening to be suitable for their purposes. Some high-threat airports even have instituted double-screening procedures. The passenger is screened before entering the concourse and again before being permitted into a sterile waiting area. This prohibits passengers from acquiring a weapon or dangerous materials from someone already in the sterile concourse but outside the gate boarding area.

Departure Gate Screening

Many security professionals consider departure gate screening the least desirable of the available alternatives. This option requires personnel to be available for screening at each individual gate, and the operating authority originally had also to provide a law enforcement officer at each gate. Consequently, personnel costs are significantly higher than under the other choices. In addition, passenger screening does not usually begin until the aircraft is actually available for loading. Because of the costs involved and the timing restrictions, this method is only practical for small airports. Making restroom facilities readily available at each gate was also a cost consideration.

This method is enhanced if storage areas can be built to prescreen carry-on baggage. Passengers can then pick up their prescreened carry-on items after they pass through the walk-through weapons detectors. However, women's purses should never be prescreened. The potential for excessive complaints of theft are likely to abound. The same precaution applies to any carry-on baggage which a passenger claims holds valuables. Furthermore, the presence of valuables should never be revealed to other passengers. Owing to potential lawsuits and extensive costs, the prescreening method is often found to be impractical. Another drawback is that the protection of time and distance evaporates. Any potential hostile terrorists are already at the gate and very close to the aircraft.

■ SCREENING CHECKPOINT AUGMENTATION

Since the first prescreening procedures came into effect, many improvements have been made. Not only have technological enhancements to the equipment been accomplished but procedural controls have been developed which have improved the process. For example, some screening checkpoints have control booths constructed behind them, which are raised above the floor for better visibility. The control booth usually has a duplicate set of monitors so that whatever the primary screener is viewing can be double-checked by a supervisor. A two-way communication system provides constant dialogue between the control booth and the screening operation. This second set of eyes increases the effectiveness of the screening.

Many of the control booths also have the capability of videotaping the activities taking place at the checkpoint. At the first sign of trouble, taping can document and protect the professional conduct of the operator. Any accusations by a passenger or visitors of inappropriate conduct on the part of security can be easily disproved. The supervisor in the booth should also have the capability of viewing the screening procedures at other gates and other x-ray machines by use of closed circuit TV (CCTV). Any attempt by someone seeking to distract security at one checkpoint while accomplices rush a second checkpoint can be more easily thwarted. Additionally, because supervisors can view screening at other gates and other x-ray machines, supervisors are more capable of monitoring the effectiveness of their employees while also engaging in security prevention themselves.

The addition of CCTV monitors at checkpoints is another effective enhancement tool. These monitors should televise the view from the cameras monitoring the line rather than the x-ray images. Placing two large-screen color monitors directly adjacent to screening points and allowing passengers in line to view themselves and each other deters misconduct. As discussed, should a difficult incident occur, the entire activity can be taped for later review or be used in any appropriate criminal or civil prosecution. The monitors also give law enforcement personnel the ability to assess an ongoing situation prior to entering the scene. Improvements in the quality of the picture have also improved the overall usefulness of this tool. A security professional in a central control booth can literally monitor the entire airport.

■ LAW ENFORCEMENT OFFICERS AT THE GATE

When Part 107.4 (former FARs) was originally drafted, it required the presence of at least one law enforcement officer at each gate, because the screening was taking place at the gate. Specifically, the regulations stated a law enforcement officer must be present:

> At the point, and prior to and throughout, the final passenger screening process prior to boarding, for each flight conducted by a certificate holder. . . . continuously until all doors on the aircraft being boarded are closed and the aircraft has taxied away from the boarding area; and in the event that the aircraft returns to the boarding area before take-off.

On 1 April 1981, the FARs were amended as Sec 107.15 to state:

> Each airport operator shall provide law enforcement officers in the numbers and in a manner adequate to support
> 1. Its security program; and
> 2. Each passenger screening system required by Part 108 or Sec 129.25 of this chapter.

49 CFR Chapter XII Part 1544.217 now requires each airport operator to arrange for law enforcement personnel meeting the qualifications and standards specified in Section 1544.21 and provide its employees current information regarding procedures for obtaining law enforcement assistance at that airport.

The first rule, FAR 107.4, was originally interpreted to require a law enforcement officer's presence during the entire process of prescreening. The responsibility for overseeing the presence of the law enforcement officer rested with the airport operator. The carriers would often suspend screening of passengers until an officer was on the scene even though nothing in the regulation prevented the airline from continuing the processing of passengers. Problems arose when a passenger could not be cleared for unaccountable metal on their person. Airlines did not want nonsecurity-trained personnel to conduct a pat-down search of passengers. The only alternative was to deny the passenger access to the aircraft. This did not endear the airline to the paying passenger.

Another area of conflict revolved around who was responsible for the added costs of such a law enforcement presence. The debate is still ongoing, especially with law enforcement officers now assuming some of the duties temporarily conducted by the National Guard to give the appearance of beefed-up security. Previously, some small communities even attempted to present the airlines with a bill. Today, they can apply to the federal government for reimbursement. Everyone was in favor of a safer airport environment, but no one wanted to bear the burden of the additional costs. Compromises had to take place, and eventually the Airport Operators Council International (AOIC) contributed to ironing out many of these issues. One of the successes of the later Air Carrier Standard Security Program (ACSSP) covered the negotiations regarding legitimate expenses attributable to the airlines and subsequent assessments as to the need for implementation of new concepts with corresponding new costs. The debate still rages.

Eventually, it became obvious that the presence of law enforcement officers at each gate was not only not cost effective but did not contribute to better security. After a trial and error period, it was soon discovered that the armed officer could even prove to be a liability being stationed so close to the actual aircraft.

Two incidents proved the point. A law enforcement officer assigned to the Baltimore airport on 22 February 1974 was positioned at a gate screening point for Delta Flight 523. Samuel Joseph Byck was armed and approached the gate. He drew his weapon and without any warning shot the police officer and entered the cockpit whereupon he shot and killed the copilot and wounded the pilot in command. After announcing his plan to fly the aircraft into the White House, he was eventually shot, but succeeded in committing suicide while still on the aircraft. The law enforcement presence at the gate failed to stop the attacker, and after the death and incapacitation of the officer, gave the attacker free and quick access to the aircraft.

Another example of the wisdom of not having an officer at the gate took place in Nebraska a few years later. In October 1977, a lone gunman casually approached the law enforcement officer at the gate of a Frontier Airlines flight. He removed a shotgun from his carry-on luggage and rapidly disarmed the police officer. After boarding the flight, he ultimately shot himself. The incident contributed to the discussion regarding the proper placement of officers within the airport complex. It was finally determined that the millions of dollars being spent to station these officers could be better spent elsewhere.

■ FLEXIBLE LAW ENFORCEMENT RESPONSE PROGRAM

The solution was named after the post-Vietnam military concept of flexible response as opposed to conventional response. Under this system, an officer was not required to be at the screening checkpoint at all. They were tasked with having to be able to arrive at the checkpoint within a given response time. The airlines were thereby somewhat assured that an officer would arrive and the police were relieved of the burden of stationing an officer at each gate. In a realistic move, the FAA was not requiring a "guaranteed" response time. The police needed some flexibility in case of multiple requests for assistance and other emergency situations. This greatly reduced the number of officers that communities had to assign to an airport. At Washington's Reagan Airport, authorities initiated the first flexible response program ironically on 11 September 1981, and the number of law enforcement officers was immediately reduced from 51 to 17.

The exact response times for each airport are part of the Air Carrier Standard Security Program, but they are not available to the public for obvious reasons.

Catering to the important public perception, the program was originally named the Strengthened Screening Point Security Program (SSPS). Few airlines or security professionals wanted to send the signal to the traveling public that it was based primarily on cost reductions. In reality, it was cost effective, but that was only the positive by-product of a legitimate security need to give the police the advantage of time and distance to the gate.

Note: *The categories of airports are generally broken down based on the number of passengers that transit the airport annually.*

Airport Categories

Category X—Any number of passengers. The designation is based on the need for special attention due to the perceived threat.

Category I—More than 2 million travelers

Category II—500,000 to 2 million travelers

Category III—Less than 500,000 travelers

Category IV—Any number of travelers

Category V—No screening

The Flexible Response Program also created the position of a Checkpoint Security Supervisor (CSS). This individual was to take over many of the functions of the law enforcement officers previously stationed at each gate. The individual was to receive special training and was to have a more extensive security background than the average contract security officer. At minimum, they were to have at least three years of prior law enforcement or private security experience. It is important to note that although it was the responsibility of the airport to provide the law enforcement officer, it was the airline carrier's duty to hire and train this "screener-in charge." The CSS, or the new equivalent substitute to the position, can use the acronym VETO.

Verify the credentials of any law enforcement officers who claim the need to board an aircraft with a weapon.

Evaluate the need to assemble law enforcement officers or station management if required.

Timely conduct pat downs and searches as required.

Organize responses to false statements by passengers, faulty communications equipment, and general supervisory duties.

Similarly, the 49 CFR Chapter XII, Section 1544.215 requires a designated Aircraft Operator Security Coordinator (AOSC). The AOSC must be designated in the airport security program. The individual appointed AOSC, or an alternate, must be available twenty-four hours a day, and is supposed to serve as the airport's primary contact for security-related activities and communications with the TSA.

■ PUBLIC AND PRIVATE SECURITY INTERFACE

The general purpose of any private security is to protect assets and people. Airport security personnel are present to create nonthreatening environments in which passengers, accompanying family and friends, employees, and airline personnel are able to conduct their business in a nonthreatening environment. All security people who work within the airport environment should be able to recognize the differences between the private "policing" function and that of the public police. In the airport, those differences are becoming more blurred, making it difficult to distinguish between those boundaries that have traditionally defined the roles of the public sector versus airport security personnel. The same overlapping parameters relate to individual versus institutional responsibilities. The most important difference relies on the fact the police can use force, whereas private security, whether contract or federal, possesses power which really relies only on persuasion.

Security personnel usually wear some distinctive clothing so they can be easily identified even from a distance. They are distinctly different than police uniforms. However, a police officer is generally armed, in uniform, and wears an insignia and badge of his or her profession. All are easily recognizable, but their responsibilities and authority are quite different. Various situations compel the expertise of both, and both need to be appreciated for the added value they bring to the overall security picture.

Airport security and local law enforcement must work in conjunction with each other in an assortment of situations. Most notable are situations when an individual threatens or attempts to board and aircraft with a dangerous weapon. The Federal Aviation Act, implemented by Section 1540.111, makes it illegal to attempt to board an aircraft while having a concealed weapon on or about one's person or a deadly or dangerous weapon in any carry-on baggage. The regulations require that passengers discovered to be carrying an undeclared weapon must be referred to a police officer. However, before that officer is ever summoned to the scene, an airport security officer makes independent decisions everyday about what exactly constitutes a dangerous weapon.

Almost anything can be used as a weapon. Swiss Army knives, knitting needles, and scissors are all dangerous in the wrong hands. The original emergency order requiring 100-percent screening of all passengers and carry-on luggage provided in part, "The certificate holder shall not permit any passenger to board its aircraft unless the carry-on baggage items are inspected to detect weapons, explosives, or other dangerous objects." What the term *dangerous weapon* encompasses is open to much dispute. Generally, the term should encompass any device or object that if its possession alone supports a reasonable presumption that it could be used as a weapon. Each decision is a matter of judgment, especially since most airlines previously provided first-class passengers with a metal knife during meals. An incident in December 1996 proves the point.

A 32-year old Algerian with an expired visa boarded a DC-10 from Detroit to Frankfurt, Germany, and about four hours from arrival, attacked a flight attendant by choking her and screaming "to Africa." The stewardess escaped, and then he attacked a female passenger yelling "whore" repeatedly. He had concealed his dinner knife in a blanket, and was extremely intoxicated after consuming another passenger's bottle of duty-free liquor. Military police on board subdued and restrained the subject, who grappled with them for several hours. The meal service had to be canceled in the back of the aircraft due to the passengers' excrement, which contaminated the aft food service area. Several crew members sustained minor injuries, and some military police uniforms were ruined. The subject became extremely violent, appearing insane and out of control during the entire incident. He was apparently trying to hijack the aircraft, but was too intoxicated to consummate the act of taking a hostage and getting control of the flight. Upon arrival in Frankfurt, the captain was denied the courtesy of discussing the matter with the police, and the subject was released without prosecution by the German authorities after three hours (Internet: http://www.alpa.org/internet/tm/tm061198.htm, 22 April 2001, Pg. 2). Even though current policy requires "plastic knives" in first class, all the passenger needs to do is grab a wine bottle, break it, and use it as a weapon.

In 1986, FAR 107.21 was amended to substitute the words "deadly or dangerous weapon" for the word "firearm." The previous regulation had stated, "No person may have a firearm, an explosive, or an incendiary device on or about the individual's person or accessible property when presenting himself or herself for screening or when entering or in a sterile area." The broadened definition permits security officials to make a determination as to what could be considered as dangerous on board an aircraft. They can evaluate the article itself and the demeanor of the individual possessing it. The regulation was amended to state, "No person may have explosive, incendiary, or *deadly or dangerous* weapons on or about the individual's person or accessible property." What exactly constitutes a dangerous weapon is often difficult to surmise. However, horror stories abound of taking nail clippers from airline pilots and knitting needles from grandmothers. Section 1540.11 now simply provides, ". . . an individual may not have a weapon, explosive, or incendiary on or about the individual's person or accessible property."

Note: *The provisions of this section with respect to firearms do not apply to the following:*

(1) *Law enforcement personnel required to carry a firearm or other weapons while in the performance of law enforcement duties at the airport.*

(2) *An individual authorized to carry a weapon in accordance with 1544.219, 1544.231, 1544.223 or 1544.211.*

(3) *An individual authorized to carry a weapon in a sterile area under a security program.*

According to Harbor Police Dispatch records, approximately 6687 armed peace officers entered the passenger boarding areas of San Diego Lindbergh Field in 2001. Their purpose was assumed to be official. Before entering the passenger areas, armed officers are required to present their documents and departmental identification to the airline and later to security. However, prior to 9/11, using false identification, FAA officials succeeded in breaching security around the nation on repeated occasions. Currently, security personnel receive no special training in the recognition of valid credentials. Department ID cards often vary in style and appearance, and improvements in technology make the duplication of documents much easier than before. This issue needs to be addressed when devising training materials for new screeners.

CRIMINAL CASE LAW EXAMPLES

US vs. James Edward Ware

United States District Court, Western District of Oklahoma, August 1970   This early case discusses whether the weapon in question was deadly or dangerous. The case ultimately determined that an unloaded .25-caliber automatic pistol in a passenger's pocket did constitute a dangerous weapon under 49 USC Section 1472 (1). Once again, the court confirmed that the primary purpose of this section is to prevent the hijacking of commercial aircraft, and it has been demonstrated many times that an aircraft can be hijacked with an unloaded gun.

The court held that the unloaded gun in question was indeed dangerous and prohibited by statute. The case set the stage for countless cases involving such "dangerous weapons" as toy guns, knitting needles, and large scissors. Generally, a dangerous weapon definition should include any firearm, whether loaded or unloaded, or any device designed as a weapon capable of producing death or great bodily harm. Additional thought should be given to adding language pertaining to combustible material or flammable liquid and any other device or instrument that, in the manner it is used or intended to be used, is calculated or likely to produce death or bodily harm.

US vs. Feldman

US District Court, Eastern District of New York, 1 May 1969   This case deals with the constitutionality of a law that imposes only a civil as opposed to a criminal penalty for falsely reporting a bomb at an air navigation facility. The court held that the statute was constitutional under the commerce clause of the US Constitution. The government argued that the elimination of all false bomb reports at airports was crucial to the safety of all air navigation. The legislative history of the law specifically cited its purpose is to eliminate the disruption of interstate commerce arising from the conduct of pranksters and jokesters.

The defendant moved to dismiss the complaint for failure to state a cause of action, and the government sought summary judgment. The defense considered this section to be unconstitutionally vague. The defendant was charged under 18 USCA Section 35 (a). The purpose of the new law, HR 6848, was to reduce the existing penalty against pranksters who falsely report the presence of bombs and the like aboard aircraft and who have no real evil intent or malice in mind. However, the court supported the contention that such comments, no matter how innocuous, must be prohibited. Their holding in the case concluded that 18 USC Section 35 (a) is clearly constitutional, and the court order denied the defendant's motion for summary judgment.

US vs. Benrus Eugene Brown

United States District Court, Western District of Texas, October 1969   In this unusual case, the court tackled the concept of what actually constitutes a dangerous weapon and the threshold of what constitutes an attempt to board an aircraft with a dangerous weapon. Generally, the court held that an unlawful attempt to board an aircraft while carrying a concealed weapon was made when the air passenger surrendered his or her ticket at the customer service agent's desk and entered the departure lounge for the flight covered by the ticket. The court also determined that statements elicited from the passenger by the arresting airport security guard were inadmissible as evidence. However, the portions of the ticket held by the passenger and the customer service representative as well as the weapon removed from the person of the passenger were admissible.

The defendant pled not guilty to knowingly, willfully, and unlawfully attempting to board an aircraft being operated by an air carrier involved in air transportation at the San Antonio International Airport while having on or about his person a concealed, deadly, and dangerous weapon—to wit a .22-caliber weapon. The defendant was charged under Title 49 USC Sec 1472. The court determined there were three main issues at trial.

1. Did the acts of the defendant constitute an attempt to board an aircraft?
2. Were statements made by the defendant at the time of his arrest admissible in view of the fact that he was not given any warnings under the rule in *Miranda vs. Arizona*?
3. Was the evidence obtained from him as the result of an unlawful search and seizure?

There is no question that the guard fully intended to take him into custody in order to determine the presence of a gun. The defendant was under arrest when the security guard began to question him in the departure lounge and that arrest was lawful. When a person is lawfully arrested, the officer has the right, without a search warrant, to make a contemporaneous search of the person of the accused for the fruits of or in the instrumentality's used to commit the crime. Consequently, the gun and the ticket components were admissible at trial. *Agnello* vs. *US*, 269 U.S. 20, 1925. The court also reasoned that he had in fact attempted to board the aircraft.

Lawrence Havelock vs. *the United States*

United States Court of Appeals, Tenth Circuit, June 1970   This particular case provides a case study on circumstantial evidence as well as illustrating an arson attempt on board an aircraft. The circumstances supported a passenger's conviction for willfully setting fire to an aircraft while in flight. The circumstantial evidence consisted of a variety of nondirect evidence. The prosecution introduced documentation concerning his demeanor during the entire flight and particularly prior to and subsequent to a fire in the restroom. They also offered his statements to other passengers, his bizarre behavior in wearing yellow gloves and the attempt to secret them, and the fact that he was the last visitor to the restroom prior to the ignition of the incendiary fire. The court also saw fit to permit the admission into evidence of similar acts, which evidenced intent or scheme, while they determined that these statements were not unnecessarily prejudicial. Mr. Havelock was convicted of setting fire to an aircraft in flight while being operated in interstate commerce.

Even evidence that is slightly prejudicial does not necessarily require a reversal. Courts have repeatedly held that not every error occurring during a trial requires reversal—only errors which affect substantial rights are prejudicial and worthy of reversal. In order to prove the defendant willfully set fire to the aircraft, the definition is well settled. Willful conduct consists of acts which are intentional and accomplished with an awareness of what one is doing. The prior acts must be similar in results, and there must be such a concurrence of common features that the various acts are naturally to be explained as caused by a general plan of which they are the individual manifestations. The sum of the total evidence illustrates sufficient fundamental features of a scheme that culminated in the fire aboard the aircraft to be admissible at the trial. Consequently, the conviction was affirmed on appeal.

Case Law Summary

All of these cases illustrate some aspect of criminal misconduct within the airline industry. Any crime that can be committed on the ground can be committed in an airport or on an aircraft. The law literally is exactly the same. The same constitutional protections apply and the same evidentiary issues come into play. The same safeguards imposed on police officers and private security guards are also applicable.

However, legislators have passed additional laws making it a crime to interfere with the aircrew, board an aircraft with a weapon or dangerous instrument, board an aircraft intoxicated, and of course, it is a crime to hijack the aircraft. Screening of people and baggage is the only way to determine whether individuals are attempting to commit some of these prohibited acts or possess the means to do so. Much litigation has been generated regarding what is a "dangerous weapon," what constitutes and "attempt to board an aircraft," and even what can constitute a criminal act versus a civil tort and what specific evidence can be used to convict someone of a crime. Even though it is not possible or desirable to turn security professionals into constitutional/criminal lawyers, it is important that they possess a basic understanding of the rules so that they can appropriately apply them.

▎INITIAL SCREENING

Everyone who has ever flown is familiar with the first safety question asked the traveler by the airlines for security reasons. Did you pack your bag yourself? Many security directors question the utility of the practice, and most travelers do not take it seriously anymore. Homer Boynton, the former Director of Security of American Airlines repeatedly claimed the question has become perfunctory and was no longer worthwhile. Admittedly, most travelers have learned to lie casually and basically ignore the question. When John Tierney, a reporter for the *New York Times*, tested the question, his bags were subjected to increased security. The official position of the TSA was better safe than sorry.

Unfortunately, there is some credibility to the concept that the question serves no real security purpose. The TSA continued to justify the policy for awhile, because bombs are still being discovered in baggage. However, the only domestic incident occurred in 1955 when a son packed his mother's bag and included a highly lethal incendiary device in order to murder her and collect insurance money. Consequently, the regulation has survived for all these years long after the original justification has faded. The TSA finally removed the requirement in August 2002.

▎SCREENING PROCEDURES

Screening procedures at the entrance to the sterile concourse have repeatedly come under close scrutiny. The FAA, and its parent agency, the Department of Transportation, had been internally reviewed by the Inspector General (IG) on the status of airport security numerous times. The results have not always been very favorable regarding the conduct of contract security personnel at airport concourse checkpoints. The IG conducted a survey in 1993 in which it discovered numerous security flaws at several US airports, especially at four major airports. According to one report, ". . . in the 1993 investigation, agents were able to pass the screening points at all four airports, and in 75% of the attempts, were able to actually board planes with the "bombs" in their carry-on luggage, as well as accessing ramp-side areas, where the planes parked" (Jim Fay, "FAA Downplays Former IG's Report on Airport Security Flaws: Reports Suppressed?", Internet: http://www.emergency.com/arprtrpt.htm., 8 Aug 2001). A follow-up survey three years later indicated that FAA agents still had access to sterile areas 40 percent of the time. Consequently, 4 out of every 10 passengers could be carrying some sort of contraband. Security procedures are very good at intercepting most contraband; however, 100 percent complete and totally accurate security has yet to be obtained and likely never will. Currently, security is better than previously but far from without flaws. There remains room for improvement in spite of recent changes.

Of course, there is no good substitute for simple good judgment. No matter how many times employees are taught proper procedures, what appears to be an exception to every rule is frequently going to happen. Unfortunately, common sense is difficult, if not impossible, to teach. Therefore, extensive, continuous, and repetitive training is an absolute necessity. Effective November 2001, all airport screeners were supposed to be required minimally to have a high school diploma and undergo government-approved training under a new federal aviation administration. The rule has been proved to be more difficult to implement totally than originally hoped.

Generally, the airport security officer will handle thousands of routine situations on a daily basis. Consequently, certain scenarios will repeat themselves, and all security personnel should be thoroughly trained on exactly how to handle them. When questions do arise, a supervisor should be called and consulted. Everyone should be encouraged to exercise caution and to think through each situation and not to simply react to it. Under no circumstances should a passenger be allowed beyond the screening point unless screening personnel are assured that the passenger is not carrying any dangerous objects. Such negligence can have serious consequences.

On July 2000, an x-ray screener at the San Francisco International Airport actually spotted a handgun, yet still allowed the passenger to proceed. He later notified the police, and several gate areas had to be shut down while 800 people and their baggage were searched. Both a Delta and a Northwest flight were delayed for quite a long period of time (ASI, *Airwise*, Internet: http://www.asi.com, 8 August 2001). In the alternative, random selection of individuals is giving the appearance that security is blatantly ineffective. For example, Al Gore, former Vice-President, in June 2002, was randomly selected for screening while other maybe more likely individuals were not. Such high-profile "apparently unnecessary" screening only deters from the real job at hand and sends the wrong signal to the public and the terrorists.

Of course, arrest situations based on probable cause should be left to the appropriate law enforcement personnel. It is neither desirable nor effective to have security personnel attempt to engage in law enforcement duties, especially when life-threatening conduct is involved. Police officers are part of a governmental enterprise better equipped to combat crime and enforce laws as well as apprehend offenders. Most importantly, they possess the statutory authority to do so. Ultimately, however, it is always wise to remember that, assuming the passenger poses no threat to the aircraft or other passengers, the final decision for boarding an aircraft still rests with the airline, not the security officer or law enforcement official. Unless, as mentioned, a dangerous situation exists where the individual involved is being arrested, all authority must indeed shift to law enforcement.

Note: *Private security officers really have no more powers than private citizens. As citizens, they certainly have the power to arrest, to investigate, and to defend themselves and to defend their own property and any property entrusted to their care. However, they have no police authority.*

There are also rare situations in which local law enforcement may clear a passenger for boarding but the airline still does not want to board them. For example, situations may arise when a passenger may have had too much to drink or even just smell offensive. They may not have broken any laws, and yet the airline may not consider them to be appropriate passengers. The government may fine the airline for boarding an intoxicated passenger even though not all intoxicated passengers are hostile or noisy and consequently obvious to identify. Airlines have different procedures in dealing with the intoxicated, offensive passenger or pregnant passengers near full term. The final decision actually rests with the pilot. Federal Aviation Regulation 91.3a states that, ". . . the pilot in command of an aircraft is directly responsible for and is the final authority as to the operation of the aircraft." The pilot can refuse to board anyone considered detrimental to flight. The actual policies regarding specific types of passengers will vary from airline to airline. The rule was put to the test when an American Airlines pilot refused to board an armed "Arab-American" secret service agent on 25 December 2001. The pilot felt that the agent did not have the proper credentials in his possession and, even though it was the second time the agent had been boarded, in accordance with airline policy, they refused to board him (Rule: 49 CFR Chapter XII, Section 1544.201).

The FAA required that airlines screen all passengers and carry-on baggage. Specifically, FAR Sec 315 (a) stated that, "all passengers and all property intended to be carried in the aircraft cabin in air transportation must be screened by weapon detecting procedures or facilities employed or operated by employees or agents of the air carrier." TSA regulation Section 1544.201 (b) and (e) provide that:

(b) Screening of individuals and accessible property. Except as provided in its security program, each aircraft operator must ensure that each individual entering a sterile area at each pre-board screening checkpoint for which it is responsible, and all accessible property under that individual's control, are inspected for weapons, explosives and incendiaries as provided in Sec 1544.207.

(e) Staffing. Each aircraft operator must staff its security screening checkpoints with supervisory and non-supervisory personnel in accordance with the standards specified in its security program.

Today, the screening is accomplished through the use of metal detectors, x-ray machines, and residue-detection equipment; all calling for airport security personnel as operators. Security personnel must remain proficient in screening all sorts of people and objects, constantly adapting to new technology as well. Screening both passengers and baggage has now become commonplace in airports all over the world, but training on explosive-detection equipment and trace-detection equipment requires sophisticated and specialized protocols. Clearly, the system is not foolproof. For example, in May 2002, the FBI labeled a man clearing security in New Orleans Louis Armstrong Airport with two loaded handguns as a "massive failure."

■ SCREENING BAGGAGE

The rules pertaining to the screening of carry-on baggage are clear. The original legislation in the Federal Aviation Act of 1958, Section 3 as amended, provided that to the maximum extent possible, the FAA administrator was mandated to require uniform procedures for the inspection, detention, and search of persons and property in air transportation and intrastate air transportation. The current rules are meant to prevent or deter the carriage aboard airplanes of any explosive, incendiary, or deadly or dangerous weapon on or about an individual's person or accessible property. The TSA defines carry-on luggage as all accessible property under that individual's control. Any articles on the person of the passenger will be subject to search by means of a walk-through or hand-held metal detector. In spite of the extensive public awareness of security screening at airports, it is surprising the number of people who either purposely or inadvertently break the law. Baggage can be screened physically by use of x-ray equipment or newer explosive-detection equipment and/or trace-detection systems. The number of weapons confiscated each year are alarming but somewhat explainable.

It must be remembered that law enforcement officers or hunters going on vacation inadvertently violate the rules when they do not clear their weapons with the airlines in advance. Additionally, some were in the possession of citizens who were violating the law, but had no real intention of hijacking an aircraft or assaulting passengers as part of a political movement. Some even claimed to be bodyguards of celebrities or individuals maintaining they needed to protect themselves. Similar to the argument relating to the exclusionary rule and the Fourth Amendment, it is hard statistically to analyze how many terrorists choose not to attack an airport or hijack an aircraft because of the procedures in place.

The proper procedure, if a weapon is detected, is to stop the x-ray machine to keep the baggage away from the passenger. It makes no sense to return the baggage to the passenger so that the weapon could be accessible to them. If discovered by a metal detector, the passenger should be asked to permit the security official or a law enforcement officer to confiscate the weapon. Under no circumstances should security personnel attempt forcibly to take the weapon. Nor should the passenger be allowed to retrieve the weapon and possibly take that opportunity to use it against security personnel or other passengers. Airport security personnel should cooperate fully with anyone brandishing a weapon. Subduing such an individual needs to be accomplished by a trained law enforcement officer.

An even more frequent scenario for screening personnel involves the potential discovery of large sums of currency or illegal drugs. The airlines do not wish to be placed in a position of law enforcement, and these situations are handled in a number of ways depending on the circumstances. It is an interesting piece of trivia that $1 million can fit into a suitcase weighing no more than 35 pounds. However, at a minimum, the security officer should either alert a US customs official or law enforcement officer immediately. At a minimum, the security officer should also take particular note of the characteristics of the baggage owner and the luggage itself for later identification. Airport security personnel should also be cognizant of the direction the passenger takes when entering the sterile concourse. In all cases, the procedures developed by the airline should be followed.

Of even more danger to the traveling public is the fact that operators of x-ray scanners can become bored and distracted, thereby missing a truly dangerous set of circumstances. It is difficult to keep focused for long periods of time, especially when the work is tedious and repetitive. Therefore, the operator needs to be relieved on a regular basis. It is best to maintain a fifteen- to thirty-minute rotation schedule if possible. In addition, bonus rewards have been proven to be effective in keeping personnel more aware and on the constant lookout for certain objects. Software to project false images to scanners is now available and in use in many airports to keep scanners alert. Suffice it to say, no x-ray machine can stop a terrorist with a weapon; the operator must see the threat and respond to it accordingly. For example, the TSA suspended a screener in Connecticut for falling asleep while checking baggage in March 2003. Finally, alert screeners are able to avoid the improbable situation where babies or animals in carriers might be inadvertently screened.

Besides fatigue, the screener may be hindered by the fact that a discrepancy exists between the width of the conveyer belt of the x-ray machine and the width of the unit's field of vision. In other words, some parts of luggage may not be fully exposed to the operator. Problems also potentially arise when luggage is folded over itself and larger objects obstruct the view to objects beneath them. Newer equipment has improved the screener's field of view as well as the clarity of the picture. However, not all airports are equipped with the most state of the art machines available.

THREAT ASSESSMENT

Every screener is only as effective as their skill in recognizing dangerous objects during the few seconds they have to observe each piece of luggage. A hair dryer might look like a gun, or the inside of a radio may just look like transmitters. Scanners must constantly be trained and retrained until they are proficient in distinguishing anything potentially dangerous from nonthreatening objects. Therefore, any doubt by the screener about the actual dangerousness of an object needs to be resolved with a physical hands-on search. Screeners must make quick assessments. A handy acronym is NOPE.

No threat exists—let the carry-on baggage pass.

Obvious threat exists—seek law enforcement assistance; stop machine, alert supervisor.

Possible threat exists—initiate physical search.

Emergency—alert supervisor, law enforcement, EOD (Explosive Ordinance Disposal) personnel.

Under certain circumstances, physical inspections are more preferable to x-ray screening. For example, plastic explosives can be rolled flat and sewn between the linings of luggage. Some articles also lend themselves to deception. Books can be hollowed out and walking canes or umbrellas can be dismantled to conceal a hidden sharp object. Alert security personnel have even dismantled a tube of lipstick to uncover a small but lethal weapon. Airport security must also recognize it is not only poor security but also bad public relations to inspect physically the contents of someone's luggage by emptying it out on a table. No one appreciates the public viewing of a change of underwear or other personal belongings. It is also particularly unwise to expose valuable jewelry or large sums of cash to the wandering and often opportunistic eyes of potential thieves. It is still important to remember that security has little defense against allegations that cash or valuables were stolen while the passenger's carry-on baggage was out of plain view. Physical searches should be accomplished with a witness nearby. The issue of the security screening officers themselves as being the thieves presents yet another problem and will be discussed in a later chapter.

Note: *More than a year after pleading guilty to federal fraud charges and being put on three years' probation, Atlanta-based Argenbright Security, Inc., was accused on 11 October 2001 by the Department of Justice for failing to complete background checks on workers. This indictment came on the heels of at least seven employees being suspended following a security breach at Chicago's O'Hare Airport approximately a month after 9/11.*

■ SCREENING COMPUTERS AND LAPTOPS

Mention needs to be made as well on the ever-increasing numbers of computers/laptops now carried by passengers. Laptop computers have become commonplace, and passengers insist on using them while waiting for flights and during flight. Before gaining entrance to the sterile concourse, these devices must be inspected. They need to be turned on and booted up if being physically screened. It should be noted that the x-ray machines on the market today have been extensively tested. They will not damage memory, destroy hard drives, or damage the computer in any way. On the other hand, a device that has been stripped of its computer components and refabricated as an explosive device poses a distinct threat that cannot be ignored. Consequently, all computers must be checked to make sure they are really computers. If necessary, checkpoint areas should be equipped with an outlet in order to boot up the computer if the laptop is not equipped with a battery. Otherwise, computers can safely be scanned by x-ray equipment; however, it is good practice to remove them from carrying cases for clearer imaging.

Security personnel need not be trained to be computer experts; however, they do need to be able to recognize when the internal workings of a laptop are really a computer and not a cleverly assembled bomb or the potential pieces of one. They should also be able to make simple distinctions between when a power source that might be more than is indicated for a laptop and consequently may pose a threat. Terrorists are very adept at smuggling the pieces of a weapon or explosive device on board an aircraft and assembling it onboard.

Discovered Contraband

Regardless of the airline and federal employee reluctance to engage in law enforcement activities, some situations are unavoidable. Should contraband be in plain view and the screener has observed it, the passenger no longer has the option to withdraw baggage from inspection. Early case law, such as the language in *US vs. Skipwith*, 182 F.2nd 1272 (1973, 5th Circuit) and *US vs. Herzburn*, 723 F.2d 733 (1984, 11th Circuit) have reasoned that once an obvious threat is observed, there is no question that passengers have forfeited the right to change their minds. They have already consented to the search, and the consent cannot be withdrawn because contraband has been found. The real issue revolves around where to proceed from that point. As stated previously, an appropriate law enforcement officer needs to enter the scenario at this moment. It is likely that federal employees will follow similar procedures in the future.

■ SCREENING PASSENGERS

Originally, passengers who could not be cleared of unaccounted-for metal were to be referred directly to a police officer for a pat-down search. This procedure proved to be impractical and time consuming. Previously, the carrier or contract agency personnel hired by the carrier performed this procedure if all other means of clearing the passenger had failed. Those other means include having the passenger remove any extraneous metal they may have on their person such as pocket change, extra large belt buckles, or the like and walk through the metal-detector portal again. A hand-held metal detector may also be utilized. In the past, airlines, always concerned about the free flow of passengers through the screening operation, also recommended that passengers who alarmed the metal detector were to be taken aside for further screening. Consequently, further procedures were automatically done behind a screen or somewhere else in private because of perceived embarrassment. Today, screening by hand-held metal detectors is so commonplace as not to warrant such measures.

Regardless of a slight delay in processing passengers, the best method of handling a passenger who alarms the equipment is politely to ask them to remove any metal in their pockets or on their person which they may have forgotten and reenter the metal-detector portal. Today, most passengers will likely do this automatically without even being asked. Should the passenger persistently alarm the machine, further intrusive measures may be required. A useful acronym for the training of new security personnel is STOP.

Send the passenger back through the walk-through detector again then;

Try a hand-held metal detector to locate the metal and only then;

Outside the view of other passengers, perform a pat-down search and only if absolutely necessary;

Perform a strip search if the passenger still believes they are clearable to board an aircraft and they consent.

Metal that is located on an individual should be removed and the passenger should always, once again, be requested to walk through the metal detector again. It should also be remembered that metal removed from a passenger that has been located by the hand-held detector does not necessarily mean that the passenger is metal free. Passengers seeking to outwit screening procedures are nothing if not creative. Some passengers have even been known to plant a piece of metal knowing they will alarm the walk-through detector. They are then scanned by a hand-held detector and happily reveal the alleged cause of the alarm, hoping the screener will let them pass. Unfortunately, a more insidious piece of metal may also have been the cause of the alarm. There is no limit to the extent of their deceit if they really want to defeat security procedures.

All airport security officers have their own war stories about the ingenuity of passengers in attempting to foil the screening process. However, one of the classic situations took place at O'Hare International Airport in Chicago many years ago. The first time the passenger alarmed the equipment he removed a knife. He was screened a second time, and security officials located a gun. Unbelievably, the third time was a charm, and .22-caliber ammunition was discovered. Stories such as these reinforce the need to keep walking the passengers through the equipment until they are absolutely clean and no longer alarm the machine. Admittedly, this can sometimes annoy the passenger enduring the process as well as those waiting in line. Regardless, it is a must, and short cuts should not be employed in the name of expediency. Federal employees, however, will not be directly subjected to airline expediency requests.

During rush hours, security personnel may feel pressure to hurry. However, when they do, oversights frequently occur. Another story, which has circulated in airport security circles for years, involved an airport in California many years ago. A woman failed to clear the metal detector. She later convinced security personnel that her bracelet had set off the alarm, but in reality, the woman had a gun in her bra. Unfortunately, the hand-held detector could not differentiate between the bracelet and the gun when she raised her hand to a similar position as the location of the gun. She was eventually permitted to board, and bragged to her seat companion that she had out foxed security. Sometimes fate does kick in though, as it turns out, she had bragged to a FAA Security Investigator. Today, hand-held detectors have become much more sensitive, but care is still needed in thoroughly covering all possible locations on a person before clearing them for entrance into the sterile concourse.

Another dangerous procedure is to skip steps in the search procedure. US law is quick to condemn a security officer that has not used the least intrusive method available to search a passenger. In *US vs. Albarado*, 495 F.2nd 799 (1974), the US Court of Appeals ruled almost thirty years ago that the "frisk" of a passenger performed immediately after he or she activates a metal detector is not lawful. This case is still good law and summarizes the need for security personnel to exhaust other efficient and available means first; namely, to have the passenger rescanned by the stationary metal detector and a hand-held detector. Overall, the use of a frisk or body search must not necessarily be a last resort to clear a passenger, but must be viewed within the context of a continuum of progressively more intrusive measures. After 9/11, the frisking of passengers has become more commonplace. It can only be reasoned that security officials are deeming these "pat downs" as consensual even though passengers are arguably intimidated into it.

Exactly who does what to whom is also an issue in today's gender-sensitive legal environment. Technically, there is no specific prohibition against a male screening a female with a hand-held metal detector, especially if the operator is careful not to touch the individual being searched. Searches of this kind have become commonplace, and the public does not really seem to mind them. Of course, searches of the crotch and breast areas need to be accomplished as discreetly as possible. Furthermore, if the operator inadvertently touches the individual with the wand, the search has changed character completely, and the legal repercussions change significantly. Professionalism is required at all times, because the crotch areas, armpits, waist, and ankles are favorite hiding places of those inclined to pass potentially dangerous articles through security. At the same time, inexperienced security personnel may be reluctant to search adequately body areas considered to be "private." Specific policies should be developed and adhered to on a consistent basis. Allegations of inappropriate touching will probably continue.

All security personnel should be trained on the proper method to search a person using a hand-held metal detector. It is simplest to start at the top of the body and to work your way down, keeping the equipment approximately three to four inches from the body. The safest method is to also ask the people being searched to raise their hands above their head, if this is practical, and to stand with their legs slightly apart. As always, the individual needs of each passenger must be taken into consideration. For example, the elderly may not be able to raise their arms very far, and those with certain physical challenges may have special needs. Individuals in wheelchairs also present some unique problems. Discretion is very important, and courtesy is required at all times. Nonetheless, security and safety is the overriding goal, and these people must still be appropriately searched.

The FAA rated numerous hand-held metal detectors in a report entitled "Screening with Hand-Held Detectors," DOT/FAA/CT-95/49. Twenty-six experienced security officers rated 14 of the most commonly used devices. The criteria included:

1. Alarm sound
2. Maneuverability
3. Ability to detect metal objects
4. Weight and length and position of controls
5. Grip comfort

Scanners should be proficient in the use of the equipment. If the device is too heavy or too large for a particular employee, either a smaller device is appropriate or a larger security officer.

Today, it is no longer an issue, but previously there was some question whether nonpassengers, aircrews, visitors, and vendors, should also be subject to search. The regulations were eventually amended to include everyone, and 49 CFR 1540.17 (formerly) FAR 107.20 reads, "no person may enter a sterile area without submitting to the screening of his or her person and property." The logic was simple. It serves no purpose to search only passengers when any of the other categories of people were perfectly capable of terrorizing an aircraft or airport. They were also capable of simply passing something dangerous to a terrorist who had already cleared security. Aircrews constantly complain about having to clear security the same as passengers and other employees. However, it is important to remember that uniforms are easily copied and or stolen and, therefore, accessible to terrorists. Wearing a uniform and impersonating a flight attendant, maintenance worker, or pilot is easy to accomplish.

Of course, none of these procedures is effective if the passenger or terrorist is successful in completely bypassing the security checkpoint. For example, Globe Aviation Security was the contract security service in the employment of Northwest Airlines at the Minneapolis/St. Paul Airport. Since around 1999, police reports at the airport documented at least seven bypassing incidents, which indicated that people do masterfully evade the checkpoint screening procedures. In another documented case, a TWA agent saw two men hastily walk right by a checkpoint without being screened. Globe personnel claimed they saw nothing, and the two men were never located. In another incident, when testing Globe Security, the FAA reported that while a screener was distracted with another passenger's baby stroller, the FAA agents were permitted to pass unchecked. Even though a supervisor did question them, they managed to convince even the security supervisor that they had already been screened. The agents eventually made it all the way to an aircraft ("Security Breach at Airport," Internet: http://www.kstp.com/index.cfm?viewer, 3 July 2001). Such incidents are occurring all over the world and are not just a problem of Globe Security in Minneapolis. Security personnel, whether contract or federal, are never going to be able to provide 100-percent protection. All that can be expected is that they do the best job they can under sometimes very difficult circumstances.

Other loopholes in the overall procedures continue to exist. Some of them simply baffle security officials as why they are permitted to exist. For example, it still amazes some security personnel that smaller knives are even confiscated. They are clearly objected to at all security checkpoints, but as soon as you clear security, some restaurants and certainly the first-class lounges have knifes available for the taking. Also, almost anything can be used as a lethal weapon. It begs the question whether knitting needles and similar items should be confiscated from someone wanting to knit on the aircraft. Furthermore, even pilots have been known to attempt to circumvent the system. They have been known to bend sharpened metal or plastic restraints inside the rim of their airline hats, rationalizing their conduct as meeting their own self-defense needs once on board. The potential use of stun guns or semiautomatic weapons by pilots in the future will add to the mix. The guns could provide a source of weapons for the terrorists.

Body Search

Should all efforts to clear an individual by means of walk-through or hand-held metal detectors fail, the possibility of a body search or pat down presents itself. Clearly, such a procedure requires consent, and the individual must be allowed the option of refusing the search. If a traveler chooses to leave the airport, that is certainly an option available to them. No force should ever be used by airport security personnel to perform a pat-down search. Certified law enforcement officers engaged in an arrest or a Terry-type or stop and frisk search certainly constitutes another matter. Again it is important to make the distinction that airport security professionals are seeking to deter individuals from gaining access to an aircraft with a weapon. They are not criminal investigators sworn to arrest and detain criminals. Additionally, a pat-down search should never be conducted without a witness being present. The potential for a lawsuit is always present. Therefore, not only for the protection of the person being searched but also the person conducting the search, a witness is a must. As mentioned, security personnel at Sky Harbor Airport in Phoenix were accused of inappropriately touching several flight attendants during the spring of 2002.

It is also important to point out that some jurisdictions around the world are not held to the requirements of the US Constitution and specifically the Fourth Amendment. For example, in Japan, people meeting certain profiles and some just randomly selected must submit to an entire body search regardless of whether they have alarmed a metal detector or not. Many other countries have laws that permit this type of conduct by local law enforcement or security personnel to meet their own stringent security needs. Generally, a gender-specific witness is usually present; however, international travelers should be aware that some areas of American sensitivity to physical contact of "private areas" are not necessarily universally recognized elsewhere.

Medical or orthopedic devices also present unique situations. Usually, the individual can be cleared by concentrating on the location of the device, such as a brace or a metal plate in the body. However, as always, such places may be ideal places to secrete a dangerous device on account of security's reluctance to hassle a person with such a disability or special need.

There are even some special situations where an individual may choose a body search over the metal detector. One such special circumstance is a heart patient with a pacemaker who, regardless of the unlikelihood the metal detector will disrupt the surgically implanted device, insists on avoiding the metal detector. Long ago scientific research failed to show any effect of metal detectors on pacemakers. However, certain individuals may still choose to request a body search in preference to walking through the metal detector. Security should permit them to do so. Another special situation concerns the deaf. It is important to be patient and explain any requests slowly and with courtesy so that they can read the lips of the person explaining the procedure. If an employee is familiar with sign language, all the better. If not, written materials should be made available to the hearing impaired. The same courtesies should be provided to the blind and non–English-speaking passengers; plus materials should also be made available in braille.

Screening Airport and Airline Employees

In the early 1970s and under an old set of rules, Air Carrier Standard Security Programs often allowed flight officers and flight crew members with proper identification and in uniform to be exempt from screening regardless of where they entered the terminal. The procedure could have led to some serious consequences, and has since been recognized as setting a dangerous precedent. Remarkably, this practice lasted up until 1987 when new rules were implemented. It is well known that many airline employees consider the security requirements to be tedious; however, the relatively small inconvenience is reasonable under the circumstances.

Since many believe that they would never engage in prohibited conduct, they also believe that none of their fellow employees would do so either. This is naïve thinking. When airlines weigh the minor inconvenience imposed on the regular screening of employees with the potential for disaster, the inconvenience is rightfully seen as minimal. The corporate culture of airlines needs to reinforce the importance of security at all times. Currently, when Federal Aviation Administration (FAA) personnel observed security violations and they attempted to warn airline personnel of the potential fines involved, airline personnel generally remained unmotivated. The current rules mandate that the airlines will receive the fine and not the individual. Consequently, because of labor issues, or corporate culture, or whatever the present rules have been proved to be ineffective in motivating regular compliance.

It should be noted as well that as of 1989, all persons entering a restricted area or the operations area are required to possess appropriate computerized access cards. Unfortunately, the airline employee identification documents are almost as easy to procure as uniforms. The advanced systems on the market today do permit airline personnel with a special form of unimpeded access. These special access cards are generally not furnished to tenants, concessionaires, or contractors, as they are definitely not considered to be airline/airport employees per se. However, as technology improves, so does state of the art duplication ability. New advances in biometric access controls have somewhat closed this loophole.

Screening Diplomats

Generally, both US and foreign diplomats must be screened and are entitled to no special privileges as relates to security. However, if a weapon or other contraband is discovered on properly documented foreign diplomats, international law provides they are entitled to diplomatic immunity. Diplomatic immunity is a concept which prevents them, in most cases, from being prosecuted in the country in which they are stationed. Diplomats have historically been afforded this protection, and the practice is not likely to be changed in regard to airports. Additionally, of importance to security personnel is the fact that a diplomatic courier also has special status. Basically, a diplomatic courier who presents official credentials is entitled to board the aircraft with the diplomatic pouch unscreened. According to long-standing international agreements, the bag is never to be inspected. Unfortunately, some diplomats have abused these exemptions. Diplomatic privilege is a well-known and necessary concept enabling proprietary and classified materials to be moved without threat of exposure. It is when embassies and diplomatic personnel use this as a tool to smuggle weapons, dangerous materials, and terrorist-related support that problems arise.

Another related unique circumstance involves the carriage of classified material by members of the US Armed Forces. Classified material is carried aboard aircraft by members of the Armed Forces Courier Service located at Fort Meade, Maryland. Formerly, FAA Advisory Circular 108 pertained to these materials and provides for transportation of them without inspection by airport security or law enforcement personnel.

▧ THEFT

Larceny at checkpoints by roving thieves is an increasing threat to passengers. Organized bands of "airport-proficient" thieves have been known to work the airports looking for absent-minded passengers willing to separate themselves from their baggage for a sufficient period of time to have it ransacked. There have been repeated claims over the years of valuable possessions going into the x-ray machine but never coming back out. Diligent efforts need to be made to protect the passengers from some very organized airport thieves preying on the unsuspecting traveler.

Two or more people usually effectuate this type of crime. Criminals well organized and quite well practiced at the crime have perfected an ingenious technique. Security personnel need to be trained, but individual passengers must also remain ever alert in the airport environment. Airports, like all other public facilities, are susceptible to criminal activity. Criminals, especially thieves, view airports as easy targets of opportunity.

For example, a woman was in line to pass through the metal detector and placed a carry-on bag and her purse on the conveyor to be scanned when a man pushed in front of her. He set off the alarm as he went through the metal detector and was forced to go around again. By the time the woman got to the other side of the security check, her purse was nowhere to be found. "A crime of this nature is a crime of opportunity" said Inspector Robert Belfiore, Commander of the Port Authority of New York police precinct that includes the airport ("Thief Who Set Off Airport Alarm Made Off With Woman's Purse," *Star Tribune*, Sunday, 28 January 2001, Pg. G2). Passengers and security personnel need constantly to remain alert for organized and well-practiced larceny.

Belfioere recommends further that passengers traveling in pairs or groups should have one person without luggage pass through the metal detector to await a companion's belongings on the other side of the x-ray machine. A passenger traveling alone should alert security personnel immediately if there is a distraction or if the conveyor stops while a personal item is out of sight.

Many security companies did not really understand the liability that they are exposed to when their own employees or crackerjack thieves help themselves to passenger property. In *Gin vs. Wackenhut*, 741 F. Supp. 1454 (D. Hawaii 1990), an airport security company was found to be liable for $140,000 when a passenger's bag, allegedly full of jewelry, was missing after it passed through an x-ray machine at a security checkpoint. Airlines who have attempted to limit liability by printing on the ticket a $1250 limitation of liability clause have also been held liable. In *Wachenhut Corp. vs. Lippert*, 591 So. 2d 215 (Fla. App 1991), the court held that an airline ticket's professed $1250 limitation on liability for baggage did not apply to a passenger's loss of $431,000 worth of jewelry in a handbag while passing through a metal detector, since negligence was found to have occurred. Federal courts have been somewhat more sympathetic to airlines and security companies at airports. In *Kabbani vs. International Total Services*, 805 F. Supp. 1033 (D.DC 1992), the court held that damages in a woman's suit against a security company at an international airport from the alleged theft of her purse containing hundreds of thousands of dollars in jewels was limited to $1000 under the Warsaw Convention. She was scheduled to fly on an international flight. The court did note that the security service would have been liable if the plaintiff could have proven "willful misconduct." All of these dicta, or judicial opinions were elaborated upon in the published decision despite the fact that the security company had not even raised the Warsaw Convention liability restrictions as a defense. Civil suits against federal employees will have to be filed under the Federal Torts Claim Act.

▨ PUBLIC RELATIONS

Airport security personnel who look and act professionally are far more effective than those who do not. Security officers are walking advertisements for the quality of the security at any given airport. It is important for security personnel to recognize the special needs of the elderly, individuals with disabilities or impairing diseases, the homeless, intoxicated or drug-impaired individuals, and those people not proficient in English. For example, a confused elderly person may have Alzheimer's disease and may appear to be intoxicated or drugged. Additionally, those with epilepsy may require special attention. Security personnel should be familiar with the symptoms of those diseases and treat such individuals calmly, quietly, and with respect.

A disability is any physical or mental impairment that substantially limits one or more major life activities. The Americans With Disabilities Act (APA), passed in 1990, states, " No individual shall be discriminated against on the basis of disability in the full and equal employment of the goods, services, facilities privileges, advantages or accommodations of any place of public accommodation." If found guilty of violating this particular law, private security firms could be potentially fined $50,000 for a first offense and up to $100,000 for subsequent offenses. Therefore, proper preparation for screening any individual with a disability covered by the Act is a wise precautionary measure. Compassion must be balanced against legitimate security needs.

▨ AIRBORNE AIRCRAFT SECURITY

Of course, once the aircraft is airborne, security becomes the responsibility of the people on board. In a move, hopefully not approved by the Department of Transportation, United Airlines has begun training pilots to use stun guns for self-defense. A United Airlines official was quoted as saying, "Our goal is to make sure we keep the bad guys off the airplane, and if they get on the airplane, to keep them out of the cockpit and if they try to get into the cockpit, that we have a way of absolutely stopping them" (Internet: http://www.cnn.com/2002/US/04/23/gen.united.stun.guns/index.html?related). In March 2002, Secretary of Transportation Norman Mineta publicly advised the Air Line Pilots Association he opposed the presence of lethal weapons in the cockpit. He did not, however, rule out the presence of nonlethal weapons. In spite of the inherent problems, Congress later went ahead and approved the use of firearms by pilots. In February 2003, Admiral James Loy accepted all of the recommendations made by a task force previously set up to study the matter. The task force recommended that pilots receive 48 hours of training on a .40-caliber semiautomatic pistol. The first class of 11 federal flight deck officers completed training in April 2003. The 48 initial pilots were required to undergo background checks and psychological testing. The guns will be carried in a holster during flight, and the pilots will only be able to use the weapons in the cockpit, not in the cabin. The TSA fully implemented the program in July 2003 initiating weekly training classes. The TSA is paying for the training as well as the weapons. TSA will spend $8 million training pilots in fiscal year 2003 and $25 million in 2004.

However, there are significant problems with the concept of stun guns. First, the gun often can only be shot once. Additionally, if there is more than one terrorist, there is the problem of recharging and reloading the gun. In all likelihood, one of the pilots would subsequently be killed. With only two or three people on board competent to fly the aircraft, this presents a huge safety issue.

As regards the arming of pilots with semiautomatic weapons, it appears more preferable to spend more money on the first line of defense—on the ground—as opposed to the last line of defense—in the cockpit. To the author, it is far more important to have the pilots concentrating on flying the aircraft.

▨ CONCLUSION

Most, if not all, passengers arriving at airports today completely understand that they will be subject to a search for weapons and explosives. The design of airports to accommodate security needs has advanced over the years. Major airports have generally accepted the placement of the security function at the entrance to major concourses, creating a sterile concourse past the security checkpoint. Smaller airports have not had the need to do this, and some of the larger international airports have chosen to establish a security checkpoint at both the entrance to the concourse and again at the gate boarding area. These decisions are based on the perceived threat at a particular airport and the perceived threat at the scheduled destination of the aircraft.

Since the 100-percent screening requirement has come into full effect, procedures have matured and been adapted to the legal requirements imposed by the courts. The courts will also scrutinize any significant changes imposed by the TSA. Screeners are given the responsibility of the safety of millions of travelers each year. They possess one of the last clear chances to catch a potential terrorist before a catastrophe occurs. Proper training and dedication to duty is absolutely required if the airports of the world stand any chance of being protected. Procedures that have already been scrutinized by the courts need to be followed. Good judgment should be exercised at all times as well. The perception of the public is still very important. Passengers may well balk at repeated pat-down searches and forced shoe removal. This is especially true if they do not feel more secure because of the procedures. Watching disabled elderly passengers randomly searched while healthy "potentially capable" hijackers walking through security uninterrupted sends the wrong signal to both the terrorist and the public.

Plus, considering the diversity present in today's traveling public, the personal attributes of each traveler, including physical, cultural, and linguistic differences, must be recognized. Admittedly, good judgment is often impossible to teach someone. However, the day-to-day security of an airport is almost totally dependent on the professionalism of the security and administrative staff charged with that responsibility. The only way to keep that security at its peak performance is to hire good people. This is often easier said than done; however, the consequences of failure to do so are catastrophic. Another issue relates to the question of more armed officers or better preflight security. Chapter 8 will discuss hiring procedures and motivation elements of the security profession.

chapter eight

Private Security Personnel Versus Transportation Administration Security Personnel: Increased Supervision

NEWS

1. **3 May 2002**: Passengers were forced to evacuate two concourses at Cleveland Hopkins International and undergo rescreening when a screening machine detected the presence of possible explosives in a carry-on bag, but the passenger was not stopped.

2. **7 May 2002**: A man carried two loaded handguns through a security checkpoint at Louis Armstrong Airport in New Orleans but was arrested after a random check before he boarded a flight to Los Angeles. The arrest came about a month after two men were found carrying knives past initial security checks at the same airport.

3. **June 2002**: Security rescreened 5000 passengers when a passenger with a knife passed through security at Dulles International Airport. Over 30 flights were delayed for as long as 2½ hours.

4. **1 July 2002**: Airport screeners at 32 US airports failed to detect replica weapons in 24 percent of undercover tests by the Transportation Security Administration.

5. **25 January 2002**: Police began cracking down on identity fraud at Miami International Airport after the airport's security admitted it failed to do background checks on more than 100 workers. New identification cards will restrict where workers can go and at what times.

6. **6 January 2003**: An airport screener was discovered asleep at his post and security personnel were forced to search all concourses. Twenty-three incoming flights were delayed.

■ INTRODUCTION

In the past, a vast majority of the people operating baggage and passenger screening systems in airport terminals were contract security guards. The airlines hired airport security firms to conduct essential searches and passengers depended on their expertise to maintain the safety of airports and aircraft around the globe. They were poorly trained and poorly paid, often only receiving minimal training. Their training often consisted of instruction on the operating systems and procedures by someone simply employed longer than the new employee. The instructor or supervisory employee probably did not have very extensive experience, considering most contract firms experienced a 100-percent turnover rate per year or more. Demographically, they were young, women, retired, and/or representative of a minority segment of the population. Frequently, English was their second language. It was ironic that the public relied so heavily on the dedication of these people for their safety and security but failed to reciprocate with appropriate compensation in order to attract more qualified personnel.

The situation changed effective 14 November 2002. The federal government has assumed this responsibility. After the tragic events of 9/11, the Bush administration has concluded that the government needs to step up to the plate and provide adequate security to the nation's airports. The government clearly had plenty of notice prior to 9/11 to remedy the problem and simply failed to do so.

The Government Accounting Office (GAO) had published a report in 2000 clearly portraying the inadequate security being previously provided. The report indicated that turnover among personnel was a huge problem. Specifically, the report stated, "from May 1998 through April 1999, screener turnover averaged 126 percent at 19 of the nation's largest airports. Five airports reported turnover exceeding 200 percent and one experienced a 416 percent turnover rate" ("Screeners Under Fire, *SMO News and Trends*, May 2000, Internet: http://www.securitymanagement.com/library/000855.html). The GAO strongly recommended that salaries and benefits be increased in order to attract more qualified personnel and to retain the competent employees.

In another report dated December 2000, The Department of Transportation's Inspector General stated that too many airport employees with unknown or questionable backgrounds are given access to secure areas. "Randomly pulling workers' files at six airports, investigators determined that 16 percent had undergone incomplete background checks and 8 percent had no checks at all" (Jim Morris, "Since Pan Am 103, a Façade of Security," *U.S. News*, 19 February 2001, Internet: http://www.usnews.com/usnews/issue/010219/safety.htm, Pgs. 1–3). Years previously, there had been some additional alarming studies on the need for improving security at US airports. In 1987, a Federal Aviation Administration (FAA) evaluation at major airports discovered that screeners missed approximately 20% of the potentially dangerous items which passed in front of them. Another study revealed the chilling statistics that screeners in European airports detected twice as many test objects as US screeners. A FAA report concluded, "people who had longer training, somewhat better pay and benefits, and better on-going testing by screening companies, had much better performance in detecting objects than comparable screeners in the US" (Carl Rochelle, "FAA Calls for Security Improvements at US Airports," Internet: http://www.cnn.ru/2000/travelnews/01/07/bomb_and_baggage, 7 Jan 2000).

In response to strong encouragement from the White House, Congress quickly met after 9/11 to draft a new Airport Security Act. It was signed into law on Monday, 19 November 2001. There has been a renewed intense focus on the role airport security screeners play in protecting passengers and crew. Consequently, the new law made provision for the establishment of government-paid airport security personnel. New federal duties will include supervising passenger and baggage security, performing background checks, and training screeners and other security personnel. Other duties will include purchase and control of all equipment and oversight of security patrols. The intent of the new law is to bolster training procedures and government supervision of all airport security personnel. The program was approved to be in place by November 2002. An evaluation of the success of the new program will remain to be seen.

Unfortunately, as of September 2002, a year after the tragic events of 9/11, problems still plagued the airport security program at most airports. Over the Labor Day weekend, reporters from the *New York Daily News* concealed potentially deadly weapons on 6 major airlines, at 11 airports, on 14 different flights. Seeking to test the more stringent requirements imposed post-9/11, the reporters carried box cutters, razor knives, and pepper spray. Not a single item was discovered or confiscated. The failures were all a result of both technological and human error. Better equipment and better training are clearly a necessity for the future.

■ CRIMINAL GUARDS: THE FOXES GUARDING THE CHICKENS

The caretakers of our security at airports, unfortunately, were not above being bribed, engaging in criminal activities, or just being noncommitted to the job. These circumstances often resulted in significant laxness in security. The situation has not really changed all that much in spite of 9/11. Security at London's Heathrow Airport was overhauled in March 2002 after two multi-million dollar heists in a two-month period. The British government announced more stringent background checks on employees, tighter restrictions on access to sensitive areas, and now requires security companies to be on an approved list.

The job as an airport security guard was not one that children aspired to become while growing up. As mentioned, more often than not, the job paid poorly, provided little chance for advancement or promotion, and most likely provided little training for those who were even somewhat dedicated to the job. Also, the screeners were frequently subjected to verbal abuse by passengers, airline employees, allegedly by FAA personnel, and by their own coworkers. In fact, a national report cited this abuse as the most regularly cited cause of leaving the job as opposed to low pay and virtually no benefits.

Of primary concern was the idea that most companies were struggling to find individuals willing to do the job at all. The government thought that it had more than enough applications to fill the first federal positions at Baltimore/ Washington International Airport in early 2002 only to realize many either would fail to show up, failed the background check, or failed the training to become a screener. Primarily, many companies either screened the applicants poorly or were simply willing to hire anyone who applied regardless of their background. Those companies that did attempt to screen their employees properly found the process to be expensive and often undependable. For example, the process of sending fingerprints off for a background check could be lengthy and time consuming. Some firms were forced to let the potential employee engage in security functions prior to receipt of a completed background check, because they were chronically plagued with understaffed checkpoints.

One company made some notable mistakes. Argenbright Holdings Ltd., the airport contract security company hired at Philadelphia International Airport, was fined more than $1.5 million for allowing untrained employees, some with criminal records, to operate security checkpoints. The employees had convictions in crimes that included drug dealing, kidnapping, aggravated assault, and theft. Also, in October 2000, the company pled guilty to two counts of making false statements to the FAA. The company had already agreed in April 2000 to pay more than a million dollars in fines and costs for falsifying training and background checks. The company was also ordered to pay $350,000 to 38 different airlines and was scheduled to be on probation for three years. Three former employees were also sentenced for conspiracy and fraud-related charges ("Airport Security Co. Fined $1.5 Million," Internet: http://www.apbnews.com/newscenter/breakingnews/2000/10/23/airport 1023–01). Unfortunately, the company once again made the news as the providers of airport security at Boston's Logan International Airport, departure point of the two jets that crashed into the World Trade Center in 2001. Since that time, the Department of Justice also has indicted them for repeated failures to run appropriate background checks on its employees and also for falsely verifying that checks had been done. Additionally, they were allegedly permitting the test scores of screeners to be falsified and high school graduation credentials to be counterfeited.

In another situation, a traveler alert was issued for O'Hare International Airport in Chicago. The alert warned passengers that an organized theft ring was operating at security checkpoints. The alert, issued in 1997, was in response to the discovery of a five-man South American organized group of thieves preying on travelers as they processed through security checkpoints. One member of the ring would carry something in a pocket in order to set off the metal detector. Consequently, they would have to walk back through, in essence, holding up the line thereby creating a distraction. Their partners in crime would walk off with someone's carry-on luggage. The gang was highly successful. Chicago Police Department Lt. Neal Sullivan of the O'Hare police unit was quoted as saying, "It's the same method of operation—the same training. Across the country, intelligence has shown they literally go to school for this" (*ERRI Daily Intelligence Report*, Risk Assessment Services, 16 August 1997, Vol. 3, Pg. 228).

Airport operators generally contracted for airport security by accepting bids from the nation's 10,000 or so private security companies. The FAA set forth regulations for air carriers, but put the responsibility of handling screening of baggage and people back on the airlines. More often than not, the lowest bidder won the contract regardless of the quality of services. Generally, the airlines do not want to pay extra for training, and the often fledgling security company can really not afford it. Critics would argue that the airlines were more concerned with profits than safety, often disregarding the shortsightedness of this approach.

Poor operator performance was another principal weakness of passenger screening systems. Airport security screeners who may be preoccupied with personal problems while on the job and may be poorly trained, are still required to identify sometimes faint indications of infrequently appearing target items. Missing such indicators can have catastrophic results if a bomb or other explosive device gets through the screening process. This problem will remain and will prove challenging to the federal supervisors.

The relationship between pay and performance is not necessarily a determinative one. Experts would argue that increased pay is not likely in and of itself to solve the problem. The government must place a renewed emphasis on attaining job-effectiveness goals. This process will likely involve the application of two types of factors. Those factors will consist of those that attract and keep people on the job (maintenance factors) and those that lead to acceptable or enhanced performance on the job (performance factors) (R. A. Guzzo, *Productivity in Organizations*, Jassey-Bass: San Francisco, 1988).

Another challenge relates to the self-perception of people hired in this field. Higher levels of pay will possibly make up for poor working conditions but do not enhance the perceived low status of the job or organization. Improved training techniques will greatly improve this aspect. Even the weekly access to "intelligence" briefings on the assessed threat by qualified personnel will improve job satisfaction. People who believe they are actually important and contributing to combating a real threat will often live up to the challenge. Those employees referred to as "rent-a-cops" will not.

The use of trace-detection technologies and explosive-detection systems will also require specialized training. Trace-detection equipment requires the use of specific protocols to be effective. Additionally, passenger screening settings may involve person-to-person contact or direct contact between the equipment and the passenger. Additionally, operators may feel intimidated by passengers. Training regarding the management of anger will also prove to be quite useful.

To facilitate training of screeners, the FAA had been deploying a computerized training system called Screener Proficiency Evaluation and Reporting System, or SPEARS. One unique aspect of the system is a concept known as Threat Image Projection (TIP), which consists of specific software to project fictitious images of bags with threat devices on x-ray screens to keep screeners alert and measure performance in real-time conditions. The government will likely continue the use of these systems.

It is also important to recognize the distinction between state-appointed law enforcement officers and "private" security officers. There are four basic differences. The significant distinctions include financial sourcing, profit orientation, goals toward crime prevention versus protection of assets, and the possession of statutory authority. Private security is employed by profit-oriented businesses. The police are statutorily appointed or sworn in to the service of the public and are paid by governments. Additionally, police officers are often focused on the investigation of crime that has already taken place or is taking place. Private security officers are supposed to focus on crime prevention and the protection of assets belonging to the business. The functions are similar and do overlap, but the motivational differences are worthy of note. Additionally, it will be very interesting to see whether the courts categorize the new federal government-paid employees as "state agents," hence triggering more stringent Fourth Amendment restrictions. The federal government is confronting the same problems which previously plagued the private security sector. For example, in May 2003 more than two dozen federal screeners stationed at Los Angeles International Airport have been found to have criminal histories. Similarly, in New York, police have uncovered at least 50 screeners with criminal pasts.

ERGONOMIC SOLUTIONS

One method of improving security at airports involves the study of ergonomics. The objective of ergonomics is to ensure compatibility between task requirements and the capabilities and limitations of the employee. First, management needs to discover better methods to recognize the performance of employees. Second, employees, especially those entrusted with the public's safety, should be provided with opportunities for a sense of job satisfaction and achievement. Those same employees are entitled to a work environment that gives them the opportunity to grow on the job either through openings for promotion or education and training.

In the United States, airport security employees did not previously have the opportunity to advance beyond a supervisory role at a security checkpoint. With nowhere to go, and theoretically no means to improve themselves, there was little incentive to improve job skills or dedication levels. Government supervisors will need to realize that some form of recognition for superior performance and continuing service is appropriate. Individuals can be rewarded with bonuses, extra vacation days, or in other ways the airlines or government consider to be feasible. Similar to flight attendants and pilots, providing them with the same air travel benefits is another option.

Additionally, the concept of ergonomics in system design should be considered by management to improve the working conditions at security checkpoints. The goal of system design is to ensure that functions assigned to humans are compatible with human capabilities. If not, assigned functions will not be performed well even if the best personnel selection, training, and motivational approaches are employed. In airports, current systems for screening carry-on baggage continue to suffer from human factors—that is, pressure to keep passengers moving. Problems' proliferate.

1. The monitors on both x-ray machines and explosive-detection equipment do not provide the operator with an adequate size reference.

2. Equipment controls are insufficiently distinguishable by shape and location coding to permit operation without looking at the control panel.

3. Data integration and image processing techniques have not been sufficiently exploited to provide enhancements for image interpretation.

4. Equipment design forces operators to position themselves improperly to view the display.

5. Work force constraints limit the ability of management to assign security personnel to tasks in accordance with their abilities.

6. Passengers, airport staff, air carrier employees, and others sometimes subject security personnel to verbal abuse ("Airline Passenger Security Screening," Chapter 5, National Research Council, Publication NMAB-482-1 National Academy Press, Washington, DC, 1996, Pg. 26).

■ POTENTIAL OPERATOR CONCERNS WITH SPECIFIC SCREENING TECHNOLOGIES

For imaging technologies, alarm resolution probably will involve either taking additional images or having a more experienced viewer or supervisor interpret the initial image.

Studies have revealed the need for three approaches:

1. Develop and apply selection methods to ensure that operators have the necessary aptitudes for the tasks to be performed.

2. Develop and administer training systems that provide operators with the needed knowledge and skills.

3. Incorporate elements into the system that enhance rather than degrade operator motivation and job satisfaction ("Airline Passenger Security Screening," Chapter 5, National Research Council, Publication NMAB-482-1, National Academy Press, Washington, DC, 1996, Pg. 27).

■ MEASURING OPERATOR PERFORMANCE

The government will have to develop means by which to test whether dangerous objects, weapons, and explosives are actually being detected. Such techniques include provisions for electronically inserting target objects on operational screening systems and a renewed focus on a human factors program.

In June 1990, EG&G Astrophysics introduced a new function for its Linescan X-Ray baggage screening system. The new concept was called the False Image Protection (FIP) program. It was developed not only to test the alertness of operators but also can be used as a training device to teach specific threat identification techniques to operators. The system gave the airport security supervisor the ability to activate the FIP randomly and to superimpose a false-threat object on the monitor screen of an operator. If the operator was alert and recognized the threat object, they would have to verify this by pressing an indicator on the control panel. The successful or unsuccessful test could be recorded for later auditing purposes and also as proof that continuing training was taking place. The FIP system is a common feature today and is used on a regular basis; however, it should be noted that Threat Image Projection on such a system as the Linescan 237 continues to be an optional feature. They should be made standard on all x-ray machines.

The documentation of individual screener testing is essential in order to avoid allegations of negligence. Management can protect itself by documenting adequate training has occurred. However, training adults should be distinguished from educating children. Overall, there are four fundamental tenets of adult education:

1. Adults prefer to be self-directed rather than instructor directed.
2. Adults have unique life experience that they bring with them to the learning process.
3. Adult readiness to learn is linked to what adults consider relevant.
4. Adults want an immediate application of knowledge rather than the postponed application indicative of youth learning (Michael E. Goodboe, "Should Security Practice Andragogy," *Security Management*, April 1995, Pg. 65).

Cycles of training will provide security personnel with the best means of continuing education. They need some instruction in all of following areas on a recurrent and documented basis:

1. Proper screening procedures, especially on new technologies
2. The threat to their specific airport
3. Emergency medical procedures
4. Anger management/conflict resolution
5. Liability issues
6. Performance appraisals for themselves and those they supervise

Transportation Security Administration

Symbol of the new Transportation Security Administration (TSA). The agency, which has been tasked by Congress with monitoring and executing security plans and procedures at all United States' transportation facilities after 11 September 2001, faces an enormous challenge. TSA swelled quickly to almost 65,000 employees in the aftermath of the 2001 terrorist attacks.

■ OPERATOR SELECTION

Historically, there were firms that maintained a rigorous screening hiring process. For example, the Guardsman Company had a 24-page application that demanded a plethora of information including residency verification. The hiring process also required interviewing neighbors and former employers. Some applicants were polygraphed, and all underwent drug screening. Guardsman's human resources personnel have confirmed that usually only 2 of 100 applicants survived the process. If you were a successful applicant, however, the job benefits included an hourly wage of approximately $16 per hour in the year 1994 as opposed to the average pay of $5.75 an hour prior to September 2001 at most other companies.

Since the US government has decided to be directly responsible for the hiring and training of airport screeners, NCS Pearson, Inc., a Minnesota corporation, was selected to assist in developing the selection process. NCS won the $103.4 million contract to develop an Internet-based system to collect applications, establish hiring standards, and oversee testing of the candidates. The firm markets the famous Minnesota Multiple Personality Inventory test and others to detect unstable or dangerous attitudes and/or personality traits. The company has publicly commented that a battery of tests will likely be used. First, the Minnesota Multiphasic Personality Inventory 2 test can identify individuals who may be emotionally unsuited for demanding public safety roles. A second test tasks applicants to compare abstract traits and colors to identify cognitive ability. A third test measures 16 personality factors: warmth, reasoning ability, emotional stability, dominance, liveliness, rule consciousness, boldness, sensitivity, distrust, abstractness, privateness, worrying, openness to change, self-reliance, perfectionism and tension. Whatever process is finally used, it must be capable of successfully screening the screeners before they are to take over security responsibilities at almost 500 airports on 14 November 2002.

An airport security guard reads a monitor showing an x-ray image of a suitcase. *Mark Richards/PhotoEdit.*

In order to avoid the nonproductive cycle of high turnover rates and inefficient performance, it is essential initially to hire qualified personnel. Generally, if people are treated well, paid appropriately, and provided clear standards and expectations, they will identify with their workplace and perform better. In conjunction with the initial screening process, one of the first steps will be to recruit security officer candidates who are reliable, have some personal pride, and are orientated toward attention to detail. All information contained in an applicant's application form should be verified. Obtaining records waivers is a good idea so that the employer can note any problems at a previous place of employment. Because security officers are invested with quite a bit of trust, they should also be trustworthy. Current law does not authorize the dissemination of arrest and non-conviction data, but it is legal to authorize the release of conviction data. Therefore, criminal background checks are essential.

In addition, the Transportation Safety Administration (TSA) has set down some specific guidelines in Section 108.31, Employment Standards for Screening Personnel. They mandate:

1. **Educational Background**—FAR 108.31 (a) (1) requires that screeners possess a high school diploma, a general equivalency diploma, or a combination of education and experience which the certificate holder has determined to have equipped the person to perform the duties of the position. Exactly what the last sentence means is open to interpretation.

2. **Criminal Background Checks**—FAR 108.33 (c) (5) does not require criminal records checks for every screener applicant, only those applicants who have specific deficiencies in their employment history, if there are other deficiencies in the application, or if the air carrier finds out that the

applicant may have been convicted of certain kinds of crimes. FBI records are reviewed, but this begs the question concerning non-US citizen screeners and foreign criminal records.

3. **Criminal History**—FAR 108.33(2) states that a criminal records check must not disclose that the applicant had been convicted or found not guilty by reason of insanity in any jurisdiction during the previous ten years of a number of crimes such as aircraft piracy, interference with a flight crew or cabin member, assault with intent to murder, rape or aggravated sexual abuse, or armed robbery, sedition, treason, extortion or distribution of a controlled substance. Consequently, with a conviction older than ten years, the convicted felon meets the criteria of an airport screener.

4. **Transportation Security Administration Criteria**—these individuals will take over for the screening at 415 of the 429 of the nation's commercial airports:

    Level One—screeners are trainee screeners who must attend and pass both classroom and on the job security screener training administered by the TSA. They will conduct screening of passengers, baggage, and/or cargo under the close supervision of a Federal Civil Aviation Screening Supervisor. These screeners must progress to Level Two or have their employment terminated.

    Level Two—screeners are fully trained and certified screeners. They will conduct screening of passengers, baggage, and cargo. They have completed all training and certification requirements and have been on the job for over a year.

    Level Three—screeners are fully trained and certified advanced screeners. They have been on the job in a Level Two capacity for over a year. They are also certified to use specialized explosives-detection equipment to screen checked baggage and cargo.

    Manager Level One Screening Supervisors—first-level supervisors of screeners who will provide direct day-to-day supervision of Level One, Two, and Three screeners.

    Manager Level Two—supervise the Manager Level One Managers and their subordinates.

▓ TOUGHER THAN THEY THOUGHT

Initially, over 4000 people applied for 600 federal airport screening jobs at Baltimore/Washington International (BWI) Airport. The new TSA promptly removed the job application from the Web site. Soon thereafter, however, hundreds of applicants either failed the government's new tests or did not even show up to take them. Starting 1 May 2002, BWI was the first airport in the nation to have federal workers manning the airport screening checkpoints. Starting pay ranges from $23,000 per year to $35,000 including paid leave, and health and retirement benefits. Federal officials have estimated that they will need to hire approximately 65,000 security employees (approximately 30,000 screeners) to main the nation's entire network of airports. By the end of July 2002, only about 5000 had been filled. In the New York City area, by mid-July 2002, only 368 people had accepted the job offer where 2300 were needed ("Airport Screeners," *Associated Press*, 29 July 2002).

As stated, applicants are being screened by NCS Pearson, a private Minnesota company. The tests include such functions as placing a hand inside a bag and recognizing by touch the contents. For another test, the applicant must watch an x-ray screen and identify guns and knives superimposed on top of regular luggage contents, like toiletries and clothes. In order to test fitness, applicants must lift boxes of various weights and walk around some cones. The failure rate has been unexpectedly high.

The Transportation Department has also awarded a Phase II contract to Lockheed Martin Corporation's Mission Systems unit. Lockheed will work on airport passenger lane reconfiguration and the addition of new security technologies. The company received the $350 million base contract in June 2002, with additional work boosting the value to $490 million. Lockheed implemented a master schedule by 31 October 2002 to integrate federal employees into the system by November 2002. The same firm was awarded a contract valued at $105 million to train approximately 30,000 new screeners. Each screener will train in the classroom for at least 40 hours and on the job at least an additional 60 hours. Generally, each screener has to be a US citizen, have a high school degree, and be proficient in English. The requirement of a high school education was relaxed very quickly also to permit those with an equivalent one-year of work as an airport screener or other security job. The TSA has also discarded the hopes of filling one-half of the positions with women. They have readjusted the figure to one-third.

There had been some concern that the job could not be accomplished in time. The TSA had planned to take over security at 15 of the nation's major airports by 1 June 2002 and initially had only succeeded in partially taking over responsibilities at three. Federal employees first staffed the Mobile, Alabama, Louisville, Kentucky, and BWI airports. As stated, government officials announced they met the congressional deadline of 19 November 2002. They relied heavily on both Boeing Co. and the Lockheed Martin Corporation to devise a way to get these federal screeners into the airports. Hundreds of employees from these two companies evaluated what needed to be done. Lockheed Martin deployed 146 teams, evaluating approximately 150,000 tasks necessary to set up passenger checkpoints. Program Manager Tim Bradley had indicated they would be hiring 15,000 to 20,000 federal screeners per month. Speeding up the process depended on cooperation between a significant number of people. Test programs are also being conducted at five airports to determine whether private companies can meet federal requirements for screening: San Francisco, Kansas City, Rochester, NY, Tupelo, MS, and Jackson Hole, WY.

The system has been functioning for quite some time and it was recently publicized that TSA would be downsizing. Admiral Loy has announced that a readjustment in the size of the work force is needed and he is right.

▪ CONCLUSION

This chapter has highlighted some of the major historical problem areas confronting airport screeners and airport passenger screening in general. Some recommendations were made on how to correct some of the deficiencies in current airport procedures and the hiring and training of security personnel. Hopefully, the attention span of the American public will remain focused on the need adequately to compensate and train airport screeners and security personnel in general. Means of measuring the performance of the screeners and how to enhance that performance were also discussed. Such tools as Threat Imaging Projections and SPEARS will continue to be critical to monitoring the performance of operators and need to be standardized globally.

It remains to be seen if government control of airport screening will improve the process. In April 2002, the US government held a boot camp for the nation's new top airport security chiefs at BWI. They stressed customer service as well as security. These top security officials need all the security training they can get; especially those with little to no prior private airport security experience. Certainly, if they do not recognize the issues discussed above, they are destined to make the same mistakes. Hopefully, they will implement appropriate procedures to avoid many of the potential pitfalls. Additionally, the decision to make airport screeners federal employees will surely incite civil libertarians to argue that the screeners are now state agents and hence answerable to the Fourth Amendment. The courts will ultimately have to determine future issues regarding the reasonableness of searches by federal employees.

chapter nine

Metal Detectors, X-Ray Inspection, Explosives Detection, and Trace-Detection Devices: Will the Public Tolerate the Intrusion?

▌ NEWS

1. **7 March 2001:** The Aviation Security Manufacturing Coalition, comprising firms from New Mexico, Maryland, Michigan, Minnesota, Utah, and California, says it has the technology needed to help major manufacturers InVision™ Technologies and L-3 Communications make and test the more than 2000 screening machines that will be needed.

2. **March 2001:** InVision™ Technologies Inc. announced that the FAA has given the company a delivery order of approximately $9 million for the company's CTX 9000 DSi™ and CTX 2500™ explosive-detection systems.

3. **7 June 2002:** The Department of Transportation awarded Boeing Co. a contract valued at up to $1.37 billion to provide explosive-detection machines at US airports.

4. **9 June 2002:** European and US experts say the Transportation Safety Administration–proposed method for detecting bombs in checked baggage will not reliably detect explosives. The British Airports Authority rejected "trace detection" devices a decade ago.

5. **30 June 2002:** The Chisholm-Hibbing Airport in Minnesota will be the first airport in the nation to receive a new type of technology to detect

explosives and narcotics. The Itemiser™ system can simultaneously monitor positive and negative ion modes for all substances.

6. **24 September 2001:** Secretary of Defense Donald Rumsfeld announced that the United States is taking seriously the potentiality that terrorists might use biological or chemical weapons.

■ INTRODUCTION

The screening of passengers and baggage is now a routine part of air travel. Travelers automatically factor into their travel plans the necessary time to "clear security" before arriving at their gate. The government is adjusting to the requirement to provide such security services. The government also intends to pass on the fee for screening passengers and carry-on baggage as another cost of doing business, which is eventually passed onto the traveler in the price of a ticket. Airport planners redesigning existing airports and drafting the plans for new ones, currently automatically reserve sufficient space at all airport facilities for adequate security arrangements. Advances in technology have supported the efforts of security and law enforcement. Research and development efforts have improved the quality and available choices of screening equipment available for purchase. New x-ray devices for carry-on baggage and new metal detectors, both portal type and hand held, have revolutionized the ability of scanners to determine quickly and easily if an individual is carrying any unauthorized dangerous weapons. Furthermore, advances have been in made in the production of explosive-detection and trace-detection devices with quadruple resonance devices and others on the horizon.

The equipment and the personnel have improved over the years. The latest controversy revolves around explosive-detection and trace-detection systems. Congress originally intended for the Transportation and Safety Administration (TSA) to buy thousands of explosive-detection systems to be installed from 2007 through 2014. After 9/11, they shortened the deadline to 31 December 2002. Soon thereafter, and again similar to what has happened in the 1970s, the Department of Transportation (DOT) concluded that it could not acquire and install enough of the machines within the required deadline. Subsequently, the government declared trace-detection equipment to be a reasonable alternative. This chapter will attempt to provide an historical perspective on some of the initial problems and supporting equipment and how they have developed and improved over the years. The changes in improved and more intrusive equipment will continue to affect everyone involved.

■ METAL DETECTORS

"Often domestic passengers are only required to pass through a simple metal detector before being allowed aboard an aircraft. Such rudimentary security measures have been shown time and again to be less than effective, but still they are used as

Florida National Guardsman stands guard at his post at an airport concourse at Jacksonville International Airport in Florida, after President Bush asked the National Guard to support security measures in the immediate aftermath of 9/11 with armed troops. *Oscar Sosa / AP/Wide World Photos.*

the first and sometimes only line of defense against a determined hijacker," say Chris Yates, editor of *Jane's Airport Security Standards and Technology* (Internet: http://www.james.com/press/pc990723.shtml). Such comments are reflective of easily recognizable deficiencies of many current metal detectors. They simply do not catch all forms of dangerous weapons. More often, their greatest weakness is cited as not detecting metals incapable of being magnetized. Since a number of US-manufactured guns are made of mostly nonferrous metals, the shortfall is quite evident. Even though no such thing as a totally plastic gun exists, if the sensitivity setting on the detector is not set properly, some guns may remain undetected. The lightest guns with polymer grips, bodies, and slides normally have enough metal in them to trigger the detector, but they still require special scrutiny.

The detectors also cannot detect the organic materials contained in explosives. Metal detectors remain one of the most important sources of security for airports. There have been significant advances in equipment, which include software programs that can suppress ferrous detection while boosting nonferrous metals. Others suppress nonferrous materials while magnifying the detection response of ferrous objects. Newer trace-detection equipment is also able to recognize organic explosive materials. However, most new technology comes with a rather high price tag. Regardless, the US government had mandated their use by December 2002.

The scientific principle upon which metal detectors work is quite simple. Passive systems detect metal by changes in the earth's magnetic field. Active detectors operate by creating their own electromagnetic field and alarming when metal objects passing through it disturb the field. Metal detectors contain one or more inductor coils that are used to interact with metallic elements on the ground. A pulsating current is applied to an internal coil, which induces a magnetic field. When the magnetic field of the coil moves across metal, the field induces electric currents called eddy currents. The eddy currents induce their own magnetic field, which generates an opposite reaction in the coil, thereby inducing a signal indicating the presence of metal ("How a Metal Detector Works," Internet: http://micro.magnet.fsu.edu/electromag/java/detector/, Pg. 1, 24 July 2001).

Active detectors use various frequencies, usually 90 Hz to 25 KHz. Hand-held units usually utilize the bands from 100 KHz to 1 MHz. Metals such as aluminum, brass, and copper are highly conductive, and hence provide greater signals at higher frequencies. Metals such as iron and steel produce greater signals at low frequencies. High-frequency detectors, which react to highly conductive metal, are more prone to false alarms. Low-frequency detectors, which react to less conductive metals, can disregard small metal objects. Low-frequency detectors (below 500 Hz) are more practical for walk-through screening.

▓ SELECTING A METAL DETECTOR

The selection of an appropriate metal detector is an important decision. Each airport has its own unique characteristics and priorities. Various factors must be weighed and considered. Unfortunately, one of the primary limitations is usually cost, and metal detectors are expensive assets that need to be maintained and routinely upgraded.

Additionally, accuracy and utility are weighty considerations. The rapid flow of passengers is of major concern to airlines seeking to keep their balance sheets on the positive side of the ledger. In order to keep on making money, the airlines have attempted to keep the passenger relatively agreeable to the delays caused by screening 100 percent of terminal traffic. Equipment causing too many false alarms, breaking down on a repeated basis, or otherwise causing delays was not marketable in this venue. Federal employees need not directly succumb to those pressures.

In order to satisfy market demand, many companies have been through eight or nine successive generations of equipment. Improvements have featured increased levels of security performance in metal-detection capability, discrimination of personal metal objects, and immunity to outside interference. Safety precautions regarding the passenger with a life-support device have also been tested and retested to protect the operator and manufacturer from prohibitive civil liability.

The calibration of metal detectors is somewhat a matter of preference. For example, Texans with large belt buckles may require a certain level of detection different from an airport in the Bahamas. Sensitivity formerly recommended by the Federal Aviation Administration (FAA) called for a maximum false alarm rate of 15 percent. The ideal metal detector should detect a gun without fail, whereas passing a person with an ordinary amount of pocket items and jewelry. Regardless, passengers are usually required to empty their pockets of any metal objects in order that the equipment can be calibrated at the most effective settings. Newer procedures scan for even the smallest amount of metal.

Another determining factor in purchasing criteria is the mobility of the equipment. Many units are now permanent fixtures, but moving them is still on occasion necessary. Consequently, the cost of recalibrating them, the time involved, and the ease of doing so are all important considerations. If the services of an engineer are required, the cost and time involved increase. Furthermore, the TSA requires that they must recertify the capability of the device if it has been moved.

Of course, the bottom line for each metal detector is whether or not it actually accurately detects guns and weapons. The actual detection rates are not published for security reasons. Suffice it to say they must possess a high detection rate. Today's hardware and software programs improve their interference rejection, discrimination, sensitivity, detection, uniformity, vibration tolerance, and orientation response. All of these factors contribute to the bottom line that increased discrimination significantly reduces unwarranted alarms. Many metal-detector manufacturers now also sell enhancement programs that help correct detection nonuniformity caused by vertically positioned external metal. Other programs allow the user to create customized security programs.

The manager reviewing the hundreds of pages of marketing materials on metal detectors still has to consider some basic concepts in determining the most appropriate system. Overall, managers need to contemplate such issues as external factors or sensitivity to environmental factors (i.e., environmental magnetic noise); physical construction or size; ease of operation (i.e., ease of calibration, self-calibration, and required frequency of calibration); and, last but not least, cost and appearance.

Additionally, development has produced machines that now have a multizone advantage. In addition to indicating the location of targeted objects, multizone systems possess a multitude of advantages. They improve discrimination between weapons and harmless objects, reduce unwanted alarms, and permit higher traffic flow rates. In high-volume airports, this translates into lower operating and capital costs. For example, pinpoint multizone detection is a concept currently utilized. One manufacturer uses a "block of real estate" example to explain the dynamics of the system. They explain that in

> most detectors the blocks of real estate, called zones, are stacked upon each other and extend the full width of the archway. When an object passes through a zone, it is detected by the zone and an alarm display shows its location. In this case, the alarm display depicts the height of the object above ground. The display can take the form of lights on the front edge of a side panel or a mimic display that represents the archway in graphic form ("Defining Multi-Zone Detection: Check Apple for Apples,"

Internet: http://www.omni-security.com/wthru2/wtindex.html, Pgs. 2, 3 May 2001).

Manufacturers do place different interpretations on the meaning of multizone detection. Appropriately, when a device claims to have 6 horizontal zones, it should mean that there are 12 detection channels with two sensors per zone. Each zone should be independently adjustable.

False alarms can be attributable to external electrical and electromagnetic interference and poor tolerance vibration. Good-quality interference rejection and mechanical design will lower false alarms. Multizone detectors reduce unwanted alarms caused by people wearing metal: jewelry, coins, and keys. Two conditions contribute to elevated undesired alarm rates. They include the cumulative signal effect and nonuniform detection. Cumulative signal effect lowers a detector's ability to separate weapons from harmless personal effects. It occurs when signals generated are processed as a single composite signal. Theoretically, in single-zone machines, the signals from someone's watch, keys, and some metal in shoes will be combined. If the cumulative signal is large enough, the machine will alarm causing delay and frustration for passenger and screener alike.

Correspondingly, in multizone detectors, if the device has 18 zone detectors, 6 horizontal zones would be divided into three blocks. The machine would then display the object's height above the ground, and also show if the object is to the right or left or in the center of the zone. Complicated mapping algorithms process the data and can very accurately tell the scanner where the object is. Because each zone has an adjustable control, the sensitivity can be focused on a particular object for a better analysis, thereby making a threat assessment easier and reducing unwarranted alarms.

Additionally, nonuniform detection can be caused by rebar in the floor or in the wall of the airport. External metal can distort a detector's magnetic field and may cause a loss in detection. In essence, a dead spot is created. This anomaly can be corrected by raising the machine's overall sensitivity level. The simple fix becomes impractical if a floor is heavily reinforced. The level of sensitivity setting may become so high that a disproportionate number of other unwanted alarms may take place. Multizone machines permit hot spots and dead spots to be eliminated with a simple adjustment to the equipment.

Although adjustable zones compensate for detection losses caused by metal in the floor, walls or ceiling, a different solution is needed to counteract metal positioned directly next to the machine. The presence of a steel girder, for example, causes deterioration in detection uniformity across the horizontal axis of the archway. Since it is not possible generally to reposition an imbedded steel girder, or to move the sterile concourse entrance, the machine will need horizontal axis adjustments. These advanced features are now readily available.

Another feature to consider before purchasing a specific piece of equipment is the information the screener receives from the alarm panel during an alarm. The alarm panel should show the height at which the detected object is carried. For example, more advertised zones are not necessarily better unless the numbers of horizontal sensitivity controls are present to adjust those zones. This is arguably more important than the actual number of zones. This significantly cuts down on the time needed actually to locate a weapon if there is one. Furthermore, the equipment should be continuously active and have self-testing diagnostics and a fast automatic reset. Electrical and electromagnetic interference rejection can be achieved through multiple frequency selection, electronic filtering, and sophisticated software algorithms.

■ HAND-HELD BODY SCANNERS

The best hand-held detectors are lightweight in construction and have a comfortable grip and a large scanning surface. The detector should have a tight detection pattern, have fast detection circuitry, and be ergonomically designed. These attributes contribute to higher efficiency and reduced operator fatigue. Another really useful feature is a switch that can transform the detector from a general-use mode to a super–high-sensitivity unit capable of detecting very small masses of metal.

Hand-held scanners should generally be able to detect a medium-sized pistol at 12 inches (300 mm), a small pistol at 9 inches (230 mm), and a razor blade at 3 inches (25 mm) and should scan about 3 to 24 inches per second. They also need to be adjustable. For example, the controls should enable the scanner to lower the sensitivity to avoid unwanted alarms for small harmless objects like key chains. Sensitivity adjustments are usually made through a screwdriver access hole in the handle. Most quality devices which should detect both ferrous and nonferrous metals and alloys encase the circuitry in a rugged high-impact case. It should be capable of not alarming when the scanner is used to screen at ankle height and in the vicinity of rebars in the floor.

Alarms are both visual and audio. They should remain activated while the search coil is over a metal object. The duration of the alarm is usually indicative of the size of the object. Most use alkaline batteries in a power source, which should last at least 80 hours. Low-voltage conditions should advise the user that the power is low by systems similar to those installed in today's cell phones. The average weight is a pound or less. Visual-only alarm indications are advisable if a weapon is detected. The screener can simply ask the individual to step to the side for the moment, giving security personnel time to respond accordingly. An audio alarm alerts the perpetrator that they are "caught," and they may respond accordingly.

No more than 15 percent of the people who alarm the detector should be false alarms. In other words, no more than 15 unarmed passengers out of 100 should alarm the detector. In order to test a particular machine, the FAA developed a gun kit that can be used to test metal detectors, but in actuality involves a tedious process. The suspicious object is placed in seven different positions and locations on the body and the detector is required to alert appropriately. Because of the cumbersomeness of the process, some airport security officials have used such things as a block of metal, large wrenches, and pairs of pliers to achieve the same adequate test results. Regardless of what metal object is used, the machines must be tested weekly if its use is continuous. If a piece of equipment fails the test, it should be replaced within 48 hours.

Additional improvements are considered to be necessary. The law enforcement community has requested improved detection performance, performance tests, and performance specifications for both walk-through and hand-held detectors. In order for advancements to be made, further research will be required to compile reliable data on the electromagnetic properties of weapons-grade metals on which to perform computer simulations of detector performance. The data on conductivity and permeability of many metals has yet to be fully researched.

Millions of travelers have processed through metal detectors and there has not been a single recorded incident of any damage to a computer, a diskette, or a CD. The allowable electromagnetic field permitted from a metal detector (1 gauss) is about twice the earth's magnetic field you experience every minute of your life. Consequently, no metal detector is likely to damage a computer, because exposure is only a few seconds' duration and the field is weak. However, it is not outside the realm of possibility that someone might seek to disguise a computer with an explosive device inside it. After the tragedy of Pan AM Flight 103, the FAA even proposed that all small computers and other electronic devices be banned from aircraft. In today's working world, however, this was not considered to be a reasonable request of business travelers, journalists, and a host of others. Early fears that the use of computers on board might interfere with navigation devices have proved to be groundless. The FAA permits their use except during takeoff and landing procedures.

Personal medical devices (PMEDs) are another story. Walk-through and hand-held metal detectors may affect some of the more sophisticated devices in medical use today. Walk-through and hand-held metal detectors might cause cardiac defibrillators, infusion devices, or spinal cord stimulators to malfunction. More research is required to develop and test an affordable magnetic field emulator, so that the medical devices could more accurately be tested for interference from the metal detectors. The Food and Drug Administration (FDA) should assess interference thresholds and issue regulatory susceptibility standards for PMEDs ("Development of Systems to Evaluate Magnetic Fields Produced by Walk-Through and Hand Held Metal Detectors," Office of Law Enforcement Standards, Internet: http://www.eeel.nist.gov/810.02/detection.html, Pg. 1, 11 July 2001). Currently, the National Institute of Science and Technology, in collaboration with the FDA are working on more accurately evaluating the effects of metal detectors on PMEDs, specifically regarding metal detector–induced failure or malfunction.

■ X-RAY INSPECTION UNITS

X-ray inspection units of carry-on luggage and people all use the low-dosage, low-energy, or low-radiation type. The x-rays are reflected from the subject to create an image. The newer emerging technologies can detect metallic and nonmetallic explosives and other contraband concealed under multiple layers of material. Current imaging technologies either scan subjects for natural radiation emitted by a human body, called passive imaging, or expose objects to radiation reflected, called active imaging.

In first-generation baggage screening units, low-dosage units produced a weak image that had to be amplified on a closed circuit television in order to be adequately used. Many units operated on a short pulse equaling about 1/120th of a second. Some units kept the image on the screen in an image-storage unit until the next image needed to be viewed. Others operated in a continuous emission mode. Both of these analog systems created poor contrast in comparison with the systems now available. Today, digital video storage enhances the ability to eliminate background radiation scatter making the picture clearer. The newest technology uses either x-ray or millimeter wavelength electromagnetic radiation usually from a pulsed x-ray source. The entire system is digital, including the image transfer mechanism.

Note: *Energy, frequency, and wavelength are fundamentally related. Energy is inversely proportional to wavelength. Basically, long-wavelength radiation is low energy and low-frequency or short-wavelength radiation is high energy and high frequency.*

■ PASSIVE MILLIMETER-WAVE IMAGING

Passive millimeter-wave imaging technology operates on the principle that any object not at absolute zero temperature emits electromagnetic energy at all wavelengths. These systems will operate in the millimeter-wave range or near 100 gHz. Any energy should be detected by an appropriate receiver and can be mathematically manipulated to produce a visible image. The system gathers information from radiation naturally emitted from a human body. Regardless of how clear the image, an operator must be trained to distinguish any threat objects from the natural clutter of nonthreatening objects.

The area of passive millimeter-wave imaging is still in development. It potentially can provide a system that offers a lot of contrast. Although there are applications in which active millimeter-wave sensing is more appropriate, passive sensing can avoid glint. Old equipment used to be quite bulky, but the new technology allows sensing from small integrated chips. In a military application, it can penetrate fog, dust, smoke, and light rain, including military target acquisition and aircraft navigation. In a civilian aviation capacity, it could be used to enhance autonomous landing guidance systems under development that might aid pilots in landing during Category III conditions. Because of the penetration of millimeter-wave frequencies, imaging systems could be used to fight fires by seeing through the smoke and for inland waterway navigation in foggy conditions. In the field of airport security, it can penetrate solids and is able to detect concealed weapons that are made of metal or plastic through as much as 0.5

inches of sheetrock. (Yvonne Carts-Powell, "Passive Millimeter Wave Imaging," Internet: http://www.spie.org/web/oer/march/mar97/passivemm.html, 13 August 2001).

■ ACTIVE MILLIMETER-WAVE IMAGING

Active millimeter-wave imaging technology functions as a short-range radar system that projects a narrow beam of millimeter-wavelength energy against the object and detects the reflected rays. The beam starts at the bottom of an object or person and scans up and produces an image of the object or person. Millimeter-wave technology uses low-energy, low-intensity x-rays reflected from the subject to create an image. The screener must interpret the image in order to determine whether a metallic or nonmetallic weapon is present. The x-rays are actually reflected off the surface of the body. When a patient is x-rayed by a radiologist, the process involves energy, which is transmitted through the body, and is a completely different set of circumstances.

■ SELECTING AN X-RAY UNIT

There are multiple x-ray units available on the market. Selecting a suitable unit for a specific airport can require a great deal of research. Of primary consideration is the picture (imaging) quality and sensitivity of the machine. Previously, no system on the market produced an acute photograph-quality image, but today's digital systems are quite good. No unit is totally effective unless the scanner can easily recognize threatening objects and quickly distinguish them from non-threatening objects. Effectiveness, in turn, substantially depends on the machine's ability to deliver a clear picture. An operator's ability to identify objects clearly and accurately that could be threatening and in a reasonable amount of time, is critical to a successful security operation. Using the equipment on the market to screen passengers and their carry-on baggage, the screener has 6 seconds to evaluate an image. A typical unit will be able to distinguish 36 AWG (American Wire Gauge) in air, 32 AWG behind 0.125-inch thickness of steel, and. 0.2 AWG behind 3 mm of steel. It can have a total penetration of 15 mm of steel ("Portable Digital X-ray Imaging System-RTR-4," Internet: http://www.americanaimpex.com/x-ray.htm, 24 July 2001, Pg. 4).

Stored image units essentially save the image information produced on a display unit where it can be viewed for as long as several minutes even after the object being viewed has passed through the machine. This furnishes the operator important time conscientiously to review the image at hand. At present, the use of digital memory devices is prolific and quite effective. In continuous-beam units, the actual x-ray beam is activated throughout the time the object is being inspected; usually 3 to 6 seconds. A smear effect can also appear from an object's continuous movement along a conveyor belt, making the system less desirable than digital storage methods. Older systems had to be stopped so the screener could maintain a clear viewing image.

It must be remembered that not all airports have the latest technology at their disposal. Much of the x-ray equipment in use today is several years old. There have even been reports that, "guards are watching black, white or snow-filled screens that would make any sort of real detection of weapons or explosives impossible" (Clark, Staten, "Airport Safety and Security: Minimal Acceptable Standards," Internet: http://www.emergency.com/airprtsc.htm, 4 June 2001, Pg. 1). A cynic might agree with highly underpaid and undereducated former contract guards when they quipped that the federal government requires that the bags and people be scanned, not that the guards are actually capable of detecting any dangerous items. Such attitudes are more widespread than expected. Congress did appropriate $100 million in fiscal year 1999 and $157 million in both 1997 and 1998 to continue deploying state of the art security equipment to airports ("Airport Security," http://www.skyguide.net/html/travelresources/security.html, 14 February 2001, Pg. 2).

In the past, it was also important to distinguish between those x-ray units that projected an x-ray horizontally and those that had the x-ray emanate from the top of the machine down vertically. If the machine projects horizontally across the viewing surface, some luggage, especially foldover bags, may be difficult to scan adequately. Newer L-shaped detector arrays provide 100-percent package screening. Most machines manufactured currently and used for checked luggage employ high-speed x-rays. They send a computed tomographic (CT) scan–like beam through the luggage to get a "slice" image of anything it is programmed to examine.

Another issue for discussion is the speed at which the system works. The FAA had established the standard flow-through rate as no more than 6 seconds per item. This equates to about 10 pieces of luggage per minute. Most machines will process carry-on baggage at a rate much faster than this, however, and the training of the screener comes into significant play in this regard. If the screener just wants to process people and baggage, they can hurriedly and negligently process a lot of people quickly. Conveyor belt speeds on most pieces of equipment are adjustable, making this possibility often very tempting. Most machines have a conveyor speed of around 48 feet per minute at 60 Hz (14.4 meters per minute at 50 Hz). They are also reversible.

■ SIZERS

Other factors to consider when purchasing a particular piece of equipment include safety, mobility, easy of maintenance, and relative cost. At issue is also the inspection size capability of the system. Some manufacturers are providing airlines with multitask machines, which combine the x-ray screener function and the ability to "size" the luggage. Not only is the carry-on luggage x-rayed, but it is sized to see if it will fit in the overhead compartments on board the aircraft. If the particular piece of luggage is larger than 9 by 14 by 22 inches, it will not fit through the x-ray machine. The passenger is encouraged to return to the check-in counter with the bag or the airline will have an airline employee "skycap" take control of the baggage right there at the security checkpoint. Unfortunately, not all the airlines agree on the acceptable size of carry-on luggage.

When several airlines share the sterile concourse, problems can arise. For example, Continental Airlines prides itself on permitting its customers to carry-on some rather large items. They are so committed to this marketing concept that they have sued Delta over the sizer issue in the San Diego airport. The lawsuit filed in a San Diego court alleged that sizing equipment had created traffic jams at the security checkpoint and forced some Continental customers to return to the check-in counter with their bags. Vice-President of Airport Services for Continental said, "Continental customers should not be penalized by Delta's imposition of its unfriendly baggage policies" (Paula Arrillage, Associated Press, *Texas News*, 25 November 1998). Delta had installed Plexiglas cutouts in front of two x-ray security machines in order to make sure all bags were small enough to fit under the seat or in the overhead bins. The lawsuit sought an injunction and unspecified damages alleging interference with contractual rights and unfair competition. It was settled out of court. Continental has also sued United Airlines for similar procedures at Dulles International Airport alleging that sizers interfere with security screening.

In September 2002, the TSA announced it intends to remove the plexiglas plates, arguing that they slow security. They did not state that it hindered the process. So far, the TSA has asked airlines to remove the plates but has not made it a requirement. The removal could delay takeoff times even further when passenger reach aircraft and their luggage will not fit into the overhead compartment.

■ FILM AND LAPTOPS

Passengers are always inquiring whether the x-ray machine is film safe and computer safe. Some travelers continue to insist that the CT scan–type beam from an x-ray machine will leave a bluish stripe or line on unprocessed slide, print, or picture film. They claim the "line" remains after the film is developed. The effect of the much stronger x-ray machines used in scanning checked baggage makes this a distinct possibility. Some experts have advised travelers that the powerful x-ray and neutron tomography machines will destroy film. They further advise airline passengers that x-ray–protection bags sold in camera stores are "absolutely useless" (X-ray Advice, Internet: http://sung3.ifsi.rm.cnr.it/~dargaud/Photo/xray.html, 3 Aug 2001, Pgs. 1, 2). Admittedly, the screener can just increase the beam on the bag until they can see through it. At least one manufacturer, SIMA, disputes this advice. They claim that FilmShield XPF bags protect film, withstanding multiple passes through high-dosage security equipment, even the CTX-5000 ("New Filmshield XPF Protects Film From High Dosage Airport Security Equipment,"

Internet: http://www.simacorp.com/xrayinfo.htm, 3 Aug 2001, Pg. 2). The best advice is not to check sensitive film.

Film in carry-on baggage would have to be repeatedly screened, up to as much as 10 times, to make any difference whatsoever. The average machine in use at today's airports is more likely to generate a dosage of only 0.1 mR. It should be recognized that not all low-dosage scanners are calibrated equally. As long ago as 1973, the Film Technical Services Division of Eastman Kodak found,

> The results of our tests thus far have led us to the conclusion that a cumulative exposure not exceeding 5 milliroentgens (mR) would seldom cause a noticeable photographic effect, providing the exposure is made in increments not exceeding 1 mR and the orientation of the film luggage combination is changed between exposures (J. K. Debenham, "A Brief Description of the Effects of X-ray Inspection on Unprocessed Photographic Film," Film Technical Services Division, Eastman Kodak, 1973).

However, much has changed since 1973. The Photographic and Imaging Manufacturers Association Inc. tested the CTX-5000SP. They concluded, "The CTX-5000SP will cause significant fogging of all color negative films with an ISO speed of 100 or higher when the film sustains a direct hit by the machine's high intensity x-ray beam" ("Technical Report Confirms Film Damage," *Air Wise News*, Internet: http://www.airwise.com/news/headlines/scanners2.html, Pgs. 1–4, 3 August 2001). The FAA, now TSA, had already addressed the issue. They amended Part 108 on 24 September 1998 to post warnings to travelers.

▓ PASSENGER X-RAY SCREENING DEVICES

Since the initiation of screening procedures, x-ray imaging, microwave holography, and acoustic detection have all been tested as a means for detecting weapons and contraband hidden in and on a human body. Some of the newest technology has become quite intrusive.

American Science and Engineering Inc., located in Billerica, Massachusetts, now manufacturers an x-ray machine which essentially sees through clothes. US Customs officials tested the devices at several major airports. The controversy has been immediate and vocal. The equipment is supposed to be targeting drug smugglers. If a passenger is considered to be suspicious for some reason, they are given the option of submitting to a traditional pat-down search or standing in front of the x-ray machine, which renders an image of the individual naked. Obviously, the equipment could be used to search for dangerous weapons as well.

The idea was to build a device less intrusive than the pat-down search. As mentioned, US Customs officials have been criticized for allegedly focusing too much on minority passengers. This type of x-ray machine was originally seen as an alternative to a pat-down search. Others have labeled it an electronic strip

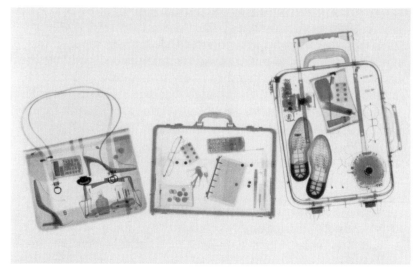

X-ray of suitcase, briefcase, and bag. No explosives or dangerous articles are observed and the bags are cleared for loading. Organic explosives appear orange on the scanner's monitor. *Nicholas Veasey / Getty Images Inc.—Stone Allstock.*

search that is extremely graphic. Some passengers, especially public figures, fear that dishonest security personnel might retain the images of them without clothes. For some people, the naked photograph of a movie star or other celebrity might be worth the deceit of selling it for publication. The temptation to a poorly paid screener might be too great.

In order to avoid raising the specter of Fourth Amendment search issues and privacy issues, US Customs officers must first obtain a signed consent form from the passenger and the viewer is supposed to be of the same sex. The advertised level of radiation is quite small, but pregnant women are not provided with this option to be on the safe side.

■ PORTABLE DIGITAL X-RAY IMAGING SYSTEMS

Police are now using portable x-ray imaging systems to search efficiently for weapons or contraband in areas either too difficult or too time consuming to search manually. The RTR-4 is one of the latest, and according to its manufacturer, it is the only fully digital portable x-ray equipment available to EOD (Explosive Ordnance Disposal) personnel. It is manufactured by the Americana Impex Consulting Co., and it weighs approximately 15 pounds. The unit can be used to investigate suspicious packages, mail, and vehicles wherever they are located. It can also be mounted on bomb-disposal robots, but it is fully operational in a stand-alone mode.

The unit could be carried on any aircraft or used to inspect a cart full of baggage while sitting on the flight line. Since it is mobile, its applications could extend throughout an entire airport environment. This tool can enhance the safety margin for innocent passengers and aircrews. It can be deployed to search the control tower and be quickly moved to a restroom where a bomb threat has been made. It is cost effective and should be considered to be a necessary tool at any major airport ("Portable Digital X-Ray Imaging System," Internet: http://www.americanimpex.com/x-ray.htm, Pgs. 1–5).

TESTING X-RAY EQUIPMENT

The government requires that all x-ray units be tested daily. This responsibility falls on the shoulders of the screening supervisor. A step-wedge testing procedure is usually used. The American Society for Testing and Materials (ASTM) step wedge reduces in size through the procedure. Ultimately, each unit must detect the 24-gauge wire under the fifth step of the step wedge, an accurately calibrated filter strip that provides a stepped range of exposures in a sensitomer. The original rationale was that the test would certify that each piece of equipment would be capable of detecting the smallest gauge of the common lead wire used for blasting in the majority of blasting caps. Today's equipment requires a more sophisticated approach. Most pieces should detect #38 AWG wire of ASTM (#30 AWG through the seventh step wedge). The units should also have a penetration of 17 mm cold rolled steel. All machines must minimally comply with former FAR 129.26 "Use of X-ray Systems."

DETECTION CAPABILITIES

It is clear that detecting and recognizing a gun either by the use of a metal detector or an x-ray machine is not an absolute and foregone conclusion. A successful detection is still dependent on the competency of the operator. In addition, a bomb is obviously more difficult to recognize than a gun. Terrorists do not submit baggage for screening with labels of "fragile bomb included" stamped in clear view. Terrorists or those seeking to do harm at airport facilities or while airborne have used advances in technology to help them evade security procedures. New "toys" like the OSA (Obshevoiskovaya Samokhodhaya Artilleriya) gun are real and deadly and have turned up at airports. They look like a key chain but are really a low-caliber gun capable of holding two bullets. The gun costs about $20, is about 3 inches long, and an inch wide, and will not set off a metal detector (Daniel Klaidman, "The New Secret Weapons," *Newsweek*, 18 May 1999, Pg. 37). In spite of its size, it can be used to kill. Interpol has even sent out a worldwide notice warning law enforcement of the potential danger. Plastic guns such as the Glock and Sigma pistols pose further threats. Even though they are not true plastic guns, because of the plastic content of the gun they can potentially evade security. An alert screener, however, can still detect the barrel, slide, and one spring, which are made of metal. Consequently, both guns and explosives are becoming more and more difficult to detect, requiring the constant vigilance of the airport screener.

Using x-rays to detect a bomb and using them to disarm it are different procedures; however, the United States lags behind many countries in research to make these systems more viable. Some unique work has been accomplished at the Police Scientific Development Branch in the United Kingdom. Equipped with a lead-lined laboratory, the Explosive and Weapons Detection Group has done extensive work on the general requirements of x-ray imaging systems as well as the related health and safety issues associated with the equipment.

▨ PRIOR X-RAY EXPLOSIVE-DETECTION DEVICES

In June 1990, EG&G Astrophysics introduced yet another option—false image protection (FIP). The purpose of the equipment was to test operator alertness. It also became useful in training operators to recognize specific threat objects. According to Kenneth Moore,

> At a location away from the operator's station, a supervisor can activate an FIP and on a random basis, superimpose a false threat object on the monitor screen showing an x-rayed bag. Thus, if the outline of a Glock 17 automatic appeared on the monitor screen, the operator would have to press the control panel to acknowledge they had seen the false threat object. The operator's actions are recorded on a diskette for auditing purposes (Kenneth Moore, Airport, Aircraft and Airline Security, Butterworth Heinemann, 1991, Pg. 137). Even more sophisticated software has been developed and will be discussed in another chapter.

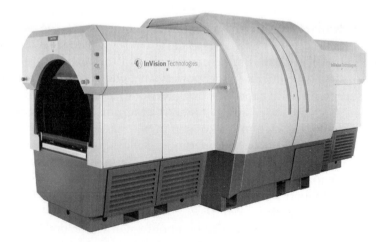

The CTX 9000DSi™ is InVision Technologies Inc. most sophisticated explosive detection system. The system utilizes core technology derived from medical Computer Tomography. The projection x-ray images initially created determine which bags or cargo need slice images taken by a rotating x-ray source which are further analyzed to compare with the properties of explosives. *Courtesy of InVision Technologies.*

Note: *The Federal Food and Drug Administration (FDA) is responsible for the monitoring of scanning devices used in US airports. They are tasked with assuring that the devices are designed so as to minimize the public and the employee's exposure to harmful rays. The contact point at the FDA is the Division of Consumer Affairs, Center for Devices and Radiological Health, FDA, Rockville, MD 20857, 301-443-4190. The National Institute of Justice sets the standards for metal detectors. Details can be viewed in NIJ Standard-0601.01, "Walk Through Metal Detectors for Use in Weapon and Contraband Detection," September 2000, and NIJ Standard-0602.01, "Hand Held Metal Detectors for Use in Weapon and Contraband Detection," September 2000.*

US STANDARD FOR RADIATION EXPOSURE

The US standard, originally developed by the National Committee on Radiation Protection, concluded that members of the public shall receive no more than 170 millirems/year from all man-made radiation sources other than medical exposures. As a point of reference, it is interesting to point out that cosmic radiation from the atmosphere can be over 200 millirems per year at high-altitude cities such as Katmandu, Nepal, and Denver, Colorado. Radiation badges worn by operators record the amount of radiation they are receiving during a work period. A control badge is kept separate and away from the area in which the x-ray machines are operating. This enables the staff to have an environmental level of radiation exposure for comparison with the badges worn by the operators. The levels are recorded and maintained.

NEW COMPUTER SOFTWARE

Newer x-ray/detection machines contain threat image projection (TIP) software. It also provides managers with the ability to test the alertness of employees. The software enables the manager to project x-ray images of weapons or bombs into the scanner monitor. The employee must signal the manager that the "dangerous object" has been recognized. The system injects these random threatening images into real bags going through the machine as well as into images of bags created by the program. When a screener detects a threat and stops the bag, the software flashes a note of congratulation. The screener's performance, good or bad, is recorded. The system allows the airport security company to monitor each and every scanner's performance. Individuals who may need more training can be identified. Those who have difficulty detecting dangerous objects can be moved to another function. As once overheard by the author, screeners should at least be able to detect the difference between an Uzi and an umbrella.

The system also allowed the FAA to oversee the performance of the airport security company. Companies could lose FAA certification if their screeners did not meet FAA standard detection criteria. On 22 May 2000, a spokeswoman for the FAA reported "About $50 million to $65 million is to be spent on the better-resolution x-ray systems with Threat Image Projection (TIP) software, and about one-third of the airports (450 of the nation's busiest) will receive new equipment in each of the next three years" ("New Airport X-ray Machines Can Train As Well As Protect," *Scripps Howard New Service*, Internet: http://www.caller.com/cfapps/printhis/index.cfm, 3 August 2001). In July 2000, the FAA announced three contracts worth a total of up to $120 million to Rapiscan, Perkin Elmer and Heimann Systems that would allow the agency to purchase up to 800 TIP installed x-ray machines from each vendor ("FAA to Receive Award for Airport Security Screener," *Air Wise News*, Internet: http://news.airwise.com/stories/2000/11/974208505.html., 3 Aug 2001).

In November 2000, Aviation Week and Space Technology's Innovation Award went to the FAA for implementing the TIP software. They received the award jointly with Rapiscan Security Products of Hawthorne, CA, and Perkin Elmer Instruments of Long Beach, CA, the two companies that developed the imaging system. The FAA Administrator announced, "We are extremely pleased to receive this award honoring the most innovative new technologies in global aerospace, especially since this is the first time the FAA has been named as a recipient" ("FAA to Receive Award for Airport Security Screener," *Air Wise News*, Internet: http://news.airwise.com/stories/2000/11/974208505.html, 3 Aug 2001).

■ EXPLOSIVE-DETECTION SYSTEMS

Screening all baggage is a gargantuan task. Screening all baggage at a reasonable throughput rate is an even greater challenge. Plainly, the vulnerability of aircraft to explosives placed in the cargo hold still poses a significant threat. In the 1970s, airline officials were forced to use technology already on the market. The most available device at the time, the explosive-detection system ION Track M97 used by the US Army Explosive Ordinance Disposal units worldwide was tested. It proved to be effective in detecting explosive materials, but was not a practical method to screen the high volumes needed at a busy airport.

The FAA, therefore, awarded several contracts to a number of firms for developing a vapor-detection device. In mid-1987, Thermedics was developing a vapor-detection device and Science Applications International Corporation (SAIC) was working on thermal neutron activation (TNA) as a detection method. However, TNA (thermal neutron activation) uses nuclear radiation, and even though it had been shown to have the highest degree of explosive-detection capability available at the time, it had its drawbacks. The system works when luggage passes through a cloud of very low-energy "thermal neutrons." The neutrons are very penetrating and cause gamma rays to be instantly produced in the luggage, consequently revealing the presence of explosives. However, in 1991, the Congressional Office of Technology Assessment told a Senate committee that the TNA was flawed, and they recommended no new purchases of the equipment.

Technology has progressed a long way in the last decade. The TSA can now certify explosive-detection equipment based on an entirely different set of scientific principles known as T-scan or CT scan technology. This technology had been under development for many years and, as previously stated, is based on the same core technology as medical CT. CT scans create a multidimensional image. As the conveyor moves each bag through the machine, the system creates a scan projection x-ray image. From this image, the computer determines which areas need "slice" images taken by the rotating x-ray source. The scanner measures density more precisely from different angles as it circles the bag. Using sophisticated computer algorithms, the machine analyzes these images and compares their CT properties with those of known explosives. If a match is found, the system alarms and displays the object on the screen. Potential explosives are highlighted in red, detonators in green, and metallic objects such as circuit boards are shown in blue. The operator views the screen image to determine whether a real threat exists and follows established protocols for threat resolution.

The InVision Technologies was founded in 1990 for the express purpose of adapting sophisticated medical CT technology for the detection of explosives at airports. The FAA Act of 1996 authorized the purchase of 54 CTX 5000™ luggage scanners. (Gregory T. Nojeim, "Aviation Security Profiling and Passengers' Civil Liberties," 13 *Air and Space Law*, 1998, Pg. 3). The company's CTX 5000™ products were the first systems to meet FAA certification requirements for automated explosive-detection systems. The CTX 5000™ was certified in 1994 and has been operating in airport environments since then. Invision's third-generation explosive-detection system is the CTX, which was certified by the FAA in April 1999. It is one of the fastest explosive-detection systems on the market and is certified to process 542 bags per hour. According to the manufacturer, the system has the lowest false alarm rate and an actual throughput rate of 800 bags an hour. In addition, its 1-meter aperture allows for smooth integration of standard airport baggage as well as oversized baggage. One of Invision's newest products is the CTX 2500EDS™. It was designed specifically for smaller airports, low-traffic areas in large airports, and mobile applications. It is smaller, lighter, and less expensive than many other models. Recently, the TSA ordered 400 model CTX 2500 and CTX 5500 DS explosive-detection systems. L-3 Communications is also certified to manufacture the machines.

The Department of Transportation's (DOT) award to the Boeing Co. included an initial contract of $508 million for the period June through 31 December 2002, the date that the Aviation and Transportation Security Act mandates that all checked luggage be screened for explosives. As mentioned, the total contract is valued at $1.37 million. Boeing is scheduled to install up to 1100 explosive-detection machines and 4800 to 6000 explosive trace–detection machines. Boeing has indicated it will utilize 14 subcontractors to fulfill the contract.

The most common machines weigh about 9350 pounds, or about the size of a sport utility vehicle. Most machines are stand-alone models and are placed near the check-in counter. Some are integrated into an airline's baggage-handling system, which greatly speeds the process. A machine can take several months to install, and some airports will need to reinforce the floors to support the equipment. The floor space must also be wide enough and be near a power source.

Both Invision and L-3 Communications had gone on record indicating that they would be hard pressed to manufacture sufficient quantities of machines to meet the government's December 2002 deadline. As it turns out, the TSA claimed compliance but in reality expanded the protocol of permitted means of screening.

■ TRACE-DETECTION TECHNOLOGY TODAY

Trace-detection technology today is based on the immediate identification of either particles of explosive or vapor containing the explosive material. Actual explosive material must somehow be transported to the equipment for analysis. The amount must be sufficient for the equipment to recognize the material for what it is. Of course, electromagnetic and imaging technologies do not require the equipment actually to analyze the weapon's chemical make-up, only its image. In order for trace-detection equipment to function, a two-step process is involved. The material must be collected and then quickly identified. All equipment must be approved by the TSA, and it is currently required that all baggage on international flights be screened (FAR Section 108.20 Use of Explosives Detection Systems, Internet: http://www.faa.gov/avr/AFS/FARS/far-108.txt, 24 April 2001, Pg. 15). The new rules under the auspices of the TSA, effective December 2002 required that all domestic cargo be screened as well.

Initially, research and development efforts focused on collecting the vapor around a person or a piece of baggage in order to search for various types of commercial and military explosives, including dynamite, Semtex, C-4, and TNT. Unfortunately, these substances do not really give off a great deal of vapor to be evaluated. Therefore, research has expanded to the breakdown of the particulates of explosive material as well. If explosive material is to be detected from an air sample or removed from a substrate (i.e., a person's clothing), the technology required is sophisticated. Both have their own pluses and minuses. Basically, "Vapor technologies are more effective for detecting explosive materials with high vapor pressures, while particulate technologies are more appropriate for explosive materials with low vapor pressure, such as military plastic explosives" ("Airline Passenger Security Screening, New Technologies and Implementation Issues," National Research Council, Publication NMAB-482-1, National Academy Press, Washington DC, 1996, Pg. 17). Samples for both methods can be acquired by having the passenger walk through a portal or by using a hand-held device.

Devices today can be either contact or noncontact. They combine chemiluminescent detection with gas chromatography. Gas chromatography is the most widely used scientific technique for the positive separation and identification of explosives in a complex mixture. Sample material is heated into gaseous form. It is added to a carrier gas and separated into its individual components by controlled temperature cycling. The components are sent to the chemiluminescent detector in the carrier gas. All nitrogen-based high explosives contain nitro chemical groups. For baggage, the operator swipes the surface of the object. In a contact device, the passenger must push on a door to get into the portal scanner. In a noncontact device, air passes over the passenger and collects the necessary material for analysis. Hand-held devices can also be used but do require a significant investment in time to process each passenger. Developmental efforts continue, because it remains difficult to extract the explosive vapors or particulates from a passenger and adequately test them for every known explosive material. An additional problem revolves around clearing the system once a positive detection has been made. A trained security officer must constantly monitor the baseline readings of the equipment in order to make sure that subsequent readings do not become cumulative and thereby false. Future technologies under development in this area include pyroluminescence, chemical sensors and ion drift spectroscopy.

▦ TRACE-DETECTION DEVICES FOR BAGGAGE

In response to the President's Commission's findings, in November 1990, Sec 108 of the Aviation Security Improvement Act amended the provisions of the Federal Aviation Act of 1958 pertaining to explosive-detection equipment. Section 320 Deployment of Explosive Detection Equipment reads:

> General Rule: No deployment or purchase of any explosive detection equipment pursuant to Section 108.7(b)(8) and 108.20 of Title 14, Code of Federal Regulations, or any similar rule, shall be required after the date of the enactment of this section, unless the Administrator certifies that, based on the results of tests conducted pursuant to protocols developed in consultation with expert scientists from outside the Federal Aviation Administration, such equipment alone or as part of an integrated system can detect under realistic air carrier operating conditions the amounts, configuration, and types of explosive material which would be likely to be used to cause catastrophic damage to commercial aircraft.

The European Civil Aviation Conference (ECAC) had mandated a deadline of 2002 for trace-detection device implementation of 100-percent hold baggage screening in Europe several years ago. Currently, in the United States, only international flights undergo 100-percent scanning of cargo, but as stated, the rule has been expanded. However, cost factors will likely be determinative of the final discussion as to when to implement them. The debate over aircraft and airport security, particularly in the cargo hold, intensified in the aftermath of the TWA Flight 800 disaster and again after 9/11. The midair explosion over Long Island, New York, in 1996 at least forged a consensus in government and by the public that drastic measures may well be needed. At the time, President Bill Clinton established the White House Commission on Aviation Safety and Security led by Vice-President Al Gore. They recommended new technology to be utilized for surveillance and screening. Unfortunately, at the time, some of the much-needed technology did not really exist.

In April 2002, the US government announced the DOT would deploy approximately 1100 explosive-detection systems and 4700 explosive trace–detection devices by 31 December 2002. The TSA has, in turn, concluded that a mix of these two technologies will provide sufficient protection. This was in reality the first example that insufficient numbers of explosive-detection systems simply did not exist to meet the deadline. DOT has determined they will decide the mix of equipment based on the following:

1. Peak bag loads
2. Ability of the airport and air carrier to integrate explosive-detection systems into the baggage handling system
3. Physical restrictions of explosive-detection systems having to do with weight and size
4. Construction cost associated with explosive-detection system installations due to excessive structural modifications needed.
5. Availability of explosive-detection systems from the manufacturers.

ENHANCING EXPLOSIVE TRACE DETECTION CAPABILITY

On 12 May 1997, the FAA/TSA announced the purchase of $12.2 million worth of trace-detection security equipment. This equipment was designed to detect extremely small amounts of explosives on such items as electronic equipment and small articles in carry-on baggage. The concept was to develop equipment that would enhance the x-ray machines already in use with little or no interruption of passenger or baggage flow. The FAA awarded contracts to Thermedics Detection Inc. of Chelmsford, MA, Barringer Instruments Inc. of New Providence, NJ, and Ion Track Instruments of Wilmington, DE. (AAR Technology R&D Fact Sheet, "Trace Detection Security Equipment," Internet: http://www.faa.gov/aar/trdfs/tdsefs.htm, 3 Aug 2001, Pgs. 1, 2). Prospective purchasers need to evaluate the systems sensitivity features, ease of use, false-positive rates, and the ability to detect ICAO taggants.

Thermedics EGIS 3000, EGIS II, EGIS III

These devices use high-speed gas chromatography with chemiliminescence detection. It is made up of a free-standing analytical unit which takes up relatively little space. Sample collection is accomplished by wiping a surface with a specially designed filter. The filter is then placed into the analytical unit and the EGIS begins an 18-second analysis to determine the presence of an explosive. If one is detected, the unit also identifies the substance. The German Ministry of Interior has selected the EGIS III system for all explosive detection at German airports. The selection was based upon the result of an ECAC (European Civil Aviation Conference) performance test. It already is used to screen passengers and freight in the Channel tunnel, which links the United Kingdom with the European continent.

Barringer IONSCAN 400B, Centurion, Sentinel II

This device uses ion-mobility spectrometry. IONSCAN is a detection-identification device designed to screen and search for trace amounts of explosives that contaminate the baggage with which it comes into contact. Sample collection is accomplished by either wiping a surface with a cotton swab or by using a battery-operated small vacuum cleaner–type device that deploys a filter card. The sample is then placed onto a sample tray and slid into an analyzer. Within 5 seconds the unit confirms the presence of and identifies explosives.

Barringer Instruments, part of Smiths Detection & Protection Systems (DPS), announced in May 2002 that it continues to receive additional orders from the TSA for its IONSCAN trace explosives detectors. Since December 2001, orders totaling approximately $9.7 million have been placed. These instruments have already been deployed at numerous US airports. The IONSCAN was widely deployed at Salt Lake City Airport for the 2002 Winter Olympics. Over 80 systems were installed at the ticket check-in counters to screen checked baggage.

ION Track ITEMISER 3, Entry Scan

This device also uses ion-mobility spectrometry. It also seeks out and detects trace quantities of explosives that can contaminate various objects. Either wiping a surface or collecting the sample with a vacuum device also accomplishes sample collection. The sample is processed through the unit and an analysis is provided within 5 seconds. Ion Track Instrument's (ITI) *ITEMISER* desktop contraband detection and identification system simultaneously detects and identifies traces of both explosives and narcotics on virtually any surface. ITI's ion trap mobility spectrometry (ITMS) surpassed conventional ion-mobility spectrometers (IMSs) in ionization efficiency and sensitivity owing to its patented ion trap. Adding high-speed switching technology that allows identification of time-of-flight peaks for substances in both positive and negative ion modes has further enhanced it. Conventional IMS detectors are restricted to operating in only one mode per sample—making screening for explosives and narcotics with one instrument a complex and time-consuming process. Extensive use of the latest computer technology software in the design of ITEMISER 3 has produced an instrument that requires no user intervention or interpretation. Consequently, operators can concentrate on obtaining good trace samples of explosives or narcotics. An operator need only sample the surface of an item that is suspected of being contaminated with traces of explosives or narcotics and insert the "sample trap" in the slot located in the front of the instrument to trigger analysis.

Nuisance alarms associated with explosive-trace detectors can be caused by the presence of actual explosive residue on a passenger as a result of their job or a medical condition; for example, construction workers, law enforcement personnel who handle explosives, or a passenger using nitroglycerine as a heart medication. Appropriate procedures need to be in place to resolve these alarms in a timely manner.

■ TAGGANTS

The practice of "tagging" or using " taggants" to render explosives detectable by gas analysis methods that are currently available have become commonplace. Their implementation was discussed earlier in relation to the successful international coordination by ICAO (International Civil Aviation Organization) to tag these materials. In 1990, a special subcommittee of the legal committee of ICAO drafted a treaty to require the addition of taggants to all explosives manufactured in one of the contracting states. The United States signed this convention on the "Making of Plastic Explosives for the Purpose of Detection" in March 1991.

Security experts generally agree that all explosives and all explosive precursors should be labeled so as to be able to identify readily the source and disposition of these kinds of materials. Some manufacturers have expressed the concern that a problem with direct labeling of explosives is the unknown effect on the stability, life, function, and sensitivity of the additive. Commercial explosives can be labeled with ceramic particles. These particles or chips are mixed with the granular support of the explosive. The chips are multilayered and the layers are colored to form a readable tag. The tag or code identifies the manufacturer and the batch number. The outside layer of the particle glows under ultraviolet light, and the particles can be easily recovered from an explosion site. This is possible chemically, because commercial explosives are not really granular; the ceramic particles are actually trapped in the mixture. Since the added particles are separate from the explosive, suspended in the mixture, the taggant does not accelerate decomposition or a change in the behavior of the active ingredients. Detonators are not labeled with taggants because of the known effects such an additive would have on the explosive's stability.

Explosives need to be distinguished from smokeless propellant and black powder. Smokeless propellants are the "granular materials that are often called smokeless powder but which are not explosives and which burn but do not detonate" (The Columbia Encyclopedia, Sixth Edition, 2001, www.bartleby.com/65/ex/explosiv.html 13 August 2002). They are used in firearms. Advocates of airport security and the international tagging of explosives are not really concerned with the tagging of materials used in firearm ammunition. They are concerned with the tagging of materials used in high-density explosives and certainly with the tracking of weapons-grade nuclear materials as well as the components of biologic and chemical weapons.

▓ CONCLUSION

New innovations in scanning equipment will only enhance airport security personnel's ability to detect dangerous weapons and explosives even in minute qualities. The equipment will be faster and more accurate than ever before. Additionally and to the dismay of opponents, they are becoming continually more intrusive. Advancements in imaging and detecting concealed weapons and explosive devices have made rapid advancements in the last few years. Current explosive-detection system nuisance alarms are usually the result of the similarity of densities of some materials with the densities of some explosives. However, detectors for locating electronically detonated bombs, improved surveillance cameras, human- and vehicle-recognition systems, and x-ray systems for bomb disarmament are all undergoing serious research and development programs. It will be interesting to follow whether both the public and the courts continue to perceive these advancements as contrary to constitutional law or acceptable intrusion. New QR (Quadruple resonance) systems can operate as a stand-alone machine or integrate into an airport's baggage-handling system. A pass/fail test immediately tells the operator whether or not an explosive threat is detected. An x-ray image can confirm an explosive devise is present. Public reaction since 9/11 has been positive. It remains to be seen how long this acceptance lasts.

Many companies receive government funds to fund their research. Others see the field as worthy of their own resources and envision the ability to make profits from the production of detection products. In other words, industry recognizes that the ongoing problem of possible terrorism at airports will be with us for many years to come.

chapter ten

Cargo Security: A Loose End

▉ NEWS

1. **19 June 2002:** Invision Technologies Inc. announced multiple orders for its CTX brand of explosive-detection systems. The order totaled approximately $6.6 billion.

2. **8 November 1998:** "They are all targets . . . Every day . . . they will receive a new corpse." *Houston Chronicle* quoting "Usama bin Ladin interview with ABC News May 1998.

3. **17 June 2002:** L-3 Communications publicized that it has successfully completed its acquisition of the Detection Systems business of Perkin Elmer, which has an installed base of over 1600 units at airports for checked and oversized baggage, break bulk cargo, and air freight.

4. **14 June 2002:** The Department of Transportation revealed that it is seeking $536,000 in civil penalties from American Airlines for multiple alleged cargo security violations uncovered in October 2000.

5. **7 May 2002:** Heimann Systems and the Belgian Customs finalized a contract for the delivery and installation of a Mobile Heinmann Cargo scanning system in Antwerp to improve security and detect dangerous materials including chemical and nuclear weapons.

■ INTRODUCTION

Cargo screening and inspection is just as important as the screening of passengers and their carry-on luggage. Even more so if it is assumed that the terrorist does not want to sacrifice their life for the cause and seeks to hide the bomb on board an aircraft unaccompanied. The catastrophe of Pan Am Flight 103 over Lockerbie, Scotland, is the perfect example. The attack on 9/11 begs the question what next? The disaster reinforces the concept that no matter how demanding the present security cargo procedures seem, under current standards, a bomb may somehow find its way into the cargo. Prevention before the event is of course a key element of any solution. However, all available efforts also need to be made to minimize the damage once the inevitable is about to happen. Speed, volume, and on-time delivery requirements drive today's cargo business strategy of supply-chain management. The increase of sophisticated threats from terrorists, international crime organizations, and cybercrime potentially could have a catastrophic impact on global trade. The new cargo criminals are nationally networked and internationally financed.

New technology needs to be developed in the specific field of cargo security. For example, blast-containment and blast-resistant technology need to be further developed. Additionally, the screening of sealed US mail must be further analyzed and addressed. Regulations and controls on indirect shippers is yet another issue worthy of follow-up research. This chapter will discuss some of the topics pertaining to cargo, air mail, unknown shippers, and the general consigning of cargo by air.

The challenge is readily apparent: how to screen literally billions of bags and consigned cargo quickly enough to prevent massive back-ups at airports, but thoroughly enough to prevent a tragedy. The task is a daunting and often frustrating one. Initial cargo scanning machines were slow, huge and were prone to false alarms. They were also very expensive. InVision's CTX 5000™ was the first and initially the only one certified by the Federal Aviation Administration (FAA). These machines are essentially the same as medical CT scanners, although they are much more powerful and connected to powerful computers. The cost for each machine remains at approximately $1 million or more. This raises the cost of cargo security considerably, especially for smaller airports unable to absorb the high cost. Therefore, the public's awareness of the need to purchase, update, and maintain this equipment before another tragedy occurs is absolutely critical. A plethora of other companies now also manufacture a variety of x-ray scanners and metal detectors. The name brand is irrelevant, but the quality of the machine and their practical use in airports is essential. The Transportation Safety Administration (TSA) has proposed rules to make the screening of domestic cargo as stringent as is already required for international cargo. However, Congress has yet to mandate an appropriate air cargo security program.

Clearly, there can be no total security guarantee given to the concept of protecting aircraft against incendiary or explosive attacks. However, if properly addressed, the risk to baggage and cargo handling can be greatly reduced. New technology pertaining to compartmented baggage containers and even more sophisticated explosive-detection and trace-detection devices will enhance

A freight cargo container on a conveyor belt rolls toward a cargo door on a Pan Am 747 at an embarkation terminal at Kennedy Airport in New York. Cargo remains a huge vulnerability in the context of overall airport security both on cargo and passenger aircraft. *Pan American Airways, Corp.*

protective efforts even further. Additionally, standardized security evaluations of manufacturers and shippers need to be immediately implemented.

■ CARGO CARRIER RESPONSIBILITY

Baggage was covered in the Federal Aviation regulations in Part 108. In particular, FAR 108.13 (b) required the baggage carried in an airplane be checked by a responsible agent and that identification be obtained from all persons, other than known shippers, who seek to ship goods or cargo aboard the airplane. Today, 49 CFR Chapter XII Part 1548.9 Acceptance of Cargo states:

a. *Preventing or deterring the carriage of any explosive or incendiary.* Each indirect air carrier must use facilities, equipment, and procedures described in its security program to prevent or deter the carriage of any unauthorized explosive or incendiary on board a passenger aircraft in cargo.

b. *Refusal to transport.* Each indirect air carrier must refuse to offer for transport on a passenger aircraft any cargo if the shipper does not consent to a search or inspection of that cargo in accordance with this part, and part 1544 or 1546 of this chapter. The indirect air carrier must search or inspect cargo, and must request the shipper for consent to search or inspect cargo, as provided in the indirect air carrier's security program.

When airlines leave the baggage unattended, the ramifications can be quite serious as occurred in Pan Am Flight 103 where the baggage container had been left unattended for over 30 minutes. Appropriate access control procedures are not only mandated by the TSA but also represent a common sense approach to security.

It is crucial that once cargo has been accepted from the passenger or shipper that it must be under continuous control. Once the airline accepts baggage at the check-in counter or curb side, it is usually placed on a conveyor belt where it is transported to a centralized sorting facility. Not every piece of baggage can be observed every minute; however, restricting access to the cargo will reduce both pilferage and unauthorized tampering. Even when the baggage is loaded onto a baggage cart from the central location for transportation to the aircraft, the baggage carts are rarely if ever sealed. Just restricting the public to the cargo/baggage area is insufficient. This is an area where the prescreening of employees and stringent access control standards are essential. It does not matter if every single piece of cargo has been screened or manually inspected if an employee who has access decides to tamper with it.

Another issue revolves around unaccompanied baggage. Anyone who travels knows that there are numerous reasons why bags become separated from their owners. Most travelers are unhappy when they arrive at their destination without their luggage; the reasons for which are often mysterious. It is the same cosmic question as where do those socks go in the dryer. However, there are many legitimate reasons why unaccompanied bags present no real threat, including the owner of the bags has taken an earlier flight or misdirected baggage has been caused by airline error. On the other hand, the separation may be deliberate, causing a hazard to flight or for the illegal movement of drugs or other contraband. These instances, although statistically insignificant when compared with the total amount of baggage processed, are highly significant when a terrorist operation is underway.

Formerly, Parts 108 and 129 of the FARs required US and foreign air carriers to adopt and carry out a security program. Each program had to have been approved by the FAA. Within the United States, the requirements for US and foreign carriers mirror each other. TSA 49 CFR Chapter XII, Part 1548.7, Approval and Amendments of the Security Program, requires the air carrier to have the TSA approve their security programs 90 days prior to implementation. Many amendments have been made to the original rules. One significant amendment changed the definition of the "known shipper" concept. Too many airlines were accepting cargo for carriage without really knowing the origination of the cargo. During 1995, the FAA started to record air carrier and airport inspection data into a new national database. The program developed the Air Carrier and Airport Inspection Reporting System (AAIRS). The system records data on all aspects of an air carrier's security obligations, including cargo security requirements. One of the greatest threats to aircraft safety remains the unauthorized shipment of hazardous and/or dangerous cargo. Shippers often tried to ship such dangerous cargo mixed in between permissible cargo attempting to seal it with black plastic, hoping the airlines or the FAA would not check it.

■ REPORT TO CONGRESS ON AIR CARGO SECURITY

In May 1998, a report was submitted to Congress in response to the requirement in Section 313 of Public Law 104-264 of the Federal Aviation Reauthorization Act of 1996. Section 313 (a) stated that the Secretary of Transportation shall transmit to Congress a report "on any changes recommended and implemented as a result of the White House Commission on Aviation Safety and Security to enhance and supplement screening and inspection of cargo, mail, and company-shipped materials transported in air commerce." The annual reports have consistently pointed out some significant discrepancies still exist within the airport security context.

The Aviation Security Advisory Committee (ASAC) created the Baseline Working Group (BWG) in July 1996 in an effort to strengthen the everyday airport security efforts in place across the nation. It was created prior to the formation of the White House Commission on Aviation Safety and Security, but its efforts were related to the recommendations of the Commission. The BWG also formed the Cargo Working Group (CWG) specifically to deal with the unique problems related to air cargo. The groups were dissolved in December 1996 when the ASAC issued the ASAC Domestic Security Baseline Final Report. The President's Commission, assembled on 25 July 1996, also recommended that the FAA implement a comprehensive plan to address the threat of explosives and other threat objects aboard aircraft. In order to consolidate all the recommendations and views, the FAA requested that the ASAC reconvene another CWG to be known as the Cargo Baseline Working Group. In 1997, this group published some expanded recommendations.

Overall, the CBWG concluded that (1) The FAA should implement a comprehensive plan to address the threat of explosives and other threat objects in cargo and work with industry to develop new initiatives in this area. (2) The FAA should place greater emphasis on the work of teams such as the Aviation Security Advisory Committee and the CBWG to address cargo issues. The FAA agreed with the two recommendations, and has pursued further cooperative efforts with the US Postal Service, the US Customs Service, and the air carriers. Some important issues persist pertaining to airmail security, indirect air carriers, unknown shippers, and international cargo standards. In fact, a Department of Transportation (DOT) Inspector General report indicates security for cargo carried on passenger planes is "easily circumvented." The report reveals a system in dire need of attention. The current air cargo system has significant security gaps in it and does not ensure that a shipper even complies with minimum security measures.

Unfortunately, security measures designed to prevent terrorists from placing bombs in the cargo holds of passenger planes have huge loopholes.

■ SUICIDES

This section may initially appear to be an odd place to discuss suicide. However, passengers checking explosive or incendiary devices who are intent on killing themselves either out of depression or to make a statement is always going to pose a threat. Individuals who have decided to attempt to leave their dependants substantial sums of money by dying in an aircraft crash also present a continued threat. Prompt investigation of such incidents has often established the death as a suicide, making most insurance policies nonpayable; however, the concept of successfully doing so continues.

Because of the potentiality for this type of criminal misconduct, the Airline Pilots Association has vigorously objected to the availability of flight insurance in airport terminals. Insurance vending machines in airports used to be a common site but are no longer readily available in the United States. The need for greater care in writing all kinds of flight insurance remains very important. The American Express Platinum Card currently has an automatic flight insurance program for anyone who purchases a ticket using the card; providing the perfect opportunity to perpetrate a fraud. Certainly, attempts to commit suicide on board an aircraft are likely to continue, especially with a payable benefit of $1,000,000 is at stake. Insurers, on the other hand, consider the risk small and the income potentially great. The Platinum Card benefit tacks on $18 per ticket, but they rarely have had to pay any death benefits.

Another problem involves the psychological health of the pilots. A suicidal pilot can be as lethal a weapon as any bomb. According to the FAA, a suicidal pilot intentionally crashed an Egyptian Airlines plane into the Atlantic Ocean in 1999. Psychologists have published warning signs criteria, providing employers with guidelines to determine whether employees are indeed suicidal. Insurers need to be alert to the same warning signs. An automatic insurance machine in an airport terminal can not evaluate any of these criteria, and does indeed provide a suicidal individual, pilot or passenger, with an unnecessarily available opportunity.

Acts of homicide should also not be overlooked. In 1955, a United Airlines DC-6B on a flight from Denver to Portland blew up minutes after takeoff. A bomb had detonated in one of the baggage compartments killing all on board. Fortunately, forensic experts were able to trace the bomb to the luggage of the mother of Jack Gilbert Graham. He had placed a bomb in her luggage and had taken out a sizable insurance policy on her life. He was eventually convicted of homicide and sentenced to death for the crime. This single occurrence literally confirmed the perceived need to ask all travelers, "Have you packed your own bags and has anyone asked you to carry a package for them?" Many people question the utility of this question. It is hard to believe under current security conditions a passenger would do this, but apparently some gullible individuals do. The TSA has announced in late August 2002 that the airlines would no longer be required to ask the question, citing the lack of effectiveness of the question.

BAGGAGE TAGS

It was not that many years ago that an individual could drive up to the curb and check a bag on an airline and simply drive away. We have unquestionably come a long way since that time. Baggage tags are viewed as valuable assets. Currently, baggage tags are locked up and far less vulnerable to pilferage than previously. Curb-side check-in can be a fast and furious operation, especially before large flights where this service is viewed as a distinct competitive marketing feature. The traffic in and around the curb-side check-in desk is often heavy, and the risk of loss is increased when sky caps are distracted. Everyone wants to check-in with as little hassle as possible. Not having to drag your baggage into the terminal and through the waiting line can be a tantalizing airline discriminating feature in a very competitive business. On the other hand, the chance for fraudulent claims and unaccompanied baggage shipments are made particularly vulnerable at the curb-side check-in point. It is fairly easy to snatch a tag, attach it to a bag, and expect it to be loaded, especially on a busy domestic flight. Currently, this service is unavailable for international flights and is sometimes made unavailable for domestic flights depending on the threat. Tracking the use of all baggage tags is an essential practice. Otherwise potentially dangerous explosives can make it to the cargo hold. For example, such a restriction was put into place at all US airports for both domestic and international flights during the Persian Gulf War and immediately after 9/11. The threat was increased and the added precaution was deemed appropriate; however, for security reasons, it should be standard procedure.

PASSENGER/BAGGAGE RECONCILIATION

As already discussed, on 21 December 1988, a terrorist in Frankfurt, Germany, loaded a portable radio packed with explosives into his checked baggage on Pan Am Flight 103. He chose not to travel with his baggage. The plane eventually exploded over Lockerbie, Scotland, killing everyone on board. President George Bush, Sr., subsequently created yet another President's Commission on Aviation Security and Terrorism. Based on the recommendations of the commission, US carriers instituted a strict bag-matching policy to remove the baggage of any passenger who failed actually to board an aircraft. The process is fairly routine in the United States; however, not all overseas airlines and airports meet the requirement of such a program.

By the end of the twentieth century, 100-percent passenger/baggage reconciliation had been made mandatory for all international flights leaving US airports. The system requires certification that a piece of luggage is not transported aboard an aircraft without the corresponding passenger on board. Before 100-percent matching became commonplace for departing US international flights, the air carrier was only required to have security maintain control over all checked baggage. That concept, established in December 1997, was interpreted to necessitate passenger luggage match-ups, x-ray screening, physical inspection, explosive-detection screening, or a combination of any number of them. However, all of them were not required. New technologies have without a doubt improved the airlines' ability to match luggage to a specific passenger. Many airlines now use a computer link between the luggage tag and the boarding pass; scanning the boarding pass when the passenger begins actually to board the aircraft and matching the individual to each piece of luggage. Again, not every airline in every city has implemented these procedures.

If the airline determines that a passenger with checked baggage does not board the flight, their bags are located and removed from the flight. The process is known in the trade as "originating" passenger/baggage match; meaning it is accomplished at the beginning of the first leg of the flight. Unfortunately, the process does not consider any bag that may already be in the cargo hold of the aircraft. If a person exits the aircraft during a flight change of aircraft or airline, the baggage may continue without the passenger on board. Consequently, an originating passenger/baggage match system is really only a partial bag match if it does not reconcile the baggage and passengers already on board the aircraft after each and every stop. This, of course, could be administratively quite costly and time consuming. A situation similar to this was a direct contributing factor of the Pan Am 103 Lockerbie crash.

As of early 2002, this major vulnerability remained. The government still does not require airlines to match passengers with their checked luggage on connecting flights. It has no specific timetable to even test such a system. In Europe, checked baggage is routinely cross matched with passenger manifests to ensure that no baggage is placed in an aircraft's cargo hold unless the corresponding passenger is on board. The government only requires that baggage be cross matched on the originating legs of the flights. A potential bomber could therefore defeat the system by checking explosives onto a multistop flight and leaving it behind at a connecting stop.

Later, President Bill Clinton established the Gore Commission, which also recommended a profile selectee or random passenger baggage match procedure until all airlines, to all destinations, could electronically track the passenger lists of boarding passengers and baggage on all flights. Currently, the process tracks only those passengers who have been singled out for some reason or randomly selected for further scrutiny. The procedure, as mentioned previously, has been the subject of much criticism. If a particular passenger meets the profile, or is selected at random, the passenger's bags receive additional screening both by x-ray and by an explosive-detection system when available. This procedure does not scan the terrorist who does not meet the profile or is not randomly selected. The Commission called for the development of a national database on passenger travel habits and history called the Computer Assisted Profiling System, or CAPS. The FAA commenting on CAPS revealed that, "soon, if not already, airline agents who enter a passenger's name at check-in will get either a red light or a green light depending on whether the passenger fits a targeted profile" ("Scanning Equipment for Customs Searches is Set for Six Airports, *Wall Street Journal*, 3

Aug 1999). The original concept proposed a database based solely on travel information; however, it could later be cross-referenced with the FBI, CIA, or criminal records even though the FAA denies that this has been done. Since then the TSA has created the Aviation Security Screening Records (ASSR) database. It is a massively broad and intrusive system. CAPS and its follow on, CAPPS II were supposed to cut down the risk. It also assumed that a terrorist is not very bright. Even though profiles are not published, their parameters can be easily guessed. At least a few computer experts have argued that a terrorist cell can defeat CAPS using an algorithm system. The entire system is currently under review. At the core of the program was an attempt to focus scrutiny on high risk passengers and reduce the imposition of low risk passengers.

▨ AIRPORT LOCKERS

Anytime a facility is open to the public, there exists at least a minimal threat that someone will seek to do some damage to people or assets at that facility. As already discussed, there had been a trend away from hijackings in favor of bombing either the terminal or the aircraft on the ground. Some incidents, of course, are nonterrorist connected and consist simply of criminal misconduct. An airport is like any other slice of the societal pie and is subject to the same ongoing criminal activity as any other location. For example, there is an ample amount of theft, damage to property, assault and battery, and general criminal misconduct that are daily occurrences at an open public airport terminal, including the parking lot.

An individual who is not necessarily suicidal but wants to disrupt the normal activities of an airport terminal has the option of a leaving a bomb in one of the self-service lockers. Most airports have at least now moved these lockers to inside the sterile concourse. The items are at least subject to screening prior to entrance into the concourse. However, prior to such measures being implemented, a bomb exploded in a locker at Los Angeles International Airport in 1974 killing 3 people and injuring more than 30 others. Again, in 1975, a bomb in a locker at La Guardia Airport in New York killed 11 people and seriously injured another 57 people. Both of these incidents took place before the government recommended more stringent rules.

Currently, the Minneapolis/St. Paul Airport is testing luggage lockers that open with a fingerprint. The TSA is permitting a six-month test program including 185 biometric lockers. All rentals are limited to forty-eight hours. The need for such lockers at all should be analyzed. The small service they provide individuals may not be worth the risk to the public.

▨ CONTAINER HARDENING

In 1993, the FAA was asked to study different types of technology designed to protect aircraft against certain explosives and to report back to Congress. Prior to that, the aircraft hardening program was initiated in 1991. The overall purpose of the project was to achieve systems that would protect commercial aircraft from catastrophic structural damage or critical system failure due to in-flight explosions. The program parameters focused on susceptibility and vulnerability. First, a determination of the probability that explosives of a particular nature and amount can be successfully placed on board an aircraft were to be standard. Second, the study concentrated on an estimation of the conditional probability that an aircraft will be destroyed or damaged by such a device.

According to the report, tasks were designed to determine and identify:

1. The minimum amount of explosives that will result in aircraft loss and
2. The methods and techniques that can be applied to the current and future fleets of commercial aircraft to decrease their vulnerability to explosive effects (Internet: http://cas.faa.gov/reports/98harden.html).

Mitigation techniques have converged on the development of blast-resistant airline luggage/cargo containers. This technology exists, but research into other mitigation techniques still will be needed, since only wide-body aircraft currently use such containers. The report concluded that it is critical to find a solution to the effects of a blast across the spectrum of aircraft being used in the airline industry. As always, the good guys will need to keep pace with future advances in criminal/terrorist explosive capabilities. The hardened container was considered to be only a near-term solution.

Currently, LD-3 containers are the most frequently used luggage container in the industry. It was extensively tested, beginning with low-charge weights and increasing the amounts until failure occurred. Results clearly indicated that the blast loading was dependent on the density of the luggage that contained each explosive, exactly where the explosive was situated in the container, and what other luggage was placed around the target luggage. After extensive analysis, it was decided that the containers had very little inherent blast-resistance capability. In other words, if a terrorist is successful in getting a bomb onboard, if detonated, it will likely bring the plane down.

▨ BLAST CONTAINMENT VERSUS BLAST MANAGEMENT

Engineers have studied the effectiveness of both blast-containment and blast-management techniques. The blast-containment design attempts completely to suppress the results of an explosion within a container. The blast-management design concept considers the container as being part of a placement system inside the cargo bay of the aircraft. They both have advantages and disadvantages.

Tests have determined that the blast-containment concept offers the best alternative for suppressing the potentially catastrophic effects of postblast fires. This system is also an independent unit. It stands alone and needs no special handling or placement within the cargo bay. On the other hand, the blast-management concept allows a container essentially to fail, and bases its control on the ability to vent the detonation products into adjacent containers. The airline must arrange the cargo appropriately for the system to have any usefulness. This could prove to be tedious and quite time consuming; another drawback as far as the airline is concerned. Consequently, early on it was decided to focus on a blast-containment container to construct state of the art high-strength composite materials with fragment penetration–resistant and fire-retardant properties.

Full-scale tests were conducted in the early 1990s, and many LD-3–type containers were tested. The Society of Automotive Engineers assisted the FAA in developing container specifications. The FAA solicited developers for designs that would meet the established requirements for blast resistance, FAA airworthiness, and airline operational requirements. Unfortunately, in 1996, no design actually met the required specification, but later models did. The newer models will also, as is to be expected, involve a higher cost. Current aluminum containers range in price from $1000 to $2000. The blast-resistant containers cost about $38,000 each; at least when they were produced as prototypes. Therefore, life cycle costs are a serious consideration in any further development of containers possessing a legitimate chance of ever seeing widespread use.

The House Subcommittee on Transportation and Infrastructure, which convened in 2000, heard testimony on blast-resistant baggage containers. Prior to that in March 1998, the FAA had approved a blast-resistant container, but as discussed, it is prohibitively expensive. One estimate from the Air Transport Association projects that such containers would cost airlines $5 billion a year. Additionally, the containers are only available for wide-body aircraft, which includes only 25% of the aircraft in service. Most aircraft are narrow-body aircraft, and 70 percent of the bombings have been directed against them (Screeners Under Fire, Internet: http://www.securitymanagement.com/library/000855.html, 11 July 2001, Pg. 3).

■ AIRMAIL SECURITY

In late 1979, an incident aboard an American Airlines flight involving a bomb inside a metal postal container prompted the FAA and the United States Postal Service (USPS) to sign a Memorandum of Agreement (MOA). It required that all direct and indirect carriers, including the USPS, implement an air parcel security program with procedures to prevent, detect, and deter the introduction of any unauthorized explosive or incendiary device into airmail parcels. Unfortunately, the USPS clung to the position that the airlines could never be allowed to screen the mail and that the USPS could only screen mail under very limited circumstances. The MOA proved to be unworkable.

Originally, standards for the security of mail were different from those of air cargo, which were also different for checked baggage. Carriers receive the mail from the USPS in already sealed bags and they are marked for destination. The FAA had literally relinquished the responsibility for airmail security, because the mail was sealed upon receipt by the airlines. The carriage of mail by commercial aircraft constituted and continues to constitute big business to the airlines. However, following the Desert Storm military action, in January 1991, USPS attempted to shift the shipment of most packages to "all-cargo" carriers instead of passenger carriers as a simple safety measure.

In the past, the USPS, by virtue of their own regulations, had taken the legal position that x-raying or other screening of mail "sealed against inspection" cannot be accomplished without first obtaining a search warrant. Title 18 USC Section 3263 requires the postal authorities to maintain "one or more classes of mail for the transmission of letters sealed against inspection." It also states, "no letter of such a class of domestic origin shall be opened except under authority of search warrant authorized by law." Postal Service Regulations, Parts 115.4 and 115.5 state, "no person may open, read, search or divulge the contents of mail sealed against inspection" without a warrant unless extraordinary circumstances create a reasonable suspicion to an inspecting authority that a letter or parcel could be dangerous. Additionally, 18 USC Section 1702 makes it a federal crime for delaying the mailing of a letter or parcel by anyone who does so "with design to obstruct the correspondence, or to pry into the business or secrets of another, or opens, secretes, embezzles, or destroys the same." These provisions severely limit the screening of the mail prior to being loaded on board an aircraft.

In May 1994, a second MOA between the FAA and USPS was signed. The agreement improved coordination between the two agencies. The purpose of the agreement was to prevent the introduction of explosive or incendiary devices into mail parcels that could be loaded onto commercial aircraft and attempted to redefine the category of "sealed against inspection" mail. One of the vulnerabilities of screening baggage intended for aircraft rested squarely on the shoulders of the USPS. Admittedly, the history behind these regulations is lengthy. It forms part of the bedrock foundation of a democratic state. Keeping the government out of private mail is an important and fundamental right. However, like many other constitutional rights, they are not absolute. There are some justifiable exceptions, and the situation of a potential bomb on board an aircraft may constitute one of those exceptions.

As a result of an extensive review of procedures by both agencies, some revisions have subsequently been made. The USPS canceled its "airport to airport" service under which a mailer could specify a particular flight. It also began a system of weekly internal security audits under which certain "profiled" mail parcels are separated from the mail tendered to air carriers. Also, the USPS modified the customs forms for outbound overseas parcels. These forms now require a "safety" certification for each parcel with a copy retained by the post office of origin. Since 1996, even stronger security measures have been implemented. Currently, a "profiled" parcel placed in a drop box is returned to the sender. The mailer must present the parcel in person if it is to be transported through the mail.

▓ INDIRECT AIR CARRIERS

An indirect air carrier is a company that is in business for the purpose of accepting and shipping items on commercial airlines. Freight forwarders typically execute all aspects of the shipping process from handling goods and paperwork to clearing shipments through customs and making delivery to the end cosignee. Significant loopholes in the system opened the airlines to specific vulnerabilities when they accept these shipments. Theoretically, a package can be forwarded through several indirect air carriers before it ever reaches an airline. This makes tracing the origin of the original shipper very difficult. FAR Part 109 was signed into law in 1979. It required indirect air carriers to develop and file for FAA approval a security program designed to "prevent or deter the unauthorized introduction of any explosive or incendiary device into any package cargo intended for carriage by air" (Internet: http://www.faa.gov/ars/AFS/FARS/far-109.txt, 24 April 2001). The goal was to place the requirement for screening at the point of acceptance rather than put the burden on the airline.

A major problem became apparent based on the fact that the FAA did really not know the identity of most of the nation's indirect carriers. In the President's Commission on Aviation Security and Terrorism, dated 15 May 1990, it was determined that the United States had between 4000 and 6000 indirect carriers, but that the FAA could only identify and track the practices of about 400 of them. Consequently, improved indirect air carrier standards were put into effect. The FAA issued a standard security program for indirect air carriers containing definitions, terminology, and requirements for the acceptance of cargo by indirect carriers. These requirements became effective in 1994. To date, more than 3000 indirect carriers have received FAA approval numbers (Internet: http://cas.faa.gov/reports/98cargo/98cargo.html, Pg. 6). The TSA now governs all indirect shipping, and specific administrative regulations will likely be improved and strengthened again. TSA 49 CFR, Chapter XII, Part 1548, formerly, Part 109, essentially detailed the security program requirements for indirect carriers. This section requires the shipper to draft a program. Forcing both carriers and indirect shippers to implement an adequate program is another issue. The TSA needs to revamp this program and implement a program similar to that in use in Europe. Manufacturers need to be held accountable for what is packed and how it is secured.

■ KNOWN SHIPPER

The known shipper rule prohibits passenger airlines from accepting cargo from customers who have not done business with them on a regular basis in the past unless the carrier visits the shipper's premises to ensure it is a legitimate operation. The FAA had already tightened the rule last fall. The FAA imposed new definitions of known versus unknown shipper. Either the manufacturer must demonstrate that it has shipped at least 24 times with the same freight forwarder since 1 September 1999 or it must have completed all of the following: The manufacturer must have a customer record with the freight forwarder; it must have a shipping record of six months or longer or a formal contract with the freight forwarder; it must ship three times with the forwarder on nonconsecutive days; and the freight forwarder must visit the manufacturer's offices and fill out the form

Aviation Security Known Shipper Revalidation. The TSA has mandated that all cargo must be screened by the 19 November 2002 deadline. However, the TSA currently permits a combination of EDS, trace detection, manual and dog-sniffing screening. Physical inspection of all cargo would be astronomically expensive. A current loophole permits the cosignee to be considered the shipper. The industry's nightmare is for the government to ban all cargo shipments on passenger flights; much the same way it had previously banned passenger flights from carrying individual pieces of mail weighing more than a pound. Postal volumes for US passenger carriers have dropped significantly, throwing airlines cargo revenues in the red. A new air cargo industry group, the Cargo Aviation Security Coalition, wants to ensure that any new security measures do not put a strangle hold on air commerce. Today, the US government requires all cargo companies to receive verbal confirmation from the end recipient before shipping goods. As a result, shipments are often delayed, especially when handling shipments with a time difference.

A known shipper is defined as a person or company that meets one of the two requirements listed:

1. Shipped with the same freight forwarder on an indirect air carrier (IAC) at least 24 times within the past 24 months and has been an active account with the freight forwarder since 1 September 1999.

2. Meets each of the following requirements: (a) The freight forwarder or IAC has a customer record (accounts receivable). (b) Established a shipping record with the freight forwarder or IAC of six months or longer or have a formal contract. A formal contract may consist of the tariff signed by both the shipper and a representative of the forwarder or IAC. (c) Shipped three times with the forwarder or IAC on nonconsecutive days. (d) The forwarder or IAC has visited the shipper location and one of its representatives completed an Aviation Security Known Shipper Revalidation form.

■ UNKNOWN SHIPPER

Some air carriers and some IACs are still experiencing difficulty identifying unknown shippers in order to review all shipping documents appropriately. The government eventually extended the previous unknown shipper rules to all cargo and required inspection of cargo from all unknown shippers and known shippers. Passenger air carriers are required to obtain a Shipper's Security Endorsement and identification check for all cargo. In the past, these endorsements were only needed for cargo from unknown shippers. In addition, foreign air carriers and indirect air carriers were also required to obtain similar information from all shippers, known or unknown, and to certify each shipment had an audit trail. The FAA also had mandated air carriers to apply security controls to cargo accepted from all-cargo flights as well as passenger flights, closing yet another loophole in providing adequate security controls on cargo. Restrictions for unknown shippers as of 9 October 2002:

1. US freight cannot be moved on a passenger flight.
2. US freight can only move on all-cargo flights subject to the carrier's acceptance.
3. Shipments from the United States cannot be consolidated with the other shipments.
4. Shipments from the United States have to be held for 7 days after the freight forwarder completes the documentation in order to move them to known shipper status.

This program remains woefully inadequate. Improvements to the program are pending in the 108th Congress.

■ VACUUM CHAMBERS

Vacuum chambers can be employed by airlines and airport authorities to minimize the dangers of barometrically detonated bombs. Before loading the aircraft, air cargo is introduced into a vacuum chamber. The flight sequence is simulated in the chamber, and the cargo is subjected to the varying air pressure expected during a normal flight. Flight details are fed into a computer which activates the chamber. Monitoring can be done locally or at a remote site.

■ INSPECTION OF CARGO

The tragic loss of Valujet Flight 592, 11 May 1996, drew attention to the tremendous growth in the shipment of air cargo. Within weeks of the accident, the FAA formed a task force to review the FAA's hazardous materials and cargo security enforcement programs. A new cargo security and dangerous goods program emerged. It was organized into nine domestic regions and one European region. Inspectors assigned to the program are still located at over 38 field offices in the United States as well as in 3 international field offices. Directed by a headquarter's staff, agents monitor the regulatory compliance of hazardous materials, shipments, and shippers throughout the transportation chain by inspecting passenger and all-cargo air carriers. They also conduct concurrent cargo security inspections to ensure that all relevant cargo security measures are being applied to all types of cargo.

The FAA combined its cargo security and hazardous materials inspection activities into a specialized discipline and staff. Authority was eventually granted to hire over a hundred specialized cargo inspectors. The program focuses on inspection/testing, trend analysis, and outreach to the shipping community. Inspections are suppose to be more in depth than those now being conducted by the generalized work force. The FAA also developed a number of courses for newly hired personnel. One course, the Cargo Security Basic Course, is standard for all personnel who are tasked with inspecting cargo. The course was developed to familiarize the newly hired cargo security and dangerous goods inspectors with the regulatory requirements placed on domestic and international shippers and on air carriers who submit and accept freight for air carriage.

As is often the case, a disaster can prompt significant inquiry into needed safety and security issues. The loss of Valujet Flight 592 also forced officials to recognize the tremendous growth in air cargo shipments and the increase in hazardous materials incidents involving air transportation. The government stepped in and created a commission to investigate the FAA's hazardous materials and cargo security enforcement programs. The screening of cargo on all-cargo carriers is just as important as air passenger flights. There are fewer humans on board, but since when do we as a society believe that it is fine negligently to kill an aircrew so long as there are no passengers on board?

■ INTERNATIONAL AIR CARGO STANDARDS

The International Civil Aviation Organization's (ICAO) security plan is contained in Annex 17. It addresses all aspects of security but also particularly addresses cargo and mail transported on international passenger flights. Chapter 4 of Annex 17 establishes controls for cargo and mail, and recommends that all governments ensure that freight forwarders are also part of a security program. US airlines operating outside the United States have only the security procedures carried out by freight forwarders in countries adopting the ICAO recommendations to rely upon. There is no guarantee or even calculated risk that what is loaded in Bombay, Hong Kong, Lagos, or Brussels is safe. US carriers must totally rely on foreign airports and freight forwarders to enforce the requirements of Annex 17. The TSA can advise and suggest but has no real jurisdiction over the operations of foreign airports. In order to enforce regulations in the United States, they can assess civil penalties and push a particularly egregious situation into the federal courts.

■ IRELAND'S AIR CARGO SECURITY PROGRAM

The Irish Air Cargo Security Program (ACSP) is a key element of Ireland's National Civil Aviation Security Program and has, as its principal objective, the prevention of acts of unlawful interference against civil aviation. The program is being updated to take note of new international requirements for civil aviation security, and is based on the aviation requirements of the ICAO and the European Civil Aviation Conference (ECAC). Additionally, the European Commission has begun to have an input into aviation security matters.

The importance of cargo security within the aviation security arena is not being underestimated in Ireland. Although traditionally the focus of aviation security resources has been on screening of passengers and accompanied luggage, the events of 9/11 displayed how these measures could prove to be inadequate. However, despite the comprehensive amount of air cargo that is carried on passenger aircraft (ranging from about 25 to 80 percent depending on the jurisdiction and the source of the statistics), the absence of effective measures for ensuring the integrity of cargo has long been an issue. The known shipper system operates in many jurisdictions including the United States. However, it has been criticized as being ineffective, principally because of the absence of detailed appraisal of known shippers and a paucity of realistic security appraisal criteria for assessing their respective security infrastructures.

Ireland's ACSP is broadly based on the unknown or known cargo principle. However, the process differs entirely from the previous system in that a known consignor applicant must now undergo a security inspection by an independent body, as distinct from being so designated by an airline, regulated agent, or freight forwarder. It is also now the case that detailed criteria exist for the conduct of security inspections. These criteria apply equally to all applicants to ensure that a reasonable standard of security exists in relation to the preparation, storage, and transportation of air cargo.

Air cargo is categorized "known" or "unknown" depending on whether it is security cleared or not. Air cargo must achieve "known" status before it will be accepted by an airline for transportation. In determining whether cargo is classified as "known," the consignment must be either security screened by an airline or regulated agent, or alternatively received by a regulated agent or airline from a known consignor who has received such a designation under the ACSP. Companies involved in exporting cargo by aircraft from any airport in Ireland or cargo that is trucked out of Ireland for transport via aircraft from an airport in another European Union (EU) member state will be subject to the new ACSP. All enterprises involved in the preparation, transport, and receipt of air cargo will now be obliged to ensure that adequate security procedures and controls are applied to all items of air cargo until final delivery to the airlines or the duly authorized handling agent for onward carriage. A checklist was designed to help applicants determine whether they are, based on their existing security infrastructure, reasonably likely to pass a security inspection. An applicant should be able to answer "Yes" to at least nine of the points in the checklist to be considered reasonably likely to pass. This does not, of course, guarantee a pass score in an actual security inspection. When an applicant is not entirely satisfied that they will pass, they have the option of having a gap analysis conducted. The gap analysis mirrors an actual security inspection by using the same methodology and considering the same criteria. Any deficiencies in the security infrastructure that may exist will be highlighted, and the report that follows will recommend any corrective action necessary to assist the applicant in achieving the required standard.

Security Inspection Criteria

It has been suggested that the actual format of the security inspection is worthy of more detailed consideration, since this is what ultimately determines whether an applicant is awarded the designation. There are 15 separate areas that are considered during the inspection. These are listed in Table 10-1.

TABLE 10-1 Security Inspection Assessment Areas

Applicants wishing to become known consignors must demonstrate that their security infrastructure is of a sufficiently high standard in the following fifteen areas:

1. Physical Security
2. CCTV
3. Intruder Alarm Systems
4. Control of Access
5. Security of Keys and Access Control Cards
6. Security Officers
7. Staff Security Awareness
8. Transport Security
9. Security of Information and Documents
10. Out of Hours Security
11. Reporting and Recording of Suspicious Activity
12. Security of Cargo Preparation and Storage Areas
13. Security of Personnel
14. Emergency Procedures
15. Sourcing and Screening of Personnel

Organizations wishing to become known consignors should note that there is no mandatory requirement to have security officers on site or to have a closed circuit television (CCTV) system. Although many larger organizations will, of course, have both as integral components of their security infrastructure, the criteria are designed also to encompass the security infrastructure of a smaller organization where a significant budget for capital expenditure on security products might not exist. Many organizations have found that capital expenditure alone does not necessarily improve the effectiveness of a security infrastructure. Rather a more robust security infrastructure is likely to result where there is also an investment in achieving optimum levels of employee security awareness, where security is a core business function, and where a security policy and written procedures exist for the guidance of employees and others who are required to visit company premises.

Bearing this in mind, the inspection criteria encompass not just elements of electronic security such as CCTV, intruder alarm systems, and electronic access control systems, where such are installed, but also elements such as the physical fabric of the premises, how access to the premises is controlled, how the premises are secured outside of normal operating hours, and so on. Furthermore, there is a particular focus on transport security. Where an applicant utilizes an external transport provider to transport its cargo to an airline, regulated agent, or freight forwarder, the applicant must ensure that the provider has in place an appropriate degree of security in terms of, among other points, the vehicles used, the training of drivers, and the safeguarding of cargo against tampering.

This is important, as each successful applicant is required to sign an aviation security declaration prior to being designated a known consigner. This declaration includes a term that agents engaged in the preparation and transport of consignments for carriage by air are sufficiently trained for them to understand and carry out their security responsibilities.

The security attaching to the actual cargo preparation, handling, and storage area is considered separately. Essentially this aspect considers the ability of other elements of the security infrastructure to safeguard the cargo that is held in these areas. The applicant must be able to demonstrate that procedures exist within the organization detailing the security measures in place to protect information. Specifically, this includes information about cargo shipments and information about the security infrastructure, as well as demonstrating that any blank *pro forma* documents used as part of the air cargo process that might be useful to those with some form of hostile intent are appropriately secured. Equally, it is a requirement that procedures exist in respect to the security of keys and access control cards, as well as a procedure to enable employees to report suspicious activity that they might encounter. The applicant must also satisfy a requirement as regards screening and vetting of employment candidates in the organization.

Finally, an appropriate degree of security must exist in respect to company personnel who could by virtue of their responsibilities or seniority in a company cause security procedures or other measures to be subverted should they be placed under duress. It is not uncommon for criminal elements to subvert comprehensive security procedures and undermine physical and electronic security products by placing persons with legitimate access to premises under duress. This form of criminal activity is known as tiger kidnap, and occurs on average three times per month in the British Isles. The two most recent examples in Ireland both occurred in Dublin on July 13 and July 19, 2002, when an employee of a bar and a postmaster's wife, respectively, were abducted from their homes in attempts to subvert normal security measures in two premises and gain access to cash. The maximum number of points that can be achieved in a security inspection is 1008. An applicant is required to score 60 percent, or 604 points, successfully to pass an inspection.

Being Awarded a Designation

The applicant receives a documented report normally within 10 days of the security inspection, and the report illustrates the overall score awarded together with the score awarded in each of the 15 assessment categories, as well as detailing, for the information of the applicant, any deficiencies that may exist. Where an applicant does not achieve a pass score, the report explains precisely why this has occurred; specifically by describing the deficient areas and indicating what the applicant should do by way of corrective action. Once the corrective action has been carried out, the applicant should book a subsequent reinspection. The option to request a gap analysis prior to the second inspection also exists.

If the applicant has passed the inspection, a *pro forma* Aviation Security Declaration is forwarded to them along with the report. The applicant is required to complete the declaration on company stationery, and the declaration must be signed by a senior executive of the company. The declaration is essentially an undertaking that the applicant will make the Security Validator aware of any future alteration made to the security arrangements as inspected. Additionally, the applicant agrees to abide by the terms of the ACSP, and agrees that the appropriate completed documentation (Statement of Compliance) will be prepared in respect of each consignment.

Once the declaration has been received, the Department of Transportation (DOT) is notified and a known consignor certificate is issued to the applicant. At this point, the known consignor's contact details, as agreed, and their known consignor number will be added to the known consignor database. Access to the database is restricted to authorized persons, such as employees of airline operators, freight forwarders, regulated agents, and the DOT. A known consignor designation applies for a two-year period, after which the known consignor's premises must be reinspected.

Appeals

An applicant may appeal the results of an inspection by contacting the DOT within two weeks of the determination of the inspection. The DOT will consider the appeal and could, for example, uphold the original finding or alternatively could overrule the original finding. Applicants wishing to appeal should state the precise grounds for appeal when forwarding their appeal to the DOT.

The most recent US development has been the Air Cargo Security Bill, introduced in the US Senate by Senator Olympia Snowe (R-ME). This Act (S.2656) would require the TSA to generate a detailed and effective cargo security regimen designed to address the shortcomings of the current system. In particular, the Act would:

- Require random screening of 5 percent of all air cargo.
- Implement an authentication policy to ensure potential terrorists can not impersonate legitimate shippers.
- Include auditing of every phase of the cargo process.
- Require training and background checks for personnel employed by cargo handlers.
- Examine the expansion of screening and detection equipment.

Unfortunately the bill did not become law. A similar bill has been introduced into the 108th Congress. However, it is clear that significant gaps exist in current US cargo security regulations.

In Canada, the Canadian Air Transport Security Authority Act became law on 27 March 2002. The Act provides for the establishment of the Canadian Air

Transport Security Authority. The Authority has responsibility for all screening equipment at airports, including explosive-detection systems, certification of screening personnel, and armed officers on board aircraft. It would appear that there are no immediate plans to introduce an air cargo security program beyond that which already exists.

Following the 11 September 2001 attacks, the EU Commission drafted a proposal aimed at establishing common rules to prevent terrorist attacks and unlawful acts against civil aviation for both international and domestic flights. Based on ECAC Document 30, the proposal provides for the mandatory incorporation of Document 30 into EU law together with the drafting of more technical standards. The proposal also provides for the adoption of national civil aviation security programs by member states, to include:

- The implementation of security measures
- The establishment of a national quality control program
- The approval and monitoring of airports and air carriers' security programs
- The implementation of a national security training program

It is expected that this regulation will be introduced soon. Notwithstanding this new measure, it would appear that Ireland is already to the fore in this area. Specifically, Ireland is ahead of many other EU member states in terms of the implementation of an effective system for the inspection and designation of known consignors.

What is clear is that the traditional known shipper system is not sufficiently robust to provide adequate safeguards against contemporary terrorist activity. Equally, developments within the EU suggest that the security standards applying to air cargo will be raised over time, and that the new arrangements should be regarded as seeking to establish baseline security standards. Although designation as a known consignor is not currently mandatory, the implications of not obtaining a designation (cargo being treated as unknown, and subject to physical search, or x-ray, or being held for twenty-four hours, and the resultant increase in costs) suggest that any organization that exports by air on a commercial basis will almost certainly take the view that obtaining a designation is an essential business requirement. The DOT fully implemented the new ACSP as of 31 December 2002.

■ TSA INSPECTION OF AIRPORTS

The FAA has begun to publish a quarterly report of enforcement actions against regulated aviation entities when a civil penalty, suspension, or revocation has been issued. The data are directly compiled from the agency's Enforcement Information System. The following text will review the actions that can be taken by the government against carriers or airports that have committed cargo-related or cargo-security violations. Most of the incidences are hazardous material related, but they still serve to illustrate the inspection criteria and the discrepancies that sometimes are discovered by an inspection.

The government has the authority to issue orders assessing civil penalties of up to $50,000 for violations of its regulations. A single violation can cost an airline up to $11,000 per discrepancy. (**Note:** *Owing to the dangers associated with hazardous materials, there is no $50,000 limitation on assessments for violations of the Hazardous Materials Transportation Safety Act or accompanying regulations.*) Once a decision has been rendered, decisions to assess a penalty can still be appealed to both the Administrative Law courts and directly to the administrator. Much negotiation can take place between the regulated entities and the government, and usually does. An entity may reach a settlement with the administration, and if the adjudication is less than $50,000, no violation is made a part of the entity's enforcement record. Hence, the regulated entities have a real incentive to settle. Any negotiated settlement is a success, since the ultimate goal is to seek compliance. Unnegotiated violations may still be referred to the US Attorney for prosecution in US District Court. It is rare, but does happen.

In addition to the assessment of civil penalties, the government has several other alternatives available as deterrents. They can also issue certificates of suspension and revocation. Suspensions of indefinite duration are issued to prevent a certificate holder from exercising the privileges of a certificate pending demonstration that the certificate holder meets the standards of a certificate holder, including security standards. Certificate revocations are issued when the government determines that a certificate holder is no longer qualified to hold the certificate at all. Fixed-term suspensions are intended to discipline the offender and to deter others from doing the same. For example, on 10 May 2001, the FAA proposed to assess a civil fine of $95,000 against KLM Royal Dutch Airlines for an alleged hazardous materials violation. Supposedly, KLM shipped an oxygen generator, which was not declared, nor was the crew informed of the cargo. Finally, the generator packing did not meet specifications (FAA Office of Public Affairs, Press Releases, 10 May 2001). According to regulations, KLM had 30 days to respond to the FAA, and they did so. In a similar situation, the FAA on 3 May 2001 proposed to assess a fine of $235,000 against Trans-Brasil Airlines Inc. (FAA Office of Public Affairs, Press Releases, 3 May 2001). They also responded as was their right. It must be reiterated that the purpose of the inspection rules and enforcement tools are to prevent the shipment of dangerous or hazardous materials. Just assessing fines is not an adequate deterrent to breaking the rules.

After an initial civil assessment, there is an opportunity for informal procedures to resolve the issues. Correcting the deficiency and resolving the problem is the most important factor. Full litigation of each and every case is just too expensive and does not really address the preeminent goal of the regulations and that is compliance. Realistically, litigation is generally punitive in nature. Consequently, the FAA frequently issues compromise orders and agrees to consent agreements so long as the airline has corrected the deficiency and projects a positive attitude toward future compliance.

■ CONCLUSION

In October 2000, the FAA conducted a special nationwide assessment of US carrier compliance with legislated cargo security procedures. Unfortunately, inspectors repeatedly found that airlines often failed to comply requirements specifically related to cargo acceptance, screening of cargo, training of screening personnel, and maintenance of training records for cargo acceptance and screening personnel. Violations took place all across the nation. In accordance with the Sensitive Security Information rule, the government does not release such information for 12 months after the events occur to avoid divulging potential vulnerabilities to terrorists. The area of cargo security continues to be a challenging one and will remain so for many years to come. Hopefully, the current security situation will motivate both administrators and the public to pursue ongoing improvements in cargo-related security.

Additionally, advancements in technology relating to blast-containment or blast-resistant containers for use on board aircraft will not solve the problem of explosives on board. On the other hand, nor should the possible feasible improvement of containers be ignored because the containers may potentially cost too much. The key is to combine efforts to contain a blast in conjunction with measures to prevent the bomb from reaching the cargo hold in the first place. Regulations pertaining to airmail are another matter of continuing concern. Regardless of the fundamental right of privacy of the mail and an individual's innermost thoughts, the law prohibits putting a bomb in the mail as well. Consequently, cooperation between the airlines and the US Postal Office need to be ongoing. Another significant and continuing problem is the acceptance of cargo from an unknown shipper. Requirements to maintain an audit trail and to pinpoint the place of responsibility for screening the cargo at the point of acceptance will greatly improve security procedures in this area. However, the solution must be international and not just domestic. This presents a gigantic diplomatic challenge but one that must be mastered if both international and domestic air travel are to be protected. Furthermore, attention must also be given to increasing the security of cargo but not at a cost that makes air cargo noncompetitive with ocean-going cargo.

chapter eleven

Security and the Rules of Law: A Slippery Slope

■ NEWS

1. **4 December 2001:** John Walker Lindh is taken into custody in Afghanistan. He fought for the Taliban in battles against US troops.

2. **12 December 2001:** Attorney General John Aschroft announced the first indictments directly related to 11 September 2001. Zacarius Moussaoui, a French citizen of Moroccan descent, is indicted for conspiracy with Usama bin Ladin to "murder thousands of people in New York, Washington and Pennsylvania."

3. **Spring 2002:** Some flight attendants are reporting that they are the targets of abusive behavior, including illicit touching by security at the Phoenix and Raleigh-Durham International Airports.

4. **11 June 2002:** The government announces that Jose Padillo, aka Abdullah Al Mujahir, was being transferred from the criminal justice system into military detention; raising some legal eyebrows. He is suspected of plotting to detonate a "dirty bomb."

5. **13 June 2002:** The judge in the case of the *US vs. Moussaoui* ruled that the defendant may represent himself.

▨ INTRODUCTION

Two years after the Algerian terrorist hijacking of a French aircraft in 1994, the police were still dealing with the unease related to the anniversaries of the incident. French law enforcement responded with a massive security operation. On a single day in December, the police stopped and questioned 6000 people. These French identity checks are similar to US "stop and frisks" and have similar goals. Both are tools used by the police to prevent crime. However, French law is distinctly different from US law, which must conform to the mandates of the Fourth Amendment of the Constitution under such circumstances. French procedures have been highly effective and bear review within the context of combating terrorism internationally, although many would ague they would not survive judicial scrutiny in the United States.

Under French law, the police are not required to have a reasonable suspicion that criminal activity is about to take place or to establish imminent danger to do a weapons frisk. Additionally, an individual stopped by French police may be detained for up to four hours based solely on police discretion. Such is not the case in the United States, and if applied to airports in the United States, would certainly raise the ire of many passengers and constitutional advocates. In order to understand the intricacies of US law, students must understand that airport security officers and police officers do not have absolute freedom in carrying out their duties even when a law has clearly been broken.

The balance between the need for effective law enforcement and for the protection of the rights of individuals remains a controversial issue. Many security officials feel that the US courts have gone too far in protecting the rights of accused criminals. On the other side, critics feel strongly that police have been given a dangerous amount of leeway in exercising police powers. Many years ago, in the majority opinion *of Mapp vs. Ohio,* Justice Tom Clark wrote, "Nothing can destroy a government more quickly than its failure to observe its own laws" (376 US 643, 1961 Pg. 649). The government contends, however, that owing to the magnitude of the danger caused by air piracy that searches of boarding passengers should be based on either mere or unsupported suspicion.

No one has ever stated that being a federal judge is an easy job. However, recently, the jobs of US District Court Judge Leonie M. Brinkema and T. S. Elliot III have taken on aspects of particular complexity. They have been assigned the cases of John Walker Lindh and Zacarious Moussaoui, respectively. For example, Judge Ellis was faced with the prickly task of balancing Mr. Lindh's Sixth Amendment right of confronting the witnesses against him versus the government's interests in protecting its security personnel and the integrity of the detainee system in Quantanamo Bay, Cuba. Walker Lindh, in a plea agreement, was sentenced to 20 years in prison. In the plea, he pled guilty to one count of supplying services to the Taliban and a criminal information charge that he carried a rifle and two grenades while fighting against US forces. Meanwhile, Judge Brinkeman was forced to deal with the defendants' in court request to represent themselves. The judge felt it was necessary to issue a four-page written order educating Moussaoui on the proper procedures to file motions under seal and *ex parte*. The judges have precious little precedent upon which to base rulings. In July 2003, the defendant Moussaoui is pitted in an intense legal battle with the government over his Sixth Amendment rights. The government is even considering yanking the case out of the civilian courts and designating the defendant an "enemy combatant." The case would then be tried in a military tribunal. In this chapter, we will examine the measures taken and extent to which the Constitution and legal precedent regulate the conduct of security officers and the police at airports.

FOURTH AMENDMENT

The Fourth Amendment reads,

> The right of the people to be secure in their persons, houses, papers and effects, against unreasonable searches and seizures, shall not be violated, and no Warrants shall issue, but upon probable cause, supported by Oath or affirmation, and particularly describing the place to be searched, and the persons or things to be seized (US Constitution, US Government Printing Office, 1989-249-097).

The Fourth Amendment itself needs to be broken down into two critical elements. First, it contains a prohibition against unreasonable searches and seizures, and second, the requirement of probable cause to issue a warrant. Case law has limited the first element to the right to be secure against unreasonable searches and seizures by government agents. The courts have yet to designate airport security officers, acting within specific parameters, as government agents. Consequently, if no search or seizure occurred or if it was done by a private entity, such as airport security, it is not even necessary to determine whether it was reasonable under the Fourth Amendment (*US vs. Morgan*, 774 F.2d 1215 [6th Circuit, 1985]). Basically, to a certain extent, airport security officials, when not considered to be agents of the state, are not technically subject to the restrictions of the Fourth Amendment. If airport security officials are considered to be functioning in the place of state agents, the constitutional protections may again be applicable. Since the FAA required airlines to institute security procedures to screen passengers (14 CFR Sec 108) some courts have reasoned that "the government's involvement in promulgating the FAA guidelines to combat hijacking is so pervasive as to bring any search conducted pursuant to that program within the reach of the Fourth Amendment" (*United States vs. Ross*, 32 F.3d 1411, 1413 [9th Circuit] quoting *United States vs. Davis*, 482 F.2d 893, 904 [9th Circuit, 1973]).

However, once it has been determined that a search has been done by the government, the Fourth Amendment requires that the search must either have been supported by a warrant or that it must fit into a few specifically and well-delineated exceptions. If airport searches are determined to be searches in the context of the Fourth Amendment, they must fit into one of three established exceptions applicable to the airport security context: the administrative search exception, the stop and frisk exception, or the consent exception. Depending on the circumstances, other exceptions to be discussed include exigent circumstances or a search incident to a lawful arrest based upon probable cause.

▓ ADMINISTRATIVE SEARCH EXCEPTION

The Supreme Court has upheld a rather broad range of searches and seizures even when they are conducted without the usual apportionment of probable cause. Collectively, the court cases reflect two kinds of departures from the traditional probable cause requirement. One situation, as in *Terry vs. Ohio*, 392 U.S. 1, 1968, is to require individualized suspicion or reasonable suspicion less compelling than that needed for arrest. The other kind of exception is to require no reasonable suspicion at all but instead to require that the search be conducted pursuant to some neutral criteria, which guard against arbitrary selection of those subjected to such procedures and which also serve a public purpose. Those searches have become known as administrative searches.

Administrative searches are justified on the basis that they serve a societal purpose other than the standard criminal law enforcement aim of detecting contraband. An example of an administrative search held to fall within those guidelines is the situation illustrated in *Veronia School District 47J vs. Acton*, 115 S.Ct. 2386, 1995. The administrative search exception enables, in this case school officials, to exercise search authority toward select groups of individuals simply because society deems it necessary and appropriate. The case upholds drug testing in schools, and notes the importance of limiting the searches to those athletes in whom the risk of physical harm is particularly high. The Court specifically stated, "by choosing to go out for the team voluntarily, student athletes subject themselves to a degree of review even higher than that imposed on students generally" (115 S.Ct. 2386, 1995:2392). This argument lends itself to the theory that passengers choose to fly instead of travel by other modes of transportation.

The Supreme Court is particularly sensitive to the exact nature of the search. In evaluating the appropriateness of these searches, they have often focused on the invasiveness of the search. In supporting drug testing of the students, Supreme Court Justice Antonin Scalia states, ". . . the student enters an empty locker room accompanied by an adult of the same sex. Each boy produces a sample of urine while remaining fully clothed with his back to the monitor who stands approximately 12–15 feet behind the student . . . no less privacy than in a public restroom" (115 S.Ct. 2386, 1995:2388).

In determining whether a particular search falls within this exception, the courts first evaluate in detail the privacy interests being violated. The first hurdle is to determine whether a search scheme falls into the administrative search exception by balancing the privacy interests sacrificed against the societal purpose or the need for which the search scheme was undertaken. It must still be determined whether the special need could have been met in a less intrusive manner and whether the particular search was really made pursuant to the special need. If it meets all these criteria, then society as a whole has agreed that the threat is worth giving up the Fourth Amendment rights of certain citizens under certain circumstances. In the case of drug testing at schools, the governmental need to detect and prevent drug usage among athletes outweighs the Fourth Amendment rights of the students.

As regards airports, the issue is whether the government's need to detect and prevent terrorist acts, implemented by airline-paid security officers and soon federal employees, outweigh the Fourth Amendment rights of passengers. So far, the courts have determined that it does. Relying on the rationale of the *Terry vs. Ohio* case, the court balanced the competing interests of law enforcement in the context of the current air piracy problem against the rights of individuals choosing air travel. They decided that airport searches could legally be conducted under less stringent standards than ordinary probable cause.

▪ BALANCING APPROACH

The challenge of airport security officials is to figure out when the courts will conclude that the intrusiveness of the search is equally balanced against the level of the threat from hijacking and therefore acceptable. The nature of the security interest will change according to the perceived threat level. If the passengers and subsequently the courts believe that the public need for protection against terrorist activity is greater than the preservation of Fourth Amendment requirements, airport searches will likely continue to be deemed to be appropriate.

Another factor balanced against those special needs of the government is the nature of the privacy intrusion. For example, at airports, "the intrusion is not insubstantial, it is inconvenient and annoying and in some cases it may be embarrassing and at times even incriminating" but is it reasonable. (*US vs. Skipwith*, 482 F.2d 1272, 1973). *Skipwith* has held in the case of airport searches that once the passenger enters the screening process, they forfeit the right to withdraw. Generally, the passenger can not withdraw simply because the search discloses items they did not want discovered regardless of a Fourth Amendment challenge. In the context of reasonableness, the *Skipwith* case involved a man convicted of possession of cocaine. He had presented himself at an Eastern Airlines boarding gate in Tampa. Florida. Clearly, the gate was a place at which he knew or should have known that he was subject to being searched. His only reason for being at the gate was to board the aircraft. An officer approached him because of his suspicious conduct and an apparent bulge in his pants, which the officer thought could have been a gun. Cocaine was discovered and the defendant contested the legitimacy of the search. The Court ruled that it had become general knowledge that citizens boarding planes are subject to special scrutiny and to weapons searches. Consequently, they determined that the defendant had little, if any, expectation of privacy and that the search was reasonable.

However, it is interesting to point out that the privacy issue has many aspects. For example, strip searches at schools, in prisons, and of airline passengers all present a variety of unique and distinct legal issues. All three may be legal under certain circumstances. The difference between them stems from the fact that all three classes of individuals, students, prisoners, and airline passengers, have much different and sometimes higher expectations of privacy than the other. Based on these expectations, the level of the perceived threat is crucial in determining what the acceptable levels of the searches will be. Prisoners clearly have a much lower expectation of privacy than an airline passenger does. Consequently, more intrusive passenger screening might not be acceptable if the government's need for ensuring air travel security can be met through less intrusive means. On the other hand, if the threat is high for a specific airport, a specific aircraft, or a whole nation, extra intrusiveness may be quite appropriate. For example, passengers seem more amenable to the very stringent requirements of El Al Airlines, especially when the aircraft is flying directly to Israel. Passengers flying from Minneapolis to Honolulu are much less patient with extra security.

■ LESS INTRUSIVE ALTERNATIVES

The courts generally have upheld the idea that a security search must be limited as is consistent with the administrative need that justifies it (*US vs. $125,740 US Currency*, 164 F. 3d 462 [9th Circuit, 1989]). If the same level of security can be maintained with a less intrusive means of search, the less intrusive means must be used. Newer technologies will have to be evaluated in these terms. For instance, to justify a passenger-screening technology that produces an image of the passenger's body beneath their clothes, the privacy of the individual must be protected as much as possible. Future security measures will also need a guarantee that the image data will neither be preserved nor archived.

No matter what the new technology, questions may arise about whether a particular search was appropriately conducted toward the legitimate objective. The human factor can change the appropriateness of any search. Regardless of the approval of the courts to a specific procedure or specific piece of equipment, an individual who steps outside the bounds of the procedure or the intended use of the equipment may still invalidate the search. Training and experience are critical to the effective and legal use of aircraft passenger screening.

The basic administrative search exception that has been extended to airports, however, is specifically limited to the search for objects that are a threat to the airport or aircraft. Other contraband, including drugs and currency, are technically not the appropriate goal of the search. However, no matter how narrowly a device or procedure is tailored to detecting safety-related concerns, other information will still be obtained in the process. The search procedure in use, therefore, may yet be acceptable for the confiscation of other contraband if the additional information is acquired inadvertently. When the information is sought specifically, however, and no concurrent safety rationale is given, the search no longer falls under the exception. A much-discussed topic is the illegal transportation of narcotics. It must be remembered that a plane cannot be easily hijacked by waiving a bag of marijuana at the pilot. Nor will a briefcase filled with cash convince most pilots to divert an aircraft. It begs the question whether airport security needs to be searching for these objects. It also raises the inquiry of the legality of police to pay airport security officers, who are already underpaid, to inform on potential drug smugglers.

The fine point of this debate is whether information on a nonthreat object is obtained in the course of the strict search for threat objects or whether action has been taken in the course of the search to broaden the scope to include a search for nonthreat objects but illegal or suspicious objects. For example, invasive searches are authorized only of persons who repeatedly set off metal detector alarms. Security personnel in some cases may even conduct an "intimate search" of such persons until the suspicion is dispelled (*US vs. Roman-Marcon*, 832 F. Supp. 24, 1993). In the *Roman-Marcon* case, the defendant passed through a magnetometer and, as he passed, the machine alarmed. Instead of remaining at the checkpoint for further screening, he kept walking. He was detained by a police officer, patted down, and packages of narcotics were found. However, the search was initiated because of an alarm from a metal detector. Since metal is the prime indication of a weapon, which can be an effective instrument with which to hijack an aircraft, the search fell within the administrative search exception to the Fourth Amendment requirements. Generally, where there is an indication of the presence of metal, the security personnel may frisk the individual.

■ STOP AND FRISK EXCEPTION

A stop and frisk exception to the Fourth Amendment requirement for a search warrant occurs when an officer or another authority has a reasonable suspicion that another person is a threat. In the context of airport passenger screening, reasonable suspicion might be that the subject fits the profile of a typical hijacker, that the screener observed something unusual, or that a metal detector alarmed. Again quoting the decision in the *Terry* case, a warrantless search was deemed reasonable when "a reasonably prudent man in the circumstances would be warranted in the belief that his safety or that of others was in danger" (392 US 1: 27, 1968). Courts since that time have also analyzed the reasonableness of searches based on profiles. It would seem that current law would allow a stop and frisk if an individual fits a narrow class of suspicious persons who are part of a "selectee" class search.

However, such procedures are subject to rigorous judicial scrutiny. A case in point occurred in 1997 in Florida. An off-duty police officer, working for the Miami-Dade county police, pulled over a car on the Florida turnpike. The police testified that the car was pulled over because it had changed lanes without properly signaling. In the course of the stop, a fight broke out. At trial, the accused,

Aaron Campbell, alleged that the officers had really used a drug courier profile to make the decision to stop him. The judge agreed ("Jury's Mixed Verdict in Cop Trial," *UPI Online*, 3 April 1998).

In essence, the court determined that the officers had stopped Campbell not because they had a reasonable suspicion that he had broken a law but because they had a "mere suspicion" based on the drug courier profile. Such profiling has adamant supporters on both sides. In a legal stop and frisk, law enforcement officers may briefly detain a person they reasonably believe to be suspicious, and if they believe the person to be armed, proceed to pat down or frisk that person's outer clothing (Karen M. Hess, and Henry M. Wrobleski, *Police Operations Theory and Practice*, St. Paul, MN, West Publishing Co., 1997, Pg. 122).

Again, it must be remembered this case law is directed at government officers whether they are local, state, or national and not private security employees such as former contract airport security. When a "passenger" can be stopped and frisked has opened up a whole new series of case law. This too may change in light of the airport screening function becoming the purview of federal employees.

▢ INDIVIDUAL STOP AND FRISK SEARCH

In the famous case of *Terry vs. Ohio*, 392 U.S. 1, 1968, the Supreme Court ruled that a policeman based on his own instincts and suspicions and on the need to protect himself and others may conduct a limited search for weapons without a warrant or probable cause if there was reason to believe that a crime had been committed. The facts of the case involved a detective named McFadden who had observed two men in downtown Cleveland acting, according to him, suspiciously. According to testimony by the officer, the men would walk past a certain store, look in, and stop at a nearby street corner and confer. They proceeded to meet again at another street corner where an additional man joined the group, one of whom was Terry. The officer detained the group and frisked them. He located two handguns, and they were charged and convicted for carrying concealed weapons.

In other words, *Terry vs. Ohio* holds that only a limited search for weapons is allowed in the absence of probable cause where the search is not incident to an arrest. The search can be permissible only if a reasonable, prudent man in the circumstances would be warranted in the belief that his safety or that of others was in danger. The rationale, as it pertains to airports and aircraft, is that the slight infringement upon individual rights should be balanced against the overwhelming need to stop hijacking.

Overall, the judicial system has refrained from placing restrictions on officers' ability to make stops. The court has basically agreed that officers do have street experience and must be given leeway to use it. In *United States vs. Cortez*, 449 U.S. 418, (1981), the Court supported an officer's discretion to stop an individual by holding that reasonable suspicion should be based on the "totality of the circumstances," which may include inferences and deductions made by a trained officer. Subsequently, the general climate of danger following the repeated hijackings of US air carrier flights was determined to be reason enough for searching all airline passengers. *US vs. Epperson*, 454 F.2d 769 [4th Circuit, 1972]). Section 202 of the Air Transportation Security Act of 1974, 49 USC Sec 1356(a) required a preboarding search of all passengers and their carry-on baggage for weapons and explosives pursuant to regulations (now TSA 49 CFR Chapter XII, Part 1544). The passing of a human passenger through a magnetometer is just such a search. The invasion of privacy constituted by a measuring of the distortion of magnetic waves around the body is so minimal as to be considered administrative. Stopping and frisking moves the level of intrusion up a notch. The search must now be reasonably related in scope to the circumstance that made the original intrusion justified in the first place.

▓ SELECTEE CLASS STOP AND FRISK SEARCH

In contrast to the individualized stop and frisk search, the selectee class category of the stop and frisk search approach requires the identification of small groups of people singled out for additional scrutiny. The suspicion only needs to establish probability, not certainty, and it can be established from the totality of the circumstances. *US vs. Sokolow*, 490 U.S. 1, 109 S.Ct. 1581, 1989. However, to prevent abuse, the attributes in the profile must be relevant to the threat being averted. In the *Sokolow* case, the defendant was stopped at the Honolulu airport by agents who knew the following: (1) he had paid $2100 for two airplane tickets from a roll of $20 bills; (2) he traveled under the name of someone who did not match the name associated with the telephone number he provided the airline; (3) his original destination was Miami, but (4) he stayed in Miami for only 20 hours; (5) he appeared to be nervous during the trip; and (6) he checked none of his baggage. The Court reasoned that these facts amounted to reasonable suspicion, and in the majority opinion, they concluded that "reasonable suspicion" was the level of suspicion considerably less than proof of wrongdoing by a preponderance of the evidence.

The Court upheld, in essence, the agent's belief that the defendant's behavior was consistent with the DEA's drug courier profile, but stated that a court sitting to determine the existence of reasonable suspicion must require the agent to articulate the factors leading to that conclusion whether they are part of a profile or not. This decision seems to set a precedent for airport passenger profiling of potential terrorists. Further decisions, however, will be required to settle the issue.

▓ CONSENT EXCEPTION

Another exception to the Fourth Amendment prohibition against unreasonable searches and seizures is evidenced by the rules relating to consensual searches. When passengers freely and voluntarily give consent to a security search, they surrender their privacy interests, and the issue of potential violations of Fourth Amendment rights is moot. *Schneckloth vs. Bustamonte*, 412 US 218, 93 S.Ct. 2014, 1973. On the other hand, if the traveler had an expectation of privacy, any consent would have knowingly to be waived in order for the consent exception to come into play.

In the *Bustamonte* case, a police officer stopped a car containing several men when he observed that one headlight and the license plate light were non-functioning. After the driver could not produce a license, the officer asked a passenger who claimed he was the vehicle owner's brother if he could search the car. The passenger replied, "Sure, go ahead." Stolen checks were found under a seat, leading to charges against the car passenger, Bustamente, whose motion to suppress the evidence at trial was denied. His conviction was affirmed on appeal but the 9th Circuit Court of Appeals set aside the district court's order. The precise question became, what must the state prove to demonstrate that consent was voluntarily given? The Court issued a very narrow decision.

The Court held that when a subject of a search is not in custody and the state attempts to justify a search on the basis of his consent, the Fourth and Fourteenth Amendments require certain conditions to be met. Namely, that the state demonstrates that the consent was in fact voluntarily given and not the result of duress or coercion, express or implied. Voluntariness is a question of fact to be determined from all the circumstances, and although the subject's knowledge of a right to refuse is a factor to be taken into account, the prosecution is not required to demonstrate such knowledge as a prerequisite to establishing voluntary consent.

As early as 1973, the consent exception to the Fourth Amendment requirement, in the context of airport searches, has been litigated. It was reasoned that if the nature of the established screening process is such that the attendant circumstances will establish nothing more than acquiescence to apparent lawful authority, some authorities have ruled that there is no real consent (*US vs. Ruiz-Estrella*, 481 F.2d 723 [2nd Circuit, 1973]). Another case went so far as to say that it could hardly be considered a voluntary consent when the passenger's only alternative was to forego their flight (*US vs. Albarado*, 495 F.2d 799, [2nd Circuit, 1974]).

Once again, the central issue revolves around the concept that airline employees, in compliance with government regulations, conduct these searches. It has already been discussed that some legal authorities contend that these "warrantless," nonarrest searches are legal because private persons administer them. Nonetheless, these searches were conducted because a federal agency has required them. Adding to the mix, in the future, the federally trained federal employees will conduct the searches. As stated, FAR 108.9 requires each certificate holder to "conduct screening under a security program . . . to prevent or deter the carriage aboard aircraft of any explosive, incendiary, or deadly or dangerous weapon on or about each individual's person or accessible property and the carriage of any explosive or incendiary in checked baggage." A passenger cannot legally board an aircraft unless the airlines conduct a search of their person and possessions.

An on-point case was *United vs. Lopez*, 328 F. Supp. 1077, 1971, which was decided before the 100-percent screening rules came into effect in 1973.

Security personnel check a passenger's luggage 18 September 2001 at Dulles International Airport in suburban Washington, D.C. Passengers, in most cases, have continued to be quite understanding and patient during the sometimes long process of screening before flying in today's threat environment. *Alex Wong/Getty Images, Inc.—Liaison.*

Regardless, it contains some interesting and applicable language. The government in this case argued that the posting of signs advising that passengers and baggage were subject to search was tantamount to "implied consent." (**Note:** *14 CFR Sec 108.17e (1995) requires notification, "posted in a conspicuous place at the screening station and on the x-ray system which notifies passengers. . . . That they are being inspected."*) The Court disagreed, and even pointedly commented that consent to a search involves the relinquishment of fundamental constitutional rights and that consent cannot be lightly inferred. In *US vs. Lopez*, which involved the seizure of narcotics, the judge wrote, "Nor can the government properly argue that it can condition the exercise of the defendant's constitutional right to travel on the voluntary relinquishment of his Fourth Amendment rights." The court extended its reasoning by providing that airport searches were not justified as searches incident to arrest either. It is also interesting that the judge referred to air travel as some sort of "constitutional right." Of course, a thorough search of the US Constitution fails to reveal such an explicit right.

Two questions regarding the consent exception remain unanswered:

1. The point at which passengers give consent
2. To what precisely are passengers consenting

As stated, some legal scholars argue that it can hardly be considered to be voluntary consent when a passenger's alternative to submission is foregoing the flight. The 9th Circuit court in *US vs. Davis*, 482 F.2nd 893, as early as 1973 also confronted this issue. In the Davis case, the Court did not specifically hold that consent to an additional search could be withdrawn after an inconclusive scan if the passenger agrees not to board the plane. Nor did it determine at what point in the boarding process a passenger might decide not to fly and thereby withdraw implied consent. Basically, the judge simply believed that the defense argument failed, because the passenger did voluntarily consent, at least to the initial search.

The law regarding the consensual search of baggage and one's person by police officers has remained fairly constant over the years. Recent case law, as in *US vs. Favela*, 247 F.3d 838, 2001, upheld the concept that police can approach and question passengers without the officer's conduct constituting a seizure. The officers had approached the defendant after observing her walk back and forth from a gate to a gift shop at the Kansas City airport. The officers asked if they could search her bag and she consented. Nothing was discovered. She was requested to pull her shirt tightly around her waist when the officers observed a bulge. One officer asked to touch the bulge, and she consented to the touching as well. She was placed under arrest. A search—incident to arrest—uncovered 1.2 kilograms of methamphetamine. The case was distinguished from *US vs. Eustaquio*, 198 R.3d 1068, (8th Circuit 1999), which involved the nonconsensual touching of a bulge in the defendant's clothing without reasonable suspicion, which was determined to have violated her Fourth Amendment rights. The defendant had argued that the officer lacked the reasonable suspicion necessary to justify a nonconsensual investigative search. The Court reasoned that the issue need not be addressed, because in this case there was not even a seizure for Fourth Amendment purposes.

Another twist to the voluntariness matter or consent question is the power relationship between the security individual and the passenger, who may be a person of color. That persons of color are subjected to a disproportionate amount of police security is hardly in doubt. This fact is especially prevalent in the context of ordinary stops even when increased security has no objective foundation; it often results in an actual search. As regards traffic stops, Justice Sandra Day O'Conner stated in a dissenting opinion, "As the recent debate over racial profiling demonstrates all too clearly, a relatively minor traffic infraction may often serve as an excuse for stopping and harassing an individual" (*Atwater vs. Lago Vista*, 121 S.Ct. 1536:1567, 2001). Such traffic stops can be analogized to stops in airports. Demonstrating whether or not a particular airport security or police officer has acted on race-based motivation is problematic at best. So much racial bias is subtle, difficult to prove, and can even be subconscious. The concept was highlighted when after 9/11, two rabbis praying in an aircraft were removed from the aircraft to be searched; presumably when a passenger presumed they were speaking Arabic and acting suspicious.

Once the passenger is singled out for whatever reason, they are often asked to consent to a search. Many courts are leaning toward requiring a law enforcement officer to have at least an articulable suspicion before even asking for consent to search. An officer often intimidates people, especially those of color. They do not completely understand their right to just say no. Even if the police do have some suspicion, the inherently coercive nature of the police citizen encounter, especially in airports, and the difficulty in proving free and voluntary

A passenger's shoes are passed through the x-ray scanner in an effort to uncover explosive concealment in the soles of footwear. The effort of Robert Reid to detonate a bomb located in his shoe on a flight from Paris to the United States alerted security professionals regarding this particular threat. *AP Photo / Cedar Rapids Gazette, Brian Tietz.*

consent may require additional safeguards. One court in Hawaii has even suggested a *Miranda*-like warning such as advising the individual:

1. The individual is free to leave and need not give consent.
2. If consent is given, any contraband found during the search will be used to prosecute.
3. Consent may be withdrawn at any time (*State vs. Kearns*, 867 P.2nd 903, 1994).

The courts will certainly continue to evaluate whether passengers have truly consented to searches in airports and that the consent they give is voluntary. In the aftermath of 9/11, passengers seemed particularly willing to consent to be searched. This attitude may well already be fading.

■ OTHER EXCEPTIONS TO FOURTH AMENDMENT REQUIREMENTS

Border Searches

At a national border, a border search is a superficial search or inspection conducted without a warrant or probable cause of persons, vehicles, and property entering the United States. The Supreme Court in *US vs. Martinez-Fuerte*, 428 US 543, 1976, upheld border searches as inherently reasonable under the Constitution. Any person entering the United States is subject to search for the simple reason that they are entering the sovereign territory of the United States. The border area is defined as any place that is the functional equivalent of the border whether it is the first airport where the plane lands or at any established inspection station near a border. Additionally, a US Customs official is allowed to stop, search, and examine any person upon whom an officer suspects is in possession of any type of contraband whatsoever (*US vs. Ramsey*, 431 U.S. 606, 97 S.Ct. 1972, 1977).

Specifically, in the *Ramsey* case, the court upheld a customs inspection of mail entering the United States, which by regulation does not extend to reading the correspondence. The mail can be searched for prohibited items, including explosives and weapons. In this case, the Court stressed:

1. That the search was constitutional under the long-standing rule generally applicable to border searches; namely, that such searches are considered to be reasonable by the single fact that the person or item in question had entered into the United States from outside.
2. That the lower court was wrong in concluding a warrant would be needed as to mail.

The lower court in the *Ramsey* case had excluded the evidence because it did not meet the "exigent circumstances test" for permitting searching without warrants. The case involved a sack of mail from Thailand being inspected at the General Post Office in New York City where heroin had been found. The Supreme Court, however, reversed and determined that the border search exception is not based on the doctrine of exigent circumstances at all. As for nonroutine border inspections, the standards are quite different. Lower courts have generally held that a "real suspicion" is needed for a strip search and a "clear indication" of the presence of some sort of contraband for a body cavity search to be acceptable. The US Customs Service has often been criticized for abusing this investigative tool. Some specific cases will be discussed in a later chapter.

Exigent Circumstances

Searches under exigent circumstances also constitute an exception and are conducted to prevent physical harm to officers or other persons, and the fruits thereof are perfectly admissible (*US vs. Sarkissian*, 841 F.2nd 959 [9th Circuit, 1988]). Certain situations may clearly justify a search of something without triggering Fourth Amendment concerns. According to the Legal Counsel Division of the FBI, there are three threats that provide that justification (John Gales Sauls, "Emergency Searches of Premises," Part I, *FBI Law Enforcement Bulletin*, March 1987, Pg. 23). They include clear dangers to life, of escape, and the removal or destruction of evidence. The requirement for searches under exigent circumstances was first recognized by the US Supreme Court in *Warden vs. Hayden*, 387 US 284, 1967.

The Court approved the search of a residence conducted without a warrant, which followed a report that an armed robber had fled into a specific building. The courts, using very interesting language, extended the idea even further in *Mincey vs. Arizona*, 437 US 385, 1978. The Supreme Court held, "the 4th Amendment does not require police officers to delay in the course of an investigation if to do so would gravely endanger their lives or the lives of others (437 US 385, 1978:392). Emergency searches, therefore, seem to be permissible when conducted by the police without a warrant on the basis of some immediate and overriding need, such as police safety. Employing this logic, airport police officers, airport security officers, and the public are certainly gravely endangered if a fellow passenger has a gun or an explosive device. How that device becomes apparent to the authorities is what is at issue. In essence, it is apparent when it is reasonable for the officer to assume that a threat exists.

▦ REASONABLENESS

Much has been written about the concept of reasonableness. Law enforcement personnel and security professionals use searches and seizures to locate and collect evidence needed to convict individuals suspected of crimes and to control the access to aircraft. Each of these searches must be reasonable. Courts, lawyers, police, and security officials have agonized over the precise meaning of this term. In *Mapp vs. Ohio*, 367 US 643, 1961, the Supreme Court found that the police did not exercise reasonable judgment in their enthusiastic seizure of alleged pornographic materials without a warrant. On the other hand, the same actions, with a valid warrant, would probably have resulted in a conviction upheld by the courts (**Note:** Mapp *vs.* Ohio *also held that the prohibitions of the Fourth Amendment were fully applicable to the states under the Amendment's due process clause; evidence obtained by illegal searches by state or federal officers was admissible in state court.*)

In airports, the reasonableness of a search must be weighed against the level of the threat. High-threat situations, such as existed during the Persian Gulf War, and after 11 September 2001 changed the degree of acceptable intrusiveness of airport searches. However, there are limits to intrusiveness. In *US vs. Afanador*, 567 F2d. 1325 (5th Circuit 1978), customs officials, acting on an informer's tip, stopped two airline attendants in Miami after arriving from Colombia, a known drug-source country. Despite finding no contraband in their luggage, the agents insisted on a strip search even though the informant's tip had only pertained to one individual. The Court decided that the strip search of the second flight attendant was just too intrusive based on the totality of the circumstances.

Another case involved a DEA agent who stopped a traveler in the Atlanta airport. The passenger had arrived from Ft. Lauderdale, a city the agent considered to be a principal source of cocaine. The suspect apparently arrived early the day when law enforcement activity is diminished and appeared to be concealing the fact he was traveling with someone else, plus he only possessed some carry-on luggage. In *Reid vs. Georgia,* 448 US 438, 100 S.Ct. 2752, 1980, the Supreme Court held, "the agent could not, as a matter of law reasonably suspect the petitioner of criminal activity on the basis of these observed circumstances" (448 US

438, 100 S.Ct. 2752, 1980:441). The Court went on to speculate that its experience with drug agents makes it wonder if there exists any city in the world that a DEA agent would not characterize as a known source of narcotics. These cases support the contention that courts will set limits on police and airport searches when they believe the authorities have simply gone too far.

■ PROBABLE CAUSE

The concept of reasonableness is linked to *probable cause*, which is another term, that has been meticulously dissected and reconstructed by the courts. In essence, the Supreme Court has ruled that any arrest or seizure is unreasonable unless it is supported by probable cause (*Michigan vs. Summers*, 452 US 692, 1981). Additionally, the burden of probable cause requires more than mere suspicion. The officer must know of facts and circumstances that would reasonably lead to, "the belief that an offense has been or is being committed" (*Brinegar vs. US*, 338 US 160, 1949).

If no probable cause existed when a police officer took a certain action, it cannot be retroactively applied. Information to support probable cause can be acquired in a number of ways. First, personal observation permits police officers to use their personal training, experience, expertise, and instinct to infer probable cause from situations, which may or may not be obviously criminal. Second, information collected from witnesses, victims, and informants, so long as it is reliable, can be used to support probable cause. Third, physical evidence, such as a gun or knife in plain view such as on an image displayed by an x-ray machine, may provide officers with sufficient credence to support probable cause. Finally, probable cause clearly exists where the police actually see a person committing the crime by concealing some sort of weapon or contraband.

Additionally, recent case law has held that a judicial determination of probable cause must be made within forty-eight hours after the arrest even if this period is over a weekend (*County of Riverside vs. McLaughlin*, 1991, Rolando V. Del Carmen, "Criminal Procedure for Law Enforcement Personnel," Monterey, CA, Brooks/Cole Publishing Company, 1987, Pg. 63). Adopting the conclusions of the courts as to what exactly constitutes probable cause is often difficult to apply in an airport setting. Airport security officers, whether police or private, are expected to make split-second decisions on probable cause. This is required regardless of the fact that the courts will dissect the decisions with a fine-tooth comb, using all the time in the world needed to do so. When an officer has over stepped what the courts consider reasonable, they are quick to implement the exclusionary rule.

■ THE EXCLUSIONARY RULE

The judiciary's most effective tool in regulating the activity of law enforcement officers is the exclusionary rule, which prohibits the use of illegally seized evidence in court. According to the rule, any evidence obtained by an unreasonable search or seizure is inadmissible against a defendant at trial (*US vs. Leon*, 468 US 897, 1984). Furthermore, any physical or verbal evidence police acquire by using illegally obtained evidence is known as the "fruit of the poisonous tree" and is also inadmissible.

The exclusionary rule forces the police to gather evidence properly. If they abuse the mandates of the Fourth Amendment, they are unlikely to get a conviction. Critics of the rule argue that it permits guilty people to go free because of simple carelessness or innocent errors. Consequently, the courts have carved out several exceptions to the rule.

■ THE LEGAL AUTHORITY OF PRIVATE PERSONS TO SEARCH

The exclusionary rule applies to all evidence presented in federal court as per the decision in *Weeks vs. US*, 232 US 383, 1914. The case held that where federal officers have made an "unreasonable" and, consequently illegal, search and seizure, the evidence obtained is not admissible in a federal court proceeding. However, in *Wolf vs. Colorado*, 338 US 25, 1949, the *Weeks* ruling was not to be applied to illegally seized federal evidence offered in a state court. Consequently, the first of many "illegal state searches" was admissible in federal proceedings. As evidenced by the case of *Lustig vs. US*, 338 US 74, 1949, the courts were inclined to admit illegal seized evidence by state officers in federal court. The Court had, for some reason not readily accepted today, ruled that, "The crux of that doctrine is that a search is a search by a federal official if he had a hand in it; it is not a search by a federal official if evidence secured by state authorities is turned over to the authorities on a silver platter" (338 US 74:79).

For approximately fifty years after the original *Weeks* ruling, state courts continued to allow illegally obtained evidence, and federal courts could admit evidence that had been illegally obtained by state officers. This practice came to be known as the *silver platter doctrine*, because each conviction was handed to the prosecution on a silver platter. The only times when the procedure was discouraged was when police actions were so extreme that they shocked the conscience of the court.

For many years, however, the silver platter doctrine was acceptable law. In essence, a search by a federal official even if the officer had a hand in collecting the evidence did not technically constitute a search by a federal official. If the evidence secured by the state authorities was turned over to the authorities "on a silver platter," it was still admissible. The Supreme Court in the decision in *Mapp vs. Ohio* (1961) finally eliminated this procedure. Whereas the Supreme Court had previously been hesitant to apply the Fourth Amendment in state courts, the *Mapp* case signaled a new willingness to apply the Fourth Amendment to both federal and state law enforcement officers.

Earlier in *Elkins vs. US*, 364 US 206, 1960, the Supreme Court had laid the foundation that evidence illegally obtained by state offices and subsequently provided to federal agents would not be admissible in federal court as per the due process clause of the Fourteenth Amendment. This was further refined in the

Mapp ruling in which the Court reasoned that the prohibitions of the Fourth Amendment were fully applicable to the states under the Amendment's due process clause, making illegal searches equally inadmissible in any court.

The Court was first convinced where, as mentioned, police actions were so extreme that they shocked the conscience of the court. The standard was created in *Rochin vs. California*, 342 US 165, 1952. In the *Rochin* case, the police entered the home of Mr. Rochin without a warrant, and testified that they saw him place what they suspected to be narcotics in his mouth. They transported him to a hospital and had his stomach pumped. Some morphine was recovered, and he was subsequently convicted of possession of illegal drugs. The Supreme Court overturned his conviction. They concluded that the police officers had gone too far and had violated the defendant's constitutional right for protection against unreasonable searches. First, the courts had made a huge distinction between state officers and federal officers. Today, they make a distinction between officers of a government entity and private security officers. It remains to be seen whether that differentiation will survive, especially when the "private security officers" are federal employees.

It should be noted at this point that as regards airport searches, which are in essence still considered private citizen searches, the courts first recognized and analyzed the issue in a landmark case as early as the 1920s in *Burdeau vs. McDowell*, 245 U.S. 465, 41 S.Ct. 574, 1921. The court specifically held that searches by private persons are separate and distinct from searches conducted under state authority. The Fourth Amendment was intended as a restraint upon the activities of sovereign authority, and it was not intended to be a limitation upon anyone other than governmental agencies. Individuals have other means of redress against those who may have illegally taken private property as part of an administrative search. This particular reasoning was reenforced again forty years later. They can sue using the law of torts as a remedy.

In *People vs. Superior Court of Los Angeles*, 449 v. P.2nd 230, 74 Cal Reporter 294, 1974. The court in California reiterated that there are no state standards for "search and seizure" by a private citizen who is not acting as an agent of the state or other governmental unit. It subsequently reasoned that, "therefore acquisition of property by a private citizen from another person cannot be deemed reasonable or unreasonable." Exactly who today is considered to be a government agent or is acting in essence or in the shoes of a government agent is still to be adequately defined by the courts; again becoming more and more complicated by the assumption of such duties by the TSA.

■ EXCEPTIONS TO THE EXCLUSIONARY RULE

Supporters of the exclusionary rule maintain that it is necessary in order to keep the police in line and as a deterrent to the police overstepping their authority. Critics have reasoned that the costs to society of losing critical evidence are higher than the benefits of deterring police misconduct. As a result, the courts eventually began to carve out exceptions to the exclusionary rule, which assisted the criminal justice system in convicting individuals even though their Fourth Amendment rights were technically violated. The rationale was based on the perceived need to get a handle on criminal activity regardless of simple mistakes or if the police would have acquired the evidence eventually anyhow. The shift in perception was also the result of more conservative law and order–type judges being appointed to the Supreme Court. The shift once again reinforces the concept that the criminal justice system adjusts to public opinion.

Inevitable Discovery

The inevitable discovery exception was first created in the case of *Nix vs. Williams*, 467 US 431, 1984. A ten-year-old child, Pamela Powers, disappeared on Christmas Eve 1968. The police's primary suspect was a religious fanatic named Robert Williams. The police eventually tricked the accused into revealing where he had buried the child using his own religious fanaticism against him. The police pressured the defendant to reveal the location of the body so she could ostensibly have a "religious funeral." The Court in *Brewer vs. Williams*, 430 vs. 387, 1977, initially ruled that the evidence, in this case the body of Pamela Powers, was inadmissible, because the accused attorney was not present during the interrogation wherein the accused revealed the location of the body. Later in the *Nix* case, the Court reversed itself and decided that the evidence was admissible, because the body would have been inevitably found by legal means. In essence, in *Nix vs. Williams*, the judges decided that although the government should not be put in a better position because of its illegal conduct, it should not be totally barred from the use of such evidence in cases either.

In *US vs. Hernandez-Cano*, 808 F.2nd 779 (11th Circuit Georgia, 1987), the courts applied the inevitable discovery rule to airport search situations. The defendant was proceeding through baggage screening when the x-ray machine revealed a large dark mass. At first, the defendant agreed to have the bag further inspected, and the airport security officer extracted a large wrapped object out of the bag. The passenger eventually objected to any further inspection. A verbal exchange took place after which the defendant agreed to give the security officer a peak at what was inside the wrapped parcel. The airport security officer later testified he thought he observed a white powder. The defendant refused to submit to a more thorough inspection, and the airport security personnel decided to summon a law enforcement officer. The police officer advised the defendant that if he refused further access to the parcel, he could not pass beyond the security checkpoint.

Consequently, the defendant retrieved the baggage with the parcel inside it and returned to the ticket counter. He advised the agent that he wished to transfer an item from his carry-on bag to the checked baggage. The airline complied. However, when returning to the checkpoint, he advised the security agent that the bundle had been thrown away; offering the explanation the bag had contained some laundry. Security proceeded to confer with the counter airline agent and was made aware of the fact that the defendant had added "something" to his checked baggage. On the theory that the agent did not know whether the bundle contained drugs or a bomb, the agent put a hold on loading the baggage. The agent also discussed the situation with the pilot and decided to open the luggage by use of a luggage passkey. Meanwhile, the officer had followed the agent to the baggage area and had been peering over the agent's shoulder. When he observed the parcel of "alleged white powder," he reached in and grabbed the bundle. The parcel was later determined to hold cocaine.

Regardless of the lack of a warrant, the court in the *Hernandez* case agreed that although the officer's warrantless search was not justified, and stated, "We hold that the inevitable discovery exception should have been applied." In an interesting note, the court described its reasoning. Under the inevitable discovery exception to the exclusionary rule, evidence is admissible that otherwise would be excludable if it inevitably would have been discovered by lawful means had the illegal conduct not occurred.

The court believed that had the police officer not reached into the bag and retrieved the parcel, the agent inevitably would have done so. Consequently, so long as the prosecution can introduce sufficient evidence to show that the information would ultimately have legally been obtained by lawful means, it is still admissible. In essence, an inevitable discovery finding is based on objective evidence concerning the scope of the ongoing investigation, which can be objectively verified or impeached.

The ultimate or inevitable discovery exception is closely related in purpose to the harmless error rule. The rule serves a very useful purpose insofar as it blocks setting aside convictions for small errors or defects that have little if any likelihood of having changed the result of the trial. On the other hand, these exemptions can provide the police with an incentive to avoid the warrant requirement. The police could seek to find the most expeditious method of obtaining evidence without regard to its illegality, knowing that so long as they could have acquired the evidence legally, the evidence will still be held to be admissible. The courts, therefore, have been required to evaluate, after the fact, many of the judgment calls made by officers in the field.

Good Faith Exception

Later, in *US vs. Leon*, 468 U.S. 897, 1984, Supreme Court Justice Byron White described the good faith exception to the exclusionary rule. In 1981, a confidential informant of unproven reliability informed an officer of the Burbank Police Department that two persons known to him were selling large quantities of cocaine and methaqalone from their residence. The informant also indicated that he had personally witnessed a sale of methaqualone by one individual at the same residence five months earlier. He also described a shoebox containing large quantities of cash, and indicated that drugs were usually stored at the residence.

The police launched a serious investigation of the residence. Cars parked at the residence were determined to belong to Armando Sanchez and Patsy Stewart. Mr. Sanchez had a previous conviction for drug possession and Ms. Stewart had no criminal record. During the investigation, officers noted a vehicle belonging to Ricardo Del Costello, a known drug dealer, arrive at the residence. The driver, later determined to be Alberto Leon, entered the house and left soon after with a small paper bag. Further investigation revealed that Mr. Leon was living at an address in Burbank as well.

Based on the observations mentioned and some others, two police officers summarized their findings in an affidavit and prepared an application for a search warrant for the addresses mentioned and a third address. The warrants were executed, and large quantities of drugs were seized. The suspects were indicted and charged, but made a motion to exclude the evidence collected during the search. The Court concluded that the affidavit was insufficient to establish probable cause, but it made clear that the officer had acted in good faith. The defense had argued that the drugs be suppressed on the grounds that the warrant had not been issued on probable cause.

The Court rejected the government's suggestion that the Fourth Amendment exclusionary rule should not apply where evidence is seized in reasonable, good faith reliance on a search warrant. The US Supreme Court disagreed and overturned the decision. The court held, ". . . the officer's reliance on the magistrates' determination of probable cause was objectively reasonable, and application of the extreme sanction of exclusion is inappropriate."

One scholar has countered the idea that police officers may use this exception to circumvent the law. He states that the deterrent to the rule's effectiveness "lies in the impetus it has provided to police training programs that make officers aware of the limits imposed by the Fourth Amendment and emphasize the need to operate within those limits" (*US vs. Leon*, footnote 20.) An objective good faith exception is not likely to result in the elimination of such programs, which are now viewed as an important aspect of police professionalism. Neither is it likely to alter the tenor of those programs, the possibility that illegally obtained evidence may be admitted in borderline cases is unlikely to encourage police instructors to pay less attention to 4th Amendment limitations.

Thus, the good faith exception to the exclusionary rule was created. The concept has been repeatedly upheld in such cases as *Illinois vs. Krull*, 480 US 340, 1987, and *Arizona vs. Evans*, 514 US 1, 1995, involving instances where the police either objectively and reasonably relied on information or where a clerical error was made.

■ POLICE PARTICIPATION

The cases of *Burdeau vs. McDowell* and *People vs. Superior Court of Los Angeles* had concluded that a search by a private security officer was not a search conducted by state officials and need not be determined to be either reasonable or unreasonable. However, the courts were not totally blind to the creative nature of many law enforcement officials. Police officers soon realized that private security officers could legally search someone without necessarily observing the stringent requirements of the constitutional parameters placed on law enforcement by the courts. Consequently, the courts came to rule on a case wherein the police officer was literally standing behind the private security officer and directing the search. The courts were quick to recognize that these attempts at legitimizing an illegal search were outside the protection of the above two cases.

In the case of *Corngold vs. US*, 367 U.S. F.2nd 1, 1966, the actions of several ingenious Customs agents were put to the test. The case involved the admissibility of evidence discovered by opening packages for inspection that had been shipped from Los Angeles to New York under an alleged false description of the contents in the shipping documents. Customs officers had originally tested the suspect package with a scintillator, advising the airline workers that the scintillator detects the radiation from watches. The Customs agents unequivocally requested that the airline agent open the package. The court ultimately held, "it would be difficult to justify any conclusion other than that the carrier employee participated in the search solely to serve the purpose of the government. There was nothing else in the record which would indicate that the package was in fact opened for any purpose of the carrier" (367 US F2nd 1:10). The watches did not pose a threat to the aircraft, and the Customs agents were aware of that fact. They were concerned with the shipment of illegally manufactured watches, not any danger to the airport or aircraft.

The *Corngold* case set the precedent that the fruits of a search conducted solely in aid of enforcement of a federal statute are inadmissible when the search fails to meet the Fourth Amendment requirements. The airline agents had merely been the pawns of the government agents. Clearly, the discovery of illegally manufactured and shipped watches does not pose a threat to the security of the airport or the aircraft. Airline officials often make much the same argument regarding the transportation of illegal drugs. As stated, the airlines consistently and vehemently have argued throughout the growth of the air transportation industry that they are not law enforcement agents and should not be forced to conduct themselves as such.

The Court in *Taglavore vs. US*, 334 U.S. 699, 68 S.Ct. 1229, 1948, further reasoned, "law enforcement agents must secure and use search warrants wherever reasonably practicable." The Court directly commented, "The violation of a constitutional right by subterfuge cannot be justified and the circumstances of this case leave no other inference than that this is what was done."

However, the courts did not completely close the door on airline personnel assisting in the discovery of contraband and the subsequent successful prosecution of smugglers. The *Corngold* court also reasoned,

> We would of course agree that if a carrier, while inspecting packages for its own purpose pursuant to a provision in the contract of carriage, discovers contraband and notifies the customs agents of that fact, and the agents then secure a warrant on the basis of this information and conduct a search, the search is entirely proper. This is precisely the procedure which the Fourth Amendment contemplates (Pg. 231).

Such a set a circumstances exemplifies the perfect legal cooperation between airline security and law enforcement. The airlines quite properly search and discover. If the contraband is illegal but not dangerous, the information they possess can be used to substantiate the issuance of a warrant. There will always be a blurring of the boundaries between public sector and private sector employees as well as a difference between individual and institutional responsibilities. The key is to find the correct balance and maintain it.

■ NONVIOLENT THREATS?

Generally, security is concerned with detecting weapons, explosives, and other dangerous materials. When security personnel do suspect such a risk, they usually call in the appropriate government agency or military personnel to handle the risks of a bomb or other dangerous device. This type of search is easily distinguishable from the normal "suspect" search due to the potential threat to the public. Arguably it could be held to be a private search, since the carrier initiated it. Additionally, it could be considered to be a lawful police search under the exigent searches exemption to the Fourth Amendment rules.

However, the search for other "nonviolent threats" has also occupied the courts. In *US vs. Pryba*, 312 F. Supp. 466, 1970, a United Airlines supervisor had authorized a package to be opened because of "peculiar circumstances" surrounding receipt of the shipment. Basically, the peculiar circumstances consisted of the fact that the shipper was nervous; he evaded questions on the actual contents of the package and admitted that the return address on the package was nonexistent. It must be remembered that this incident took place in 1970. The airline employee was arguably just being cautious, since the airlines were being held to the standard of exercising due diligence in uncovering explosives. After opening the package without a warrant, the contents turned out to be films of alleged hard-core pornography, which were turned over to the FBI. The search was considered to be legal.

Other examples of closer judicial scrutiny was exhibited in *Wolflow vs. US*, 391 F.2nd 61, 1968, where police participation at the request of the carrier was at issue once again in a case of the nonviolent contents of certain luggage checked for carriage. The ticket agent accepted two "overweight" suitcases for a flight scheduled to fly between Los Angeles and Las Vegas. The agent testified that he held them off the flight based solely on the excessive weight of the two suitcases. The agent's superior, for whatever reason, called a Los Angeles policeman to witness the opening of the bags. The contents revealed 3500 watch movements that the airline turned over to customs agents. This 1968 case upheld the admissibility of the fruits of the search as falling within the exemption created by *Burdeau vs. McDowell*, 256 U.S. 465, 41 S.Ct. 574, 1921. However, it is unclear how the weight of baggage actually accepted for shipment was suspicious in and of itself.

Earlier the courts had bolstered once again the concept that law enforcement agents must secure a warrant whenever reasonable. The judges categorically restated the basic idea of unreasonable searches when they said, "It is a cardinal rule that, in seizing goods and articles, law enforcement agents must secure and use search warrants whenever reasonably practicable." This rule rests upon the desirability of having the magistrate rather than police officers determine when search and seizures are permissible and what limitations should be placed upon such activities." *Trupiano vs. US*, 68 S.Ct. 1229, 334 U.S. 699, 1948. Overall, airline agents now leave the contraband exposed so that law enforcement can visibly see the contraband and are not forced to reopen the luggage, which would necessitate the acquisition of a warrant.

Therefore, the courts have sought to rule on searches wherein the airline agent locates contraband and summons the police. Is the police activity, with respect to the same object, a separate search subject to Fourth Amendment constraints? In *US vs. Jacobsen*, 466 U.S. 109, 104 S.Ct. 1652, 80 L.Ed.2nd 85, 1984, Federal Express employees opened a damaged box. They discovered newspapers covering a tube. After the tube was cut open, they observed plastic bags of white powder. They immediately summoned the federal authorities. However, prior to the federal agent's arrival, the airline employees had put the plastic bags back into the tube and the tube and newspapers back into the box. They did keep the box open. A federal officer reopened the box and exposed the smaller bags of white powder. He field tested the contents on the spot and determined the white powder to be cocaine.

Justice John Paul Stevens concluded that the agent's actions were not a significant expansion of the earlier private search, and also concluded that subsequently no warrant was required. He stated, "Respondents could have no privacy interest in the contents of the package, since it remained unsealed and since the Federal Express employees had just examined the package and had, of their own accord, invited the federal agent to their offices for the express purpose of viewing its contents." The agent's viewing of what a private party had freely made available for their inspection did not violate the law. It remains in dispute whether the suggestion that the owner of the container had no legitimate expectation of privacy in its contents, and that government agents in opening that container without a warrant on the strength of information provided by a private party would not violate the law.

The subject of joint operations between private security, the airlines, and/or law enforcement personnel remain blurred and are generally decided on a case by case basis. In a very early case during Prohibition, *Byars vs. US*, 47 S.Ct. 248, 1927, a federal agent who had been invited to accompany a state officer participated in a search that turned up counterfeit strip stamps of the kind used on whiskey bottled in bond. The Court once again set the precedent that such joint operations dictate the need strictly to follow Fourth Amendment protections and held the contents of the baggage, therefore, to be inadmissible.

In summary, in the *Burdeau* case, the exclusionary rule was characterized, "as a restraint upon the activities of sovereign authority and not a limitation upon other than governmental agencies" (256 U.S. 465:1921), and on this basis, courts have declined to exclude evidence in criminal cases when obtained by private persons. However, the Fourth Amendment becomes applicable when this private officer or citizen is acting as an instrument of government agents. Whether a private individual has been encouraged to cross the line is determined by a "totality of the circumstances" test. Circumstances to consider include the motive of the private security officer or airline agent, any compensation or other benefit the private individual receives from the government, and the advice, direction, and participation of the government agent. This test would therefore apply to airline security officers who receive a bonus for discovering certain kinds of the contraband and who may be receiving bribes from law enforcement to inform them of suspicious activity.

It is significant to point out that certain circumstances can jeopardize an individual's status as a private airport security guard or simply a private citizen. Of particular concern is the moonlighting of off-duty police officers. In *People vs. Tarantino*, 45 Cal. 2nd 590, 290 P.2nd 505, 1955, the court resolved that a police officer working during his off-duty hours as a security guard is still a deputized police officer. In the *Tarantino* case, the Court concluded that the *Burdeau* ruling was inapplicable. They distinguished the case by recognizing that an officer employed by the district attorney and paid with public funds as part of his regular daytime employment obtained the evidence.

■ AIRPORT ADMINISTRATIVE SCREENING SEARCHES AT AIRPORTS

As repeatedly mentioned, the concept of police participation in private searches takes on a whole new aspect when combined with the idea of searches conducted by federal employees. Much has been written about the idea that airport security officers are not agents of the state and that they are in essence private citizens. However, they would never be stationed at airports searching baggage unless mandated by federal regulation. The government and the airlines consider the threat real, and have regulated the equipment used in the searches and have made it obligatory that airport operators and airline carriers maintain and implement stringent search procedures precluding the introduction of dangerous weapons and materials onto airplanes and into airplane terminals.

FAR 108.9 required each certificate holder to conduct screening under a security program. They must prevent or deter, by appropriate procedures approved by the FAA, the carriage aboard airplanes of any explosive, incendiary, or a deadly or dangerous weapon on or about each individual's person or accessible property and the carriage of any explosive or incendiary device in checked baggage. An Assistant Attorney General of the United States testified before Congress in 1973 that even though private employees of airlines are doing the search, it is indisputable that they are ordered to do so by the federal government. This issue is again amplified by the transfer of private security jobs to federal employees.

Cases prior to the mandatory 100-percent screening of all passengers and baggage requirement explain the concept. In *US vs. Lopez*, 328 F. Supp.1077,

1971, discussed earlier, the courts were critical of airline employee abuse in airport searches. The case involved a narcotics seizure and turned on the issue of consent. Government attorneys contended that because airport officials had posted signs advising passengers that they and their baggage were subject to search, they could search on that basis alone. The idea of "implied consent" is not a new one, but it is based on some stringent requirements.

The *Lopez* case was one of the first airport search cases to raise the issue of consent by prior written notification. The idea simply of posting signs advising that passengers and baggage were subject to search was tantamount to implied consent, neglects to recognize that the passenger is not free to leave if contraband is suspected or that access to air transportation is effectively denied. Everyone knows that to reach the aircraft or gate concourse each passenger, visitor, crew member, or vendor must submit to a search of their person and effects. Early cases were extremely critical of the concept. Most courts have consistently held that consent to a search involves the relinquishment of fundamental constitutional rights and that this consent should not be lightly inferred. In fact in *US vs. Meulener*, 351 F. Supp. 1284, 1974, a passenger opened a suitcase only after he was ordered to do so by the marshal at a time when he was not free to leave or to avoid the search. The Court therefore concluded that, under these particular circumstances, the search was inherently coercive.

US vs. Blalock, 255 F. Supp. 268, 1966, another earlier case, discussed the requirement of an "intelligent consent," which implies that the subject of the search must have been aware of his or her rights. The logical extension of this reasoning was that for an intelligent consent to be present, it could only embrace the waiver of a known right. In other words, if the individual is not aware of the fact they have a right, it is difficult to conclude that they knowingly waived it. Remember again that this case was decided prior to the 100-percent screening requirement. Second, note that the *Lopez* case also did not support the contention that airport searches were justified on the basis that they are searches incident to arrest. In traditional legal language, simply because a search discovers evidence of a violation of a law does not render the search justifiable. The end does not justify the means. A police search conducted in violation of the Constitution is not made lawful just because they find something illegal.

Returning to the discussion relating to *Terry vs. Ohio*, legal scholars have also sought to use the concept of probable cause to warrant an airport search. The *Terry* case was the first case to recognize the need for police officers to search individuals for the sheer need of protecting themselves and in the interest of public safety. In the *Terry* case, the Court reasoned, "A police officer may in appropriate circumstances and in an appropriate manner approach a person for purposes of investigating possible criminal behavior even though there is no probable cause to make an arrest." The Court, however, made it perfectly clear that the police officer's conduct must be limited in scope and be reasonable. So what constitutes the probable cause? Officers have used everything from alerting the magnetometer to an individual fitting a specific profile.

In the *Terry* case, the Court also commented on whether or not mere government observation constitutes a search regulated by the Fourth Amendment. They concluded the decision rests on whether or not the defendant had a legitimate expectation of privacy in the place or thing searched (*Terry vs. Ohio*, 392 U.S.1, 1968:9). Based on the above reasoning, it appears there is no search if the government observation reveals information only relating to illegal activity. This kind of rationale has also been used to substantiate the legality of canine searches.

US vs. Place, 462 U.S. 696, 707, decided in 1983, contained the language that the warrantless use of a canine did not violate the Fourth Amendment, because the sniff of a dog only discloses the presence or absence of drugs or explosive residue. The dog cannot reveal a plethora of unlimited information about the items or person searched. The logic is based on the concept that a defendant has no legitimate expectation of privacy for drugs, explosives, or other contraband. Some legal analysts have extended this logic to reach a conclusion that more sophisticated and precision oriented search equipment at airports may be free of the Fourth Amendment concerns of the past. In the *Place* case, the Court concluded that the canine search was not very intrusive and also did not expose the person to much embarrassment or inconvenience.

The courts have relied heavily on determining just how intrusive is the search. There are competing values at play. Certainly, the courts have recognized the need to maintain public safety. As the courts and public further understand the continuing need for stringent security measures, the more likely the courts will justify the newer less intrusive means of airport searches. As early as 1971, in *Barrett vs. Kunzig*, 331 F. Supp. 266, 1971, the judges supported the government's substantial interest in conducting a cursory inspection at federal buildings, determining that the intrusion outweighed the personal inconvenience suffered by the individual. Such searches have now become commonplace. Further supporting the idea that "some" government observation does not even rise to the level of a search, the court commented, "The term search has been used by plaintiffs. To the extent that term is applied to more than a casual visual inspection, it has no meaning and is without foundation in this record" (331 F. Supp. 272, 1971).

The courts have applied the above reasoning to magnetometers at airports. They once again weighed the minimal invasion of personal privacy and the reasonableness of the security search in the light of the known risks. As early as 1972, the Court in *US vs. Epperson*, 454 F.2d 769, 1972, simply and concisely analyzed the legality of a search by use of a magnetometer. The growing threat to combat terrorism was self-evident. Consequently, the court expressed the view, "the danger is so well known, the government interest so overwhelming and the invasion of privacy so minimal, that the warrant requirement is excused by exigent national circumstances." The court was quick to recognize that the public viewed the searches as a welcome reassurance of safety to passengers traveling domestically and abroad. Specifically the court stated,

> The reasonableness of any search must be determined by balancing the
> governmental increases in searching against the invasion of privacy,

which the search entails. . . . It is clear to us that to innocent passengers the use of the magnetometer to detect metal on those boarding and is not a resented intrusion on privacy, but, instead, a welcome reassurance of safety. Such a search is more than reasonable; it is a compelling necessity to protect essential air commerce and the lives of passengers (454 F.2nd 772, 1972).

The Court considered the use of magnetometers perfectly legal right from their initial operation. It is worthwhile to point out that the Constitution does not forbid all searches, just those that are unreasonable. The same reasoning applied to magnetometers was soon applied to x-ray machines searching carry-on baggage at airports. X-ray machines are minimally intrusive of privacy and are also minimally embarrassing, if at all, to passengers. This is true at least as to the machines currently in use.

Soon thereafter the court in *US vs. Henry*, 615 F.2d 1223 (9th Circuit), 1980, differentiated between the x-ray scan and the magnetometer search. The judges resolved that the x-ray scan is a more intrusive search than the magnetometer and that both were subject to Fourth Amendment controls. At the time, they also recognized that if the passenger wanted to, they could have decided to avoid the x-raying of their carry-on baggage by merely consigning any baggage they did not want searched to the baggage compartment. The magnetometer does not provide such an option—passengers cannot ship themselves via the baggage compartment. It is simply a different set of circumstances when the only way to avoid a search is not to fly. With the advent of 100-percent screening of checked baggage, this rationale will become moot.

■ PASSENGER'S RIGHT TO TERMINATE A SEARCH

According to many legal analysts, passengers are deemed to have given consent when they place their bags on the conveyer belt for luggage screening (*US vs. Pulido-Baquerizo*, 800 F.2nd 899, 1986). The judge's decision includes the language,

> Those passengers placing luggage on an x-ray machine's conveyer belt for airline travel at a secured boarding area gave implied consent to a visual inspection and limited hand search of their luggage even if the x-ray scan is inconclusive in determining whether the luggage contains weapons or other dangerous objects (800 F.2nd 902:1986).

From a security officer's perspective, if passengers were allowed to withdraw after setting off the security system, the deterrent effect of the security system would be undermined. It may even be reasonable to argue that there is no guarantee that they might not return and be more successful later. The greater threat may even be the very fact that since a safe exit is available, it would be diminishing the risk and in essence encourages attempts.

The alternative question is more difficult to answer. Implicit consent derives much of its justification from the fact that it is a privacy invasion that free society is willing to tolerate as long as the scope of the search is limited to discovering weapons or explosives and is limited in a manner that produces negligible social stigma. It appears the law is still somewhat unsettled. In *US vs. DeAngelo*, 584 F.2d 496 (4th Circuit, 1979), a traveler submitted his briefcase to be searched. The security officer noticed an opaque object, which could not readily be identified. The traveler was advised that his bag would have to be manually searched. The passenger protested the further search of his briefcase, and said he would prefer not to take the flight. He was not afforded that option, and narcotics were ultimately found.

The Court believed that the circumstances were sufficiently suspicious to cause a reasonably prudent man to conclude the defendant might endanger security officers and passengers. Later in the opinion, the judge specifically stated, "allowing him to withdraw his luggage when the x-ray raised the suspicions of the security officers would frustrate the regulation's purpose of deterring hijacking." The *De Angelo* case was decided before *US vs. Pulido Baqerizo*, where the court extended the earlier decision. The opinion added the concept that placing luggage on the x-ray machine conveyor machine automatically provides implied consent not only to scan but also to conduct a manual search if deemed by security personnel to be necessary.

The idea that potential passengers may avoid the search by electing not to fly is somewhat loosing favor. Even though there certainly exists no constitutional right to fly, there has been some softening of the hard-core position that passengers have indeed consented to searches in order to fly but only when the search is directly related to the safety of the flying public. As stated before, marijuana or counterfeit money does not have the ability to bring an aircraft down or provide the means to hijack it.

In the course of litigating these issues, some passengers and later defendants have more vigorously sought to avoid being searched. In *US vs. Herzburn*, 723 F.2d 773 (11th Circuit), 1984, clearly involved a more determined and forceful attempt by a passenger to terminate the search. The defendant had placed a shoulder bag on the conveyor belt, and the examiner observed a large dark mass on the bottom of the bag. The defendant insisted he did not want the bag searched further, but the airport security officer reached into the bag. At this point, the defendant exclaimed, "I don't want to fly," grabbed the bag and retreated to the nearest exit. Later the bag was searched after a dog alerted and authorities obtained a warrant. The Court opinion referred to the *Skipwith* case discussed earlier, and restated that an unimpeded exit would diminish the risk to skyjackers and increase attempts.

▧ ALTERNATE VIEWPOINT

Not all courts have supported the decision contained in the *Skipwith* case. The court in *US vs. Albarado*, 495 F.2d 799 (2d Circuit), 1974, took a diametrically opposed position. They reasoned that the prospective passenger may refuse to submit to a frisk and instead forfeit his or her ability to travel by air, because this serves the purpose of the whole search procedure, which is not to catch criminals but rather to keep armed hijackers from getting on airplanes. As previously mentioned several times, airlines are loathe to act as law enforcement officers. They do not believe that they are responsible for the confiscation of all forms of contraband. On the contrary, the Federal Aviation Regulations only required them to search for potentially dangerous weapons and materials.

Courts in the past have also wrestled with a similar issue. Remember, in the *Meulener* case, the court determined that the defendant's Fourth Amendment rights were indeed violated. They concluded that when he was not told at the time the search was initiated that he had a right to refuse to submit to the search provided he did not board the airplane, he had not knowingly waived his rights and consented to the search. Case law appears to mix the concepts of implied consent and just how far the passenger has agreed to be searched without the need for some other substantial government need. Some defense attorneys continue to argue the language contained in the *Meulener* ruling that the government interest which justifies a physical search of the person or hand baggage of a passenger in the process of boarding is lacking in cases where the prospective passenger declines to board the plane.

Attorneys taking the opposite view have honed in on some additional language in the case of *US vs. Davis*, 482 F 2d. 893 (9th Circuit), 1973. In this case, the court used a different justification for the searches. They supported the searches on the bases of an "administrative" search theory. They alternatively rationalized that the essential purpose of the scheme is not to detect weapons or explosives or to apprehend those who carry them but to DETER persons carrying such material from seeking to board at all.

Future case law will need to engage in a balancing test to determine if and when a passenger can actually revoke their consent if consent is the most accepted justification for making airport searches consistent with the Fourth Amendment. Some common sense must also be thrown into the mix. Everyone knows now that they will not be boarded unless they submit and consent to a security check at the entrance of a sterile concourse. Common sense dictates that the alternatives presented to a potential passenger approaching the screening area are so self-evident that an election to attempt to board necessarily manifests acquiescence in the initiation of the screening process. In other words, it is unlikely any one in the twenty-first century arrives at an airport unaware that they will be searched. They still have plenty of alternatives before they reach the airport. Additionally, they can check their luggage or they can leave. When they do place their luggage on the conveyor belt or walk through the magnetometer, some would argue they have clearly consented to a search.

Additionally, the courts will also have to contend with whether or not airport searches are simply administrative searches and therefore exempt from all Fourth Amendment restrictions. The courts will have to determine whether the airport administrative search incorporates a screening process that is limited sufficiently in its intrusiveness as to be consistent with the requirement that the administrative need justifies the search. Courts will also surely consider whether the risk of successful hijacking is not necessarily enhanced by allowing a potential passenger to avoid a search on a particular occasion by electing not to fly because the potential hijacker or terrorist will just be searched on the next attempt.

One additional case deserves some collateral discussion and mention. The case of *US vs. Henry*, 615 F2nd. 1223 (9th Circuit, 1980) decided in 1980 involves some unique security considerations. In this particular instance, a passenger first offered his briefcase to the ticket agent in order to check it. In the process he asked for the briefcase back and allegedly nervously went to the men's room. Apparently the passenger was wearing an ill-fitting wig and extra clothing, which caused some extra suspicion. After getting the briefcase back from the agent and seeking to resubmit it, the agent advised the defendant he could no longer check baggage. This was a subterfuge to get the defendant to submit it to screening by x-ray. In some interesting language, the Court opined, "that under the totality of the circumstances Henry, freely and voluntarily consented to the search." Additionally they reasoned, "In determining whether Henry freely and voluntarily consented to the search we believe the crucial factor is whether Henry could have freely withdrawn the briefcase and avoided the search." Defendants are likely to litigate these issues extensively in the future.

■ THE WAR ON DRUGS

Continuously, airline officials have attempted to reiterate the fact that the airlines are not in the law enforcement business. They repeatedly argue that the carrier's only legal obligation is to locate weapons. On occasion the courts, in frustration, have gone further. Certainly, procedures for handling attempts to smuggle contraband when discovered by the airlines need to be addressed. Criminal activity cannot just be overlooked. Difficult issues arise, however, in determining just how far the airlines need to go to fulfill their duty to every citizen to maintain a safe and lawful atmosphere at airports and aboard aircraft. These difficult situations are passed along by the airlines to the security officials, who are expected to understand and interpret the law in every situation and to conduct themselves accordingly in every instance. Of course, constant correct decision making constitutes a tall order in that attorneys and judges alike struggle with these issues.

In 1973, the federal courts were becoming distressed over the amounts of illegal drugs being smuggled into the United States on commercial carriers. Consequently, in a US District Court in Brooklyn, New York, a judge ordered the US attorney to seize a Braniff DC8. The aircraft, which had carried three persons smuggling drugs from South America, was technically used in the illegal transportation of controlled substances. The federal government had already passed laws to combat the increasing influx of drugs into the United States by statutes that provided for the actual confiscation of vehicles used in transporting narcotics. This well-known law, on the other hand, had previously not been enforced against commercial carriers. The seizure in this instance did get the attention of the airlines.

This particular federal action prompted carriers to reexamine corporate policy regarding contraband items. The original legislation permitting federal agents to confiscate boats and small aircraft was passed in 1986. It also imposes stiff penalties on owners and operators of aircraft found to be involved in smuggling or in other fraudulent activities. The legislation was intended to take away the smugglers means of transporting the illegal goods as well as the tangible results of extremely profitable drug business. However, airlines had not considered themselves subject to this law.

They based their interpretation of the law on theories argued in other case law. Some state courts had reasoned that a common carrier aircraft should not be seized in connection with drugs unless the carrier had been negligent in locating the contraband. Generally, the courts agreed that the carrier was not responsible for drugs found on passengers, in their luggage, or in the cargo found to be properly manifested unless the carrier had knowledge of the violation or was "grossly negligent" in preventing or discovering it. Other judges concluded that the aircraft may not be seized and forfeited unless neither the owner, pilot, nor any other employee knew or through the exercise of the "highest degree of diligence" could have known that the contraband was aboard.

It is well-accepted law that no carrier is required to embark upon a full-scale law enforcement effort to discover contraband. The carrier must take steps to ensure that proscribed articles are not knowingly transported. Extraordinary measures to identify contraband items are not required, but just what constitutes reasonable measures will continue to be litigated. Airlines are not often able to analyze and know what courts will determine to be sufficient effort to locate contraband on an air carrier. Judges are usually willing to permit searches in the name of airport security, citing a special need that benefits all of the traveling public. Extending police power simply to search for drugs has not been authorized and will not likely be authorized in the future.

▓ PASSENGER RIGHTS

Airport security officials who go beyond what the courts consider reasonable searches are subject to 42 USC Section 1983. The legislation passed in 1976 authorizes a person deprived of any constitutional right as a result of state action to bring civil suit against the person who deprived him or her of that right. Even though neither the airlines nor airport security officials have yet to be considered to be engaged in "state action," they have repeatedly been sued for allegedly violating a passenger's constitutional rights.

Clearly, not ignoring contraband is much different than actively searching for it. As discussed previously, the issues are once again cloudy when the airlines refuse to cooperate. Sometimes law enforcement officers monitor passenger screening and pay airline employees to be informants without the knowledge of the carrier. When airport security personnel have a police officer standing and looking over their shoulder and are encouraged to engage in a search that the officer would not be permitted to effectuate, the courts will raise a red flag and exclude any evidence of contraband found. Airline security officials must not encourage employees to engage in this activity, and when it is discovered, it must be stopped. Otherwise the airlines and contract security officials will be approving of the conduct of the informants, and the courts will not look kindly on the activity. Such conduct could result in the carrier being sued.

One of the most recent cases in this area tried to answer the question, "Can law enforcement authorities use airport security inspections to look for contraband that is unrelated to safety?" The US Court of Appeals for the Ninth Circuit in *US vs. $125,740 Currency*, 873 F 2nd 1240 (9th Circuit 1989) analyzed the actions of Bonnie Boswella, a Flight Terminal Security Officer at the Seattle International Airport when she noticed a dark mass in a briefcase. On 5 Jan 1987, Wayne G. Campbell put his locked briefcase on the airport x-ray scanner. After noticing the dark mass, Officer Boswella asked Campbell to open the briefcase. At first, he was reluctant, but agreed to open it in a private area behind a screen. Karen Kangas, another airport security officer, searched through the briefcase and located a huge sum of money. After inquiring as to his destination, security released him. Officer Kangas called Steve Symms, a US Customs Service Officer, and informed him about the briefcase and its contents. In addition, Customs was provided with a description of Mr. Campbell. Consequently, for their efforts, they received a reward of $250 for locating currency of over $10,000. Later, Mr. Campbell arrived in Los Angeles, where two DEA agents met him. During questioning, he admitted that he had about $130,000 in his briefcase, but that the money belonged to a friend of his who had hired him to ransom a stolen painting.

The two DEA agents confiscated the briefcase. They advised Mr. Campbell he was free to go, but he decided to accompany the agents to the DEA office. At the office, the agents asked Campbell to open the briefcase. He was told that if he refused, they would simply obtain a search warrant and open it in any case. Mr. Campbell, therefore, opened the briefcase, and a significant amount of money was discovered as well as a lot of cigarette rolling papers and a receipt from a Seattle hotel. On the following day, a drug-detection dog alerted when brought into contact with the money; indicating that drugs had come into contact with the currency. As per administrative procedures, the United States filed a civil forfeiture action pursuant to the currency. In response, Mr. Campbell filed a claim to suppress the evidence uncovered by the search. The District Court denied the motion to suppress and ruled the currency was rightfully subject to forfeiture, which decision was later appealed to the 9th Circuit Court of Appeals.

The judge, Alex Koziniske, was concerned with two issues. He considered the idea that the flight terminal security officers were looking more carefully for currency in carry-on baggage because of the potential $250 reward rather than concentrating on searching for items relating to air safety. The second issue the judge considered was whether Mr. Campbell had voluntarily consented to the search at the airport, because his expectation of privacy was waived only as it related to the search for weapons or explosives. The judge ruled that the search at the airport had not been conducted within the narrowly construed objectives permitting airport searches solely to ensure airline and airport security. The judge reversed the lower court and vacated the order of forfeiture. Basically, the judge had reasoned that the Air Transportation Act of 1974 requiring all passengers and carry-on property to be screened by security does not extend an exception to the Fourth Amendment to search for contraband or currency.

Notes: *Law 1990s*

United States vs. Scales *903 F.2nd 765 (1990) Tenth Circuit. Law enforcement authorities with reasonable suspicion that a piece of luggage contains narcotics may detain luggage briefly to investigate the circumstances. Seizure of the suitcase exceeded law enforcement's authority when the suitcase was seized for approximately seven hours before a drug-sniffing dog alerted to the suitcase.*

United States vs. Riley *927 F.2nd 1045 (1991) Eight Circuit Police only need reasonable suspicion, not probable cause, to separate a narcotics defendant's suitcase from others at an airport and subject it to a dog sniff.*

United States vs. Hooper *935 F. 2nd 484 (1991) Second Circuit Briefly detaining a defendant and his suitcase and exposing the luggage to a narcotics-detection dog, if conducted diligently, only requires reasonable suspicion.*

■ NEW LAW IN THE AREA OF SEARCHES

In a departure from recent rulings supportive of police in drug interdiction efforts, the US Supreme Court in *Indianapolis vs. Redmond*, 531 U.S. 32, 121 S.Ct. 497, 2000, has held that the use of road blocks designated to uncover ordinary criminal activities like drug trafficking are unconstitutional. The decision stems from a situation where police stopped a motorist at a roadblock in a high drug crime area. The man was arrested after police discovered drugs in the car. The motorist challenged the arrest, arguing that there was no probable cause for the search.

In the decision, the Court distinguished between roadblocks used to deter drunken driving and illegal immigration from those used to check for random criminal activity. Whereas the previous roadblocks carry implications for public safety and immigration, the latter searches were reasoned to amount to an unreasonable search under the Fourth Amendment. Specifically, Justice Sandra Day O'Conner stated, "We have never approved a checkpoint program whose primary purpose was to detect evidence of ordinary criminal wrongdoing." The case evidenced the scrutiny by the Court in distinguishing between searches which serve a public safety purpose, like airport searches, and searches specifically conducted in order to detect criminal activity unequivocally unrelated to public safety.

Earlier caught in a fire of controversy over "racial profiling," the US Customs Service began imposing limits in 1999 on its screening of airline passengers to intercept illicit drug shipments. They have implemented rules that prohibit agents from detaining airline travelers suspected of drug smuggling for more than four hours without specific approval of a federal magistrate. The policy guidelines also require Customs officers to notify an attorney or friend of the passenger, if asked, if the passenger is detained for longer than two hours. In cases where no drugs are discovered, the agents must also assist the passenger in resuming their journey.

The high-technology crime landscape is another area of expanding law. Experts closely watched a racketeering case against Nicodemo S. Scarfo. FBI agents used a warrant to break into his place of business and put either a program or some sort of "electronic bug" into his computer. According to Scarfo's lawyer, the procedure enables law enforcement to capture every keystroke made on a user's computer (*US vs. Scarfo*, 263 F.3rd 80, [3rd Circuit, 2001]). They use a software system called TEMPEST by which the FBI has the means to recreate a picture on a computer screen from its electromagnetic energy. Another program, called DCS 1000, enables investigators to follow a suspect's Web browsing and e-mail.

In the federal court case in New Jersey, Mr. Scarfo was using a publicly available software program named Pretty Good Privacy, which is a free-encryption program that is usable for e-mail and files. The FBI wanted the password to those files ostensibly so they could collect information on gambling and loan-sharking operations. The government argued that what they did does not rise to the level of a wiretap. Mark Rausch, former head of the Department of Justice's computer crime section, said, "You really need to understand at what point it captured things, and how it got it back to the government, in order to figure out what the Fourth Amendment concerns are" (*Associated Press*, "FBI's Electronic Snooping Headed for Court Test," *Star Tribune*, Minneapolis, Sunday, 29 July 2001, Pg. A13). The defendant's motion to suppress this evidence was denied (*US vs. Scarfo*, 180 F.Supp 2nd 572; 2001). In October 2002, a federal judge issued a Protection Order in favor of the government permitting them to withhold the classified nature of the technology. The case was affirmed in December 2001.

Permitting law enforcement to peek into computers is the wave of the future. Providing such a tool to airport security would enable them to snoop into the computers of passengers and possibly detect information on potential terrorist activity. However, civil libertarians and the courts will likely heavily scrutinize this kind of exploratory investigation.

■ NEW TECHNOLOGIES AND THE LAW

Sometimes new technologies change everything. The use by drug enforcement officials and law enforcement in general of forward-looking infrared radar devices, or FLIR, is one of those innovations. Law enforcement has used the equipment, often mounted on helicopters, not only to assist ground law enforcement during dangerous chases but also to establish evidence of indoor marijuana cultivation. The device detects differences in the surface temperature of objects, and because marijuana needs high-intensity grow lights successfully to grow indoors, FLIR can detect the huge amount of heat radiated.

The constitutionality for the use of the FLIR has been upheld on several occasions. The circuit court in the case of *US vs. Pinson*, 24 F3d 1056 (8th Circuit, 1994) believed that the defendant had no legitimate expectation of privacy in the heat emanating from his house. The court took into account the fact that the only information acquired by the FLIR was data. The 8th Circuit developed a two-prong test for determining what constitutes an expectation of privacy. A legitimate expectation of privacy is considered to exist where ". . . the individual manifests a subjective expectation of privacy in the object of the challenged search and society is willing to recognize that subjective expectation as reasonable." The Supreme Court, however, recently ruled that special heat-seeking devices require a warrant when seeking to find home-grown marijuana plants; changing the legal landscape completely.

The courts have analogized the expectation of privacy argument to the use of canines and also the placement of garbage left at the curb. These situations have been thought not to have a reasonable expectation of privacy attached to them. In the case of the garbage, it is left out to be taken away. In the case of the dogs, the court compared the dogs to the FLIR by claiming that the dogs merely sniffed the odor emanating from the bags. The Court also specifically stated, "none of the interests which form the basis for the need for the protection of a residence, namely the intimacy, personal autonomy, and privacy associated with a home, are [*sic*] threatened by thermal imagery." Consequently, the use of the FLIR could easily be utilized for airfield security without much concern about constitutional challenge.

As is common in the law, other courts have disagreed. The 5th Circuit Court in *US vs. Ishmael*, 843 F. Supp. 205, affirmed 48 F.3d 850, 1995, reached an opposite conclusion. They reasoned that the FLIR cannot tell the difference between legal heat and heat being used to grow marijuana. For that matter, even the excessive heat radiated from grow lights could be being used to grow basil or a host of other legal plants. They, therefore, reached the conclusion that the FLIR is more intrusive than a dog. Additionally, the dog's sense of smell is clearly not as technological precise as the FLIR, which can detect miniscule heat graduations. Reviewers of both arguments have tended to continue to support the concept that dog-sniffing, FLIR, and garbage searches are all fair game for law enforcement as investigative techniques. Both the dogs and the FLIR especially involve sense-enhancing equipment. The degree of that detectability is really not an issue.

Other technological innovations have presented additional court-reviewable topics. US Customs officials at six US airports are currently using the Body Search X-ray to examine drug-smuggling suspects. The system basically sees through clothes. Specifically, passengers who cause Customs officials to become suspicious are required to choose between a pat-down search or to stand in front of a machine that arguably renders an image of the suspect naked.

Customs officials ". . . had hoped that the new technology would help quiet a controversy over the agencies searches, which civil libertarians contend focus too much on minority passengers. A hands-off approach, customs officials reasoned would seem less intrusive" (Michael Allen, "Are These X-Rays Too Revealing?, Targeting Drug Smugglers. Airport Screening Device Sees Right Through Clothes," *Wall Street Journal*, Thursday, 2 March 2000, Pgs. B1, B4). However, the technology is so good it reveals just about everything. In other words, airport security officials might be able to view a little more than the average citizen is personally inclined to show to a stranger. This modesty has nothing to do with the carriage of weapons. Pulsed radar scanners, which pretty much produce an image of an individual's naked body, are clearly intrusive.

In summary, the courts currently do not require a physical intrusion in order to determine that a search has taken place. However, how much of an intrusion, what degree of expectation of privacy is involved, and the reasonableness of the search will all play into any future court analysis. The problem evolving is that as technology improves, it becomes easier to characterize information as being exposed, because technology can now expose it. By systematic practice, expectations of passengers have been conditioned to expect some sort of search. Just how intrusive a search is permissible is still the question to be fully litigated.

■ CONCLUSION

Admittedly, the law is a complicated matrix of sometimes conflicting legislation, policies, and opinions. However, every security official, whether a state agency or privately employed individual, should have a basic understanding of the Fourth Amendment and how it applies to airport searches. Since the Fourth Amendment is currently only applicable when a state agent is conducting the search, private security must be careful not to wander into discretionary authority that rightfully belongs to the police. Whether contract airport security personnel continue to fall into the non–state agent category, has so far generally been decided in the negative. However, the distinction between private and public "policing" are blurring, and it will remain to be seen if this decision persists. The issue becomes even murkier when the airport security officer is an off-duty police officer or soon to be federal employee.

The Fourth Amendment also only protects passengers against unreasonable searches and seizures, not all searches. Additionally, just what is considered to be reasonable is often defined in terms of how serious the threat is conceived to be. During the Persian Gulf War, the threat was accepted as being significantly higher than normal, and the public and the courts were willing to adjust the expectations of privacy. This acceptance was clearly expanded again after 9/11. Another issue pertains to how much privacy a passenger expects to receive at an airport. They expect to be searched for dangerous weapons and explosives, because that is the public policy function of the search. Therefore, it may be perfectly acceptable to have a passenger screened by a metal detector and their carry-on luggage scanned. Having them "undressed" by an x-ray machine may result in a different conclusion. The courts, consequently, will likely continue to evaluate the extent of the permissible intrusion. Advances in technology will likely strain the courts patience with the airline wish for speed versus the level of intrusion.

There are outright exceptions to the Fourth Amendment including administrative searches, border searches, and consent searches. Generally, the judiciary has concluded that passengers do consent to airport searches, but also seem to accept that they are administrative in nature and serve a distinct public need. If the courts believe that security has gone too far, the exclusionary rule may come into play. It is meant to keep the state, via its police function, at an appropriate distance from individual rights. If the state chooses arbitrarily to overstep its bounds, the rule will deny them the success of a conviction against the perpetrator of the alleged crime. According to many criminologists, the rule has proved to be an effective deterrent, but the rule has also undergone much criticism. It is difficult to account for just how many police officers or federal agents restrained their conduct fearing the implications of the exclusionary rule. Consequently, some exceptions have been carved out. Most importantly, the good faith exception, the inevitable discovery exception, and the exigent circumstance exception are the most frequently utilized. Whatever the ultimate decision of the courts regarding a particular search or procedure, the public's attitude toward the search will play a large part in determining its acceptability.

The reasonableness and extent of that attitude from the public can become strained even in today's tense environment. The perception that it is unreasonable to search "little old ladies" while "suspicious characters" are permitted to board unhindered will continue to pose a challenge to security officials. Additionally, any legal search can quickly become illegal when security goes outside the boundaries of reasonableness. The allegation of the selection of only "good-looking" flight attendants for pat-down searches at Sky Harbor Airport in Phoenix is a good example. Most people do not mind being searched in order to feel more secure when they fly. However, when the searches provide neither security nor a sense of security, they lose their public safety purpose and the support of the traveling public.

chapter twelve

Foreign Airport Security: US Law and Foreign Domestic Law Comparison: Lessons Learned

▌ NEWS

1. **1987/1988:** The US Department of Justice filed suit (*PLO* vs. *US*, 695 F. Supp. 1456, 1987) in federal district court seeking to close the PLO's observer mission in New York City. Four members of the IRA successfully challenge the British Anti-Terrorism Law in the European Court of Justice.

2. **1988:** An Italian court sentenced Abu-Nidal to life imprisonment for his role in the 1985 massacre at the Rome airport in 1985. He was tried *in absentia*. He was found dead in Iraq in August 2002.

3. **20 October 2000:** A French Appeals Court ruled that Libyan leader Muammar Khaddaffi could be prosecuted for the bombing of a French DC-10 airliner over Niger in 1989 in which 170 people died.

4. **February 2001:** A Saudi court sentenced an army officer to 70 lashes for using his mobile phone on a domestic flight despite warnings from the crew to desist from using it.

5. **2002:** Attorney General John Ashcroft announced that US prosecutors will seek the death penalty against Zacarias Moussaoui, who is charged with a six-count indictment of conspiring with Usama bin Ladin to carry out the events of 11 September 2001 causing the death of over 3000 people.

■ INTRODUCTION

Certainly, the quality and quantity of security in foreign airports varies from country to country. Title V of the International Security and Development Act of 1985 authorizes the US Secretary of Transportation to determine that an airport maintains effective security measures. Basically, if a condition exists that threatens the safety or security of passengers, aircraft, or crew traveling to or from a foreign airport, the Secretary of State is supposed to be notified. The Transportation Security Administration (TSA) assesses, in conjunction with local host government authorities, the security of airports that are served by US carriers or served by foreign carriers flying directly to the United States. Assessments are based on the provisions of International Standards and Recommended Practices of Annex 17 of the Chicago Convention.

The Federal Aviation Administration (FAA) annually evaluated many of the airports worldwide, usually around 200 in any given year. The US has no jurisdiction to mandate that foreign airport managers comply with US regulations or suggestions. Many foreign airports simply refuse to accept US standards or ICAO (International Civil Aviation Organization) Annex 17 requirements, and others do not have the financial resources to implement any well-intentioned efforts. An example of the difficulty can be shown by a particularly complex choice for some policymakers: The reason an airport in a developing country had no x-ray equipment or scanning devices was because its government was currently saving money to purchase an x-ray machine for the hospital. Aircraft from these impoverished nations still fly into the larger and more industrialized nations' airports and present significant security challenges. The United States has taken a hard stand against terrorism and has legislated laws to support that proactive stand. The level of precautions taken at US, European, and other industrialized country airports is not the universal norm, and even those standards have not prevented terrorist attacks. The government attempts to assess foreign airports using several criteria. Ground security is one of them.

■ GROUND SECURITY

Adequate security on the ground has increased in importance over the years. It is clear that hijack attempts or incidents had been moving from the actual aircraft to the more open terminal. In spite of the 9/11 hijackings, the terminal remains a high threat area. The killing of 25 people and wounding of another 76 at Tel Aviv's Lod Airport on 31 May 1972 was one of the first indications that passengers on the ground were easy targets of machine gun–wielding terrorists. Additional attacks in the Rome and Athens airports in December 1973 and the Rome and Vienna killings in December 1985 finally woke the world up to the increased need for sufficient ground security. The incident at Los Angeles

International Airport over the July 4th weekend of 2002 reminded the public once again of this particular threat. Unfortunately, it is often the wrenching pictures on the television and in newspapers that awake the general public to the need to spend the funds to provide satisfactory protection. It is also significant to point out that the above airport incidents in Rome, Vienna, and Tel Aviv were the result of terrorists spraying automatic weapons fire in the terminal while passengers were checking in. Consequently, efforts to screen passengers and their carry-on baggage would not have avoided the consequences of the attacks.

Some airports, owing to the fact that they have been previous targets, have implemented improved and demanding security procedures. At the Frankfurt International Airport, for example, security appears tight even to the most casual observer. Armed guards patrol the entire airport, and their presence is obvious to any passenger arriving to check in initially. Additionally, only passengers with tickets are permitted outside of the main check-in area. At arrival, no curbside checking is available. All passengers must check in at the counter to receive a boarding pass. Once through the first screening, passengers must also clear immigration and customs, where their identities can be again checked and verified. These added procedures, required for international travel, all have secondary security benefits. However, individual airlines have added even more security. In Frankfurt, Delta Airlines rechecks carry-on baggage at the gate and reverifies passenger identities on other international flights before proceeding to the aircraft.

Some other overseas airports also take security quite seriously. At Narita Airport outside Tokyo, armored personnel carriers are stationed around the entire facility, indicating to everyone that they mean business. Singapore, Sydney, and Seoul all also have taken special efforts to make their airports safe. The same cannot be said for Manila, Lagos, and many others. Athens airport has repeatedly come under severe criticism for the ineffectiveness of its security processes. Ever since the hijacking of TWA Flight 847 in June 1985, Athens officials have attempted to upgrade its security. Travel advisories have been published and lifted over the last twenty years; however, laxity is still prevalent. In October 1986, the Greek government received a $5 million loan for security improvements, after which perimeter fences were upgraded and armored cars were stationed at exits. However, the Greek government has still not given the needs of Athens Hellenikon Airport much priority in their budgeting process regardless of the thousands and thousands of international passengers transiting this particular airport. The new airport, which opened in March 2001, is still plagued with problems, especially concerning the access roads to the airport ("Athens Sparta Airport Not Ready to be Opened," *IATA Press Release*, 9 February 2001, Internet: http://www.iata.org/pr/pr01febb.html, 10 July 2001). Experts have continued to criticize the Athens airport management, and concerns have abounded especially in light of the upcoming Olympics. The US government regularly publishes their assessment of airports serving US aircraft and aircraft servicing US ports of entry.

▓ AMERICAN ASSESSMENTS

On 8 August 1985, Public Law 99-83, the Foreign Security Act, was signed into law. Title V, Part B amended Section 1115 of the Federal Aviation Act of 1958. It directed the Secretary of Transportation to assess the effectiveness of security measures at all foreign airports. The legislation covered all airports being served by US air carriers, those foreign airports from which foreign air carriers serve the United States, those foreign airports that pose a high risk of introducing danger to international travel, and other airports as the Secretary should assess. The Act also obligates the Secretary to take appropriate action with respect to airports that do not maintain and administer effective security measures. The Secretary subsequently delegated the FAA the responsibility to implement the provisions of Public Law 99-83; now amended to task the TSA the same function.

As stated, in order to effectuate their responsibilities, the government conducts periodic inspections of the applicable airports. Assessments are made and threats are analyzed in conjunction with the Department of State. US authority is limited by the fact that the foreign airport authorities must be willing to cooperate. The United States really only acquires some specific jurisdiction over foreign carriers on the last leg of their flight directly to the US. All other evaluations are done on a cooperative basis. Over 300 airports were evaluated and met the criteria established by the FAA for a safe airport during the year 2000. Hundreds more have been evaluated since that date. Obviously, owing to limited resources of funds and personnel, not every airport that should be periodically assessed can be as often as the government would prefer.

▓ DIVERSION AIRPORTS

Stansted Airport is the London area's third largest airport. It is little known to the international traveler, since most passengers normally arrive at the gateway airports of Heathrow, outside London, and Gatwick, south of London. Located slightly east of London, Stansted Airport, has become the choice of airport security officials dealing with a hijacked aircraft. In an effort to handle a developing hijacking incident without disrupting the major airports, authorities have attempted to hornswoggle the terrorist demanding that an aircraft be flown to one of the two larger airports by diverting it to Stansted. In combating a hijacking, it is an obvious and valuable tool to be able to direct the hijacked aircraft to the airport of choice of the security officials as opposed to the hijackers. In spite of the perceptions 9/11 has created, few hijackers are expert aviators.

Stansted was first used to receive a hijacked aircraft in 1975, when a BAC-111 was hijacked on an internal flight between Manchester and London. The pilot, as part of a prebriefed alternative in case of a hijacking, managed to divert to Stansted instead of Heathrow. The hijacker had demanded money and wanted to be flown to France. Not being a pilot, the hijacker was convinced that the aircraft had actually been flown to France when in reality it was still in England.

Stansted is London's third international gateway and is one of the fastest growing airports in Europe. The airport currently handles over 14 million passengers and plans to grow to a capacity of 25 million passengers by 2010. It is also an exceptional diversion airport manned by trained and coordinated anti-terrorist security teams. *From the BAA Aviation Photo Library.*

Many lessons were learned from this initial effort to be in more control of an ongoing hijacking situation.

For example, it became imperative that airline personnel and ground security needed to be able quickly to coordinate their responses. Security officials began to work out the number of police on hand to deal with a specific emergency and to create rendezvous points for emergency services. As a result of lessons learned communications between pilots and ground personnel security were greatly improved, and designated command posts were firmly incorporated into procedures.

The importance of training all personnel and maintaining a high level of response capability was reinforced during a second hijacking. The hijacked aircraft, originating in central Africa in 1982 aboard an Air Tanzania Boeing 727, eventually made its way to Stansted after traveling a circuitous route throughout Europe. In this particular situation, a fully coordinated response team awaited the aircraft. The team consisted of a combined police and military operation with the elite British Special Air Service (SAS) standing by to mount a hostage-rescue operation if negotiations failed. In protracted negotiations including the Tanzanian

High Commissioner, the crisis was settled peaceably approximately twenty-four hours after it began.

By 1996, the hijacking team was ready and waiting for a Sudan Airways A310 Airbus originating in Khartoum that had been hijacked by Iraqi terrorists. They had demanded that the plane be flown to Italy, but owing to insufficient fuel, the plane was forced to land in Cyprus. After becoming airborne again, the pilot flew the aircraft to Stansted and a well-prepared team settled the crisis peacefully and professionally. Such prearranged diversion airports and supporting teams should become standard procedure. Not only does a well-trained and prepared team meet and greet the hijacked aircraft, but also the entire situation is centered away from other standard airport facilities, precluding the need to stop air operations and take other precautionary measures.

▓ TRANSPORTATION SECURITY ADMINISTRATION INTERNATIONAL AVIATION SAFETY ASSESSMENT PROGRAM

Foreign airport assessments will continue to be handled by the former Civil Aviation Security section of the FAA, which is now a part of the TSA. The Office of Inspections within the FAA will also continue to assist with some functions and review the effectiveness of all TSA programs. There are only two choices for the inspectors when assessing airports overseas. The foreign airport either complies with ICAO standards or does not. A Category 1 airport exists when a country's civil aviation authority has been assessed and has been found to license and oversee air carriers in accordance with ICAO aviation safety standards. On the other hand, Category 2 airports do not. A determination is made whether the airport does not provide safety oversight of its air carrier operations in accordance with ICAO standards. The government recognizes the following deficiencies:

1. The country lacks laws or regulations necessary to support the certification and oversight of air carriers in accordance with minimum international standards.
2. The country's Civil Aviation Authority (CAA) lacks the technical expertise, resources, and organization to license or oversee air carrier operations.
3. The country's CAA does not have adequately trained and qualified technical personnel.
4. The country's CAA does not provide adequate inspector guidance to ensure enforcement of, and compliance with, minimum international standards.
5. The country's CAA has insufficient documentation and records of certification and inadequate continuing oversight and surveillance of air carrier operations (Internet: http://www.faa.gov/avr/iasa/iasadef5.html, Pg. 1). Each airport's overall safety and security procedures are reviewed. Trained inspectors make determinations whether the in-place programs are effi-

cient and fully supported by the local CAA. Safety and security programs in name only do not withstand scrutiny.

The assessment program became official policy in August 1992. It was published in the *Federal Register*, Vol. 57, No. 164, 24 Aug 1992. The purpose of the overall program was to ensure that all the foreign carriers that operate to and from the United States are competent to do so. The program was determined to focus on the country's overall ability to adhere to international standards as established by the ICAO and not on individual airlines. After a trial period, the formal rules were formulated and implemented. Any foreign air carrier desiring to conduct air operations into the United States needs to file an application with the US Department of Transportation (DOT). The foreign carriers apply for a foreign carrier permit in accordance with the Federal Aviation Act, 49 U.S.C. 41302, Parts 211 and 302. The Code of Federal Regulations (CFRs) implements and codifies the rules in 14 CFR 211, 302. Additionally, 14 CFR Part 129 specifies that the carrier must meet the safety standards prescribed in the Chicago Convention, Annex 6. Before the DOT actually issues the permit, the government evaluates the candidate's capability to provide safety and continuing oversight for its international carriers. Assessment teams are regularly sent to the CAA of the applicant country and evaluations are forwarded to the DOT for review and action.

▓ LEGAL REMEDIES

International treaty efforts to combat terrorism have already been discussed. The US domestically legislated approach has not necessarily been adopted by other nations. In other words, other nations have legislated quite different domestic legal tools to address the problem. It is worthwhile to explore the US legislation as well as some of these different methods. Some have arguably been more successful than others. Additionally, the ever-increasing threat from nuclear, biological, or chemical terrorism has heightened the attention the public has given to law enforcement and general criminal justice efforts.

On the eve of the bombing of the federal building in Oklahoma City, Congress sent a compromise version of antiterrorism legislation, The Anti-Terrorism and Effective Death Penalty Act of 1996 (AEDPA), to President Bill Clinton for his signature. He signed it into law. As discussed, just how to define terrorism and who exactly should be considered a terrorist has created much controversy. In the last five years, the federal government had once again become focused on terrorism, both domestic and international. Prior to 11 September 2001, this renewed attention was already the result of an increased threat from nuclear proliferation, ethnic cleansing, and continued religious wars. Many nations unfortunately have been brutally forced to refocus on the shady world of terrorism. No country is immune.

The AEDPA was formally adopted on 24 April 1996. In addition, the United States is party to over 100 extradition treaties (Mark Janis, *Introduction to*

International Law, 2nd ed., 1993, Pg. 348). Overall, "extradition treaties provide that a state is obligated to extradite persons to another state when the other state shows that the person is sought for trial for a crime allegedly committed within the jurisdiction of that state for punishment for a crime committed in that state after conviction and flight from that state" (*Restatement of Foreign Relations Law of the United States*, 1987, Pg. 475). However, extradition has historically been subject to several exceptions, including the concept of when the offense is shown to be political in nature. Terrorists have used this exception to their advantage. Persons accused of terrorism have claimed that they are engaged in political activities and fall within the exception. The tradition has survived many challenges and remains in effect because of the strong inclination of several nations to provide refuges of political asylum.

How the treaties define political offense is open to interpretation. In essence, the requirements of the exception include:

1. The conflict for which the accused claims support is ongoing
2. The act in question is part of the conflict
3. The accused is a member of an organization of defined structure and command.
4. The accused is acting on orders from someone within the organization.

Because the Irish Republican Army (IRA) claims to fall within this definition, naturally, the British have failed to recognize it. The United States and Britain amended their extradition treaty accordingly. In 1985, the Supplemental Extradition Treaty went into effect (Mark Janis, *Introduction to International Law*, 2nd ed., 1993, Pg. 349). The new version excludes several offenses from the "political exception" parameters. Specifically, the law permits extradition in cases of politically motivated crimes of murder, manslaughter, kidnapping, hostage taking, and the manufacture of explosives and use thereof. It effectively discounts the political offense exception. As is usually the case, powerful nations can interpret international law how it suits them. The British have taken a hard stand against the IRA, and during the Reagan administration, every effort was made to support the British; hence the new extradition treaty.

Even after passage of the AEDPA, the Clinton administration sought stronger legislation against terrorism. In July 1996, the administration reintroduced two measures previously removed from the AEDPA. The administration sought expanded federal roving wiretap authority and the required use of taggants in explosives (Terry Atlas, "GOP Balks over Wiretaps, Tagging Explosives; US Allies OK Counterterrorism Initiatives, *Chicago Tribune*, 31 July 1996, Pg. 3; "Airline Security Crackdown Is Stalled on the Runway: Despite Federal Rhetoric Little Has Been Accomplished," *Los Angeles Times*, 19 August 1996, B4). Simultaneously, Vice-President Al Gore was heading the commission to review all aspects of aviation safety. After the commission published its findings, the Aviation Security and Anti-Terrorism Act of 1996 was passed. Unfortunately, the House version, under pressure from the National Rifle

Association and the American Civil Liberties Union, dropped the wiretap and taggant provisions. The British and others have been much more successful in enacting stronger antiterrorism legislation.

Legislation After 11 September 2001

The Aviation and Transportation Security Act established a new TSA within the DOT responsible for security for all modes of transportation and headed by a new Under Secretary. The bill provided that the federal government would assume responsibility for all passenger and baggage screening at commercial airports in the United States as soon as possible. Within a twelve-month period, the TSA hired, trained, and deployed federal screeners, federal security managers, federal security personnel, and federal law enforcement officers. In addition, five airports have been allowed to participate in a pilot program to experiment with private contracting. After two years in the program, all airports will be allowed the option of having the federal government contract with private firms to provide aviation security services if the Secretary of Transportation determines that this will provide an equal or greater level of security. The law is supposed to require the administration to adopt new stricter standards for screeners. All screeners will be US citizens. It also requires the federal government to conduct background checks on all individuals with access to secure areas within an airport. The measure allows for expedited procedures to be used to get important

President George W. Bush presenting the 2003 State of the Union Address on Capital Hill. He discusses the creation of the Department of Homeland Security, mobilizing the government in efforts to combat the threats of the 21st century. President Bush promises to answer every danger and every enemy that threatens the American people. *Alex Wong / Getty Images, Inc.—Liaison.*

security directives in place including a provision that 100 percent of checked baggage be screened by explosive-detection equipment. It also requires the deployment of Federal Air Marshals. It also directs the new Under Secretary, in consultation with the FAA, to take action to strengthen cockpit doors and now provides for pilots to carry firearms to defend their aircraft.

In conjunction, the legislation mandates a fee to be charged to cover the cost of providing the aviation security services. The fee will be based on the number of times a passenger boards a plane during the course of travel, but will be capped at $5.00 per one-way trip. Any additional funds needed will be authorized to be appropriated or may come from a fee imposed directly on the airlines. The intent of Congress was also to establish an aviation oversight board composed of representatives from other agencies (DOT, Department of Defense, Department of Justice, Treasury, the CIA, the National Security Council, and Homeland Security) of the federal government to share intelligence information and oversee the actions of the new Under Secretary. The bill, S. 1447, authorizes funding and provides flexibility in the use of Airport Improvement Program (AIP) and Passenger Facility Charges (PFC) funds to help airports pay for the increased security costs. The bill was signed into law 19 November 2001.

Another piece of legislation, H.R. 3210 creates a temporary industry risk–spreading program to ensure the continued availability of commercial property and casualty insurance. The intent was to establish a means for insurance companies to reinsure for terrorism-related risks to limit immediate market disruptions, encourage economic stabilization, and facilitate a transition to a viable market for private terrorism risk insurance. According to the legislative history, in the event of a terrorist attack, the Secretary of the Treasury will determine when losses from one or more acts of terrorism result in insurance claims industrywide of over $1 billion and up to $20 billion during the coverage period of the measure. This provision is modeled in part on existing state insurance programs for solvency guarantee funds and catastrophic disaster pools. After such a determination, the Treasury will pay 90 percent of the claims (with 10 percent of losses retained by the insurers) on the first dollar of the coverage. The Secretary of the Treasury must thereafter assess all commercial property and casualty insurers to recoup the costs of the Treasury payments. If losses in the coverage period are less than $1 billion industrywide, the bill provides company-specific trigger levels for cost sharing with a per company deductible to protect smaller insurance companies. If losses exceed $20 billion industrywide, the Treasury will pay 90 percent of all claims up to financial assistance of $100 billion over the covered period. The legislation gives the Secretary the power to recoup these payments through surcharges on commercial property and casualty policy premiums upon a weighing of economic conditions and other factors. These provisions expire at the end of 2002, although the Secretary may extend the program through 2004.

Additionally, H.R. 3004, the Financial Anti-Terrorism Act of 2001, provides the United States with new tools to combat the financing of terrorism and other financial crimes. The measure contains provisions to strengthen law enforcement authorities, as well as to enhance public-private cooperation between government and industry in disrupting terrorist funding. Specifically, the measure: (1) makes it a crime to smuggle over $10,000 into or out of the United States, and to transport more than $10,000 in criminal proceeds across state lines; (2) gives the Justice Department new prosecutorial tools to combat terrorist-related and other money-laundering activities through US financial institutions; (3) provides statutory authorization for the Financial Crimes Enforcement Network (FinCEN), which analyzes reports filed by financial institutions on currency transactions and suspicious financial activity; (4) sets up a unit in FinCEN directed at oversight and analysis of hawalas and other underground black market banking systems; (5) makes it a crime knowingly to falsify one's identity in opening an account at a financial institution and directs the Treasury to develop regulations to guide financial institutions in identifying account holders; (6) directs the Treasury Department to establish a secure Web site to receive electronic filings of suspicious activity reports (SARs), and provides financial institutions with alerts and other information regarding patterns of terrorist or other suspicious activity that warrant enhanced scrutiny; (7) requires the Treasury to report quarterly to industry on how SARs are used to assist law enforcement in combating terrorism and other crimes; (8) authorizes intelligence agency access to reports filed by financial institutions, and expands government access to consumer financial records and credit histories; (9) creates a public-private task force on terrorist financing; (10) sets a 31 December 2001 deadline for proposed regulations on SAR reporting requirements for broker-dealers and authorizes the Treasury to require SARs of commodity futures traders; (11) authorizes the Secretary of the Treasury to impose "special measures" if a foreign country, financial institution, transaction, or account is deemed to be a "primary money-laundering concern"; (12) prohibits US financial institutions from providing banking services to "shell" banks that have no physical presence in any country nor any affiliation with a financial institution; (13) requires greater due diligence for certain correspondent and private banking accounts; (14) authorizes the Treasury to regulate concentration accounts; (15) requires financial institutions to have anti–money laundering programs; (16) authorizes the President to impose certain sanctions (including limiting access to the US financial system) against foreign governments that refuse to cooperate in law enforcement efforts against terrorism and money laundering; and (17) updates US anticounterfeiting laws.

Antiterrorism Legislation in the United Kingdom

Because of continued violence in Northern Ireland, the British considered a criminal justice means of handling the prolonged situation. In 1972, Lord Chief Justice Diplock was sent to Northern Ireland to review the processes in place and to make recommendations. He investigated how to use criminal law to combat terrorism. His recommendations were implemented, and they became some of the most controversial antiterrorism policies in the world.

The police and the courts were given increased powers—some would say excessive. Security forces were given the power to arrest and jail individuals suspected of being terrorists without a warrant or a trial. In conjunction, courts were given the power to hold secret trials and collect testimony without any opportunity to cross examine. A special type of martial law to supplement the procedures, the Special Powers Act (1922), was first enacted by a semiautonomous Irish parliament and renewed each year until 1933 when it became a permanent part of the legal code in Northern Ireland. After the Diplock report, the Emergency Powers Act was passed; taking only a slightly different approach. It remained in existence from 1973 to 1995. This law united the police, the military, correctional departments, and the courts into a cohesive antiterrorist unit. This Act was not legislated in an "Irish parliament" but came directly from Britain. According to one scholar, the purpose of the Act was to shift the burden of proof from the state to the defendant and to shift more control away from the judicial branch of government and channel it toward the executive branch (John E. Finn, "Public Support for Emergency Legislation in Northern Ireland: A Preliminary Analysis," *Terrorism*, 1987 Pgs. 113–124).

The United Kingdom Prevention of Terrorism Act of 1984 granted some extraordinary powers to the executive branch. They were granted the powers of arrest, detention, and exclusion. They also "proscribed" membership in the IRA and the INLA (Irish National Liberation Army). The Act made contributions to acts of terrorism and withholding information about acts of terrorism outright criminal offenses, and expanded the powers of police in carrying out searches of travelers. Internment became an administrative process. The suspect could be held for 28 days unless a police official decided there was reason for further detention. No criminal charges had to be filed, because the individual was not under arrest. It came under serious review in 1985 and again in 1993 after the Anglo-Irish Peace Accord. The law was extensively criticized, not just for its sweeping violations of civil liberties, but many argued it was totally ineffective as well.

In 1988, the European Court of Human Rights found the amended law to be in violation of the European Convention on Human Rights. The act still allowed individuals suspected of terrorism to be held for seven days without any sort of court appearance. Opponents of the law alleged that the seven-day holding provision is simply a means of harassment and is used in efforts to intimidate and obtain information. According to these same opponents, thousands of people are affected by it each year, and only a tiny percentage are ever charged with anything. The exclusion provisions of the law enable the UK Secretary of State to issue exclusion orders against British citizens and noncitizens from entering the United Kingdom. The authorities were seeking to limit IRA flexibility in moving around the United Kingdom. It is clear that such provisions would not likely survive judicial review in the United States because of long-standing freedom of movement expectations.

Another distinct difference between US and British law was the fact that wiretapping was not illegal in Britain until 1985. Under pressure from the rest of the European community, the British passed the Interception of Communications Act of 1985, which limited the government's indiscriminate tapping of telephones and interfering with the mail. It is relevant to acknowledge the fact that the United

Kingdom is one of the few democratic nations that does not have a written constitution or a Bill of Rights that guarantees the rights of individuals.

The United States and the United Kingdom have taken different paths to reach the same end. Both hope to control the proliferation of terrorism. Also, because of the absence of separation of powers between a judicial, legislative, and executive branch, the functions of drafting and implementing laws are somewhat merged. Consequently, there is no real judicial review of British antiterrorism legislation. Hence, the scrutiny which has cropped up originated in the European Court of Justice.

The United States has also historically approached the problem from a criminal code perspective. When people died in terrorist acts, the crime of murder was committed. The terrorist acts were forced to fit within the already existing criminal code. Later under AEDPA, the approach was changed somewhat singling out terrorists as people unworthy of certain civil liberties. The Bush Administration has expanded this concept even further. Some would argue that the new approach is inappropriate, because it impinges on basic civil liberties and is therefore not worth any advantage it may give law enforcement in stopping terrorism.

Canada's War with the Front du Liberation du Quebec

Canada decided on yet another approach. The Canadian government concluded the best way to handle terrorism was both swift and limited in scale. Canada was forced to deal with a violent native terrorist group. The Front du Liberation du Quebec (FLQ) sought an independent Quebec and was willing to create anarchy and commit murder and kidnapping to accomplish it. The era culminated in the kidnapping of James Cross, a British diplomat, and Pierre Laporte, Minister of Labor in the Quebec provincial government.

The then Prime Minister, Elliot Trudeau, who had been so eloquently outspoken about terrorism at the Bonn Conference, invoked the Canadian War Measures Act in 1970. The law empowered him to call in the army when the Prime Minister felt it was necessary. (The Posse Comitatus Act prevents this alternative in the US.) At the time of the kidnappings, Trudeau agreed to negotiate with the terrorists. In return for the release of Cross, the terrorists were permitted to fly to Cuba. Laporte, however, had already been murdered. As the British had learned years before when British citizens were held captive, bargaining with terrorists is often antiproductive. The Canadians vowed to never negotiate again. After the kidnappings, Trudeau wanted to rid Canada of the FLQ by whatever means necessary.

He inundated Montreal with troops after the Royal Canadian Mounted Police concentrated on locating them. Suspending some of the normal Canadian protections against unreasonable search and seizures, the police used their new broad powers to arrest and search about 300 suspects (Christopher Dobson and Ronald Apyne, "*Counterattack*, The West's Battle Against Terrorists," New York, Facts on File, 1982, Pg. 113). Trudeau's troop saturation of Montreal took nine weeks, but successfully tracked down those responsible for Laporte's death.

When it was over, the troops disappeared from the streets, the police went back to normal democratic search and seizure protocols, and the government sought to address some of the issues that contributed to terrorism in the first place. Canada, at the time, chose to focus on a specific group for a specific period of time. The United States, on the other hand, must deal with a multitude of international and domestic threats.

German Antiterrorism Laws

When the German antiterrorism laws were first enacted, many considered them to be fairly moderate considering the seemingly overwhelming problems the authorities were having with the Baader-Meinhof gang and later the Red Army Faction. Germany decided to enact what came to be known as the "contact ban" and the "propagation of violence laws." The contact ban law was intended to restrict the flow of communications between imprisoned terrorists and their comrades on the outside of Germany's prisons. The German authorities believed that the attorney's visiting the imprisoned members of terrorist organizations were passing information back and forth. Consequently, the German correctional authorities suspended the right of prisoners to confidentially discuss their cases with their lawyers. "To many experts on German law, this made it appear that a fundamental principle of due process was being sacrificed without any appreciable benefit" ("Report on Domestic and International Terrorism," Subcommittee on Civil and Constitutional Rights of the Committee on the Judiciary, First Session April 1981, Washington, DC, Government Printing Office, Pgs. 6–23).

The provocation of violence law stirred up a bit of controversy. The law was used against student protestors as well as those engaged in terrorism. For example, it made it very easy for the police to infiltrate a student demonstration and arrest anyone they thought might be planning to riot or resist. It gave them almost blanket authority to arrest whom they saw fit, without any restraint, under the pretense that any situation was prone to violence.

Terrorism has been severely curtailed in Germany not only because of these laws but also the "declassified" files of the former East German Stasi, or secret police. When those files were opened after the reunification of Germany, many terrorists formerly financed and protected by the East Germans lost their cloak of protection. The secret police were no longer able to circumvent the police efforts of the West Germans to track them down. As mentioned previously, on occasion, some German antiterrorism units have allegedly gone too far.

Italian Antiterrorism Laws

When Aldo Moro was kidnapped and killed, Interior Minister Virginio Rognoni, assumed the office of Prime Minister. At the time, the Italian Red Brigades were at their peak. "Statistics issued by the Interior Ministry indicated that in 1978 there were 2,498 terrorist attacks in Italy. Between 1968 and 1982, 403 people were killed in terrorist incidents and another 1347 were injured" (Cindy Combs, *Terrorism in the 21st Century*, 2nd ed., Prentice Hall, Upper Saddle River, NJ, 1999, Pg. 185). In response, the Prime Minister unleashed a Carabinieri general named Carlo Alberto Della Chiesa. He created an antiterrorism unit, which was supported by legislation with teeth. The Italian laws, like some of their European counterparts, strengthened the maximum sentences for convicted terrorists, suspended search and seizure laws, and legislated terrorism as a crime.

The Italian authorities also made use of the fact that the population was tired of terrorism. Even the terrorists began to think that their efforts were gaining little. In 1982, a law that promised "repentant" terrorists lighter sentences if they confessed was passed. One of the most famous "Penniti" was Patriz Peci. He was a commander of a Red Brigade from Turin, who provided the police with some important intelligence. Italy balanced strict police enforcement measures with the ability to confess and be somewhat forgiven. The mix worked, and Italy is currently relatively free of terrorism.

■ PROFILING

As discussed, critics are inclined to denounce the practice of profiling. The basic concept behind a profiling system is to use trained security agents to detect patterns and behaviors that warrant closer scrutiny of certain passengers and their baggage. The system is not designed to detect weapons or explosives. It is designed to detect the person who is carrying such devices. A terrorist is absolutely convinced that the cause, whatever it is, has been betrayed and that he or she has been victimized. The cause can be based on ethnic, religious, economic, or ideological convictions. Because they feel exploited by forces usually more powerful than their group, they feel they can victimize others. Their psychological characteristics do not easily transform themselves into physical attributes. However, many terrorist groups are anti-Western. Consequently, many members of racial minorities repeatedly complain that they are unfairly singled out for questioning and searches.

Using similar techniques, the US Customs Service also uses computer profiling and plainclothes and uniformed officers to prevent contraband from entering the country. That agency, in particular, has been heavily inundated with complaints that its officers select a disproportionate number of blacks for strip searches. The agency has been sued often, but just a short while ago it was sued by the American Civil Liberties Union representing a 33-year-old advertising agent returning from a vacation in Jamaica. As a result, Raymond Kelly, Customs Commissioner, recognized the need for a response and instituted a mandatory sensitivity training program for Custom's officers who engage in these types of searches.

Similarly, the FAA implemented a computerized profiling system to help identify potential hijackers. The details of the system have not been disclosed. It is, therefore, impossible precisely to determine whether the profiles now in use involve illegal conduct or not. However, David Harris, a law professor at the University of Toledo, has said that the system scans for passengers' destinations, how they paid for the fare, and when they booked their reservations (Martha Carr and Keith O'Brian, "Profiling at Airports Warranted, Say Officials Who Screen People," *Star Tribune*, 4 February 2001, Pg. G2.) The Computer-Assisted Passenger Screening, or CAPS system, and later CAPS II, was supposed to rely solely on information that passengers already provide to air carriers for reasons unrelated to security. It was not intended to depend on gathering any additional information from the traveler, nor was it connected to any law enforcement or intelligence database. The government had repeatedly and emphatically denied that race, ethnicity, gender, or religion played a role in the process. They have stated, "it has to do with people's travel patterns and how well they're known in the system" (Interview with FAA Officer James Paget, Gore Commission participant, 6 November 1998, Michael Higgins, Looking the Part, *A.B.A. Journal*, Pg. 52). It is difficult to ignore that a person's personal, ideological, and psychological characteristics do not play an important role in "profiling" them. After the TWA 800 disaster in mid-1996, it is alleged by some that the FAA issued an internal confidential memo to select all individuals who were Iranian or carrying an Iranian passport to be singled out for special scrutiny ("ACLU Against Airport Profiling," Internet: http://www.antidiscrimination.org/airlineprofileform.html, Pgs. 1, 21, August 2001). In response, the ACLU has created a form for people to fill out who believe they have been discriminated against. Literally hundreds of complaints had been filed.

In reality, abuse of such collected information would be almost inevitable. It puts every person in the situation that a "virtual" identity overshadows our corporeal selves. It also raises the issue that those individuals who are determined enough to construct a bomb and carry it onboard an aircraft are almost certainly intelligent enough to avoid behavior likely to single themselves out for special scrutiny. Regardless, the Gore Commission was responsible for reviewing airline passenger safety and making recommendations on how to improve the system. The Commission wholeheartedly embraced profiling of terrorists specifically used in conjunction with some other controls.

In the Final Report to President Bill Clinton, the Commission stated, "the threat of terrorism is changing . . . it is no longer just an overseas threat from foreign terrorists. People and places in the United States have joined the list of targets, and Americans have joined the ranks of terrorists." The Commission recognized the need for sophisticated technology for detecting the presence of explosives in checked baggage. However, since those machines are expensive and not readily available for use in many airports, the report also recommended that the FAA implement programs for bag matching and passenger profiling by 31 December 1997 in order to enhance overall airport security. Additionally, the commission recommended that the FAA should develop the automated system for passenger profiling over the legal objections of the ACLU and many Arab-American groups.

In mid-1996, the FAA, using a grant to Northwest Airlines, introduced the first automated passenger profiling system. In April 1997, the FAA and Northwest completed programming changes to a prototype CAPS system. The system as stated became known as the Computer-Assisted Passenger Screening (CAPS). It used information directly acquired from the airline reservation system. If the system decided that someone was high risk, that person became subject to more stringent security review as per the discretion of the viewer. The system could also randomly select individuals for specific scrutiny. The system was not supposed to maintain a permanent database, and the airline was required to delete all information shortly after a flight lands. However, the profiles used in the system were not based on data about actual terrorists. The FAA developed the criteria based on "consultations with a large number of security and terrorism experts, who gave their assessments of the likely patterns of behavior of individuals intending to attack civil aviation" (Anthony Fainberg, "Aviation Security in the United States: Current and Future Trends", 25 *Transportation Law Journal*, 1998, Pg. 200). The parameters themselves were therefore open to criticism.

In the mid-1970s, the FAA began using manual passenger screening to combat hijacking and to prevent explosives or incendiary devices from being placed aboard aircraft on international flights. This kind of screening relied on an employee of an air carrier to use personal judgment on whether a passenger meets the profile of a terrorist. Even though the factors used in conducting the manual screening are not supposed to be biased, there is a distinct chance that the employee may be either consciously or unconsciously biased. There can be a thin line between profiling and discrimination.

Indeed, profiling has failed in the past. For example, the German SS profile for the potential bomber of the von Hindenburg airship made Jewish and dissident passengers the preferred suspects. The alleged culprit turned out to be a German patriot. Prejudice, whether it is overt or less consciously implemented, does play some part in "profiling." Profiling should augment technological safeguards such as high-tech bomb detectors, trace-explosive detectors, and bomb-sniffing dogs and should not be considered to be an independent tool. In and of themselves, profiling systems would be incapable of protecting airports from a terrorist attack.

The specific format of future airport programs remains uncertain. The system was designed to remove some human subjectivity by eliminating the choices of the personnel who identify persons targeted for heightened security. As stated previously, after each passenger's name is entered into the computer, the system makes an independent determination and flashes red or green. The passenger is totally unaware of the event. The process is focusing on checked baggage and other travel-related information. If the person's bags appear to be suspicious, they should be opened or scanned. The level or intensity of the search would depend on the level of suspicion. The choice initially to scrutinize the baggage is made by the computer, but the field officer must decide whether to halt or continue the search process through any additional steps. They view the images on the scanner and have complete discretion to choose the subsequent intensity of the search. Theoretically, they could just have a hunch or maybe they decide to seek other contraband not dangerous to flight. In order for it to work, the terrorist must be unaware of its criteria. Additionally, terrorists are likely to continue to seek innovative ways to place bombs on aircraft without having to carry it onboard themselves. The Department of Justice recommended that the FAA conduct periodic reviews of the CAPS system, required domestic airlines to obtain approval before adding to or enhancing the system, and required airlines to train employees responsible for the passenger screening system to respect individual civil liberties.

On 19 April 1999, the FAA proposed new regulations pertaining to security profiling (*Federal Register*, 19 April 1999, Vol. 64, No. 74, Pgs. 19219–19240; *Federal Register* On-line via GPO access, wais.access.gpo.gov). The FAA proposed that each certificate holder be required under Section 108.5 to adopt and implement an FAA-approved security program to screen checked baggage or conduct passenger bag matching for scheduled passenger operations. (The regulations are to apply to aircraft configured to seat more than 60 passengers.) The proposal mandated that the screening of checked baggage on domestic flights may be accomplished by screening the checked baggage of every passenger with explosive-detection equipment (EDS), by 100% positive bag matching (PPBM), or by utilizing the FAA-approved CAPS system. Unfortunately, the improvements were not implemented in a timely manner. The FAA argued that CAPS was based on the same concept as the manual screening system, which was designed to exclude from extra security measures the vast majority of passengers. It supported the system and supported its decision in spite of allegations it was discriminatory or that a potential terrorist could circumvent the system. In order further to justify the merits of the system, in addition to selecting persons pursuant to the profiling standards, it randomly selected a limited number of passengers for heightened security measures. The FAA determined that this random selection in which each passenger had a chance of being a selectee has a valid deterrent effect. However, alternatively, it is arguable that the chance of the system selecting a terrorist by means of random selection was about as likely as winning the powerball lottery. New legislation initiated by the Bush Administration has now revamped the program completely empowering it with intrusive powers not originally conceived of prior to 11 September 2001.

International Views of Profiling

Much of the hijacking originally had been taking place in the Middle East, and the Israeli Airline, El Al, eventually developed some of the best security in the world. Security officials for El Al have made profiling of passengers a necessity since 1968 (*Security Management*, May 1992, Vol. 36, No. 5, Pg. 26). Dan Issacharoff, former head of El Al, said the El Al security system emphasizes the identification of people who would be a threat rather than the detection of objects that could be used to hijack or destroy the airplane. Their system recognizes five types of passengers, who are labeled: naïve passenger, partly naïve passenger, framed ter-

rorist, terrorist, and suicide terrorist. They have developed procedures specifically to deal with each of those types of individuals. The procedures in other
countries vary depending on the perceived threat in the geographical region
where the airport is located. Additionally, it should be noted that many countries
are not bound by the proscriptions found in the Fourth Amendment of the US
Constitution.

BOMB-SNIFFING DOGS

Dogs have a great sense of smell. Their noses are about 100,000 to a million times
more sensitive than a human's nose, and a well-trained dog can detect up to 20
different kinds of explosives. Furthermore, the legality of their use is well established and does not seem to be significantly limited by the Fourth Amendment. In
the case of *United States vs. Place*, 462 US 696 (1983), the Supreme Court held
that the warrantless use of a canine did not violate the Fourth Amendment,
because the dog disclosed only the presence or absence of narcotics and nothing
more. The opinion reasoned that the dog was less intrusive than a typical search,
and the limited disclosure exposed the property owner to a minimum amount of
inconvenience.

Canines are also less expensive than other means of explosive detection.
Dogs cost about $6000 to train, and a piece of equipment can cost more than
a million dollars. According to Techmit.edu (2 October 2002), ". . . the Bureau
of Alcohol, Tobacco and Firearms is developing a plan to train and provide
bomb-sniffing dogs for up to 50 of the nation's largest airports in a proposed
new step toward tightening security for air travelers." The White House
Commission on Aviation Safety and Security had recommended in 1996 that
the number of bomb-sniffing dogs and handlers needed to be increased.
Consequently, Congress provided $8.9 million for reimbursements to airports
that used the dogs. In response, by the end of 1998, there were about 150
teams working at 40 airports. Bomb-sniffing dogs are not without their problems, which include short attention spans, false alarms, sickness, and the distraction of male dogs by female dogs in heat. Therefore, the FAA and the
Bureau of Alcohol, Tobacco, and Firearms (ATF) teamed up to conduct a joint
research pilot project to determine the best method to train these dogs and
their handlers. Testing was done at Dulles International Airport and Ronald
Reagan Airport in Washington, DC.

To pass the certification test used by the ATF, the dogs must receive a score
of 100% accuracy. They must convince the handlers that they can successfully
detect at least 20 known explosive compounds, which enables them to identify
over 19,000 varied explosive combinations. Their training system is based on a
food reward program. The method rewards the dog for detecting a compound.
To reenforce the conditioning, they are never fed without some exposure to an
explosive's odor. This keeps the dogs highly motivated to sniff out the explosive,
because food is always available if they do.

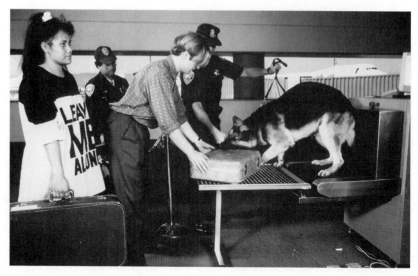

A police dog sniffs the baggage of a traveler. Trained dogs continue to represent a vital tool within the overall security toolbox at airports around the world. *Kermani / Getty Images, Inc.—Liaison.*

The ATF and the US Department of State have provided dogs and training to numerous airport authorities around the world. The program was successfully used by the Australians before the 2000 Olympic Games, and has been in operation at high-threat airports for a number of years. Dogs are compact, mobile and capable of working in a variety of environments including confined spaces. More importantly, in the airport environment, they can reduce the manpower needed to screen huge quantities of cargo.

■ CONCLUSION

Most countries have taken a "legal" or "criminal" approach to prosecuting terrorists. They assess the results of an attack and pursue a public legal remedy based on the specific misconduct already deemed criminal in a standard penal code context. Murder, kidnapping, and assault by terrorists are treated exactly the same as murder, kidnapping, and assault by any other type of criminal. Other sovereign nations have chosen to create the offense of terrorism. They have legislated laws that apply directly to the antiterrorism effort. Some have been in place for quite a long time, as in Northern Ireland and the Middle East. Others like those enacted in Canada have been short lived. The United States is adjusting its efforts in the fight against terrorism by moving away from the use of state and federal penal codes, and has moved to an all-out effort to pass the necessary legislation to more aggressively combat terrorism by the use of specific contextual and procedural laws. Like in all other criminal cases, the US legislation is subject to review by the judiciary and is bound by the fundamental civil rights dictated in the Constitution. Other countries are not held by those same constraints.

Many nations have tried many remedies to control terrorist activity. New technologies become available with increasing speed to assist authorities in providing security at airports and onboard aircraft. However, all of these available technologies used by security personnel or antihijacking/rescue squads must be viewed in perspective and in the proper focus. Technology is not the bottom line. The human effort behind the security demands scrutiny as well. The current political sentiment has justified massive budget expenditures to militaries, police forces, and other agencies. Such actions also have challenged constitutional personal rights to travel, to privacy, and to equal protection under the laws. It is clearly within every nation's best interests to harness the concern for airline safety. The key is to do so within acceptable democratic norms.

Each airline previously determined what procedures were appropriate for its own operation. In the recent past, however, the airlines have all come to realize that the threat is obviously very real. Additionally, this very real threat has made it clear that security is cheap in comparison to the costs of a major security breech. The airlines have been forced to think the unthinkable; namely, that the cockpit is not secure, the terminal is not secure, and the aircraft is not secure unless proper procedures and equipment are used to make them secure.

In accordance with the concept of awareness of the threat, the airlines need to take one step further and recognize that quick stopgap measures will prove to be insufficient. Furthermore, more of the unthinkable thoughts need to be addressed. These unthinkable thoughts, including the threat of nuclear, biological, or chemical attack, will continue to plague the airlines and airports. New procedures and policies must be developed to meet these threats. If the Ebola virus were released in an aircraft and transported thousands of miles across an ocean, it could potentially kill millions of people.

chapter thirteen

Technological Improvements: Some Intrusive and Some Not

▨ NEWS

1. **27 April 2001:** Perkin-Elmer Instruments announced a $6.2 billion contract award for the development of ARGUS, a certified automated explosive-detection system.

2. **9 May 2002:** Airbus, the European jet manufacturer, is considering a set of tiny, concealed cameras above the passenger seats. The pilot will be able to be a spy in the sky in order to spot a potential hijacker.

3. **17 May 2001:** More than 100 terrorist organizations around the world have succeeded in obtaining elements for the construction of a nuclear bomb.

4. **2 February 2002:** A passenger tried to force his way into the cockpit of a United Airlines plane on a flight from Miami to Buenos Aires. The copilot hit him over the head with a small ax.

5. **17 June 2002:** The US Department of Transportation made public a rule that foreign airlines must install flight deck doors on aircraft serving the United States by 9 April 2003. Temporary locking devices were authorized until that date.

■ INTRODUCTION

With the need for safety increasing in the airline industry by leaps and bounds, new technology is constantly and rapidly being developed. With technological change also comes concern from the public about health- and intrusion-related factors. When purchasing new high-tech equipment, the security manager must be aware of the availability of more and more sophisticated equipment as well as the public's reaction to it. The most sophisticated and effective technology in the world is unacceptable if the traveler will avoid travel in order to avoid the equipment.

Improved x-ray imaging, microwave holography, and acoustic detection are just a few of the many technologies recently put into service for detecting weapons and other contraband. All of these systems can be utilized in many formats such as wand-type metal detectors, x-ray imagers, and microwave radar imagers.

Other rapidly expanding advancements will certainly tend to improve security at airports. The costs will be correspondingly high. Under former law, each airline passenger paid a $3.00 passenger facility charge (PFC) for the use of the airport facilities and the costs associated with airport maintenance (14 CFR 158; 1998). Many believed that the charge should have been increased to $5.00 to provide for increased funds for security measures at that time. (FAA Reauthorization Bill 106th Congress 201, 1999). In light of 11 September 2001 and the new Airport Security Act passed in November 2001, the fees are even higher and will likely continue to rise.

However, nothing will replace a human being's overall situational awareness. Regardless of massive and critical improvements in technology to be used at airports, if a human operator cannot properly utilize the new technology, it is useless. Additionally, as stated above, with technological change also come concerns from the public.

In 1996, The National Research Council published a study on the future implementation of new passenger screening technologies. One of the primary tasks of the research was to assess aspects of each method that might generate concerns over health risks and to consider ways to maintain effectiveness while increasing public acceptance. In the 1970s, the first introduction of equipment that x-rayed baggage was met with alarm from some segments of society. The initial alarm was due, in part, to a lack of information. However, it is likely that the introduction into air terminals of more powerful and intrusive systems of both baggage and personal screening may evoke a similar prompt response. The key to avoiding a negative public reaction will depend on efforts to educate the public prior to their use.

As repeated many times in this text, the responsibility for aviation security was shared between the Federal Aviation Administration (FAA), the airlines, and the airport operators and now by the Transportation Security Administration (TSA) and the new Department of Homeland Security. The government sets guidelines, establishes procedures, and relies on the intelligence community for information on threats to aviation. In addition, the government sponsors the development of new security technology, such as improved explosive-detection equipment, and it also oversees the implementation of such equipment. Generally, airlines were responsible for screening checked baggage, carry-on bags, passengers, and cargo, whereas airports were responsible for the security of the airport facilities. Even though the FAA set the standards and approved the equipment, it generally remained the responsibility of the airport and air carriers to obtain and finance new equipment. Everything has changed.

■ GORE COMMISSION

A catalyst for taking important steps in aviation security was the July 1996 crash of TWA Flight 800. As stated previously, the crash prompted the August 1996 creation of the White House Commission on Aviation Safety and Security (the Gore Commission). A further result of the Gore Commission was congressional approval of $198 million for aviation security initiatives. As part of the $198 million, $144.2 million of it was for the deployment of advanced security technologies, $18 million to hire 300 additional FAA security personnel, $8.9 million for additional canine teams, $5.5 million for airport vulnerability assessments, and $21 million for aviation security research and operational testing.

One piece of new equipment, which was a direct development of the Gore Commission, was the CTX 5000SP™. The machine was developed to improve the capability of explosive trace-detection equipment. The equipment is supposed to increase security by safely collecting, analyzing, and identifying trace amounts of many different types of explosives.

These analyzers, produced by Perkin-Elmer Instruments and Invision Technologies, have high-detection probabilities with low false-alarm rates and allow for rapid baggage screening; however, initially they did not. Employing transmission x-ray data, the system acquires an overall map of objects in luggage and uses strategic computer tomography to identify objects that may be explosives. An EDS is automated, using red and green lights to indicate the presence or absence of a threat. When a potential threat is detected, the operator is alerted and can use the instrument's threat-resolution features to validate the threat.

The complexity of the installation and the number of entities involved slowed deployment of the initially purchased CTX 5000SPs™. At some airports, the CTX 5000 SPs™ were installed in locations not conducive to efficient and effective security operations. Another contributing factor to delays and nonuse has been the initial inexperience of the integration contractors, airline indecision on site surveys, and delays experienced due to airport permits, approvals, and construction. In contrast, because of smaller size and portability, implementation of trace-detection devices for screening carry-on baggage has been smoother.

The industry has found that integrating new explosives detection systems with day-to-day operations is more complex than first imagined. Making this task more difficult is the fact that each airport is unique, and airline-operating philosophies differ as well. The success of industry and government efforts will rely on the development of an effective security plan that includes the cooperation and commitment of all facets of the aviation security community. The events of 9/11 have speeded up the process.

The White House had urged the FAA to purchase and deploy the latest technology for detecting explosives. In 1997, the FAA purchased 54 CTX 5000SPs™ to scan checked baggage. Initially, they were installed in Atlanta, San Francisco, Chicago, New York, and Miami. As it turns out, the CTX 5000 SPs™ performance in airports differs from its performance during certification testing. Expert analysis indicated that FAA-certified CTX 5000 SPs™ currently deployed at airports were experiencing high false-alarm rates and slow baggage processing speeds. From the operational data reviewed, the false-alarm rates were up to 169% higher than the standard established during certification testing. Test bags used for certifying false-alarm rates in the laboratory environment were not fully representative of passenger baggage. Many of the items, such as food, that cause false alarms were not included in the bags used for certification tests. Also, the certification testing procedure for determining the machine's baggage processing rate does not take into account "alarm resolution." Resolution is the time it takes for an operator to determine if an alarm is real. Without improvements in performance, the early EDSs could not facilitate the goal ultimately to screen 100 percent of checked baggage. Based on some estimates, this goal will also not be achievable in the immediate future.

Furthermore, the analysis indicates air carriers had initially underutilized the EDS. For example, daily usage rates on 10 of 11 units installed and operating during the review were significantly less than the certified processing speed of about 225 bags per hour. At five locations, 10 CTX 5000SPs™ were screening less than 200 bags per day. The machine has a tremendous throughput capability but some airlines formerly ran as few as four bags an hour through the $1 million machines according to the *Chicago Tribune* (The Associated Press, "Bag Screening Underutilized Airlines Slow to Use Bomb Detection Equipment," *Chicago Tribune*, 11 Aug 1999). At the time, the goal was to run 2 to 20 percent of all checked baggage through the machines depending on the threat at a particular airport. It has been reported that nationally the machines actually screened less than 1 percent. This was in part due to complaints by the airlines that more extensive use would disrupt flight schedules. The scan is relatively quick; however, if the machine alarms, the process takes longer. The machines also sometimes give off a false alarm, frustrating the scanner, the airlines, and ultimately the passengers. As previously noted, 100% screening was mandated effective 31 December 2002.

Human factor issues associated with the new equipment deployment also cannot be underestimated. The government believes screeners are absolutely critical in improving security. The CTX 5000SP™ is a very complex piece of equipment that has taken countless man-hours to design and implement into the everyday workings of an ever-increasing busy airport environment. Additionally, with every new piece of equipment such as the 9000 series comes the ever-increasing expense related to training, as well as an enormous amount of money for future development and upkeep. Without such maintenance and training expenses, operators will be unable to use the equipment effectively.

■ MICROWAVE HOLOGRAPHIC IMAGING

Microwave holographic imaging is a portal-type device that scans individuals using microwave energy. Some of its drawbacks will cause airlines to resist purchasing them. Drawbacks include an inability to search for weapons or contraband in body cavities, the person being scanned must stop and be scanned, and the portal is claustrophobic for some people.

On the other hand, the system provides a means to see through optically opaque mediums. In an ordinary system, the microwave field is scattered from a stationary object. The object is illuminated from a stationary transmitter, which is mapped over a prescribed hologram recording aperture by means of a detector that is scanned over the aperture. The simplest machines need a fixed reference beam to interfere with the object wave that creates a wave-field pattern that can be measured by an internal sensitive detector. More sophisticated pieces of equipment use phase-locked receivers with local oscillators, which act as synthetic internal reference beams. Sometimes, in detectors using low-intensity applications, the detected wave-field is considerably disturbed, giving false or distorted readings. This can be overcome by using modulated scattering techniques including mechanical, electrical, and optical modulated signals. Equipment used today for discovering metallic objects generally employs a scatterer in the form of a selected high-speed photodiode which is modulated optically via a plastic fiber collecting and performing image reconstruction digitally.

Summing up some complicated scientific language, this type of technique for obtaining two-dimensional microwave holographic images of objects uses a light-modulated scatterer that can produce highly distinct images of metal objects. The technology would show an extremely dissimilar image to the operator, making it very simple for the scanner to recognize a potentially dangerous object. Microwave holographic imaging has the potential to provide crystal-clear images that a screener could hardly miss. However, currently, having each passenger step into a closed portal is not conducive to airport use.

■ BODY ORIFICE SECURITY SCANNER

According to the manufacturer, Omni Security, the Body Orifice Security Scanner (BOSS™) is a safe, nonintrusive method of detecting objects concealed in body cavities. Currently, it is commonly used in correctional facilities to scan inmates for weapons and contraband, but it clearly has potential applications elsewhere. The equipment looks much like a chair and is capable of detecting objects hidden in oral, nasal, vaginal, and anal cavities. Both federal and state correctional facilities personnel have extensively tested it.

Because the equipment is highly sensitive, it is capable of detecting such objects as razor blades, knives, and other potentially dangerous but small weapons. BOSS is also able to detect metal foils and detonator caps. This particular piece of equipment minimizes the need for intrusive manual searches. It also increases the safety of not only airport security personnel but ultimately passengers by eliminating the liability and safety issues associated with manual searches. Additionally, it saves time and the expense of using portable x-ray machines to achieve the same result.

BOSS™ is considered to be a powerful deterrent. It can be used not only to scan people, but is also useful in viewing small objects inside pens and lipstick holders. BOSS™ has been well tested. According to Jim Krane, a new staff writer, in an article entitled "Prisoners' Weapons No Match for BOSS Chair," in 1990, 1500 stabbings occurred in New York City jails, but after using the BOSS chair, they dropped to 229. BOSS™ is also mobile and is equipped with wheels.

The procedure is medically safe and completely efficient. Magnetic sensors located in the seat of the chair and the oral sensor assembly automatically scan for the presence of metal. Audible and visual alarms respond when metal is carried into the magnetic field. The measurement detects both ferrous and nonferrous material even if it is moving. The manufacturer claims it will detect contraband that might go undetected by a hand-held detector. There is even a briefcase-sized model. The BOSS™ chair does require a power source of 110/240 VAC. Each piece of equipment weighs 68 pounds and is $53 \times 32 \times 30.5$ inches ("Body Orifice Security Scanner, B.O.S.S.," Internet: http://www.omni-security. com/product2/boss2.html, Pgs.1–6).

■ FLIGHT VU™ AIRCRAFT DATA SCANNER

AD Aerospace is now creating the Flight Vu Aircraft Data Recorder (Flight Vu). This device combines a flight data recorder, cockpit voice recorder, and a flight video recorder. It is designed for large aircraft weighing over 12,000 pounds and for helicopters weighing over 6000 pounds. Future air accident investigation teams could use the information for postincident investigation, but it also has security applications.

Flight Vu™ can engage up to eight channels of video pictures from inside and outside the aircraft. In the cockpit, the equipment will help investigators understand what occurred or provide a real-time picture of what is occurring in the cockpit area. Reviewers could also get an idea of why an aircraft has had an accident or monitor an ongoing hijacking situation. This digital recorder is protected in a "crash-free" environment and possesses a one hour "fire-free" environment feature. This protects the flight data that has been recorded, as well as the cockpit voice and video from the external and internal cameras.

Airport and aircraft security is as important on the ground as it is in the air. Because Flight Vu™ offers up to eight cameras for internal and external use, the Flight Vu Defender™ constantly gives visual security for the aircraft, personnel,

Flight Vu Witness™ is a system of covert or overt CCTV cameras fitted throughout the cabin and cargo holds of aircraft. The cameras provide real-time security surveillance and can also deter violent or disruptive passengers. As depicted in the photos, they can maintain an accurate and clear digital recording of activity in any area of the plane, inside or out.
Photographs provided courtesy of AD Aerospace.

passengers, and the aircraft itself. While the aircraft is parked, protective measures are taken with Flight Vu™ to make sure the aircraft is safe and secure. Certain areas around the aircraft are constantly supervised, and when an incident occurs in these areas, the motion is taken note of by video motion detection (VMD) technology. An onboard camera records the movement, and the picture is transmitted by a low-power microwave spread spectrum to a ground station location. These pictures can be transferred all over the world by continental telephone links whether they are mobile or stationary. This transfer only takes seconds to complete and could be very useful to interconnected airports for security reasons; especially for terrorist acts. The Flight VU Defender™ permits security personnel to view the internal and external parts of the aircraft from any of the eight cameras giving them a pretty accurate depiction of an overall situation. Flight Vu™ also allows security personnel to monitor and keep track of airport workers such as those who handle luggage and mechanics who work to fix and maintain the aircraft. The cockpit crew, flight attendants, and passengers may also be monitored. Using the Flight Vu™ witness system could also prevent passenger disturbances on the aircraft. It contains closed circuit television cameras that are attached to a digital video recorder. These cameras could prevent litigation if passengers are ejected because of "rage" incidents or disturbances. These cameras promote the safety and protection of passengers and the crew by letting potentially enraged people know they are being videotaped. The cameras cover the inside of the aircraft, which can record all of the passengers because of the wide angle. The camera can record during the entire flight or just when personnel desire it. A panic button can also activate the witness system. Because Flight Vu™ is a recorder, the video can be viewed anytime—while on board the aircraft or at a different time. Digital recording means that these videos are state of the art and are precise. They also can be rerecorded or copied for other purposes such as litigation.

Cabin security is a rising threat against flight attendants. There has been a significant increase in assaults. Flight Vu™ would not only have evidence but also protect the crew from allegations of any misconduct. Additionally, Airbus is considering the purchase and installation of a set of tiny concealed cameras above some of its passenger seats. The aerospace division of Goodrich is developing the technology. The newest video cameras have lenses no larger than a pinhole. The signal can travel up to 30 meters, and the transmitter will be surrounded by a small ring of infrared light emitting diodes to send a readable signal in both daylight and darkness. The pilots will be able to monitor small screens in the cockpit.

NEW GENERATION OF VIDEO SECURITY SYSTEMS PROVIDES IMPROVED RELIABILITY AND IMAGE QUALITY

A third generation of IP-based, digital video security systems has been developed by Boundless Security Systems, Inc., in Monroe, CT. The *Boundless Security System*™ is a new generation system because it is controlled differently and has a different flow of digital video throughout a local area network than previous IP-based systems. The new architecture has been developed specifically to provide much higher system reliability as well as improved video quality, ease of local and remote access to live and recorded video, and ease of installation.

The *Boundless Security System*™ is completely controlled from its edge, or perimeter, for superior reliability, fault-tolerance and video quality. It is a platform for third-party video-understanding applications. It is an *enterprise-class system* that is network-friendly so it can be used on corporate networks rather than requiring a dedicated local area network. It can handle a wide range of jobs, from a few cameras to thousands of cameras, and from 100's of gigabytes to 100's of terabytes of disk storage. MPEG-4 variable bit rate, video compression is used.

The *Boundless Security System*™ merges access via a local area network and the Internet to both live and recorded audio, video and data. Networked access to live and recorded information does not affect recording. The viewing of any live digital video stream via a network can be paused, and the corresponding point in the recorded stream can be viewed within a few second for detailed analysis. Each camera is recorded and live-forwarded with multiple resolutions and frame rates simultaneously to optimize the formatting of video displays, provide data rates most-suitable for remote and wireless access, and improve forensic analysis of recorded information. Fully distributed, fault-tolerant control of the *Boundless Security System*™ is provided by Boundless' *Storage Operating System*™. Every detail of recording on Boundless' Linux-based *Multi-Servers*, networked record and live-forward devices, are controlled by every one of Boundless' *CamPuters* and *CamServers*, digital audio/video/data input devices.

The network protocols used ensure that transient network and server faults have no impact upon recording. Hard failures in the network and *Multi-Servers* are detected within a few seconds by the *CamPuters* and *CamServers*, which automatically select alternate *Multi-Servers*. Normal system operation is restored within seconds. Any video in the interim is buffered in the *CamPuters* and *CamServers*, and automatically recorded on the alternate *Multi-Servers*.

Boundless' *CamServers* enable standard CCTV cameras to be used with the *Boundless Security System*™. Boundless' *CamPuters* provide higher resolution, wider image dynamic range, and better capture of the images of moving objects than is possible with CCTV cameras. The *CamPuter* provides extremely high image resolution, in the range of HDTV to $8 \times$ HDTV.

Live and recorded video are accessed by Boundless' *Video Player* software. It runs on PC's and PDA's running Microsoft Windows. The *Video Player* supports Boundless' *Storage Operating System*™, which provides full storage virtualization, even when many *Multi-Servers* are distributed throughout a network. The user sees a single, seamless pool of storage regardless of the number and location of *Multi-Servers*, and hard disks and disk partitions used within them.

■ BIOSIMMER™

Sandia National Laboratories has brought virtual reality into the realm of airport security. This particular virtual reality application allows rescue personnel to practice responding to a terrorist attack. The simulation involves the release of a biological agent in a small airport. The responding security or health personnel are immersed into a three-dimensional computer-simulated setting of virtual patients in a virtual disaster. The program seeks specifically to aid medical personnel to make instantaneous and correct decisions and to avoid becoming victims of the terrorists themselves.

Like video games, the simulation can be run over and over again. Mistakes can be corrected and appropriate responses ingrained in the student. Such instinctive responses are difficult to teach, especially in a potentially contaminated environment. The computer simulation engages the user's eyes and ears by wearing sensors on the arms, legs and waist. All of the user's actions are fed back into the simulation. Users are also taught the significant lessons of self-protection by learning initial decontamination procedures for themselves and the victims.

The airport used in the simulation is a one-story, simple three-gate facility. The software program recreates the disbursement of the biological agent, in this case staphylococcal enterotoxin B (SEB), throughout the airport. The program, although simulating a small airport explosion, would still be particularly useful for larger airport personnel as well. The Defense Advanced Research Projects Agency (DARPA) funded the research. The program is still a prototype, but its potential benefits are self-evident. The Department of Energy's Office of Science and Technology Pilot Projects in Biomedical Engineering Program is also working to make the program even more realistic.

QUADRUPLE RESONANCE DEVICES

Quadruple resonance devices, or QR technology, are a variation of the commonly used magnetic resonance imaging (MRI) technology used in hospitals and already in some baggage scanning equipment at airports. MRI machines utilize large magnets, which affect the magnetic properties of the nuclei of the water in the human body. Those magnetic properties enable the machine to generate an image. QR technology does not use a magnet. It operates on the principle that a magnetic resonance signal can be detected from explosives without applying a large external magnetic field.

- A transmitter emits pulses of low-intensity radio waves.
- Nuclei within the explosive are momentarily aligned with the radio waves.
- After each pulse, the nuclei emit a characteristic radio signal, like an echo.
- The signal is picked up, amplified, and analyzed.
- A computer issues a warning if it identifies a signal that is emitted only by explosives.

One of the problems with virtually all the existing technologies used to find hidden explosives, such as x-ray or radar, is that they pick up too many ancillary objects. A gun may give off a signal, but a rock or any piece of metal also may give a signal. QR sensors pick up the so-called resonance frequency, which is quite specific for different explosives. Additionally, unlike electromagnetic systems, QR sensors can detect plastic-encased explosives.

Pioneering developments in QR technology took place in the 1980s at the Naval Research Laboratory (NRL). The FAA came to the NRL in 1983 looking for advice on how to use the QR technology for detecting explosives in luggage. Since 1987, funding for QR work came from the FAA and the Department of Defense. NRL patented the technology, but in 1993, it gave an exclusive license to Quantum Magnetics, a San Diego–based company. One scientist explained, "the beauty of QR is that it is highly sensitive to the chemistry of explosives. If a bag containing explosives is scanned using QR, the machine flashes a red light. And so far, tests have shown that the technology accurately detects the presence of explosives without false alarms" (Sandra I. Irwin, "Bomb-Detection Technology Useful for Countermine Ops," Internet: http://nationaldefense.ndia.org/article.cfm?Id=442, Pgs. 1–5, 9 August 2001).

INTELLISCAN™ 12000 METAL DETECTOR

The Intelliscan 12000 metal detector has 18 horizontal and vertical zones, and is one of many metal detectors on the market. This particular model is manufactured by Ranger Security Detectors located in El Paso, TX, and exhibits some of the newest state of the art metal-detection equipment currently available

(Internet: www.rangersecurity.com). According to the manufacturer, the Intelliscan 12000™ was one of the first walk-through detectors to pinpoint accurately the exact location of weapons. Intelliscan 12000 is a continuous-wave multiple-zone detector. In other words, it is continuously active and cannot be switched or programmed to a deactivated mode. This detector provides a high level of protection and function in difficult environments, because it is equipped with six computer-controlled horizontal zones of detection that perform as independent metal detectors. The vertical segments monitor the left, center, and right side of a person while the horizontal zones determine the height at which a weapon is carried.

As a weapon or contraband object is transported through a zone, the zone's receiver channels the data and sophisticated mapping software compute its position within the archway. Security personnel can quickly and accurately locate the material identified. The equipment has a detection enhancement option. This option is designed for sophisticated users who wish to design and optimize their own detection programs. It allows customized detection profiles to be created for advanced weapon and asset protection applications. The design procedure is implemented using a microprocessor. A software program analyzes metal objects that are passed through the detector. It generates a characteristic signature for each object. Once a signature has been created for an object, its detection response can be precisely manipulated. Difficult to detect ferrous, nonferrous, stainless steel, or composite objects can be specifically targeted. As is usual, the equipment's low-intensity magnetic fields have been certified as being safe for users of heart pacemakers and implanted defibrillators.

■ BIOMETRIC SYSTEMS

When an employee requests access to a restricted area, that person's identity needs to be verified before entry is granted. A guard has historically performed this process manually. However, the current generation of biometric identification devices offers numerous cost and performance advantages over manual security procedures. These innovations in technology have dispensed with the requirement of a human being present at all access points. Modern identification-verification systems have greatly improved in the last decade and now include newer biometric recognition features.

Some of the available applications have been expanded to include physical access control at portals, computer access control at terminals, and telephone access control at central switching locations. An airport may have a single, stand-alone verifier or it may have a large networked system consisting of numerous verifiers that are controlled at a single central security site. In choosing the most suitable biometric device, serious consideration needs to be given to the performance criteria of a particular piece of equipment.

Essentially, biometric security systems recognize unique physical traits such as fingerprints, signatures, voices, and retinas. Another popular biometric access control system employs a technique of recognizing three-dimensional data about a person's hand geometry. Biometric systems are basically of two types: verification and recognition. A biometric identification device automatically verifies a person's identity from measuring a physical feature or repeatable action of the individual. However, the human factor significantly affects the performance. Each mechanism can also be affected by environmental factors such as noise, light, moisture, dust, temperature, and electromagnetic radiation (Karyn Hodgson, "Hot and Cold Biometrics Heat Up Again," *Security*, Cahners Publishing Company, Newton, MA, Vol. 31, No. 11, 1994, Pg. 17).

Verification systems require that the individual seeking access have some sort of identification, such as a card, that is matched with some physical characteristic of that person to make the verification. A reference measurement of the biometric feature is obtained when the individual is programmed into the device. According to one expert, only retinal scan systems have the practical capability of operating as a true recognition device, not requiring a personal identification number or code to corroborate the biometric search process (Kim Bowers, "Premises Security Without Keys, Codes, Cards and Combinations," *Security Concepts*, December 1994, Pg. 19).

There are now numerous biometric systems on the market and they vary in performance capability. Of course, performance is a very critical issue, but it is not the only factor to consider in choosing an appropriate biometric system. The best device for each particular environment must be determined and the device must be suitable for the facility in which it is installed. The newest systems have computer interfaces, and state of the art software provides effective security management with real-time control, transaction recording, and audit capabilities. As mentioned, the current generation of devices is both reliable and cost effective, but the greatest challenge to the industry is to create product familiarity and acceptability.

In determining reliability, false positives are a key indicator. False rejection is the rejection of an individual who makes an honest attempt to be verified and gain entry. These are considered Type I errors. False acceptance, or Type II errors, are the acceptance of an imposter. Some systems do indeed permit access to individuals without the proper authorization. False acceptance attempts are generally considered to be passive; meaning that the intruder has used their own biometric features as opposed to simulated or mechanically produced biometrics. Even if a system has a 2 percent false-positive rate, it means that there is a 98% probability that an imposter will be unable to access the system, resulting in fairly good security management. Users seem to prefer a system that produces the fewest false rejects and takes the least time to use.

Most users would rather have the system slightly slower than have a high false-rejection rate; but those who have to wait to gain access often get impatient. When evaluating systems, it is best to consider the average transaction time to enter a PIN number, to present the biometric feature, and to receive the verification or rejection result. In practice, the device must be effective and sufficiently quick not to annoy those using it. From a security prospective, prevailing computer interfaces and software provide real-time control, an audit trail, and sophisticated transaction records.

One of the first commercial passenger applications of a biometric system was tested at London's Heathrow Airport in fall 2001. The system, manufactured by Eye Ticket Corporation of McLean, VA, encompasses a scanner that scans the eyes of arriving passengers in about 2 seconds. Frequent fliers were encouraged to enroll in a six-month test program. "A similar Eye Ticket™ System Has Screened Airline and Airport Employees at North Carolina's Charlotte Douglas International Airport Since May 2000" ("Heathrow to Try Eye Scanner, *Los Angeles Times*, reprinted *Star Tribune*, 26 August 2001, Pg. G5).

▨ FACEIT™-ACCESS CONTROLS

Super Bowl XXXV (2001) questioned the morality of a new biometric face-recognition technology. Fans questioned whether the authorities had the right to use a public event to identify individuals by a mere photograph without any probable cause whatsoever. Cameras monitored fans as each ticket holder passed through the turnstiles. The Tampa Police Department had decided to use the new technology to scan for known criminals and terrorists as they entered the stadium. Civil libertarians wondered where this surveillance technology would lead and how such an intrusive system would affect the right to privacy of the average noncriminal fan.

One such system is commercially known as FaceIt™. Developed by Visionics Corporation, it uses face-recognition algorithms to process facial images and match them to known criminals and terrorists. One competitor, Visage Technology, developed a similar system commercially known as "FaceFinder™," which was the actual system deployed during the 2001 Super Bowl ("Face off Over Super Bowl Spying," Security Focus.com, Internet: www.securityfocus.com). Other suppliers of the technology include Graphco Technologies (Face-trac™), Raytheon, and Veltek International. All of the systems consist of computers that use a face-recognition software engine accurately to detect and recognize faces in a matter of seconds.

The system utilizes software called local feature analysis that codifies the face into different features. It operates from the statistical representation of universal facial shapes. In other words, the software comprises various programming languages that turn numerical data into useful information, including digital photographs. The new technology uses both the characteristic facial shapes and facial features and the geometric pattern in which they are combined on a face. The software employs a complex mathematical formula to develop a map of an individual face, called a faceprint ("FaceIt Face Recognition—the Technology," Internet: www.faceit.com/faceit/tech).

Once a particular face has been recognized, it is put through a process that normalizes the image. This process takes into account the expression, position, lighting, and size of a face and transforms the image into the faceprint. A faceprint has the ability to take into account the intrinsic features of facial shape and cannot be inhibited by attempts to alter one's appearance, such as glasses, hair, and facial expression. However, the identity of an individual is only acquired when it is compared against a faceprint already in the system. FaceIt™ can perform identity matches against a database of set individuals and individuals it has been programmed to recognize from its databases.

Common ways in which the FaceIt™ technology is used is in identification, verification, monitoring, and surveillance. Identification or one-to-many searching is used to determine someone's identity against a database of individual facial images. FaceIt™ can return a list of possible matches, those that resemble each other, or the exact identity of the subject. Verification or one-to-one matching matches the live faceprint to a stored faceprint. If the confidence level of the match exceeds a certain percentage of certainty, the match is considered to be successful and identity is verified. Monitoring uses FaceIt's™ ability to follow the presence and position of a person in its field of view. Surveillance can continuously track an individual and select them out of the field of view. The system also has the ability to detect an individual on a specific database, give notification of their presence, and track their actions.

FaceIt™ has been tested for accuracy against false-acceptance rates, false-rejection rates, and equal-error rates that are dependent on the database used to perform a facial analysis. These rates are a mathematical function similar to a calculus function with trigonometric sine and cosign graphs showing how they intersect. The point at which the two curves intersect represents the equal-error rate; the rate at which the number of people incorrectly accepted and correctly rejected is determined. For FaceIt™, the equal error rate is 0.68 percent. Automatic facial alignment failure occurs between 1 and 2 percent of the time.

The courts have yet to decide if the technology, when deployed in a public forum, should be considered unconstitutional as a violation of the Fourth Amendment's prohibition against unreasonable search and seizure. The Fourth Amendment only restricts the actions of government officials. It does not prohibit private firms such as banks or stadiums from face scanning. It is likely the courts will note that citizens have the least amount of expectation of privacy when they are in public, including airports.

■ IMAGING TECHNOLOGIES

Imaging technologies generally involve the use of ionizing radiation (x-rays) to produce images of individuals and objects that may be concealed under layers of clothing. The images are produced using computer analysis of either reflected, absorbed, or scattered radiation (active imaging) or of natural radiation emitted from the human body (passive imaging). Both processes are currently being used in airports. As mentioned previously, for active imaging, small doses of radiation are used in the imaging process. The level of exposure to x-rays in passenger screening in order of magnitude is well below the x-ray levels used in medical diagnosis and represents a fraction of 1 percent of the natural background to which the US population is exposed annually.

Trace-Detection Technologies

Trace-detection technologies for passengers have their own medical drawbacks; hygiene being the most basic shortcoming. Personal contact may be a vehicle for transmitting various microbial diseases from one individual to another. A trace-detection device that requires the passenger to actually touch the door before entering the trace detection equipment means that the individual could leave some disease-producing microorganisms behind. Experts have reasoned that if the transfer of infectious diseases in the passenger screening setting were to occur, it would most likely result from the hand-mediated transfer of disease-producing microorganisms. The likelihood of disease transmission during passenger screening is dependent upon numerous disease specific factors. They include the integrity and cleanliness of the skin and other host factors, such as the virulence of a disease-causing microorganism and the actual amount of organisms transferred.

Cleanliness is the key. The new trace detection equipment should be designed to allow frequent cleaning to minimize disease transmission from passenger to passenger. Passengers will demand it, and the airlines will not want to expose themselves to any unnecessary liability. The use of small wands that can sniff traces of explosives presents an interim alternative. Ion Track Instrument sells the small computer-enhanced wands for around $40,000. They are currently being used in Salt Lake City where officers pass the wand over luggage while passenger's wait in line at the ticket counter.

▓ CONCLUSION

New technology will ultimately completely change the face of all airport screening whether it be cargo or passenger screening equipment. No airport or airline is completely secure and likely never will. The advances made in technology will have both positives and negatives related to them. The public will have to decide just what is too intrusive or unsafe in the long run.

Scientific experimentation has determined that health issues are primarily a perception of risk rather than an actual health threat. Passengers are suspicious of any device that can potentially cause cancer, interfere with their pacemakers or mechanical hearts, or hinder the development of their children. Any new technology on the market will have to take these perceptions into consideration.

Overall, the real risk is insignificant to the perceived risk. Consequently, airlines and the manufacturers of screening equipment need to educate the public. Airport security personnel also need to be trained on the basic principles of each device so they can answer basic questions asked by passengers. They are not required to understand all of the technical theories relating to radiation, electricity, or possible medical repercussions, only enough to reassure the public. Written material should also be available for distribution if the passenger should request it. This type of resource material will be essential in convincing the public to accept even more intrusive screening methods.

chapter fourteen

Airport Operator Concerns and Other Safety and Security Issues: The Foundations of Security

▓ NEWS

1. **6 May 2001:** A passenger forced a plane to return to the terminal at the Minneapolis/St. Paul Airport. Flight 1479 pulled out of the gate, and a man continued walking up and down the aisles, refusing to take a seat. He appeared to be intoxicated. Although it is a federal offense to disrupt a flight, it is unclear whether the man was taken into custody.

2. **16 May 2001:** The National Transportation Safety Board (NTSB) named runway incidents as one of the nation's top transportation safety issues each year since 1990.

3. **6 July 2001:** The Federal Aviation Administration (FAA) listed 306 reported incidents involving unruly passengers in 1999, 314 incidents in 2000, which was up from 46 in 1995.

4. **7 July 2002:** The Transportation Security Administration (TSA) said it will place armed law enforcement—uniformed and plain clothes— throughout the public areas of airports in response to a shooting at the El Al check-in counter at the Los Angeles International Airport.

5. **23 April 2002:** United Airlines began training its pilots to use stun guns for self-defense in the cockpit. The idea that "frangible" bullets might be loaded into handguns carried by cockpit crews also represents a new turn. They are 30 percent lighter than normal bullets and shatter on impact, thus being unlikely to penetrate aircraft panels.

6. **19 July 2003:** The TSA has selected German firearms manufacturer Heekler & Koch to supply the .40 caliber semi-automatic handguns the agency will use to arm pilots.

■ INTRODUCTION

Airport security managers are responsible for the safety of huge numbers of people and very expensive aircraft in addition to airport terminals and surrounding areas. Clearly, the burden is a difficult one and requires the possession and mastering of numerous skills. Passengers and luggage must undergo screening; building, ground crews, and maintenance people must keep things running safely and smoothly; and security guards must maintain the peace in lobbies, terminals, and parking areas. Security managers must be aware of threats not only from terrorists and common criminals but also a myriad of other safety aspects of any complicated air terminal environment. The challenge is significant, and any lapses can be costly in terms of human life and assets.

Much concern should be given to the problem of the proliferation of nuclear weapons. The International Atomic Energy Commission (IAEC) held a conference in Stockholm, Sweden, in May 2000. They reported more than 370 confirmed incidents of nuclear trafficking since 1993. The General Director of the Commission was quoted as saying, "Looking toward the future, it is clear that real international cooperation will be needed to upgrade security measures, to improve capabilities

United passengers at O'Hare Airport Terminal 1 after a security breach forced authorities to evacuate the terminal. Lapses in security can create huge inconveniences for passengers and airport personnel. Such delays generate a ripple effect when planes are late and passengers miss connecting flights and landing arrival times are disrupted. *Ralf-Finn Hestoft/Corbis / SABA Press Photos, Inc.*

for intercepting and responding to illicit trafficking, and to enhance the protection of facilities against terrorism and sabotage" (*World Tribune*, 17 May 2001; Internet: http://www.worldtribune.com/worldtribune/Archive-2001/ss-terror-05-17.html, 10 August 2001). Unquestionably, the time and production capabilities to build a nuclear bomb are considerable. However, according to some leading scientists, the production of sophisticated devices is conceivable. A nationally supported program or a very wealthy terrorist group could produce a bomb if they are provided the necessary resources and facilities and an established working place with the time to build it (Carson Mark, Theodore Taylor, Eugene Eyster, William Maraman, and Jacob Wechsler, "Can Terrorists Build Nuclear Weapons," Internet: http://www.nci.org/k-m/makeab.htm, 10 August 2001, Pgs. 1–13).

As the potential threat of chemical, biological, and other unconventional weapons grows at the local, state, and federal levels, preparation for such an event is rapidly becoming a significant issue to the private sector. Private security managers and law enforcement officials at all levels now need to address the age-old question of "what if."

It has become clear that airport security officials need to be educated to the fact that biological, chemical, and nuclear threats are not just the concern of international policymakers and national level law enforcement. More specifically, the silent partner of the weapons of mass destruction (WMD) triumvirate, "biologicals" could become the most insidious danger of the three. In March 1996, the President of the International Association of Fire Chiefs informed the US Senate that it would be the responsibility of local firefighting, police, and emergency personnel to cope with any attack by biological weapons, and that unfortunately they were likely not up to the task.

During the Cold War, the United States and the former Soviet Union amassed thousands of nuclear weapons and stockpiled thousands of tons of chemical weapons. The Soviets, among others, were also developing a comprehensive biological weapons program designed for use against their potential enemies. With the disintegration of the former Soviet Union, thousands of technical specialists and an extensive array of biological weapons are still out there. Furthermore, there is very little being done to collect intelligence on "biologicals" issues and even less being done to share the information between agencies. If any effective management of an incident is to be successful, renewed interagency cooperation and communication will be crucial. In conjunction, private sector and airport security managers must recognize the threat as a viable one and take reasonable precautions to prepare for it. Conventional weapons remain a considerable threat, although knowledge of the entire terrorist toolbox is essential for defeating them.

■ AIRPORT/RUNWAY INCURSIONS

The FAA definition of a runway incursion is an "encounter at an airport between a plane that is taking off or landing, and any other object or person that creates a risk of collision, or results in less than the recommended separation distance."

Runway incursions have been an issue in aviation for more than three decades, but have become one of the primary safety concerns at modern airports as air traffic and congestion increase. Airport security obviously cannot control miscommunications between a pilot and air traffic controllers, but other incursions onto a runway can be monitored and controlled.

Incursions onto runways continue to increase, rising from 186 in 1993 to 325 in 1998. About 56 percent are admittedly related to pilot error; the rest are operational errors caused by controllers or vehicles and pedestrians who enter restricted areas (Alan Levin, "Runway Incidents Called Top Hazard," *USA Today*, 16 May 2001, Pg. 4A). Overall, controllers at most large airports believe that understaffing and heavy workloads contribute the most to safety problems. Controllers are forced to work longer hours under tremendous amounts of pressure for unreasonable periods of time. According to the controllers union, a majority of runway accidents occur on the fourth or fifth day after a five-day tour when fatigue is a major factor (Ricardo Alonso-Zaldivar, "LAX Leads US in Close Incursions," *The Los Angeles Times*, 2000, Pgs. 1, 3).

The FAA has issued numerous "safety action plans," but little improvement has been seen. In addition, the airport surface system, or Area Surface Detection Radar systems, around the United States have been neglected for years. They need to be upgraded and improved. Recently, the FAA agreed to allocate $5 million to companies for developing new systems to improve security aspects such as better lighting, surface surveillance, and improved markings and signs. In May 2001, the FAA approved a new runway collision warning system. The system is currently only operating in San Francisco and Detroit but is expected to be deployed at many other major airports in the near future. The system utilizes radar to track airplanes and airport vehicles on the airport field. It alerts air traffic controllers to the potentiality of a collision but not the pilots ("New Technology Targets Runway Safety", *USA Today*, 30 May 2001, Pg. 7a). This system alone will improve the runway traffic system, but is not the total answer to the problem.

In a recent report on access control at airports, the Inspector General of the FAA criticized security measures and suggested greater use of access control equipment, more detailed training, and better-implemented oversight programs. In other words, controlling access to the runway is very important and remains the domain of airport security officials. It is advisable that all members of the security staff have at least a cursory understanding of the operational controls of the runways and taxiways so as not to interfere with them and to keep others from inadvertently intruding.

▪ PASSENGER INTERFERENCE

Passenger misconduct on flights is a growing problem and becoming more serious, as the passengers sometimes interfere with the ability of the crew to maintain a safe aircraft. Interference by passengers during and prior to flight operations includes everything from verbal abuse to outright assault, and is usually caused by excessive alcohol consumption, but it can also be just the result of simple air rage. When the disruption in flight operations is between two passengers, the airline is in a very difficult position and may even be liable depending on a court's interpretation of current law. In any case, airport security must be prepared to assist the crew both before takeoff and after landing.

The Association of Flight Attendants has adamantly criticized both the US Justice Department and the FAA for alleged failure to require airlines to report all incidents and to train aircrew members to handle these hostile situations. Additionally, the FAA has yet to levy and collect fines as a deterrent to such incidents (Thurston Hatcher, *CNN.com*, 6 July 2001, Pg. 1). The US Justice Department has yet to empower local law enforcement or airport security formally to arrest perpetrators of air rage when it occurs on the aircraft. Jurisdiction of the crime is strictly federal. The flight attendant's association argues that because of this dereliction the government is failing to protect passengers and to promote cabin safety. Contrary to published statistics, the flight attendants believe there were more like 4000 incidents of air rage in 2001, but the total number must be analyzed in light of the fact that more than 600 million passengers flew the nation's airlines in 2001. Consequently, the incidents were relatively isolated.

According to flight crews, passenger interference with flight crews has already reached epidemic proportions. Captain Stephen Luckey, Chairman of the National Security Committee of the Air Line Pilots Association, testified before the US House of Representatives on 11 June 1998 about the seriousness of this issue. He testified regarding the increasing problem of passenger interference with flight crews and the Carry-On Baggage Reduction Act of 1997. Specifically,

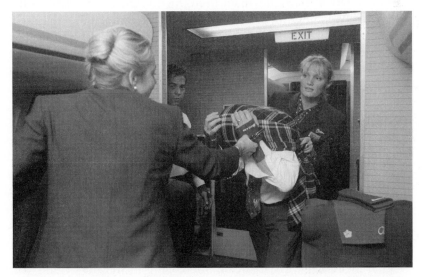

Learning to disarm a violent passenger—British Airways. All airline personnel should be required to undergo extensive training in protecting themselves and other passengers in light of not only the terrorist threat but the rising threat from disruptive passengers. *London Evening Standard / Solo Syndication Limited.*

he stated, "passenger interference is the singularly most pervasive security problem facing the airline industry, not only in the US but around the globe" (Internet: http://www.alpa.org/internet/tm/tm061198.html, 22 April 01, Pg. 1). He clarified the concept that such interference poses demonstrably real hazards to the safety of passengers, crews, and the flight. He reasoned that newer aircraft now have only two pilots in the cockpit. Therefore, sending a pilot into the cabin to resolve a dispute could seriously diminish the safety of the flight; especially if the pilot is injured.

He attested to the following incidents at the hearing:

- July 1996: Shortly after takeoff on a flight from Savannah, Georgia, to Charlotte, North Carolina, a man created an altercation with other passengers and flight attendants after his demands for more alcohol were not met. During this episode, he tried to break down the cockpit door. He also grabbed the lead flight attendant and threw her against the cockpit door, and then attempted to throw her off the plane through an emergency door. The perpetrator was eventually sentenced to 51 months in prison, 200 hours of community service, and was ordered to pay $611 in fuel costs.

- June 1996: A visibly inebriated professional wrestler boarded an aircraft in San Francisco and was subsequently asked to disembark before takeoff. He was a gigantic man, who was obviously intoxicated. The crew clearly viewed him as potentially dangerous because of his physical condition and obvious signs of alcohol-induced misconduct. He left the aircraft as requested, but became combative in the jetway and several people, including police, were required to help restrain him.

- June 1996: On a flight from Frankfurt, Germany, to Dulles International Airport, Washington, DC, a German tourist complained that the flight attendant had bumped him with the food cart. The flight attendant apologized, but the passenger nevertheless threw the flight attendant against the emergency exit and hit him on the head and face. Three other passengers eventually pulled the attacker off the flight attendant.

- July 1997: Two passengers boarded a flight at Los Angeles International Airport and became disruptive after being denied a request for an upgrade to the first-class section of the airplane. One of the passengers went to the galley and grabbed two coffee pots, which he wielded as weapons. He poured hot coffee on two flight attendants, causing second-degree burns on the hand of one of the crew members. A female passenger then joined the fray and banged on the cockpit door yelling that she had a gun (Internet: http://www.alpa.org/internet/tm/tm061198.html, 22 April 01, Pg. 2).

Such incidents are statistically increasing in frequency and volatility. The passengers, who do not have political goals like terrorists, are creating unpleasant and potentially dangerous incidents prior, during, and after flight. Airport security is currently simply "unavailable" once the flight is airborne. The crew needs to be prepared to handle the situations. Of course, all of the resources available to control assaults on the ground are still on the ground. Some airline pilots, however, have been known to conceal plastic hand restraints inside their designated uniform hat, successfully getting them by security for use in the air if necessary. The limited resources the aircrew has to handle a potentially serious incident are sealed inside with them.

FAR Part 91.17 or FAR 121.575 makes it illegal for airlines to board someone who appears to be drunk, but unfortunately it is not very easy to determine who exactly is drunk. Excessive alcohol consumption can be hard to detect during the boarding process. Not all "drunks" are initially boisterous and loud. Even if an individual is not technically intoxicated upon boarding, it is fairly easy to become so while airborne. Disproportionate alcohol consumption on board aircraft, particularly in first and business class where it is free, is probably the most often-cited reason for passenger interference. However, other causes include narcissistic passengers, authoritarian business executives, passengers with a flying phobia, celebrities with an attitude, and increased crowding onboard the aircraft. The Association of Flight Attendants has recommended more responsible alcohol policies. They would prefer that drinks not be offered prior to takeoff, permitting the service of only one drink at a time and never using free drinks as compensation for delays. It is unclear, however, if alcohol is really the primary cause of most air rage incidents.

It is also not unheard of that the aircrew may have had too much to drink. Amendments to the Department of Transportation's (DOT) rules in August 2001 require flight crew, instructors, mechanics, and others involved in the operation and maintenance of commercial aircraft to undergo routine testing for drugs and alcohol usage. The DOT has described the changes as, "Increased protection measures for the employee if an initial test result indicates that a specimen may have been altered or substituted; a plan to make validity testing mandatory; a procedure for employers to remove employees from their jobs temporarily while a test is under review; greater authorization powers to contract services providers; and enhanced training requirements for testing personnel" ("DOT Amends Drug and Alcohol Rules," *AIN Weekly*, 20 July 2001, Pg. 4). It is unfortunate, but true, that airline employees are just as susceptible to alcohol and drug abuse as any other segment of the population. Permitting them to fly is dangerous and prohibited but difficult completely to eradicate. Some would argue that the drug and alcohol problems in America have been greatly underestimated, and there are no safe sectors from which to draw absolutely drug-free employees (Charles R. Carroll, "The Dilemma of De-toxing the Work Force," *Security Management*, May 1992, Pg. 54).

Additionally, airlines are held responsible for passengers getting hurt by other passengers. In *Stone vs. Continental Airlines*, 905 F. Supp. 823 (Hawaii 1995), a court relieved Continental Airlines from any liability relating to an incident where a passenger punched another passenger. The court held the Airlines Deregulation Act barred the plaintiff a remedy. The court also pointed out that the plaintiff was also barred from any recovery under the Warsaw Convention, because the act was not an accident as defined by the Act. Other airlines have not been so lucky. In *Romano* vs. *American Trans Air*, 56 Cal. Reporter. 2d 428 (Cal App 1996), a California court ruled just the opposite, and held that a passenger could hold the airlines liable for allegedly failing to prevent one passenger from assaulting another.

It should be pointed out that falsely accusing a passenger of misconduct can also bring the plaintiff's attorneys down on airlines and security companies. In *Curley vs. American Airlines, Inc.*, 846 F. Supp. 280 (S.D.N.Y 1994), a court ruled that neither the Warsaw Convention nor the Federal Aviation Act pre-empted an airline passenger's lawsuit for negligence and false imprisonment. The plaintiff claimed that the airline falsely identified him to Mexican authorities as having smoked marijuana on the plane.

Air Rage and Passenger Involvement

An additional serious and new threat, exacerbated by crowded aircraft, is the concept of air rage with passenger involvement. Since trained security personnel are not aboard most flights, passengers have voluntarily jumped into situations to assist. On occasion, such involvement has resulted in unexpected grave reper-cussions. On 11 August 2000, an incident occurred aboard Southwest Airlines Flight 1763 that had deadly results. The plane took off from Las Vegas at about 9:30 PM and was scheduled to land about an hour later in Salt Lake City. The first thirty minutes of the flight were uneventful. Then a young man, Jonathan Burton, began to pace back forth in the aisle. At first, he was just talking to himself and walking around, but later he became more hostile. He ran up to the cockpit and started to pound on the door. He succeeded in kicking a hole in the door and proceeded to attempt to climb through it. A group of male passengers saw fit to intervene.

They returned him to his seat, but in a few moments, he lunged toward the emergency exit and tried to open it in flight. The same group of male passengers attempted to restrain him and drag him to the back of the plane. Burton responded violently. In the ensuing scuffle, someone stood on his neck and he went limp. Everyone involved believed that the passenger had been brought under control and waited for security to remove him from the plane. When the plane landed, the paramedics were called, and it was discovered that Burton was dead. Just how much force one passenger exerts over another is difficult for the aircrew to monitor, let alone control. Most crews just want to see the unruly indi-vidual brought under control.

Incidents of this nature have been increasing. They range from a German body builder who broke into the cockpit and grabbed the controls to a Japanese rock star choke holding a stewardess. In the first example, the plane plummeted 2000 feet before an onboard dentist tranquilized the body builder. In the second case, another passenger hit the rock star over the head with a flashlight.

Air rage has proliferated in the terminal as well. As more and more flights are cancelled or delayed, passengers have turned violent. One family on its way to Walt Disney World experienced several delays in their flight. When they did start to board, the ticket agent indicated that something was wrong with their tickets. Meanwhile their child proceeded down the jetway. When the mother went to retrieve him, the agent pushed the mother. The father and the agent became entangled, and the agent's neck was broken. The father was accused of aggravated assault and was later tried but was found not guilty. The airlines were clearly not pleased with the result of the trial. The proliferation of the problem is quite evident, and the airlines have had difficulty in inhibiting it.

Air Rage and Civil Liability

In essence, the terms *air rage* and *sky rage* have come to mean conduct occurring during air travel which can fall anywhere between socially offensive words involving inappropriate threats, racial epithets, or curse words to criminal misconduct. Air rage is also described as intentional acts that are out of proportion to the usual frustrations related to air travel. They potentially endanger the crew and other passengers. Crew and passengers alike manifest these types of acts. One judge has reasoned, "air travel in modern society presents formidable safety and security concerns and often passengers with criminal intentions are the source of that threat. But even passengers with merely bad tempers are as dangerous in some respects as any would be hijacker" (*Smith* vs. *ComAir*, F.3d 254, 258, 4th Circuit, 1998). As mentioned, the frequency of these events are increasing exponentially. Some airlines even estimate that 50 percent or more of all incidents involve the excessive use of alcohol (Asra K. Normani, "Airlines Tell Boozers to Put a Cork in It," *Wall Street Journal*, 28 August 1998, Pg. W1). The remedy is prevention. American air carriers already have the right to refuse to transport a passenger if the airline determines that safety is an issue (Sec 49 USC 44902[b] 1994). In order to protect themselves from liability, the airline must always act reasonably in refusing someone access to the aircraft or removing them from one. However, beyond preventing access to the aircraft, little organized prevention of in-flight incidents exists. The Senate Commerce, Science and Transportation Committee increased the maximum civil penalty for interference with aircraft safety from $1100 to $10,000 per incident (Richard Powelson, "Bill Boosts Civil Penalty for Unruly Air Travelers," *The Times Union*, Albany, NY, 12 February 1997, A7). Passengers who are charged under federal law must fall into the definition contained in 14 CFR 91.11, which states, "no person may assault, threaten, intimidate, or interfere with a crew member in the performance of the crew member's duties aboard an aircraft being operated" (*Federal Aviation Administration* vs. *Hench*, No. CP97SO0004, 1998, 27 January 1998).

Civil remedies include:

1. *Warsaw Convention:* Makes an airline liable for damages sustained if a passenger is wounded, suffers any other personal injury, or dies onboard an aircraft (Article 17).

2. *Death on the High Seas Act:* Allows recovery by the personal representative of a decedent whose death was caused by the wrongful act, neglect, or default occurring on the high seas. Aircraft that crash into the sea fall into this category. It limits recovery to pecuniary losses and precludes recovery for predeath pain and suffering (46 USC 761–768 (1994).

3. *Workman's Compensation:* Depends on each state's applicable law.

An adequate means of appropriate redress currently does not exist. A better understanding of the causes of air rage and better legislation to protect the victim is needed. That victim could be either the passenger or the aircrew member depending on the circumstances. International law is conflicting, and finding the proper jurisdiction to even hear the case is also a problem during international travel.

■ CONVENTIONAL WEAPONS

Terrorists have always been capable of acquiring manufactured weapons on the open market and also of improvised firearms bought from professional arms dealers. Intelligence agencies and law enforcement agencies have been able to document that terrorists groups have come into possession of small arms, medium-size infantry weapons, and heavy infantry weapons.

Small arms weapons include those which are not belt fed. They are now mostly semiautomatic or self-reloading, and were originally designed for military use. Considerable quantities of small arms are diverted to the black market each year. Manufacturers, including Beretta, Glock, and Kalishnikov, have failed to stem the flow of weapons, but not because they have not tried. The AK-47 is probably the most available automatic weapon for terrorists. During the Cold War, the Russians supplied the weapon to any and all left-wing insurgency organizations. The AK-47 has been replaced with the new AKM, which is available to anyone with the hard currency to buy it.

RPG-7s (rocket propelled grenade) were issued to the troops of the Warsaw Pact and in China and North Korea. They are easily manufactured and are a very functional weapon. They play an antivehicle antiarmor function when used against a stationary or moving target. RPG-7s vary in quality but generally have a range of about 300–500 meters. They are easily available to the terrorist.

The United States–made Stinger missiles have proliferated in the underground international arms market. It is a man-portable infrared-guided surface-to-air missile capable of bringing down a commercial aircraft. It has an effective range of about 5500 meters. The United States generously supplied them to the "freedom fighters" during the Afghan war, and they are now available to terrorists, including Usama bin Ladin. The Russians have sold sophisticated weapons and continue to sell such materiel. Thousands of SA-7 Grail missiles were sold which were equipped with optical sight and tracking systems. They have effective ranges up to 6125 meters and are designed to target aircraft.

■ EXPLOSIVES

Explosives are chemical compounds that undergo quick burning or decomposition with the generation of large amounts of gas and heat accompanied by the inevitable production of sudden pressure effects. Explosives do have many commercial applications and are therefore mass-produced for civilian purposes. The military and, unfortunately, terrorists and criminals also acquire the same materials for destructive purposes. Explosives are also used as propellants for projectiles and rockets and as bursting charges in bombs.

Gunpowder has been available since the thirteenth century. Nitrocellulose and nitroglycerin were developed in the mid nineteenth century. Since that time nitrates, fulminates and azides have been the ingredients most widely used either alone or in combination with a fuel. Xenon trioxide became available in the early 1960s.

Such materials are categorized into two separate classes. Low-grade explosives burn at rates of inches per second and high explosives undergo detonation at rates of 1000 to 10000 yards per second. In addition, some explosives are more or less susceptible to conditions of heat, cold, and humidity. The shattering effect, known as brisance, depends on the velocity of detonation. Explosives used as propellants in guns need to burn slowly, because they are required to deliver a steady increasing push to the bullet rather than a sudden shock which would make the gun explode instead of ejecting the projectile. High explosives, such as dynamite, are often mixed with inert materials to reduce sensitivity and, therefore, lower brisance.

Other explosives need to undergo detonation to explode. For example, TNT, trinitrotoluene, has a very high resistance to shock and can therefore be handled quite easily without fear of an unintended detonation. Nitroglycerin, on the other hand, is so sensitive that it has to be mixed with something else to maintain stability for practical use. Technology has improved the quality and efficiency of newly developed explosives. Two developed during World War I include cyclonite and pentaerythritol tetranitrate. Cyclonite, or RDX, is often used as a detonator in bombs when mixed with TNT.

Since the 1950s several types of high explosives have replaced dynamite. A mixture of ammonium nitrate and fuel oil has been proven to be quite effective. Unfortunately, it is extremely easy to acquire and produce a bomb. For detonating bombs, compounds are used that will themselves detonate from a shock or some heat in order to force the explosive of the main charge. For many years, mercury fulminate (Hg (ONC) 2) mixed with potassium chlorate was used. It takes some training and skill to use these materials, plus the combination cannot be stored in heat without some decomposition taking place. Today, diazodinitrophenol, lead azide ($PbN6$), and mannitol hexanitrate are most commonly used. These combinations have brisance and high–explosive-strength values.

Terrorists can buy explosive devices on the international black market or they can improvise them fairly easily. All they need is a charge, a fuse, and a triggering device. They acquire the necessary materials by stealing them from mili-

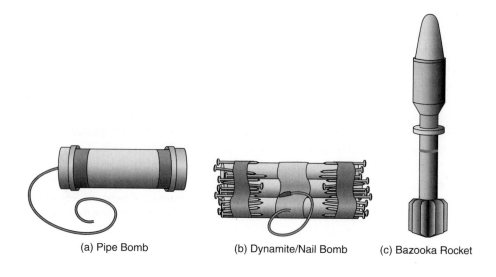

(a) Pipe Bomb   (b) Dynamite/Nail Bomb   (c) Bazooka Rocket

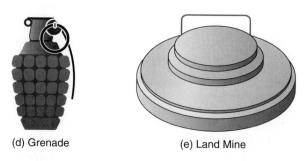

(d) Grenade   (e) Land Mine

Depiction of various bombs and explosive devices provided courtesy of the Bureau of Alcohol, Tobacco, and Firearms.

tary supplies or legitimate commercial users. They can make effective crude devices by purchasing the components at a hardware store. Terrorists are known to possess Semtex, cyclonite, C-4 plastic, TNT, dynamite, and, of course, common fertilizer. They have been known to assemble the materials into pipe bombs, Molotov cocktails, fertilizer truck bombs, and barometric bombs.

■ NUCLEAR WEAPONS/BIOLOGICALS

In order to build a nuclear weapon, the manufacturer would need a critical mass of uranium or plutonium or uranium oxide or plutonium oxide. As a substitute, it is possible that an oxide powder might be used. The process would require a highly trained technical team with specialized equipment. Fuel elements of any type would have to be subjected to chemical processing to separate the fissile material they may contain from the inert cladding material or other dilutents. Spent fuel from power reactors would contain some plutonium but at such low concentrations that it would have to be separated from other materials in the fuel. The fuel would contain enough radioactive fission fragments that the chemical separation process would have to be carried out by remote operation: a complicated undertaking.

Terrorists have three options: they can build a very crude nuclear weapon or use a sophisticated design similar to the nuclear weapons built by industrialized nations. Terrorists, however, do not care whether the bomb looks pretty or whether it makes as large a crater as a hydrogen weapon. They only want the weapon to explode or to have the authorities think that they have the ability to make one explode. As the ancient Chinese said, "Kill one, scare 10,000." In the case of a nuclear weapon, the concept of to threaten one and scare a million is highly applicable. The third option involves lacing a conventional weapon with radioactive materials creating a "dirty bomb."

A crude design is one which deploys either a gun-type or the implosion-type device similar to those used on Japan during World War II. In a gun-type device, a subcritical piece of fissile material is fired speedily into another subcritical piece such that the final assembly goes supercritical without a change in the density of the material. In an implosion-type device, a near-critical piece of fissile material is compressed by a converging shock wave resulting from the detonation of a surrounding layer of high explosive and becomes supercritical because of its increase in density.

The proliferation of nuclear weapons is a fact. The disintegration of the Soviet Union and its subsequent inability to control its own stockpiles of weapons-grade nuclear material has been well established. Out-of-work nuclear physicists and technicians are also abundant. Their expertise is a valuable commodity to terrorists, and owing to exorbitantly high unemployment in Russia, they are also available. Additionally, whether or not a security practitioner believes or does not believe a terrorist organization can build a nuclear weapon, experts cannot assure that the possibility does not exist. Consequently, the threat of the use of such a weapon is sufficient to "scare a million."

There are two basic categories of biologicals. The first category, microorganisms, consists of living organisms, like the bacterium that causes anthrax. The second category includes toxins that are the by-product of living organisms such as botulism. The US Biological Weapons Act of 1989 defines a biological agent as any "micro-organism, virus or infectious substance capable of

1. Causing detrimental changes in the environment.
2. Harming or damaging food, water or equipment supplies.
3. Causing disease in humans, animals or plants or other living organisms.

Nonetheless, all biological agents need to be weaponized to be effectively used as a tool in a terrorist or hostile situation.

Even though biological incidents have taken place throughout history, technological advances of the twentieth century have changed the threat considerably. Previous uses were clumsy by comparison. Today, one incident could kill millions. Challenges to the potential perpetrator most singularly relate to the manufacturing process. Even the most virulent agent needs to be stabilized and made predictable. Therefore, the criminal actor is particularly vulnerable to discovery in this acquisition and preparation phase.

Regardless, in part owing to a lack of resources targeting biological threats, individuals and groups can now rather easily create a workable delivery device filled with a deadly agent free from detection. Many officials merely dismiss the idea as just too horrific to consider and fail to pursue it. The threat is clearly out there even though not well publicized, as evidenced by discoveries in France and Japan.

In 1984, French police raided a safe house of the German Red Army Faction terrorist group and located a bathtub containing flasks filled with Clostridium botulinum, which secretes botulin, one of the most lethal toxins known. More recently, Japanese police confirmed that the cult Aum Shinrikyo had been stockpiling biological agents. Adding to the seriousness of the situation, the current revolution in biotechnology may well produce other agents that could be even more toxic and resilient.

Even the acquisition of seed stock of pathogens no longer poses a significant challenge. For example, some pathogenic organisms are simply endemic to specific geographical regions and are found in natural reservoirs. All that is required is a plane ticket and some basic knowledge of microbiology. In addition, agents can be bought from the American Type Culture Collection or the Microbiological Research Establishment in weakened form or from financially strapped Russian labs. It should be noted that controls in Western labs have been strengthened since the Iraqis bought their initial supply. Those control improvements, however, do not change the fact that almost anything is probably available on the Russian black market.

On another scary note, future genetic research may be able to pinpoint the genetic characteristics of both the target population and the potential agent. In other words, the agent would target specific individuals genetically. This could lead to an "ethnic" agent. The ramifications of this are almost unspeakable in the hands of a terrorist group or a deranged individual.

The problem is further intensified by the fact that these agents are *almost* impossible to detect. The same production facilities can produce toxic agents in something as legitimate as dried milk. In addition, the technology to detect a biological agent in transit is not readily available. The inability to detect such agents is only worsened by the fact that once located and identified, medical prophylactic measures have been proven to be inadequate. Furthermore, considering the fact that security managers are already fighting tooth and nail for their part of budgetary resources, personal protection equipment has not been considered to be essential additions to private security equipment supplies.

Realistically, it is both expensive and impractical to vaccinate personnel against all agents, equip personnel with individual protection suits or even to have decontamination kits, respirators, and other response tools. Even if victims are provided with emergency medical care and later hospitalization, it is unclear whether these agencies are up to the task. Clearly, the technical community needs to expend considerably more effort to develop effective detection equipment to work as well as metal detectors.

Some efforts have been made. For example, *New Scientist* revealed in 1998 that Washington's Naval Research team had tested a plane weighing 42 lbs that is capable of detecting minute quantities of biological agents. The planes were designed to fly into suspected contaminated areas and detect up to four separate bacterial agents.

An onboard sampling chamber has been designed to allow air to pass through and thus creating a vortex in a pool of water. Every five minutes the water in the chamber washes over a sensor comprised of four optical fibers. The optical fibers have a probe affixed to the core of each fiber. Each of the probes is coated with an antibody for a particular bacterium, allowing for the adhesion in water if the presence of the spore of a particular bacterium comes in contact with the probe.

At a minimum, security managers should review all procedures with biologicals in mind. For example:

1. Get Outside Help! The effectiveness of appropriate liaison with authorities such as the Federal Emergency Management Agency (FEMA), Department of Defense (DOD), FBI and Centers for Disease Control and Prevention (CDC) is crucial. Telephone: 404-639-1293.

2. In the event of an incident, control and contain any further release of any suspected biologicals as much as possible. Determine the actual nature and extent of the threat.

3. Evacuate personnel to a safe distance. Ascertain the actual identity of the agent. Both a primary and secondary secured perimeter must be established.

4. Always control physical security and access to your premises. Periodically review security procedures for detecting and reporting suspicious delivery of devices or packages.

5. Emphasize employee training in response to specific telephone threats: Always attempt to determine, for example, the type of biological agent, location, and dispersal mechanism. Review decontamination procedures.

6. Staff awareness to this type of threat needs to be regularly reenforced.

7. Determine whether appropriate procedures for a terrorist-type attack include a search plan, an evacuation strategy, a postincident recovery plan, and a crisis communication strategy.

8. Reevaluate the effectiveness of surveillance systems in deterring, detecting, and documenting suspicious activity.

9. Be prepared to make a complete after-action report.

Furthermore, it will be important not to overlook the psychological reaction of the public to such an incident. They will certainly react to feelings of being unprotected and helpless. Those reactions could present issues of crowd control, rioting, or opportunistic crimes. Consequently, a close working relationship between public affairs officers and the media must be developed. Security managers must preplan how they will deal with a panic mentality on the part of the public and maybe even their own employees. Senior managers must keep local, state, and federal officials informed and seek early intervention by experts and government authorities.

If both private and public security officials take a biological threat seriously, a major effort will be needed to develop contingency plans and initiate coordinated and mutually supportive programs across a broad spectrum of agencies. Currently, major health professional organizations are a long way from providing adequate training and education to their own health care community, let alone the rest of the population. Adequate diagnostic and identification will require a major push. Public health, intelligence, and law enforcement agencies as well as the private sector should recognize the threat for what it is—a national priority considering the potential consequences.

■ CONCLUSION

Airborne criminal activity nonrelated to terrorism is a growing problem. It is not limited to alcohol-related incidents but includes aspects of air rage and the involvement of other passengers in the fray. Unfortunately, all security assistance available is locked into the plane with the aircrew and passengers. Crews need to be trained to handle these situations and ground security needs to be immediately available to take over control of the incidents. Additionally, local security and local law enforcement must acquire concurrent jurisdiction along with the federal authorities.

It is undisputed that many modern terrorist organizations are extremely well financed. They can afford a nuclear weapon, and they can also afford the components of a poor man's weapon of mass destruction, both biological and chemical. One of the primary goals of the terrorist is fear. Terrorists hope the public will panic if nuclear, biological, or chemical (NBC) weapons are deployed against commercial air carrier passengers. The second goal of the terrorist is publicity. The media would be drawn to an actual or threatened NBC attack in droves; assuming they felt they could protect themselves from the danger. Some security experts would argue that terrorists would not use these methods for fear that they could not protect their members or control the outcome. However, this type of analysis reflects the fears of the security practitioner rather than any fears of the terrorist. Fanatical terrorist are not necessarily concerned with a rational approach. This is why the study of terrorism, the terrorists themselves, and the causes behind the terrorism is so important.

chapter fifteen

Access Control and Perimeter Security: Another Foundation

■ NEWS

1. **April 1999:** A Transportation Department report noted that investigators deliberately set off 25 emergency exit alarms. Security personnel never responded to 10 of them.

2. **18 January 2000:** A driver who had lost his way at the Auckland International Airport was arrested and charged with illegal entry into restricted airport zone, driving on the runway, and assaulting a police officer.

3. **July 2002:** The US government issued a warning to airlines to be on the alert for people in stolen uniforms after numerous reports of stolen aircrew and airline employee uniforms were received.

4. **Today:** Communication is crucial to good security. The common phrase "out of sight out of mind" loosely translates into Russian as "invisible idiot."

5. **14 May 2003:** Officials at Boston's Logan International Airport have begun testing an integrated software-based perimeter security system manufactured by Vista Scope Security Systems which uses thermal imaging.

◼ INTRODUCTION

Sometimes the most basic measures can prevent real tragedy from happening. However, sometimes the most basic measures are often overlooked or underutilized. Basic physical security equipment consists of three items: locks, lights, and alarms. The three basic lines of physical defense at an airport are:

1. Perimeter (fence around the airport)
2. Buildings (the terminal and collateral buildings, both interior and exterior, including the runways, taxiways, and their surrounds)
3. Aircraft (the airplane and jetway)

The degree of security required will determine exactly just how sophisticated these three options and areas need to be. For example, at airports, access to the sterile concourse is not controlled only at the security checkpoint. Access to jetways, restricted areas, and the airport itself require some consideration. When considering interior security, the airport security professional must address not only sterile concourses but also doors, windows, ducts, and any other openings large enough for someone to go through. The initial step in any risk-assessment program is to determine where the airport is most vulnerable and assess the likelihood that its security will be breached at that point. Each area identified as a problem area requires an appropriate degree of attention depending on its criticality and vulnerability. Access control is always a primary issue.

Police officers observe security monitors in the police control center at Hancock International Airport. Close coordination between federal screeners, local law enforcement and other supporting agencies must be maintained in order to sustain effective security within the airport environment. *Kevin Jacobus / The Image Works.*

■ ACCESS CONTROL

The Office of the Inspector General for the Federal Aviation Administration (FAA) issued a report on airport access control in November 1999. They identified several vulnerabilities, but generally confirmed that there were four general reasons for concern:

1. Airport operators and air carriers not successfully implementing procedures for control
2. Employees not meeting their responsibilities for airport security
3. FAA not successfully implementing its oversight program for ensuring compliance with programs
4. FAA policies that contribute to weaknesses in access control (Report No. AV-2000-017, Internet: http://www.securitymanagement.com/library/faa1299/txt).

In the past, the primary means of gaining access to a controlled area was merely to be wearing whatever was considered to be the ramp uniform. Clearly, apparel and uniforms can no longer be safely accepted as an appropriate means of identification. The uniforms of airline, flight operations, and security personnel are too easy to duplicate. Additionally, in May 2002, the FBI reported that a truck containing airport worker uniforms was stolen from a Kansas City, MO, uniform company. The truck was recovered but the uniforms, from Delta, Midwest, and Vanguard Airlines, were not. You can even buy a duplicate copy of airport security sleeve patches in some airport gift shops. Consequently, security badges, constantly being improved by advances in technology, have replaced uniforms as a standard identification security practice.

The government obligates that airport access control systems must:

1. Enable only those persons authorized to have access to secured areas to obtain that access
2. Immediately deny access at the access point to individuals whose access authority has changed
3. Have the capability of zone coding, so that it can admit or deny access by area
4. Have the capability of time coding, being able to admit or deny access by time and date (FAR 107.14; TSA 49 CFR Chapter XII, Part 1540).

Locks

Locks are probably the most commonly used means of controlling access to an area (the airport), a building (the terminal, control tower, or hangers), a room (package area), or a container (an aircraft). Locks are one of the oldest means of security in use in that the Egyptians used them more than 4000 years ago. Variations on the general theme, however, have been expanded. A proficient thief or terrorist will boast that any lock can be opened. However, locks are still very valuable in that they increase the time an intruder needs actually to gain access. That time can be used to increase the probability of being detected. Locks include those that are key operated, combination type, card activated, and electronically operated.

The concept of using a key is simple and efficient but will not likely protect assets very well. First of all, keys can be easily duplicated. Unless a closed circuit TV system monitors every door or access point, a key will also not enable security to document who and when an individual enters. It also becomes quite expensive to change all of the keys when an employee is terminated, quits, or retires and administratively to track them. Keypads with access codes have some of the same problems. Even doors with codes require downtime when replacing old codes and having employees memorize the new codes.

Card-operated locks make use of a card reader installed near a door or restricted passageway. When an appropriately authorized card is inserted, a minicomputer unlocks the access. More sophisticated card-operated locks record the time a lock was opened and who opened it. These types of locks are very useful in areas that are restricted to the general public but must still be made accessible to large numbers of employees or workers. In 1000 BC, the Chinese required servants at the Imperial Palace to wear rings engraved with unique intricate designs identifying palace areas they were permitted to enter. Historians credit this method by the Chinese as the first comprehensive access control system (John Naudts, "Access Control; It's in the Cards," *Security Management*, 1987, Pg. 169). Advancement in science and technology has improved on the Chinese system. Some systems can be programmed to lock and unlock access points at specific times and on specific days.

Electronic Locks

Electronic locks are also an option at smaller airports without a twenty-four–hour access requirement. It is important to recognize that there are two kinds. A failsafe lock will remain unlocked when the power is off. Such locks are usually used on doors in the path of a fire exit and a fail-secure lock, which remains locked when the power is removed. Historically, the most common form of protection from an intruder penetrating these interior systems was "magnetic contacts." They were placed in a position so that if a door or access point was opened without the proper authority, a signal was sent to a control panel and an alarm activated. Today's locks withstand forces that range from 650–1,500 pounds and can be controlled and monitored individually, sequentially, or simultaneously from one or multiple locations.

Access Cards

Wiegand, magnetic strip, and proximity cards previously dominated the market. Today, optical memory cards and smart card technology is the way of the future in the field of access cards. They possess one or more integrated circuit chips capable of storing a great deal of information and interpreting it. Military ID cards now use similar technology to encode someone's entire medical history onto the card. Weigand cards have metallic rods or wires embedded inside the card. Named after their inventor, the cards have the data encoded in the embedded wire, which has been twisted under tension and heat tempered. The manufacturing process gives the treated wires unique magnetic properties. The cards are difficult to duplicate and are also resistant to moisture and temperature. Radio frequency interference or external magnetic fields do not affect these cards (Protective Technologies International, Inc. Access Control System, Internet: http://www.pti-world.com/Access control.html, 3 May 2001, Pg 1).

Magnetic strip cards use a strip similar to those on credit cards. A magnetic strip is affixed directly on the surface of the card and the data are recorded magnetically just like tape recording. They can be encoded on site, but they are also subject to being easily copied and/or modified and are easily damaged when placed near magnetic media. Watermark cards also use a magnetic strip but have a permanently encoded number that cannot be altered. Barium ferrite cards or magnetic sandwich cards contain information encoded in a soft pliable magnetic material positioned between layers of plastic. Rows and columns of spots on the magnetic sheet are magnetized to create a code that is read by magnetic sensing heads. Infrared cards use a pattern of shadows inside the card and a low-level infrared light in the reader to detect the pattern and determine if entry should be granted.

Smart cards have embedded computer chips in them that consist of either a microprocessor with internal memory or a memory chip with nonprogrammed logic. Two general categories of cards exist. One is a contact card requiring direct physical contact to a conductive micromodule on the card. The other type is a contactless card requiring only close proximity to a device designed to read the card. Original research on the card was done in both Europe and Japan where the first patents were filed. Advances in technology in the 1980s enabled the card to transmit commands, data, and other information. The micromodule is embedded in the plastic substrate of a credit card–like piece of plastic. Glue is used to affix the micromodule to the card ("Smart Card Overview," Internet: http://www. scia.org/knowlefgebase/aboutSmart Cards/primer.html, Pgs. 1–5).

Proximity cards are either active or passive. "The active technology card has an embedded lithium battery and transmits the signal; a passive card has no battery and relies on the strength of the receiver's signal to retransmit the encoded number" (Roy N. Bordes, "Pick a Card, Any Card," *Security Management*, 1994, Pg. 74). They are very difficult to duplicate and correspondingly rather expensive. The system uses a radio receiver plus transmitter implants. The reader, usually mounted on the wall, transmits a low-frequency radio signal. The card receives the data and interprets it sometimes from as much as a couple of feet away. Some manufacturers claim the card does not even need to be removed from a wallet to be used. Since proximity cards use radio frequency signals, personal identification numbers (PINs) or frequencies are also a means to gain access in some sophisticated systems.

None of these cards provides effective security in the wrong hands. The card does not know who is holding it, and the machine reading the signal or data does not know either. An access card simply cannot identify a specific individual using the card. It is only wishful thinking to assume that every time a card is used that the person using it is actually the person authorized to use it. As frequently occurs, piggy backing is also a problem. One person opens the door or access point and several people follow them through. Another issue arises when terminated employees fail to turn in their security badges. One company, TEMTEC, Suffern, NY, has overcome this problem with identification badges that expire. Its VOIDbadge™ is a plastic badge printed with the word *void* that becomes valid when a two-part authorization sticker automatically expires by turning red. Currently, the technology is only being used on photo identification cards, but it forecasts a future concept (Marketplace, *Security Management*, August 2001, Pg. 142).

Sensors

If a glass door or window is breached, glass-breaking sensors can detect either the acoustic or the seismic breaking of the glass and also send a signal. Newer microprocessor-based glass-break pattern analysis ensures detection reliability and prevents false alarms. One system, manufactured by Rokonet Electronics Ltd., based in Israel, manufacturers a product containing audio discriminators which sample the environment 40,000 times per second, and the microphone analyzes a combination of low and high frequencies against 30 specific sound patterns (Marketplace, *Security Management*, August 2001, Pg. 141). Infrared and temperature alarms have also become more popular. A ceiling-mounted detector works on the same principle as a smoke detector. They both can cover a 360-degree field of review. Wall units have a field of vision of 180 degrees but are usually equipped with a longer range. Corner placement is sometimes the best, but each room must be evaluated individually.

Biometric Doors–Security Systems

Biometric security systems have been hailed as a major advance in access control. The newest systems can accurately verify an individual's identity through fingerprint scans, hand geometry, iris scan, retinal scan, voice patterns, and facial scan. A biometric system needs three functioning components including (1) enrollment of the individual into the system providing baseline information, (2) entry into the biometric device by the person seeking access, and (3) acceptance or rejection by the device based on technical comparison with the enrolled data.

Retinal Scans   Retinal scans are actually one of the oldest and most accurate biometrics. Researchers in the early 1930s discovered that patterns of blood vessels on the back of the eye are unique to each individual. EyeDentify™ is the primary manufacturer of the devices. They are expensive and the public has generally not accepted their use.

Fingerprint Verification Readers Fingerprint readers read an encrypted template in a smart card or a biopatch. Systems are either semiconductor chip based or optical. Optical prisms resist distortions caused by dirt, oil, or moisture build-up. Semiconductor systems are susceptible to damage from electrostatic energy, especially near carpets. At least one manufacturer claims the false rejection rate is 0.1 percent and the false acceptance rate is 0.001 percent.

Voiceprint Identification This method can be defined as a combination of aural and spectrographic comparison of one or more identifiable voices with an unknown voice for the purpose of identification. The first factor in determining voice uniqueness lies in the vocal cavities and vocal cords. The second factor depends on the use of speech articulator use patterns. The system is

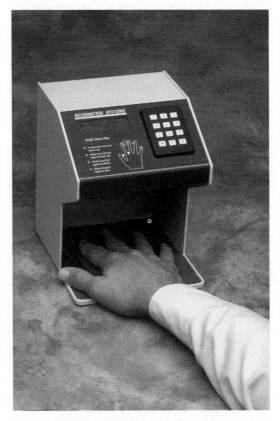

Biometric security device scans hand for security clearance into a restricted area. Such biometric access control devices will continue to become more and more essential within the airport security context. *Recognition Systems, Inc.*

widely used within the criminal justice system but has so far not been extensively used in an airport environment.

Hand Geometry   This system uses the geometric shape of the hand for authenticating a user's identity. However, individual hand features are not descriptive enough for accurate identification. It takes a three-dimensional measurement of 90 different points on your hand. The measurement is turned into a unique algorithm and stored in the reader. At San Francisco International Airport more than 30,000 employees are enrolled in Recognition Systems Inc.'s Hand-reader™, which controls access to over 180 doors.

Iris Scan   Iris scans use video cameras to scan the iris—the colored ring that surrounds the pupil in the human eye. The system translates the 266 independent characteristics of the iris into a 512-byte digital code. A 30-frame/second, black and white video camera is used to take a picture of the eye from 6 to 36 inches away. EyeTicket Corp., McLean, VA, began initially to register passengers at Charlotte/Douglas International Airport in North Carolina and Flughafen Frankfurt Airport in Germany. Others have adopted similar systems since. The scans can confirm a person's identity in less than 30 seconds.

Facial Scan   Facial scans require the use of a digital camera to develop a facial image of the end-user for authentication purposes. Eye scans are similar to

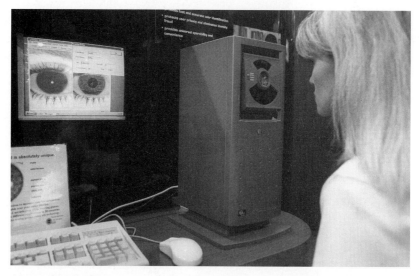

An employee of Iriscan Inc. looks into an iris scanner which projects her eye scan into a computer for comparison within a sophisticated database. Iris recognition technology identifies people by the patterns in the iris. Programs have been tested at several airports around the world. © *Liaison / Tim Chapman/Newsmakers/Online USA.*

facial scans. Face recognition is a complex process and has proven to be somewhat unreliable. Detection is the process of locating a human face in an image and isolating it from other objects in the frame. After the face is isolated, the process of recognition begins, which compares the face being captured with a database of faces to locate a potential match. During detection, the hardware/software combination isolates the facial elements of an image and eliminates extraneous information. The software examines the image for typical facial structures (such as eyes and nose), and once it has found them, it calculates the remainder of the face. It then cuts away background details, leaving a close-up of a face inside a rectangular frame.

Signs

Areas identified as those needing to be restricted, especially air operations areas, should be so designated. A sign should make even the casual observer aware that a specific area is restricted to authorized personnel only. They must be large enough and sufficiently eye catching to alert the most absent-minded traveler. Furthermore, international airport officials must be acutely aware that not everyone speaks English. Many airports absolutely require that critical information be communicated in several languages. Such signs will obviously not deter the determined terrorist. However, those travelers accidentally straying near an area can be deterred. Signs should be posted at intervals of no more than 100 feet.

Signs are also extremely important on the flight line. It is a busy and constantly moving area. Signs are crucial for the safe flow of traffic. Both aircraft and servicing vehicles must know where they are at and where they are going. Owing to the noise on the flight line, signs are an important means of communication. Security personnel also should always be trained in understanding the hand signals used on the flight line. Signs at the entrance to the field and along any perimeter road or access road are also important. Inadvertent access to the flight line needs to be minimized. Although seemingly incredible, it is always possible that a wayward traveler may seek to drive directly to the plane or somehow drive across the flight line. In most jurisdictions, trespassing prosecutions require that a legible sign has been posted in clear view of the public.

Perimeter Fencing and Lighting

Some airports have huge areas to monitor—covering acres and acres of land. Monitoring these perimeters can prove to be extensively manpower and cost intensive depending on the equipment used to patrol the circumference of an airport. According to the National Crime Prevention Institute (NCPI), perimeter barriers are, "any obstacle which defines the physical limits of a controlled area and impedes or restricts entry into the area. It is the first line of defense against intrusion. . . . At a minimum a good perimeter barrier should discourage an impulsive attacker" (National Crime Prevention Institute, *Understanding Crime Prevention*,

Stoneham, MA, Butterworth, 1986). Fencing will deter the wanderer, but the determined terrorist could easily breach the fence. However, they can be slowed down, and the fence can give security the benefit of time and distance to reach the intruder if detected soon enough. The general purpose of the fence is to define the airport's perimeter and to channel passengers and employees to authorized gates.

The fence itself needs to be sufficiently high. Chain link fence is the most commonly used, is cost effective, and it should stand at least 8 feet from the ground level with a mesh no larger than 2 inches. It should also be topped with some type of barbed wire extending at an outward angle. Security personnel, however, must be thoroughly aware of all local ordinances, because some communities have restricted the use of outward-extending barbwire. Outrigging, like razor wire, must also be appropriate to the height of the fence. A 6-foot fence could easily be brushed by a 6-foot-tall individual, causing some serious bleeding. Anyone panicking could be cut severely and possibly fatally if they do not receive assistance. Concertina wire also can create a formidable barrier. Concertina wire is often used in emergencies to block access when a fence or gate is no longer secure.

The fence must be at least 11-gauge wire. Cost is always a factor, but the stronger the fence the better. Plus the larger the mesh in the fence, the larger the wildlife that can cross through it. Critical areas may need double fencing. This is especially true of the fuel farm area. This crucial area is a highly desirable target for a terrorist seeking to get attention, cause a lot of damage, and kill a large number of people. Another highly vulnerable area is the power source access points. Double outrigging of the fence would be most appropriate, including razor wire if permissible.

The fence must always be flush with the ground. If the airport is located in a sandy soil or loose soil area, the fence needs to extend down into the ground. Embedding the fence into cement would be even better, although costly. Intruders should not be able to tunnel directly into the airport, especially near the fuel farm, power sources, or navigational equipment. The fence should also have a clear space of at least 20 or so feet on both sides, providing a full field of vision for security. On the field side, the grass near the fence must be maintained or mowed at regular intervals. Snow should not be piled high near the fence. Nearer the terminals and hangers, cargo should not be permitted to be piled up near the fence enabling an intruder literally to step over it. Fences can also be electrified, but issues of liability present themselves when this method is chosen. If budgetary constraints permit, fiberoptic sensors can be mounted on a fence, which present a safer alternative.

Adequate lighting on the perimeter is also a mandatory security function. An unobstructed 20-foot view is useless if it is cloaked in complete darkness. Four types of lights are commonly available. They include floodlights, streetlights, fresnal units, and searchlights. Inside the perimeter, lights should be positioned about 30 feet from the boundary, 50 feet apart, and 30 feet high. If a security officer cannot read the headlines of a newspaper, some additional light is needed. When dark areas remain unlighted, security may be required to investigate in the shadows with a flashlight, a function that is both time consuming and dangerous. Providing night-vision goggles to security personnel can also be effective, but is another costly measure.

FAR Part 139 requires that lighting must, ". . . show that all surface apron, vehicle parking, roadway, and building illumination lighting. . . . is so designed, adjusted, or shielded as not to blind or hinder air traffic control or airport operations." Perimeter lighting deployed in conjunction with a chain link fence should project light toward the fence, preferably from inside the fence, keeping control over the source of the light to airport authorities. The illuminated zone outside the fence should reach about 20 yards or more.

Parking lots can often present some unique problems. They are compounded by the scarcity of space and the need for travelers and employees to be provided with long-term and short-term parking. When possible, privately owned vehicles should be parked at a distance from the terminal; even though this is quite unpopular. Vehicles should be parked outside the perimeter in a parking lot with its own fence, gate, and lights. Obviously, the potential for assault and theft in these areas is significant. Consequently, either an escort service or other appropriate security measures deserve some attention. Emergency call boxes are useful in these areas. Lighting is a crime prevention measure that is an absolute requirement.

The number of gates providing access should be limited to the number of essentially required entry points. Gates either need to be guarded by a security officer or constantly viewed by some sort of electronic equipment, either closed circuit TV (CCTV) or by the use of a card activation system to gain access. The earlier methods involved simply padlocking the gate and providing keys only to those truly needing them. Advances in technology enable security now to utilize electronically generated controls, key card access, keypad access, and others depending on the budget of the operation. Dogs are also a viable option.

It should also be remembered that natural boundaries of airports also deserve some attention. Lakes and rivers will not stop a well-equipped terrorist. Additionally, any opening greater than 96 square inches is considered to be large enough for a human to pass through. Larger openings should be secured with metal bars of sufficient strength to deter an intruder. Whatever method is utilized, fences and gates in whatever configuration need to be periodically inspected. Security should always be alert to wear and tear on a system or man-made damage to it.

Security experts unfamiliar with airport operations sometimes view the air traffic control tower as a security tool. This is a misleading perception. Air traffic controllers are kept busy enough controlling air traffic on the ground and in the sky. Tower operations personnel cannot be expected to perform a continuing security role. Most controllers will alert security to anything they observe that is either unusual or dangerous. Permanently stationing airport security personnel in the tower is another matter. Certainly, there is an expanded field of vision from the tower.

▪ EXTERIOR ALARM SENSORS

A fence provides minimal protection. Lighting adds to the protection level. However, the combination of a fence, proper lighting, and at least two sensors greatly increases the probability that an intruder will be detected. Sensors can be expensive, and the actual threat must be weighed against the cost. A professional should be consulted. Product knowledge, proper installation techniques, site surveys, and choice of the correct protective device are critical to satisfactory performance. Such factors as weather, terrain, area to be covered, and electromagnetic interference need to be evaluated. Sensors come in all shapes and sizes and the technology is constantly improving. Such devices are either mechanical, electronic, or a combination of both.

Sensors in alarm systems range from simple magnetic switches to sophisticated Doppler radar. There are literally thousands of differing types of magnetic switches. The simplest sensors are electromagnetic devices in which an electric circuit is broken or closed. There are varying degrees of integrity. Shock sensors are also still available on the market today as piezoelectric sensors and can be installed directly on a fence. They originated as mechanical or acoustical vibration detectors. Some sensors are pressure devices that respond to the weight of an intruder. Taut wire detectors are also quite functional. Any change in the tension of the wire activates the alarm. Photoelectric sensors are activated when a light beam is interrupted. Some sensors currently on the market include the following.

Motion Detectors

Motion-detector devices are based on the simple concept of detecting motion. Earlier models were referred to as ultrasonic motion detectors and used the Doppler effect to work. Each unit had an emitter and a receiver. The detector would flood the designated area with ultrasonic sound waves not detectable by the human ear. The sound waves would span outward and bounce off of any inanimate objects and returning the wave to the receiver. A human intruder would interrupt the constant flow of sound waves, triggering an alarm. These devices do not function in an open area, and unfortunately various natural phenomena will also set them off.

Microwave Motion Detectors Microwave motion detectors also operate on the Doppler effect using an emitter and a receiver. They function in the gigahertz band of the radio frequency spectrum. Unlike ultrasonic motion detectors, wind currents or changes in temperature do not especially affect them. The greatest drawback is that sometimes they are "too accurate." Owing to their extremely high radio frequency, the microwave-detection pattern can see "too much," causing confusion as to what is actually a threat. Additionally, microwaves reflect metal easily, setting off the alarm. Line of sight is required, and blind spots can occur between the transmitter and receiver.

Charged Coupled Devices Charged coupled devices are solid-state image sensors that convert light into an electrical signal. There are numerous types on the market. Such a device is sometimes referred to as a chip camera, because it has a small, photosensitive unit that has replaced the imager or tube in a CCTV.

Portal Coax System This system involves the use of two cables. One cable transmits and the other receives. The detector senses any changes in the electromagnetic field surrounding the coaxial cables.

Electric Field Device Electric field devices used to be quite popular. They require a field generator that includes a long field wire and a sense wire, which are placed parallel to each other. If an intruder approaches the fence, the signal is interrupted. Electric fences are a different system all together. The potential for inadvertent severe injury to "wanderers" as opposed to intruders has made electrified fences impractical and outdated. Fiberoptics mounted on fences has replaced this concept of protection.

Vibration/Stress Detectors These units can detect someone simply walking into a protected area from a completely concealed unit. Near fences they can be installed underground in order to follow along the terrain, and the actual weight of the intruder affects the system. Most systems can be adjusted for sensitivity so that small animals do not trigger it. Depending on the need, they can be extremely sensitive. In one interior setting, an alarm at a restricted military facility was repeatedly initiated when geckos ran across the device. The sensors are also referred to as seismic sensors or buried line intrusion detectors. Vibration detectors can be mounted right onto the fence at specific intervals and will detect anyone trying to climb or cut the fence.

Once the exclusive domain of sophisticated aerospace and military imaging systems, high-quality infrared (IR) focal plan arrays have been refined to give security professionals affordable see in the dark technology. Designed to integrate into existing CCTV systems or operate alone, these new high-resolution cameras are rugged, easy to operate, and portable. IR cameras can be put to work wherever poor visibility hampers the performance of visible CCTV cameras. With IR cameras in place, as much as 50 percent of a facility's night lighting costs can be eliminated for both interior and exterior surveillance (Jeff Frank, "Out of Darkness," *Security Management*, 1991, Pg. 45).

Infrared Motion Detectors There are two types of infrared motion detectors: active and passive.

Active infrared systems: These are photoelectric using visible or invisible pulsed infrared beams. They are not lasers. The alarm is actually triggered when someone breaks a beam of light being sent from a transmitter to a receiver. Most systems utilize dual beams, and the system requires that both beams be broken at the same time before an alarm is set off. This significantly cuts down on false alarms. Line of sight transmission is required for satisfactory operation. Beam ranges vary from 10 to 800 feet.

Note: *Except for a very few highly specialized fiberoptic systems in military or government use, no laser beam technology is currently available on the mainstream commercial market.*

Passive infrared detectors: Infrared detectors were the next generation motion detectors after sound waves. Largely as a result of research done as part of the space program, they became more commonly used and reasonably priced. However, in reality, they do not really detect motion. An infrared detector literally sets a "virtual" barrier along a path. Passive infrared detectors (PIR) do not emit any energy. They are in the strictest sense only receivers that detect the body heat of an intruder. The device detects and registers the "normal" ambient temperature of infrared energy in a particular zone. When an intruder violates that space, the temperature changes and an alarm is activated. Generally, they work best indoors. The best devices incorporate two different sensors in the same equipment; for example, infrared and Doppler combined.

Closed Circuit Television

Closed circuit television (CCTV) has become the security device of choice in many applications, not just along a perimeter. They can be used in corridors, entrances, and secured areas. Cameras can instantly monitor activity near a fence and record the intruder if needed. Some are equipped with motion detectors to alert a guard that a camera has detected an individual near the fence. They have become indispensable in today's security world and come in all shapes, sizes, and budget requirements.

A significant enhancement to CCTV came with digitization. For example, now a QUAD can compress images from four cameras into a single frame of VCR tape or DVD, allowing the operator to view all four cameras on a four-way split screen. Video multipliers also allow the system high-speed, full-frame recording from multiple sources. Infrared cameras are used for night surveillance.

Glass-Break Detectors

There are two categories of glass-break detectors. One attaches directly to the glass being protected and a second space-coverage type of acoustical sensor that protects all the glass in a specific area. They are extremely sensitive, and modern ones can distinguish between glass actually being broken and noises similar to glass breaking. They have advanced electronic detection circuits, which are not fooled into making annoying false alarms like older models were wont to do.

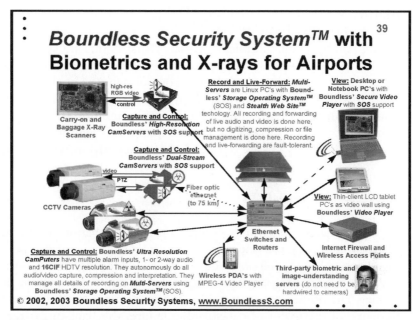

Boundless Security System™ combines biometrics with state of the art surveillance and x-ray equipment to provide a total security access control and monitoring regime for airports. *Used with permission of Boundless Security Systems, Inc., Monroe, CT,* www.BoundlessS.com.

■ THE CONTROL ROOM

All of the unique devices installed in an airport security system need to be controlled from a central point. A control panel in a control room is generally considered the heart of the system. Today, most control centers have alarm device inputs or zones:

1. Reporting device outputs
2. Timing circuitry
3. Power supplies
4. Back-up batteries
5. Programmable microprocessor
6. Memory for user codes
7. Memory for activity logs which can be displayed locally or downloaded
8. Digital communications
9. Supervisory circuits to monitor zone status, AC power, battery power, phone line integrity, self-diagnosing programs, and fuse integrity (Internet: http://www.aloha.com/~sednat1/prod02.htm#detection, 14 August 2001).

Alarms

Alarms can be silent, audible, or visual. Visual alarms are specifically designed to catch someone's attention to a potential problem. A blinking red light is the classic example—either mounted on a control panel console or at the site of the alarm involved. Audible alarms are intended not only to alert security but also to scare the intruder. Any noise is acceptable, including bells, sirens, whistles, chimes, or music. One system actually plays the "Star Spangled Banner" at 118 decibels. Silent devices are designed to alert security as well as law enforcement.

■ NO POWER—NO SECURITY

Unless a security system has power, it is severely handicapped, to say the least. The power supply provides the necessary voltage to operate not only the command center but also all of the devices installed throughout the airport to provide security. Most alarm panels are connected to a primary current through a transformer. The power supply provides constant power to all systems and their components. In the event of catastrophic failure, the back-up battery system takes over. Alarm systems should always be programmed to report a current failure or low-battery conditions. Testing of the back-up system is critical.

■ MEDIA INTRUSION

The role of the media has become a significant factor in all hijackings. Margaret Thatcher, former Prime Minister of Britain, referred to "the oxygen of publicity" as constituting a vital requirement of any terrorist undertaking. Photographs of armed police lying in wait near an aircraft could pose considerable problems for police negotiators should the photos reach the hijackers. Consequently, the police and the media are often at odds. The public is eager to soak up any sensational and newsbreaking pictures, and the press seems willing to do whatever it takes to get them regardless of the delicacy of any negotiations. In any democratic society, the value of the press and its principal focus of news gathering must be weighed against the impact on the situation at hand. Cooperation with the media is necessary and sometimes difficult but must be addressed. Airport security must always be prepared to handle, some say massage, the media.

Some would take the point of view the media is only interested in sensationalism. They are allegedly interested only in what sells. Arguably, they make terrorism possible and profitable. Large terrorist organizations, like the Irish Republican Army (IRA) and the Palestine Liberation Organization (PLO) have well-developed press sections within the organization. They have well-planned and well-organized long-term strategies for the use of the media to project their central message. These press specialists can respond immediately to an event, feeding material to a sympathetic journalist and making attempts to justify any violence. The security forces at airports must operate in the same way. Media management and propaganda features are important policy considerations in determining the appropriate response.

Some scholars have reached the conclusion, ". . . media does not cause terrorism, but they can make it worse by poor reporting practices, by allowing themselves to be manipulated by interested parties, and by not giving audiences a better understanding of the issue" (Robert G. Picard, *Media Portrayals of Terrorism*, Iowa State University Press, Ames, IA, 1993, Pg. 29). The most important function of the media when a terrorist act is occurring is not to describe the acts but to explain the meaning assigned to the acts by the terrorists. In order for violence to become a terrorist act, there must be witnesses. Airports provide the victims and the witnesses in one package.

■ COMPUTER SECURITY

Although the issues behind terrorism are usually national, regional, or issue specific, the impact of terrorist campaigns is international. Domestic terrorism often has spillover effects. Combating terrorism has encompassed efforts to use the law, efforts to infiltrate and destroy, and efforts to remedy the underlying cause of the violence. However, with the dawning of the computer age, terrorism can now be accomplished by individuals thousands of miles from the target. Airports, airlines, and their computer networks are no less vulnerable than anything else. In fact, they may be one of the softest targets available to terrorists, whereas offering the least amount of physical risk to the perpetrators. They present an easy and potentially massively destructive tool to create panic. Completely to shut down the airways or to cause several aircraft to crash or have mid-air a collision is a real danger that has been somewhat ignored by the airlines. The FAA is aware of the problem and has made significant strides to establishing fail-safe systems.

On the other hand, airport security and airlines in general need to stay on top of state of the art computer security systems. Computer crime includes, but is not limited to, accessing a computer's database without authorization for the purpose of sabotage or fraud. Obviously, the information revolution is here and electronic access to information is the wave of the future. Electronic kiosk systems are one of the key means by which to acquire this access. The benefits include providing connectivity and flexibility of access while avoiding the security-related problems of using personal computers. Problems arise because technologies that give access enable fraud. All computer systems suffer from security vulnerabilities that can threaten the integrity of the services they provide and can infiltrate any computer to which they are connected. Airport security officials must recognize the full risks that information and service computer systems represent. Terrorists could also seek to access the computer systems upon which a nation's entire air traffic control is based. To hack into a signal circuit could give the intruder the ability purposely to collide aircraft on the ground or in the air.

The CIA has admitted its concerns as regards their ability to stop hackers and sophisticated technology–smart terrorists. Lawrence K. Gershwin, the CIA's top advisor on science and technology issues, admitted, ". . . we end up detecting an attack after it's happened" (Ray Schroeder, "CIA Can't Keep Up With Hackers," *The Associated Press*, 21 June 2001). He went on to testify that despite a major increase in intelligence efforts dedicated to computer security, potential hackers still develop means to get into the system faster than the authorities at the CIA can detect and nullify them. The CIA does believe that the threat from computer infiltration is greater from foreign governments than it is from terrorists, but that does not mean that the threat does not exist (Internet: http://news.cnet.com/news/0-1003-200-6344815.html?tag=prntfr). A "cyberattack" from a terrorist organization is always possible. It is a well-accepted concept in criminology that crime is strongly linked to opportunity, and computers at airports offer some unprecedented opportunity for easy access. Once terrorists have mastered the technology, it is likely that they will use it. More than likely, they will seek to disrupt the financial networks or communication networks upon which the industrialized nations and their airports are so dependent.

Kiosks

A kiosk is a publicly accessible computerized unit that gives information and services to authorized clients who are not particularly computer proficient. Most airlines have already implemented automated kiosks that deliver information to users. Passengers can now purchase tickets, locate flight information, and even print out boarding passes. Kiosks are a cost-effective means of providing services to clients. Every transaction performed on a kiosk is one that an employee does not have to perform. The shift represents a savings in not only the costs related to personnel but also the costs of building and maintaining offices and infrastructure. They also have a security price in that they expose the airlines to problems of ticket theft and fraud. The Electronic Communications Privacy Act of 1986 makes it illegal intentionally to access, without authorization, a facility providing electronic communication services or intentionally to exceed the authorization of access to such a facility. However, successful prosecutions are rare, and the damage is already done; that is, the fraud has taken place or an incident has occurred. Security measures for computer systems include logical controls such as encryption, physical controls, administrative controls, and protecting the equipment from fire and heat.

Logical controls are unique programs written into the software of the system. The most common, of course, is the use of passwords. Multilevel access capability allows some operators to access some information, with only a limited number of people having access to the entire system. A callback modem is also a good logical control. A user attempting to access the system enters an identification code after dialing the computer, and the modem scans its directory for the appropriate code and phone number and calls back. After the code is verified, the connection is completed and the user is connected to the computer system.

A corollary is the use of encryption. The device puts the data into code before it enters the transmission line and it is decoded at the receiving end.

Computers need adequate physical controls as well. At airports, they should be located in restricted areas with locked doors and equipped with alarm systems. If the public has access to them, a supervisor should be on duty to monitor their usage at all times. Always remember SAM—secure it, alarm it, and mark it.

Cybersecurity officials have praised the administration's efforts to have an Information Analysis and Infrastructure Division within the Department of Homeland Security. The new office will combine elements of the FBI's Cyber division and the Commerce Department's Critical Infrastructure Assurance Office. The National Infrastructure Protection Center's multiagency analysis and warning function would also be combined into the new office.

■ CONCLUSION

Access control to an airport is vital. Locks, alarms, and sensors best control that access. A mixture of these measures is usually the best approach. Key and lock controls, placement of the devices, electronic access cards, fences, and signs all play an important part in managing the flow of people through an airport. The use of computers has greatly facilitated this effort. Using computers, manufacturers of access controls can create huge systems providing security with a tremendous amount of flexibility. All access control systems should be based on a risk-assessment analysis in concert with the latest versions of access control technology and computerized systems. The media is just one of many potential intruders that need to be reasonably controlled. Also important is strict control of computer and kiosk access.

Epilogue

Over two years has passed since one of the worst acts of terrorism in American history. The site has been cleaned up but the scars remain, and fear of another attack lingers. That fear is well justified. Another attack will undoubtedly take place, and the transportation industry is still a prime target. In order to avoid such a tragedy, an independent group consisting of security experts should advise policymakers and members of Congress on what measures can best serve the interests of the industry. These recommendations should subsequently not be amended on the basis of political or profit-making goals. Much money has been thrown at the problem. Unfortunately, airline security continues to consist largely of window dressing, possessing gapping holes. The vulnerabilities appall serious aviation experts.

During the fiscal year that ended in September 2002, airline passengers paid the federal government nearly $1 billion for security. Each passenger was charged a $2.50 security fee added onto the price of a ticket. Additionally, the airlines in turn paid approximately $160 million, which will likely double by the end of 2003. However, it does not appear that the money has been particularly well spent. For example, controls over airline employees, service and maintenance personnel, and cargo continue to be weaker than they should be. Many solutions have been offered, yet many of them contain aspects of corporate or personal gain or political motivation and manipulation. Arguably, the American public is being duped into a false sense of security.

CHANGES

There are still many changes contemplated by governments to combat the threat of terrorism specifically as it relates to aviation. Some are temporary fixes, like locks on cockpit doors, and some are more long range, such as more sophisticated explosive-detection systems and improved preventive law enforcement. The Transportation Security Administration has focused considerable effort on attempting to ensure that a passenger does not carry a bomb or weapon onto a commercial aircraft. Unfortunately, about one-half of the cargo hold is usually filled with nonpassenger cargo. In spite of a report issued by the General Accounting Office in December 2002 recognizing the potential problems, little has actually been done. Such vulnerabilities threaten the entire transportation network and provide terrorists with a target of opportunity.

▓ THE MORE THINGS CHANGE THE MORE THEY REMAIN THE SAME—SCREENERS ARE SCREENERS

The Transportation Security Administration is facing the same challenges that private security incurred prior to TSA involvement. So far, they have not been able to avoid the same missteps that private security firms have encountered for years. If administrators do not address these issues, the same potentially disastrous results will eventually occur.

The quality and caliber of air baggage and passenger screeners represents a persistent problem. Not long after the holidays in December 2002, at Seattle's International Airport, a baggage screener was found sleeping on the job. Two years ago he simply would have been a private security company employee sleeping on the job. Twenty-three incoming flights were delayed while dogs and security personnel checked the concourses. Employee training and dedication levels are often less than optimal. Scores of instances of weapons and potentially dangerous instruments passing through checkpoints have been well documented by the press in the past two years. Screening at most airports in reality remains a sieve.

On top of this, screeners want to unionize. The Bush Administration announced it would deny 56,000 federal airport security screeners the right to negotiate for better working conditions and higher pay. Admiral James Loy, Agency Chief of the Transportation Security Administration, proclaimed that mandatory collective bargaining is not compatible with the war on terrorism. The American Federation of Government employees promptly threatened to sue. In surrebuttal, the Administration denies that there is widespread dissatisfaction among screeners. This approach may well be shortsighted. Screeners are also complaining that they are suffering from back and knee injuries from lifting heavy bags, which they are required to carry from conveyor belts to newly installed screening machines. They also have expressed displeasure at the placement of the machines, indicating they are often in dark and dirty terminal base-ments. A TSA spokesman has confirmed the injuries and claims the agency is addressing them. However, some of the same problems of employee dissatisfaction that plagued private airport security are resurfacing.

The Transportation Security Administration is growing by leaps and bounds. Starting with about 13 employees, it has grown to more than 64,000. Congress originally imposed a 45,000-member employee cap. Admiral Loy has requested nearly $6 billion for the 2004 budget. Early in January 2003, agency executives met to determine just how they were going to pay their employees. Congress would prefer the agency focus more on equipment and airport modifications than staffing. The TSA is part of the new Homeland Security Department, which employs 170,000 people. Consequently, with size comes bureaucracy and with bureaucracy ultimately comes inefficiency.

▧ ARMING PILOTS

An additional change proposed involves arming airline personnel. Stephen Luckey, chairman of the National Flight Security Committee of the Air Line Pilots Association, told Congress that pilots are willing and prepared to assume this responsibility. That's probably true. Regardless, problems have already emerged. Claiming he did not know it was not appropriate, in January 2003, a Northwest Airlines pilot was arrested at New York's LaGuardia Airport with a loaded gun in his bag. The overeager pilot claimed it was all a big mistake.

The key to effective airline security is on the ground. Security experts learned this in the 1970s, and apparently it needs to be relearned. The argument that the aircrew is the last line of defense is an emotional, but not a particularly realistic, approach. Hopefully, no aircrew member is going to let a passenger or fellow crew member die in order to retain a weapon the terrorists has demanded be given up. A firefight at the cockpit is a really bad idea. Shooting a terrorist before they take over a flight and drive the aircraft into a populated building or neighborhood will not prevent an already horrendous situation from playing out.

Other experts have indicated that arming pilots will serve as a deterrent. More than likely it will serve to provide a ready-made armory for the terrorist. Why risk secreting a weapon through airport security when you can take one off an aircrew member? As mentioned, the terrorist will present a no win situation to the aircrew. Die, have a hostage or hostages killed, or relinquish the weapon. In a worse scenario, the terrorist will simply kill the aircrew members. Five terrorists versus two pilots is not a particularly winnable fight, especially while continuing to fly the plane. One pilot standing guard at the door while the other pilot flies the plane is a good movie scene. It does not represent an effective tool to stop a terrorist either determined to explode an aircraft or to produce a cabin full of dead passengers.

Last but not least, dismissing the concept of the airline civil liability as a nonissue because a litigious society exists in the West does not make it disappear. A gunslinging pilot could theoretically bankrupt an airline. Again, the key to effective aviation security is on the ground. Realistically, once the aircraft is airborne, it is too late to avoid some sort of a disaster.

THE FEDERAL AIR MARSHAL PROGRAM

The original Sky Marshal Program has changed considerably over the years. As long ago as the 1970s, administrators recognized that the program was one tool in the airport security toolbox but not the absolute solution to airport security. As recently as a year ago, the program had a $4 million budget and about 33 armed officers who flew on international flights. A year later, thousands of marshals and a budget of over a billion dollars have not resulted in concrete proof that the well-intentioned officers have foiled a single hijacking attempt. On top of that, just because an officer is onboard, does not mean the aircraft will not be hijacked or destroyed.

A major problem is that it is logistically impossible to have an officer on each and every flight. It is even impossible to have an officer on every aircraft considered to be at some higher risk. In an attempt to cover more aircraft, the program rushed to hire marshals. However, in the rush to grow, the agency got ahead of itself. Marshals have complained that poor scheduling, inadequate training, insufficient supervision, and cutbacks in the marksmanship training have diminished the force. Indeed, at one point, the program was hiring approximately 800 marshals a month. The administration of such a process carries its own problems. The question therefore that presents itself is whether the public is getting sufficient protection considering the cost.

EMERGING TECHNOLOGY

There are so many emerging technologies with applications to airport security it is impossible to discuss them all. What is relevant boils down to what technology will provide the most security for the most reasonable price within the context of a complex airport environment. For example, literally hundreds of unique devices previously applicable within a broad private security context are available for use in an airport. The challenge is to determine what will suitably add to the appropriate mix of gizmos in the overall big toolbox.

For instance, Imaging Automation's document checker matches documents against a database that indicates what the document should look like. They are already in use at airports in Dallas–Fort Worth and Boston. They essentially compare driver's licenses, passports, and other IDs against the real thing. The system was developed to weed out job applicants with forged identification documents. The company would like to convince the TSA that the scanners, the size of a small toaster, could perform the same check on passenger documents.

Another issue relates to the sophistication of more expensive pieces of equipment. Many explosive-detection devices, trace-detection devices, biometric access control devices, and others are undergoing intensive research and development. Again, cost is a gigantic issue. Because the technology exists does not mean it can adequately be integrated within the airport context for a reasonable cost. Some experts have questioned the decision to pour billions of dollars into baggage screening equipment that is error prone, labor intensive, and extremely expensive for smaller airports to finance. The TSA claims to have met its deadline of 100-percent baggage screening by 31 December 2002. However, they did so by weakening the requirements; using a combination of explosive-detection systems, explosive trace-detection systems, dogs, and manual inspection. The whole issue begs the question whether spending $12 billion on already outdated, but approved, technology with error rates as high as 30 percent and slow throughput is the answer.

Consideration of the European model of a several-tier baggage screening system must be reviewed. Additionally, Heimann's EDS machines scan 1000 bags per hour and are cheaper. However, US manufacturers are balking at the purchase of foreign-produced machines. In conjunction, the detection of high-risk people, not baggage, is critical. The Israelis and the Europeans have recognized this for years. Airport security officials need to be smarter, more efficient, and more realistic in approaching the security needs of airports in the twenty-first century. Not to heed the lessons learned of the past and not to recognize the successes of the Europeans and Israelis condemns the air transportation industry to a constant threat of disaster.

■ CIVIL LIBERTIES

In January 2003, a federal appeals court ruled that the Administration has the authority to designate US citizens as "enemy combatants." This enables the government to label citizens and detain them in military custody if they are considered to be a threat to national security. In the case of Yaser Hamdi, a Louisiana-born American citizen who was captured in Afghanistan fighting for the Taliban, a lower court had ordered the government to release more information to the defense. The government has been able to deny him access to his public defender and has not filed charges against him. The court opinion says, "Because it is undisputed that Hamdi was captured in a zone of active combat in a foreign theater of conflict, we hold that the submitted declaration is a sufficient basis upon which to conclude that the commander in chief has constitutionally detained Hamdi pursuant to the war powers entrusted to him by the United States Constitution" (advance sheets). The ruling comes from one of the most conservative jurisdictions in the nation.

This case parallels but is easily distinguishable from *Padilla vs. Bush*. Jose Padilla, the alleged "dirty bomb" suspect, has also been designated an "enemy combatant." However, he was captured on US soil after arriving at Chicago's

O'Hare International Airport as part of an alleged scheme to explode a conventional bomb laced with radioactive material. His attorneys contend that the government should be forced to comply with standard criminal court procedures including the right to counsel. So far, he has been denied that access. On the civil side, a Pakistani businessman from Los Angeles has lost a discrimination suit he filed against United Airlines. He had been blocked from boarding a plane following 11 September 2001. The jury reasoned that the discrimination was justified.

■ SUMMARY

Better management and better utilization of resources is needed. An independent committee of experienced security experts could help policymakers to determine the best methods of creating an effective toolbox of assets to combat the threat to aviation. The threat is not going to evaporate anytime in the near future. Good judgment and common sense aspects need to be integrated into a system that is devoid of personal, political, or corporate profit.

Select Bibliography

Adams, James (1986). *The Financing of Terror*, New York: Simon & Schuster.

Alexander, Yonah (1976). *From Terrorism to War: The Anatomy of the Birth of Israel*. International Terrorism, New York: Praeger.

Alexander, Yonah (1994). *Middle Eastern Terrorism: Current Trends and Future Prospects*. New York: Chapman & Hall.

Alexander, Yonah, and Kenneth A. Myers (eds.) (1982). *Terrorism in Europe*. New York: St. Martin's Press.

Anderson, Sean and Stephen Sloan (1995). *Historical Dictionary of Terrorism*, Lanham, MD: Scarecrow Press. Internet: *http://www.securitymanagement.com/library/000248/html*.

Anderson, Teresa (15 February, 2001). "Airport Security, All Systems Go," Pg. 1–8, Internet: *http://www.securitymanagement.com/library/000539.html*.

Aris, Stephen (May 1980). "Terror in the Land of the Basques." *New York Times*. Basque Fatherland and Liberty (ETA), Internet: *www.ict.org.il/*.

Bahgat, Gawdat (1994). "Democracy in the Middle East: The American Connection." *Studies in Conflict and Terrorism* 17:87–96.

Barton, John H. (1980). "The Civil Liberties Implications of a Nuclear Emergency." *New York University Review of Law and Social Change* 10:299–317.

Bassiouni, M. Cherif (ed.) (1983). *Terrorism, Law Enforcement and the Mass Media*. Rockville, MD: National Criminal Justice Reference Service.

Becker, Julian (1984). *The PLO*. New York: St. Martin's Press.

Beckwith, Charlie, and Donald Knox (1985). *Delta Force*. New York: Dell.

Berkowitz, B.J., et al. (1972). *Superviolence: The Civil Threat of Mass Destruction Weapons*. Santa Monica, CA: Advanced Concepts Research.

Bill James A., and Carl Leiden (1984). *Politics in the Middle East*. Boston: Little Brown.

Blumberg, Abraham S. (1979). *Criminal Justice and Ironies*. New York: New Viewpoints.

Bollinger, Paul P., Jr., "Airport" World Book Online Americas Edition, Internet: *http://www.aolsvc.worldbook.aol.com/wbol/wbpage/na/ar/co/0009760*, 24 July 2001.

Bolz, Francis (May 1984). Hostage Negotiation Training. Grand Rapids Police Department, Grand Rapids, MI.

Boyne, Sean (11 April 2000). "Uncovering the Irish Republican Army-Organization and Command." *Frontline*.

Bruce, Steve (1985). "Paramilitaries, Peace and Politics: Ulster Loyalists and the 1994 Truce." *Studies in Conflict and Terrorism* 18:187–202.

Bullion, Alan J. (1995). *India, Sri Lanka, and the Tamil Crisis, 1976–1994: An International Perspective*. London: Pinter.

Bureau of Alcohol, Tobacco, and Firearms, U.S. Department of the Treasury (1995). *Violent White Supremacists Groups*. Washington, DC: ATF.

Cameron, Gavin (1999). *Nuclear Terrorism*. Macmillan Press, New York, NY.

Chubin, Shahram (1997). "Iran and It's Neighbors: The Impact of the Gulf War." *Conflict Studies* 204:1–20.

Clark, Robert. (1984). *The Basque Insurgents*. Madison: University of Wisconsin Press.

Clutterbuck, Richard (1975). *Living with Terrorism*, London: Faber & Faber.

Coates, James (1987). *Armed and Dangerous: The Rise of the Survivalists Right*. New York: Hill and Wang.

Cobban, Helene (1984). *The Palestine Liberation Organization: People, Power, and Politics*. Cambridge, UK: Cambridge University Press.

Combs, Cindy (2000). *Terrorism in the Twenty First Century*, 2nd ed. Upper Saddle River, NJ: Prentice-Hall.

Costigan, Giovani (1980). *A History of Modern Ireland*. Indianapolis, IN: Bobbs-Merill.

Cranston, Alan (1986). "The Nuclear Terrorist State." In Benjamin Netanyahu (ed.), *Terrorism: How the West Can Win*. New York: Avon.

Crozier, Brian (1975). "Terrorist Activity: International Terrorism." Hearings Before the Subcommittee to Investigate the Administration of the Internal Security Act and Other Internal Security Laws of the Committee on the Judiciary, 79th Congress, 1st Session, Washington DC, US Senate.

David, B (1985). "The Capability and Motivation of Terrorist Organizations to Use Mass Destruction Weapons." In Ariel Merari (ed.), *On Terrorism and Combating Terrorism*. Lanham, MD: University Press of America.

Debenham, J.K. (1973). A Brief Description of the Effects of X-ray Inspection on Unprocessed Photographic Film," Film Technical Services Division, Eastman Kodak.

Dobson, Christopher, and Ronald Payne (1982). *The Terrorists*. New York: Facts on File.

Donnelly, Sally B. (2001). "A Safety Fight at the FAA," *Time*. Internet: *http://www.atag.org/ECO/default.htm*.

D'Oliviera, Sergio (1973). "Uruguay and the Tupamaro Myth." *Military Review* 53:25–36.

Duff, Ernest, and John McCamant (1976). *Violence and Repression in Latin America*. New York: Free Press.

Ehteshami, Anoushiravan (1995). *After Khomeini: The Iranian Second Republic*. London. Routledge.

Finn, John E. (1987). "Public Support for Emergency Anti-Terrorist Legislation in Northern Ireland: A Preliminary Analysis." *Terrorism* 10:113–124.

Flynn, Kevin, and Gary Gerhardt (1995). *The Silent Brotherhood*. New York: Penguin, Internet: *http://www.front14.org/rac/88pre2.htm*.

Fooner, Michael (1989). *Interpol Issues in World Crime and International Criminal Justice*. New York: Plenum Press.

Friedlander, Robert (1979). *Terrorism: Documents of International and Local Control*. Dobbs Ferry, NY: Oceana.

Gesell, Laurence E. (1981). *The Administration of Public Airports*. Daytona Beach, FL: Coast Aire Publications.

Getler, Michael (18 July 1978). "Move to Combat Air Piracy is Viewed as Toughest Yet", *Washington Post*.

Hill, Jim (3 July 2000). US News, "New Airport Security Means Dogs, Better Scanners," Internet: *http://www.cnn.com/US/9711/23/airport.security/*.

Hiro, Dilip (1987). *Iran Under the Ayatollahs*. London: Routledge and Kegan Paul.

Hodgson, Karyn (1994). "Hot and Cold Biometrics Heat Up Again." *Security*. Newton, MA: Cahners.

Holden, Bruce (1995). *Historical and International Perspectives on Right-Wing Militancy in the United States*. Las Vegas, NV: American Criminal Justice Society.

Horchem, Hans Josef (1986). "Political Terrorism: The German Perspective." In Ariel Merari (ed.), *On Terrorism and Combating Terrorism*. Frederick, MD: University of America Press.

Horchem, Hans Josef (1987). "Terrorism in West Germany." *Conflict Studies* 186. Spring 1987, Pg. 186.

Interagency OPSEC Support Staff (May 1996). *Intelligence Threat Handbook*, Section 4, *http://www.terrorism.com/terrorism/IntelOperations.shtml/*.

International Security Council (1986). *State Sponsored Terrorism*. Tel Aviv: ISC.

Israeli Foreign Ministry (1996) "Hizbullah." Internet: *http://www.israel.mfa.gov.il)*.

Iyad, Abu (1978). My *Home, My Land: A Narrative on the Palestinian Struggle*. New York: Times Books.

Jenkins, Brian (1980). "Nuclear Terrorism and Its Consequences." *Society* July/August:5–16.

Jenkins, Brian (1975). *Terrorism: Will Terrorists Go Nuclear?* Santa Monica, CA: Rand.

Juergensmeyer, Mark (1988). "The Logic of Religious Violence." In David C. Rapaport (ed.) *Inside Terrorist Organizations*. New York: Columbia University Press.

Kane, Robert M., Vose, Allan D. (1999). *Air Transportation*, 11th ed. Dubuque, IA: Kendall/Hunt.

Kennedy, Tom, and David Phelps (22 September 2001). "NWA will lay off 10,000; $15 billion airline aid OK'd." *Star Tribune*.

Klaidman, Daniel (18 May 1999). "The New Secret Weapons." *Newsweek*.

Kupperman, Robert H., and Darell M. Trent (1979). *Terrorism, Threat, Reality and Response*. Stanford, CA: Hoover Institution Press.

Laquer, Walter (Sept/Oct 1996). "Post Modern Terrorism." *Foreign Affairs*.

Lochmuller, C.H. (16 August 2001). "Fact Sheet: Tagging and Taggants for the Detection and Identification of Explosives, Smokeless Propellants, Black Powder. Internet: *http://www.ca-rkba.org/ncrkba/nccda—taggant.html*.

Mario, Leo, Stanley Stewart, and Michael Sharpe. (December 1999). *Air Disasters: Including Dialogue from the Black Box*, Barnes and Noble Books.

Melman, M. (1986). The *Master Terrorist*. New York: Adams.

Moore, Kenneth (1991). *Airport, Aircraft and Airline Security*. Burlington, MA: Butterworth-Heinemann.

Nambisan, Shashi Sathisan (September 1999). *The 2020 Vision of Air Transportation: Emerging and Innovative Solutions*. American Society of Civil Engineers.

Nojeim, Gregory T. (1998). "Aviation Security Profiling and Passengers' Civil Liberties." 13 *Air and Space Law* 13. Vol 23, Pg 13.

Pan Am Flight 103 Disaster (April 1992). United States Department of State, US Government Printing Office, Internet: *http://www.emergency.com/panam103.html*, 13 March 2001.

Panghorn, Alan (5 May 1996). "How Far Has Europe Come Since Pan Am 103." *Intersec,* Vol. 6:195.

Richardson, David B. (17 March 1980). "Basque Country: Violence is a Way of Life." *US News and World Report*.

Rose, Paul (June 1986). "Terror in the Skies." *Contemporary Review* June 1986, P. 248.

Schroeder, Ray (21 June 2001). "CIA Can't Keep Up With Hackers." *The Associated Press.*

Sharpe, Michael (September 1999). *Air Disasters: The Truth Behind the Tragedies*. London: Brown Partworks.

Simonson Clifford E., and Jeremy R. Spindlove (2000). *Terrorism Today, The Past, The Players, The Future*. Upper Saddle River, NJ: Prentice-Hall.

Sjursen, Katie (2000). *Globalization*. The Reference Shelf, Vol. 72, No. 5, H.W. Wilson Publishing.

Spence, Charles F. (August 2000). *Aim Far Aeronautical Manual, Federal Aviation Regulations*. New York: McGraw-Hill.

Steinberg, Matti (1988). "The Radical Worldview of the Abu-Nidal Faction," *The Jerusalem Quarterly*. 1 October 1988, No. 48, Fall, 1988 Pg. 3–26.

Study and Report to Congress on Civil Aviation Security Responsibilities and Funding (1998). US Department of Transportation, US Government Printing Office, Washington, DC, *http://cas.faa.gov/reports/98study/98study.html*.

Taylor, Qualye, E. (1994). *Terrorists Lives*, London: Brassey's Publishing.

Tibon, Jack (1998). "Customs Hunt Air Smugglers." Government Computer News, Internet: *http://www.pals.msus.edu*.

US Department of State (1984). *Patterns of Global Terrorism*. US Printing Office, Washington, DC.

US Department of State (1996). *Patterns of Global Terrorism*. US Government Printing Office, Washington, DC.

US Department of State (2000). *Patterns of Global Terrorism*. US Government Printing Office, Washington, DC.

Washington File (2001). "Justice Department on Verdict of Pan Am 103 Bombing," *http://www.usembassy.org.uk/terr127.html*, 13 March 2001.

Wells, Alexander T. (1998). *Air Transportation and Management Perspective*. Belmont, CA: Wadsworth.

White, Jonathan (1998). *Terrorism: An Introduction*. 2nd ed. Belmont, CA: Wadsworth.

White, Jonathan (2002). *Terrorism: An Introduction*. 3rd ed. Belmont, CA: Wadsworth.

Whiteman, Marjorie (1998). Digest of International Law. Department of State, Vol. 11, Chapter 35, Article 2, 3518–3520, Washington, DC.

Index

References to photos or figures are indicated by *f*, tables by *t*.